Volume 96 Number 4 December 2024

American Literature

New Citizenship Studies

Edited by Carrie Hyde and Derrick R. Spires

Essays

Books

Review Essay

Reviews

Carrie Hyde and Derrick R. Spires

New Citizenship Studies: An Introduction

The legal and cultural history of citizenship is fundamentally fraught. In the popular imagination, citizenship has long been idealized prospectively through impassioned dreams of democracy and rights not yet realized. Yet, citizenship also depends on and produces nightmares of violence, dispossession, and disappointment.[1] The very existence of the United States is predicated on the occupation of Indigenous lands, the enslavement of African and African descended peoples, and ongoing assaults on Indigenous sovereignty. US citizenship rests on settler colonialism, antiblackness, racism, sexism, heteropatriarchy, xenophobia, ableism, class, capitalism. . . . The list goes on. All too often citizenship functions as a "common-sense category of the social regime of white supremacy," to quote Nicholas De Genova's (2017: 37) entry on citizenship in *Keywords for Latina/o Studies*. And yet, because exclusion from the benefits associated with citizenship is so consequential, citizenship continues to be a touchstone for an array of people who seek to envision the world otherwise: within, against, and beyond the settler nation-state.

This special issue develops, defines, and seeks to give momentum to a "New Citizenship Studies" that grapples with the "both/and" of citizenship: its violent histories and imaginative possibilities; its political importance and limitations. Building on our own work and other recent scholarship that takes citizenship as a fraught but productive field of interdisciplinary inquiry, New Citizenship Studies examines the literatures, practices, and expressive cultures that legalistic approaches to citizenship often devalue, paying special attention to political imaginaries that operate outside of or in contradistinction to the violent logics of white supremacy and the settler nation-state. New

American Literature, Volume 96, Number 4, December 2024
DOI 10.1215/00029831-11587026   © 2024 by Duke University Press

Citizenship Studies does not treat citizenship as a universally desirable political goal nor as a guarantor of rights; instead, it understands citizenship as a vexed but potent juridical and imaginative concept that organizes ideas about belonging, access, and resources. In the spirit of David Walker's *Appeal to the Coloured Citizens of the World* (1829) and other texts that use the language of citizenship even as they criticize its exclusionary histories, New Citizenship Studies approaches citizenship as a contested and malleable political and aesthetic form that writers and activists have used to challenge the existing state of things and to imagine alternatives to it. By attending to the aesthetic dimension of citizenship as well as its political limits, New Citizenship Studies recognizes the formative role that literature and other expressive traditions play in the cultural making and unmaking of citizenship.

Over the past several decades, scholars have disrupted celebratory, progress-oriented narratives of citizenship that seek to remedy the failures and limitations of citizenship by expanding its scope rather than rethinking its structures and epistemologies. Whereas earlier work critiqued citizenship in binary terms through the paradigm of inclusion/exclusion, scholars in a number of fields have begun examining the fundamental limitations and violence of formal citizenship—in which inclusion and protection often double as code for absorption and assimilation. Recent scholarship in Indigenous studies, Black studies, Latinx studies, Asian American studies, critical refugee studies, disability studies, queer theory, critical race studies, and a range of other fields has opened up new approaches to citizenship by rethinking the meanings of inclusion, access, community, rights, and equity.[2] For instance, as Jodi A. Byrd (Chickasaw Nation) (2011: xxiii) notes, when "inclusion into the nation-state" is posed as the telos for Indigenous communities, "there is a significant failure to grapple with the fact that such discourses further reinscribe the original colonial injury." Work by Saidiya Hartman (1997, 2022) and others has unsettled the association between citizenship and freedom by excavating the afterlives of enslavement, the ongoing violences of settler colonialism, and the forms of subjection that fetter nominally free individuals, often through the mechanisms of citizenship and the language of rights.[3] This scholarship has contributed to a heightened recognition of the violence of liberal notions of citizenship. It also has spurred a critical resurgence and reconceptualization of citizenship. For example, Audra Simpson (2007, 2008, 2014), Edlie L. Wong (2015), Martha S. Jones (2007, 2018, 2020), Koritha Mitchell (2020), Dennis Tyler (2022), and others have begun rethinking citizenship from the perspectives and practices of those whom the state routinely refuses to recognize or protect.

This work across the humanities presages a New Citizenship Studies. Our gambit in characterizing this new node and critical mass in the ongoing interrogation of citizenship as "New Citizenship Studies" is to give voice and velocity to a shift that has not yet crystalized as a critical movement per se. By identifying New Citizenship Studies as an emergent movement, with multiple genealogies, we are inviting other scholars to join the conversation and, in some instances, to see themselves as already engaged in this work.

We have inherited not a single sense of citizenship, but multiple, often Janus-faced notions of the concept. For many in the United States, writing and thinking about citizenship at any point in US history produces a sense of dread. It can mean staring at one's own abjection, rejection, exclusion—and the abjection of others—and understanding this violence and the redoubled pain associated with it as among the constitutive features of citizenship. Nonetheless, many writers and activists are drawn to the term *citizen* because it provides a recognizable legal and cultural framework for claiming rights, access, and protection—and because legal recognition as a citizen has been and continues to be a matter of life or death. In such cases, *citizen* often functions as a rhetorical placeholder and political starting point for imagining new formations that have yet to be enacted or named. However, because citizenship is a technology of state power, even the most radical and creative uses of the term are haunted by its ties to the state. In this respect, the practical hope that draws many to the language and project of citizenship can entail disappointing tradeoffs in which expansive visions of community (the possible) are instrumentalized into the logic of the state (as it is).[4]

New Citizenship Studies approaches literature, the arts, and other expressive cultures as crucial sites of knowledge production that shape understandings of citizenship. This approach to literature requires a critical reorientation, a shift of vision and of method. Typically, scholars treat the law as citizenship's master discourse, and they privilege the state as citizenship's most important field of play. Similarly, accounts of the relationship between literature and citizenship traditionally frame literature as a response to and protest against the state. This approach celebrates the revisionist power of literature, but it also privileges the state as the primary arena for defining citizenship. In so doing, it treats literature as a secondary (and presumptively ineffectual) form of political expression. When scholars privilege legal sources and historically empowered authors (white men) as the source of the meanings of citizenship, they fail to recognize the cultural significance of traditions that theorize and enact conceptions of citizenship that exceed the epistemes and interpretive paradigms of the US nation-state and Anglo-American political thought writ large. This epistemic hierarchy is especially pronounced for a range of literary traditions outside of a white Euro-American canon whose cultural significance is often articulated through the framework of protest, resistance, and response.[5]

New Citizenship Studies recognizes the formative role of literature in creating (rather than reimagining) the meanings of citizenship; in so doing, it moves beyond the paradigm of literature as *only* resistance.[6] In order to fully understand the history and present of citizenship, we need to attend to its cultural practice, as well as its speculative making in a variety of subjunctive forms—including but not limited to literature. As Carrie Hyde (2018: 9, 16) argues, literature and other "subjunctive formulations" of citizenship can be understood "as historically activated genres of political theory," "where the possible (what might or could be) and the prescriptive (what should or ought to be) collide." Understood thus, literature and other subjunctive forms do not merely point to alternate worlds not yet realized; they "create a scene for happening" that projects and calls forth new conditions of possibility (Quashie 2021: 59).[7]

Examining politics from a confined number of sources and (largely European) traditions reinforces white supremacist metrics for recognizing where and how theorizing about citizenship happens.[8] The kinds of questions we can ask about citizenship change fundamentally when we approach the concept through the works, methods, and practices of those who cannot presume the protections of the state—people whose exclusion from formal citizenship has been the state's condition of possibility. "What happens to our thinking about citizenship," Derrick R. Spires (2019: 2) asks, if "instead of reading black writers as reacting to (or a presence in) a largely white-defined discourse . . . we base our working definitions of citizenship on black writers' proactive attempts to describe their own political work"? What happens when we approach citizenship through Indigenous writing and organizing? Or from the perspectives and literatures of migrants, refugees, and asylum seekers?[9] How have writers and activists engaged the framework of citizenship to develop something more just and sustaining? And when does the framework of citizenship sap energy from articulating and enacting something more fulfilling that has yet to be named? The answers to these questions vary, but they offer different "angle[s] of vision" (Wright in Spires 2019: 16); they also require different approaches to the archive as we have received it.[10]

New Citizenship Studies limns the speculative possibilities of citizenship and attunes us to the forms of worldmaking and community that writers build as practitioners of political *poiesis*. This issue begins with the premise that an approach to citizenship grounded in literary studies can offer new insight into the past, present, and future of citizenship. This attention to literature is all the more urgent today in light of the marginalization of literary studies, the humanities, and higher education more broadly. Attacks on higher education, book-ban initiatives, and the defunding of the arts have the cumulative effect of foreclosing and constraining our capacity to imagine, collectively, more equitable visions of the world as it is and could be. What new stories and methods emerge when we engage with, learn from, and make connections among traditions that have historically imagined citizenship otherwise?

Origins and Principles

Every era makes new conversations about citizenship urgent. The 1990s, for example, witnessed an outpouring of reassessments of citizenship that sought to rethink citizenship in the wake of transformative work on race and gender in a number of fields, an expanding literary canon, and the cultural and political aftermath of the Reagan era.[11] This special issue emerges, in part, from a series of formal and informal conversations we had beginning around 2017, when our books about citizenship and literature were in production.[12] The 2016 Presidential election brought into view with sharper clarity for a wider range of people the ongoing realities of white supremacy, inequality, and exclusion. For some, the outcome was met with a mix of surprise and disappointment. For others, it represented an eerily familiar (even predictable) backlash—an illustration of misogyny and racism resonant with what Koritha Mitchell (2020: 2, 4–5) has termed "know-your-place aggression."

The history of US citizenship is characterized not by inexorable progress but by switchbacks, reactionary declensions, and dreams deferred. The years following the 2016 election underlined this dynamic in a number of ways, including a series of anniversaries related to the legal history of citizenship. 2018 marked the one-hundred-fiftieth anniversary of the ratification of the Fourteenth Amendment in 1868, which codified the modern legal framework of birthright citizenship in the United States. 2019 marked the one-hundred-year anniversary of the Nineteenth Amendment—which formally prohibited denying the right to vote "on account of sex." These anniversaries mark events of Constitutional and legal consequence, but they also index what has not changed.[13] They coincided with the increased visibility of the ongoing violence against a host of people: the police killings of Michael Brown, Sandra Bland, George Floyd, and others; conversations around misogyny and sexual violence under the umbrella of #MeToo[14]; the buildup to what would become *Dobbs v. Jackson Women's Health Organization* (2022); the resurgence of anti-Arab and anti-Muslim racism, anti-Asian violence, and queer- and trans-phobia; the fights over the Dakota Access Pipeline; the growing documentation of state-sponsored violence in boarding schools for Indigenous children; the heightened instability of Deferred Action for Childhood Arrivals (DACA) protections; the renewed political currency of explicit appeals to white supremacy and Christian Nationalism; and ongoing voter suppression—all of which mark with stark clarity the exclusions and limitations of formal citizenship. They remind us of the disjuncture between legal definitions of citizenship and the everyday experiences of a range of citizens and noncitizens in the United States. They also remind of US citizenship's "changing same."

Citizenship is a conceptual palimpsest with many ideas and practices mapped onto it that exceed its legal uses. Its meanings are messy, polyvalent, contradictory, and fraught. We take the following principles to be core to New Citizenship Studies:

1. New Citizenship Studies understands that ideologies about whose voices and lives matter are as consequential as legal definitions of citizenship—and that literature and literary studies contribute to these ideologies. Literature and the speculative arts play a formative role in shaping the grammars, practices, and imaginaries of citizenship and other forms of collectivity. They illuminate possibilities for sovereignty, personhood, and community that US law and state-centered thinking tend to foreclose; they also provide ways of telling new stories about ourselves and for reexamining archives not built for articulating such stories.[15]

2. New Citizenship Studies recognizes narrative forms as dynamic sites of theorizing that embed impactful stories about citizenship, belonging, rights, protection, kinship, care, affection, and the collectives we form. It moves beyond the romance of resistance and

attends to the immanent meaning-making practices people have developed proactively for themselves, paying particular attention to the voices, forms, and methodologies that Euro-American canons, epistemologies, politics, and institutions try to marginalize or silence.[16] Examining citizenship through the works of those who cannot presume the state's protections challenges deterministic and triumphalist accounts of legal history; it also provides new ways of reading the law itself.

3. New Citizenship Studies wrestles with the ongoing failures of citizenship—failures that for many Americans, especially white Americans, have historically not been failures at all. It does *not* approach US citizenship as a universally desirable goal nor as an equally empowering structure; it recognizes the historical and ongoing importance of citizenship without idealizing it. The legal status of citizenship is often a matter of life or death, but the mere fact of being a US citizen has *never been enough* to *guarantee* protection from either state agents or nonstate actors. And, in some instances, US citizenship entails the loss of sovereignty, identity, and agency.

The Essays

This special issue takes citizenship as a flashpoint for theorizing the dynamic ways people have shaped and imagined the ideas, practices, and aesthetics of community. The essays examine citizenship through a variety of sources and across a range of genres, including fiction, poetry, periodicals, sketches and treatises, testimonies, and legal documents. The essays also track how writers draw on and improvise on established literary tropes, modes, and traditions, including sentimentalism, the bildungsroman, occasional poetry, and periodical culture. These works exemplify the wide array of venues through which people collectively imagined citizenship; they also dramatize the important role that literature and other extralegal forms play in the cultural constitution of citizenship.

Many of the essays consider formal citizenship, but they are also invested in articulating other ways of belonging and relation that people have created for themselves. When the essays do take up formal citizenship they do so not as a mechanism for liberation but rather as a technology of power that has reinforced subjection—save for brief moments of potential reset that have, to date, been followed by backlash and retrenchment. The works gathered here also challenge the ongoing tendency to periodize American literature around events (antebellum/postbellum, Civil War, Reconstruction, interwar years, etc.) that privilege chronological progress narratives constructed largely in the service of white nationalist mythologies.[17] The multiple origin points in the essays highlight the overlapping temporalities and spaces of citizenship: the durée of the long emancipation, ongoing settler colonial violence and occupation, queer time and relationality.[18] Collectively, these sources reveal the at times contradictory, at times interconnected, and at times parallel ways writers engage with citizenship—ranging from desire and reform to refusal and inoperability.

Recognition is core to the way critics have conceptualized citizenship and the politics of literature more broadly. In the sentimental tradition, for example, characterological identification is often understood and valued as a stepping stone to political recognition and enfranchisement. And yet, as Xine Yao (2021: 14) argues, "To acknowledge sympathy only as feeling across difference erases its violent origins in the matrices of domination that produce the system of racial difference." Insofar as sympathy is a precondition for belonging, it demands a level of transparency that elides what Édouard Glissant (1990: 189) terms the "right to opacity": a right to refuse legibility and therefore incorporation on terms set by white colonial and settler power. The meanings of opacity vary within different histories of racialization. As Erin Suzuki observes in "Transparent Citizenship: The Racialization of Privacy in Post–World War II Japanese American Fiction," the "ascription of inscrutability or 'unfeeling' to the figure of the Asian American" exposes the "limits of the politics of recognition." Suzuki draws on Hisaye Yamamoto's short story "Wilshire Bus" (1951) and John Okada's novel *No-No Boy* (1955) as case studies for rethinking the "transparent citizenship" of Japanese Americans, who are subject to "racialized surveillance and policing in the name of national security." Suzuki argues that these midcentury Japanese American texts offer "an aspirational, if often elusive, model for both Asian American and multiethnic solidarity movements whose constituents continue to occupy an ambivalent or ambiguous relationship to the figure of the rights-bearing citizen."

Several contributors examine the centrality of print culture to the making of citizenship. Kathryn Walkiewicz's "The Sentimentalist Terrain of Ora V. Eddleman Reed's *Twin Territories* Fiction" identifies Ora V. Eddleman Reed—editor of and contributor to *Twin Territories* (1898–1904), a magazine in the Muscogee Nation, Indian Territory—as a "vital contributor" to "Indian Territory's rich literary and media landscapes." Reed's fiction uses "sentimentalist tropes to assert the necessity of tribal autonomy," but, as Walkiewicz observes, her representation of "Indian Territory as a space of regenerative domesticity—a sentimentalist terrain" also reinforces "racialized notions of Indigeneity." In light of the lack of evidence that Reed was an enrolled member of the Cherokee Nation, the essay conceptualizes Reed as a "good territorial citizen"—a concept that draws meaning from Reed's literary advocacy for Indigenous sovereignty over Indian Territory (rather than from her own citizenship status). Sidonia Serafini's "'Unquestioned Citizenship': History, Poetry, and Black and Native Military Service in Hampton Institute's *Southern Workman*" takes up the politics of print culture through its engagement with poems published by Black and Native historians and poets in the Hampton Institute's *Southern Workman* (1872–1939), including Sarah Collins Fernandis (1863–1951), Paul Laurence Dunbar (1872–1906), Arthur C. Parker (Seneca, 1881–1955), and Hen-toh (Wyandot, 1870–1927). These writers stress that military service should guarantee formal citizenship, but they also develop what Serafini terms *unquestioned citizenship*: a sense of citizenship that "place[d] value on the formation of social, cultural, racial, and familial coalitions within—but separate from—the larger American nation." These writers saw themselves as "soldiers, fighting not with a gun on the battlefield but fighting with the pen in the public sphere to claim Black and Native peoples' place as unquestioned citizens." By conceptualizing literature as a form of warfare, even in times of "ostensible peace," Serafini also brings to light the "female figures on the periphery of the war effort."

Xiomara Santamarina, Ajay Kumar Batra, and Eve Eure show how Black Americans and Black Cherokees in the nineteenth century improvised modes of affiliation through and against formal citizenship and racial capitalism. Santamarina's "Market Nation: Forging Economic Citizenship in Nineteenth-Century African America" draws on two mid-nineteenth-century proto-sociological sketches by Joseph Willson and Cyprian Clamorgan to examine the benefits and perils of deploying "an ideal of economic citizenship that translated Black material successes and social mobility into an extra-legal symbolic citizenship." These sketches are part of a larger tradition of writing by free African Americans that sutures citizenship, labor, and economic uplift. Whereas Santamarina's "Market Nation" examines economic success as the measure of proper citizenship for free Black Americans, Batra's "Becoming 'Fellow-Servants': Slavery, Theft, and Improper Fellowship in the Nineteenth-Century South," examines theft—rather than private ownership or possessive individualism—as the basis for building fellowship among fugitive slaves. In the 1863 deposition by Octave Johnson that Batra discusses, theft is more than a tactic for survival amid hostile conditions; it is a creative practice of "improper fellowship" that forged "bonds of communal reciprocity" outside of enslavement's predatory racial capitalism. In a moment of extreme flux—when the possibilities for Black freedom, let alone Black citizenship, were unclear—Johnson and his compatriots point us toward an alternative to the "burdened individuality" (Hartman 1997: 115) upon which Reconstruction eventually hinged.

Where Batra and Santamarina focus on enslaved and free Black people engaging with US citizenship and enslavement in the middle of the nineteenth century, Eure examines how a Black Cherokee family navigated kinship, citizenship, and the legacies of enslavement at the turn of the twentieth century. In "Intergenerational Testimonials and the Politics of Black Cherokee Belonging," Eure examines a Black Cherokee family's attempt to claim formal Cherokee citizenship in a series of applications and appeals that spanned multiple decades. Eure reads these documents as *intergenerational testimonials*: "an emergent literary practice that created a Black Cherokee politics of collective belonging defined by intergenerational community and family knowledge and relationships." These testimonials show how forms of fellowship deemed improper between enslaved Black people and Indigenous people haunt future generations.

What does it mean to live under "the double-bind of choice under settler colonial conditions"? Florencia Lauria's "More than 'A Matter of Deciding To': Citizenship, Border Positionality, and Irresolution in Louise Erdrich's *The Night Watchman*" examines irresolution as a form of refusal. Building on the model of refusal developed in Audra Simpson's *Mohawk Interruptus* (2014), Lauria uses the term *border positionalities* to describe "the unresolved and *un*settled tension between the characters' Indigenous and settler political identities." For the Chippewa characters in Erdrich's *The Night Watchman* (2020), Lauria argues, "all choices are irresolute, inadequate, and contaminated." Refusal, as Lauria frames it, is not about whether one accepts or declines; rather, it is "a demonstration of the difficulty of absolute choice" amid the unresolved tensions of settler colonialism.[19] These tensions subtend US imperialism more broadly. Joseph Isaac Miranda's "The Suspended States of Latinx Literature" examines the impositions and inadequacies of US citizenship in the context of the Insular Cases (1901–25), which "legitimized the suspension of Puerto Rican sovereignty in the aftermath of the Spanish-American War" and created a qualified form of citizenship. Drawing on Justin Torres's *We the Animals* (2011), Miranda shows how the "legal maneuvers" of the Insular Cases are "entrenched in the representation of Latinx Literature." Miranda reads Torres's novel as a distinctly Puerto Rican bildungsroman, in which the protagonist's "suspended maturation" and "infantilization" mirrors the US empire's investment in keeping Puerto Rico in a perpetual state of childlike pupilage.

Taken together, the essays highlight the "lived contradictions between US citizenship and citizenship" in other communities (Lauria), on other terms, and in other sites. The essays track the various ways writers and practitioners have engaged with citizenship, as well as related frameworks such as fellowship, kinship, relation, and entanglement. They point to not one literary history of citizenship, but rather multiple, overlapping traditions, temporalities, and aesthetics. By tracking plural idioms, imaginings, and practices of citizenship across multiple critical traditions, this special issue invites a reading practice based on "connection." To invoke Sunny Xiang's review essay in this issue, "by reimagining comparison as connection," critics can "give new meaning to a politics of recognition, one in which seeing each other is more important than being seen."

We bring this introduction to a close not knowing the future world into which it will enter. It is hard to write about citizenship without considering the meanings it will take on in the future, because it is haunted backward and forward in time. Given the political problems that already beset the moment in which we write, we cannot help feeling a sense of foreboding. Yet, the uncertainties that surround each act of writing about citizenship are part of what has drawn so many writers to the term, even as they seek to write beyond its meanings in the present. Ultimately, this introduction, too, is one incitement—in a longer history of incitements—that looks ahead to new connections, collaborations, and beginnings.

Carrie Hyde is an associate professor of English at the University of California, Los Angeles. She is the author of *Civic Longing: The Speculative Origins of U.S. Citizenship* (2018).

Derrick R. Spires is associate professor of English and John and Patricia Cochran Scholar of Inclusive Excellence at the University of Delaware. He is author of *The Practice of Citizenship: Black Politics and Print Culture in the United States* (2019).

Notes

1 See Hughes 1994; Rusert 2015; Fuentes 2016; Shklar 1991; Hildebrandt et al. 2019.

2 For a sampling of related scholarship published in the last ten years, see: "Contested Citizenship: Legacies of American Slavery," an online forum (hosted by *Black Perspectives* and the Gilder Lehrman Center in 2021); Altschuler 2023; Best 2018; Blackhawk 2023; Brady 2022; Bruce 2021; Byrd 2021; Crawford 2023; Escobar 2023; Espiritu et al. 2022; Field 2014; Fleming 2022; Greer 2019; Han 2019; Hardison 2014; Hirschmann and Linker 2015; D. Jones 2021; M. Jones 2018 and 2021; Kazanjian 2016; King 2019; Mitchell 2020; Nguyen 2012; Le-Khac 2020; Miles 2015; Pegues 2021; Pexa 2019; Pickens 2019; Pinto 2020; Ponzio 2022; Roberts 2021; Roh 2021; Saguisag 2018; Saldaña-Portillo 2016 and 2019; Schalk 2022; Schlund-Vials 2016; Sépulchre 2021; Simpson 2014; Stanciu 2023; Stanfield 2022; Tyler 2022; Walkiewicz 2023; Wong 2015.

3 See, for instance, Best 2004 and 2018; Crawford 2023; DeLombard 2007 and 2012; Dayan 2011; Mansouri 2020; Miles 2015; Roberts 2021; Sharpe 2016; Sirenko 2023; Staidum 2022; Tillet 2012; Walcott 2021; Wong 2009 and 2015.

4 Here we take inspiration from José Esteban Muñoz's (2009) use of "educated hope" and Lauren Berlant's (2011) and Nancy Bentley's (2018) use of "cruel optimism."

5 See Quashie 2012: 3–5; Mitchell 2020: 40–42; Spires 2019: 25–26.

6 Hyde 2018: 15–16; Spires 2019: 25–26.

7 Kevin Quashie argues that "subjunctive utterances, through their wishfulness, seem to create or manifest a scene for happening, as if the subjunctive is a spell that casts its subject into the suspension of an imaginary" (Quashie 2021: 59).

8 This method follows from African American literary critical traditions and Barbara Christian's (1987: 58) insight: "For people of color have always theorized—but in forms quite different from the Western form of abstract logic. And I am inclined to say that our theorizing (and I intentionally use the verb rather than the noun) is often in narrative forms, in the stories we create, in riddles and proverbs, in the play with language, because dynamic rather than fixed ideas seem more to our liking."

9 How, for example, "could historical struggles over borders, citizenship, and identity by Latina/o and immigrant groups help to contextualize and challenge our thinking about these important and contemporary topics," asks Josue David Cisneros (2014: viii)? And what if we theorize citizenship from the vantage of refugees and others for whom the so-called "gift of freedom" is used coercively by the state to elicit and demand gratitude and loyalty (Nguyen 2012)? How can an attention to "homemade" models of citizenship, kinship, and placemaking reorient understandings of political membership, community, and belonging (Mitchell 2020; Brooks 2008; Bentley 2009; Fielder 2020)?

10 See, for instance, Hartman 2022; Nunley 2023; Trouillot 1995.

11 See Berlant 1991 and 1997; Burgett 1998; Castronovo 1995; Delany 1999; Harris 1993; Isenberg 1998; Kerber 1997 and 1998; Moon and Davidson 1995; Morrison 1992; Nelson 1998; Reid-Pharr 1999; Smith 1997; Shklar 1991; Wald 1995; Warner 1990. As the decade came to a close, Hartman's *Scenes of Subjection* (1997), among other works, provided a fundamental and radical reorientation in our understanding of citizenship and the law as mechanisms of subjection.

12 These conversations developed across a range of forums, including: "Re-Framing the Constitution: Futures of the Fourteenth Amendment" (organized by Keith McCall and Scott Pett at Rice University, October 5–6, 2018); a roundtable on Citizenship and Nineteenth-Century American Literary Studies (organized by Gordon Fraser and sponsored by MLA's Nineteenth-Century Literature Forum, January 9, 2021); and a roundtable and seminar on citizenship that we co-led at C19 on October 17 and 23, 2020. (The response to the C19 CFP was so robust that we had to divide the seminar into two sessions.) These forums revealed the breadth of thought on and ongoing interest around citizenship.

13 This way of understanding the history of US citizenship is informed by Hartman's (2022: chapter 4) analysis of the "nonevent of emancipation"; Christina Elizabeth Sharpe's (2016: 12) observation that "the means and modes of Black subjection may have changed, but the fact and structure of that subjection remain"; and Keeanga-Yamahtta Taylor's (2022: xiii) reminder that the long afterlives of enslavement function "as affirmation of a kind of deeply constrained and compromised conception of democracy and liberty in the first place."

14 Tarana Burke coined the phrase *Me Too* in 2006.

15 For related work on archives see, for instance, Hartman 2022; Keith 2013; Nunley 2023; Trouillot 1995. Our use of *grammars* draws on Spillers 1987.

16 Our attention to imminent meaning-making practices draws on Brown 2009; Foreman, Casey, and Patterson 2021; Foster 2005; Mitchell 2020; W. Johnson 2003.

17 For recent work rethinking these chronologies, see Marrs 2015 and "Revisioning Reconstruction," a special issue of *ALH* (2018).

18 On the "long emancipation" and the durée of emancipation, see Walcott 2021 and Staidum 2022.

19 On refusal more broadly, see, for instance, Bernstein and Er 2022; Campt 2019; Harney and Moten 2013; Moten and Hartman 2016.

References

Altschuler, Sari. 2023. "Babo's 'Mute'-ny: Deaf Culture and Black Testimony in Antebellum America." *PMLA* 138, no. 5: 1149–64. https://doi.org/10.1632/S0030812923000949.

Bentley, Nancy. 2009. "The Fourth Dimension: Kinlessness and African American Narrative." *Critical Inquiry* 35, no. 2: 270–92. https://doi.org/10.1086/596643.

Bentley, Nancy. 2018. "Reconstruction and the Cruel Optimism of Citizenship." *American Literary History* 30, no. 3: 608–15. https://doi.org/10.1093/alh/ajy029.

Berlant, Lauren Gail. 1991. *The Anatomy of National Fantasy: Hawthorne, Utopia, and Everyday Life.* Chicago: Univ. of Chicago Press.

Berlant, Lauren Gail. 1997. *The Queen of America Goes to Washington City: Essays on Sex and Citizenship.* Durham, NC: Duke Univ. Press.

Berlant, Lauren Gail. 2011. *Cruel Optimism.* Durham, NC: Duke Univ. Press.

Bernstein, Sarah, and Yanbing Er. 2022. "Gestures of Refusal: Introduction—Post45." *Post45* (website), October 27. https://post45.org/2022/10/gestures-of-refusal-introduction/.

Best, Stephen Michael. 2004. *The Fugitive's Properties: Law and the Poetics of Possession.* Chicago: Univ. of Chicago Press.

Best, Stephen Michael. 2018. *None like Us: Blackness, Belonging, Aesthetic Life.* Durham, NC: Duke Univ. Press.

Blackhawk, Ned. 2023. *The Rediscovery of America: Native Peoples and the Unmaking of U.S. History.* New Haven, CT: Yale Univ. Press.

Brady, Mary Pat. 2022. *Scales of Captivity: Racial Capitalism and the Latinx Child.* Durham, NC: Duke Univ. Press.

Brooks, Lisa Tanya. 2008. *The Common Pot: The Recovery of Native Space in the Northeast.* Minneapolis: Univ. of Minnesota Press.

Brown, Vincent. 2009. "Social Death and Political Life in the Study of Slavery." *American Historical Review* 114, no. 5: 1231–49. https://doi.org/10.1086/ahr.114.5.1231.

Bruce, La Marr Jurelle. 2021. *How to Go Mad without Losing Your Mind: Madness and Black Radical Creativity.* Durham, NC: Duke Univ. Press.

Burgett, Bruce. 1998. *Sentimental Bodies: Sex, Gender, and Citizenship in the Early Republic.* Princeton, NJ: Princeton Univ. Press.

Byrd, Jodi A. 2011. *The Transit of Empire: Indigenous Critiques of Colonialism.* Minneapolis: Univ. of Minnesota Press.

Byrd, Jodi A. 2021. "Not Yet: Indigeneity, Antiblackness, and Anticolonial Liberation." In *Antiblackness*, edited by Moon-Kie Jung and João Helion Costa Vargas, 309–24. Durham, NC: Duke Univ. Press. https://doi.org/10.1215/9781478013167-020.

Campt, Tina Marie. 2019. "Black Visuality and the Practice of Refusal." *Women and Performance: A Journal of Feminist Theory* 29, no. 1: 79–87. https://doi.org/10.1080/0740770X.2019.1573625.

Castronovo, Russ. 1995. *Fathering the Nation: American Genealogies of Slavery and Freedom.* Berkeley: Univ. of California Press.

Christian, Barbara. 1987. "The Race for Theory." *Cultural Critique*, no. 6: 51. https://doi.org/10.2307/1354255.

Cisneros, Josue David. 2014. *The Border Crossed Us: Rhetorics of Borders, Citizenship, and Latina/o Identity.* Tuscaloosa: The Univ. Alabama Press.

"Contested Citizenship: Legacies of American Slavery." 2021. Online Forum. *Black Perspectives*, July 26. https://www.aaihs.org/online-forum-contested-citizenship-legacies-of-american-slavery/.

Crawford, Margo Natalie. 2023. "African American Citizenship in the Post–Civil Rights Era." In *The Cambridge Companion to Contemporary African American Literature*, edited by Yogita Goyal, 31–45. Cambridge Companions to Literature. Cambridge: Cambridge Univ. Press.

Dayan, Colin. 2011. *The Law Is a White Dog: How Legal Rituals Make and Unmake Persons*. Princeton, NJ: Princeton Univ. Press.

De Genova, Nicholas. 2017. "Citizenship." In *Keywords for Latina/o Studies*, edited by Deborah R. Vargas, Lawrence La Fountain-Stokes, and Nancy Raquel Mirabal. New York: New York Univ. Press.

Delany, Samuel R. 1999. *Times Square Red, Times Square Blue*. New York: New York Univ. Press.

DeLombard, Jeannine. 2007. *Slavery on Trial: Law, Abolitionism, and Print Culture*. Chapel Hill: Univ. of North Carolina Press.

DeLombard, Jeannine. 2012. *In the Shadow of the Gallows: Race, Crime, and American Civic Identity*. Philadelphia: Univ. of Pennsylvania Press.

Escobar, Guadalupe. 2023. "The Critical DREAMer Memoir: Educational Mobility and the Limits of Meritocratic Citizenship." *American Literature* 95, no. 1: 29–58. https://doi.org/10.1215/00029831-10345351.

Espiritu, Yến Lê, Lan Duong, Ma Vang, Victor Bascara, Khatharya Um, Lila Sharif, and Nigel Hatton. 2022. *Departures: An Introduction to Critical Refugee Studies*. Berkeley: Univ. of California Press.

Field, Corinne T. 2014. *The Struggle for Equal Adulthood: Gender, Race, Age, and the Fight for Citizenship in Antebellum America*. Chapel Hill: Univ. of North Carolina Press.

Fielder, Brigitte. 2020. *Relative Races: Genealogies of Interracial Kinship in Nineteenth-Century America*. Durham, NC: Duke Univ. Press.

Fleming, Julius B. 2022. *Black Patience: Performance, Civil Rights, and the Unfinished Project of Emancipation*. New York: New York Univ. Press.

Foreman, P. Gabrielle, Jim Casey, and Sarah Lynn Patterson, eds. 2021. *The Colored Conventions Movement: Black Organizing in the Nineteenth Century*. Chapel Hill: Univ. of North Carolina Press.

Foster, Frances Smith. 2005. "A Narrative of the Interesting Origins and (Somewhat) Surprising Developments of African-American Print Culture." *American Literary History* 17, no. 4: 714–40. https://doi.org/10.1093/alh/aji042.

Fuentes, Marisa J. 2016. *Dispossessed Lives: Enslaved Women, Violence, and the Archive*. Philadelphia: Univ. of Pennsylvania Press.

Glissant, Édouard. 1997. *Poetics of Relation*. Translated by Betsy Wing. Ann Arbor: Univ. of Michigan Press.

Greer, Brenna Wynn. 2019. *Represented: The Black Imagemakers Who Reimagined African American Citizenship*. Electronic resource. American Business, Politics, and Society. Philadelphia: Univ. of Pennsylvania Press.

Han, Shinhee. 2019. *Racial Melancholia, Racial Dissociation: On the Social and Psychic Lives of Asian Americans*. Durham, NC: Duke Univ. Press.

Hardison, Ayesha K. 2014. *Writing through Jane Crow: Race and Gender Politics in African American Literature*. Charlottesville: Univ. of Virginia Press.

Harney, Stefano, and Fred Moten. 2013. *The Undercommons: Fugitive Planning and Black Study*. New York: Minor Compositions.

Harris, Cheryl I. 1993. "Whiteness as Property." *Harvard Law Review* 106, no. 8: 1707–91. https://doi.org/10.2307/1341787.

Hartman, Saidiya. 2022. *Scenes of Subjection: Terror, Slavery, and Self-Making in Nineteenth-Century America*. New York: W. W. Norton.

Hildebrandt, Paula, Kerstin Evert, Sibylle Peters, Mirjam Schaub, Kathrin Wildner, and Gesa Ziemer, eds. 2019. *Performing Citizenship: Bodies, Agencies, Limitations*. Cham: Springer International Publishing.

Hirschmann, Nancy J., and Beth Linker, eds. 2015. *Civil Disabilities: Citizenship, Membership, and Belonging*. Philadelphia: Univ. of Pennsylvania Press.

Hughes, Langston. "Harlem." 1994. In *The Collected Poems of Langston Hughes*, edited by Arnold Rampersad, 426. New York: Knopf.

Hutner, Gordon, ed. 2018. "Reenvisioning Reconstruction." Special Issue, *American Literary History* 30, no. 3.

Hyde, Carrie. 2018. *Civic Longing: The Speculative Origins of U.S. Citizenship*. Cambridge, MA: Harvard Univ. Press.

Isenberg, Nancy. 1998. *Sex and Citizenship in Antebellum America*. Chapel Hill: Univ. of North Carolina Press.

Johnson, Walter. 2003. "On Agency." *Journal of Social History* 37, no. 1: 113–24.

Jones, Douglas A., Jr. 2021. "Pragmatics of Democracy: A Political Theory of African American Literature before Emancipation." *American Literary History* 33, no. 3: 498–509. https://doi.org/10.1093/alh/ajab046.

Jones, Martha S. 2007. *All Bound up Together: The Woman Question in African American Public Culture, 1830–1900*. Chapel Hill: Univ. of North Carolina Press.

Jones, Martha S. 2018. *Birthright Citizens: A History of Race and Rights in Antebellum America*. Cambridge: Cambridge Univ. Press.

Jones, Martha S. 2021. *Vanguard: How Black Women Broke Barriers, Won the Vote, and Insisted on Equality for All*. New York: Basic Books.

Kazanjian, David. 2016. *The Brink of Freedom: Improvising Life in the Nineteenth-Century Atlantic World*. Durham, NC: Duke Univ. Press.

Keith, Joseph. 2013. *Unbecoming Americans: Writing Race and Nation from the Shadows of Citizenship, 1945–1960*. New Brunswick, NJ: Rutgers Univ. Press.

Kerber, Linda. 1997. "The Meanings of Citizenship." *Journal of American History* 84, no. 3: 833–54.

Kerber, Linda. 1998. *No Constitutional Right to Be Ladies: Women and Obligations of Citizenship*. New York: Hill and Wang.

King, Tiffany Lethabo. 2019. *The Black Shoals: Offshore Formations of Black and Native Studies*. Durham, NC: Duke Univ. Press.

Le-Khac, Long. 2020. *Giving Form to an Asian and Latinx America*. Stanford, CA: Stanford Univ. Press.

Mansouri, Leila. 2020. "Slave Narratives, Black Disenfranchisement, and the Electoral Limits of Black Freedom." *J19: The Journal of Nineteenth-Century Americanists* 8, no. 2: 355–62. https://doi.org/10.1353/jnc.2020.0019.

Marrs, Cody. 2015. *Nineteenth-Century American Literature and the Long Civil War*. New York: Cambridge Univ. Press.

Miles, Tiya. 2015. *Ties That Bind: The Story of an Afro-Cherokee Family in Slavery and Freedom*. Oakland: Univ. of California Press.

Mitchell, Koritha. 2020. *From Slave Cabins to the White House: Homemade Citizenship in African American Culture*. Urbana: Univ. of Illinois Press.

Moon, Michael., and Cathy N. Davidson, eds. 1995. *Subjects and Citizens: Nation, Race, and Gender from Oroonoko to Anita Hill*. Durham, NC: Duke Univ. Press.

Morrison, Toni. 1992. *Playing in the Dark: Whiteness and the Literary Imagination*. Cambridge, MA: Harvard Univ. Press.

Moten, Fred, and Saidiya Hartman. 2016. "The Black Outdoors." John Hope Franklin Humanities Institute at Duke University, October 5. https://www.youtube.com/watch?v=t_tUZ6dybrc.

Muñoz, José Esteban. 2009. *Cruising Utopia: The Then and There of Queer Futurity*. New York: New York Univ. Press.

Nelson, Dana D. 1998. *National Manhood: Capitalist Citizenship and the Imagined Fraternity of White Men*. Durham, NC: Duke Univ. Press.

Nguyen, Mimi Thi. 2012. *The Gift of Freedom: War, Debt, and Other Refugee Passages*. Durham, NC: Duke Univ. Press.

Nunley, Tamika. 2023. *The Demands of Justice: Enslaved Women, Capital Crime, and Clemency in Early Virginia*. Chapel Hill: Univ. of North Carolina Press.

Pegues, Juliana. 2021. *Space-Time Colonialism: Alaska's Indigenous and Asian Entanglements*. Chapel Hill: Univ. of North Carolina Press.

Pexa, Chris. 2019. *Translated Nation: Rewriting the Dakhóta Oyáte*. Minneapolis: Univ. of Minnesota Press.

Pickens, Therí A. 2019. *Black Madness:: Mad Blackness*. Durham, NC: Duke Univ. Press.

Pinto, Samantha. 2020. *Infamous Bodies: Early Black Women's Celebrity and the Afterlives of Rights*. Durham, NC: Duke Univ. Press.

Ponzio, Alessio. 2022. "Queer Citizenship: Between Desire to Belong and Impulse to Dismantle." *Journal of History* 57, no. 3: 325–35.

Quashie, Kevin. 2012. *The Sovereignty of Quiet: Beyond Resistance in Black Culture*. New Brunswick, NJ: Rutgers Univ. Press.

Quashie, Kevin. 2021. *Black Aliveness, or a Poetics of Being*. Durham, NC: Duke Univ. Press.

Reid-Pharr, Robert F. 1999. *Conjugal Union: The Body, the House, and the Black American*. New York: Oxford Univ. Press.

Roberts, Alaina E. 2021. *I've Been Here All the While: Black Freedom on Native Land*. Philadelphia: Univ. of Pennsylvania Press.

Roh, David S. 2021. *Minor Transpacific: Triangulating American, Japanese, and Korean Fictions*. Stanford, CA: Stanford Univ. Press.

Rusert, Britt. 2015. "Disappointment in the Archives of Black Freedom." *Social Text* 33, no. 4 (125): 19–33. https://doi.org/10.1215/01642472-3315874.

Saguisag, Lara. 2018. *Incorrigibles and Innocents: Constructing Childhood and Citizenship in Progressive Era Comics*. New Brunswick, NJ: Rutgers Univ. Press.

Saldaña-Portillo, María Josefina. 2016. *Indian Given: Racial Geographies across Mexico and the United States*. Durham, NC: Duke Univ. Press.

Saldaña-Portillo, María Josefina. 2019. "The Violence of Citizenship in the Making of Refugees: The United States and Central America." *Social Text* 37, no. 4 (141): 1–21. https://doi.org/10.1215/01642472-7794343.

Schalk, Sami. 2022. *Black Disability Politics*. Durham, NC: Duke Univ. Press.

Sépulchre, Marie. 2021. *Disability and Citizenship Studies*. New York: Routledge and CRC Press (accessed November 9, 2023).

Sharpe, Christina Elizabeth. 2016. *In the Wake: On Blackness and Being*. Durham, NC: Duke Univ. Press.

Shklar, Judith N. 1991. *American Citizenship: The Quest for Inclusion*. Cambridge, MA: Harvard Univ. Press.

Simpson, Audra. 2007. "On Ethnographic Refusal: Indigeneity, 'Voice' and Colonial Citizenship." *Junctures: The Journal for Thematic Dialogue*, no. 9: 67.

Simpson, Audra. 2008. "From White into Red: Captivity Narratives as Alchemies of Race and Citizenship." *American Quarterly* 60, no. 2: 251–57.

Simpson, Audra. 2014. *Mohawk Interruptus: Political Life across the Borders of Settler States*. Durham, NC: Duke Univ. Press.

Sirenko, Valerie. 2023. "Destroyed Documents and Racial Vulnerability in the Literature of Slavery's Legal Afterlife." *American Literature* 95, no. 1: 1–28. https://doi.org/10.1215/00029831-10345337.

Smith, Rogers M. 1997. *Civic Ideals: Conflicting Visions of Citizenship in U.S. History*. New Haven, CT: Yale Univ. Press.

Spillers, Hortense J. 1987. "Mama's Baby, Papa's Maybe: An American Grammar Book." *Diacritics* 17, no. 2: 65–81. https://doi.org/10.2307/464747.

Spires, Derrick R. 2019. *The Practice of Citizenship: Black Politics and Print Culture in the Early United States*. Philadelphia: Univ. of Pennsylvania Press.

Staidum, Frederick C., Jr. 2022. "The *Durée* of Emancipation and the Crisis of Freedom in Antebellum Black Writing." *South Atlantic Quarterly* 121, no. 1: 33–51. https://doi.org/10.1215/00382876-9561517.

Stanciu, Cristina. 2023. *The Makings and Unmakings of Americans: Indians and Immigrants in American Literature and Culture, 1879–1924*. The Henry Roe Cloud Series on American Indians and Modernity. New Haven, NC: Yale Univ. Press.

Stanfield, Susan J. 2022. *Rewriting Citizenship: Women, Race, and Nineteenth-Century Print Culture*. Athens: Univ. of Georgia Press.

Taylor, Keeanga-Yamahtta. 2022. Foreword to Hartman 2022: 12–29.

Tillet, Salamishah. 2012. *Sites of Slavery: Citizenship and Racial Democracy in the Post–Civil Rights Imagination*. Durham, NC: Duke Univ. Press.

Trouillot, Michel-Rolph. 1995. *Silencing the Past: Power and the Production of History*. Boston: Beacon Press.

Tyler, Dennis. 2022. *Disabilities of the Color Line: Redressing Antiblackness from Slavery to the Present*. New York: New York Univ. Press.

Walcott, Rinaldo. 2021. *The Long Emancipation: Moving toward Black Freedom*. Durham, NC: Duke Univ. Press.

Wald, Priscilla. 1995. *Constituting Americans: Cultural Anxiety and Narrative Form*. Durham, NC: Duke Univ. Press.

Walker, David. 1829. *Walker's Appeal, in Four Articles: Together with a Preamble, to the Coloured Citizens of the World, but in Particular, and Very Expressly, to Those of the United States of America, Written in Boston, State of Massachusetts, September 28, 1829*. Boston.

Walkiewicz, Kathryn. 2023. *Reading Territory: Indigenous and Black Freedom, Removal, and the Nineteenth-Century State*. Chapel Hill: Univ. of North Carolina Press.

Warner, Michael. 1990. *The Letters of the Republic: Publication and the Public Sphere in Eighteenth-Century America*. Cambridge, MA: Harvard Univ. Press.

Wong, Edlie L. 2009. *Neither Fugitive nor Free: Atlantic Slavery, Freedom Suits, and the Legal Culture of Travel*. New York: New York Univ. Press.

Wong, Edlie L. 2015. *Racial Reconstruction: Black Inclusion, Chinese Exclusion, and the Fictions of Citizenship*. New York: New York Univ. Press.

Yao, Xine. 2021. *Disaffected: The Cultural Politics of Unfeeling in Nineteenth-Century America*. Perverse Modernities. Durham, NC: Duke Univ. Press.

Erin Suzuki

Transparent Citizenship: The Racialization of Privacy in Post–World War II Japanese American Fiction

Abstract Written in the wake of the Japanese incarceration and the emergence of new Cold War discourses around race, privacy, and democracy, Hisaye Yamamoto's and John Okada's works mark a shift from the specific targeting of Japanese Americans as individuals whose citizenship was contingent upon enforced transparency to the broader suspicion of the more generalized "Oriental" as a figure whose opacity becomes an excuse for racialized surveillance and policing in the name of national security. As formerly interned or imprisoned individuals, Yamamoto's and Okada's protagonists begin their stories already understanding the contingency of their right to privacy and the expectations of transparency that attend their reentry into the mainstream of US society. This article argues that Yamamoto's and Okada's depictions of this transparent citizenship not only critique the limitations and burdens of proof that it places on racialized (and otherwise minoritized) individuals, but also articulate ways to think differently about citizenship itself. What if US citizenship were understood as a formation that did not fetishize the role of individual agency in the process of self-determination? What if the goal of transparency was not to expose or condemn the individual but to better illuminate the parts that individuals play in the construction of our society, and the complexity of their connections to others? And how might transparent citizenship be reconceptualized to empower, rather than infantilize, citizens vis-à-vis the state, by giving us information we might need to imagine and remake the power dynamics of this relationship?

Keywords opacity, transparency, Asian American literature, citizenship

On June 26, 2018, the US Supreme Court officially repudiated and overruled *Korematsu v. the United States* (1944), the court case that notoriously upheld the lawfulness of the forced removal and incarceration of Japanese American citizens during World War II. Ironically, however, the overruling of *Korematsu* came as part of a decision that sustained discrimination against a *different* class of racialized persons in the name of national security. Executive Order 13780, issued shortly after President Donald J. Trump took office in 2017,

American Literature, Volume 96, Number 4, December 2024
DOI 10.1215/00029831-11557497   © 2024 by Duke University Press

created an effective block on travel to the United States from several Muslim-majority nations; it banned new visas and required all individuals traveling from Iran, Libya, Somalia, Sudan, Syria, and Yemen to be subject to heightened background checks, surveillance, and scrutiny. The State of Hawai'i and three other plaintiffs brought a lawsuit against the Trump administration, arguing that the executive order was unlawful in its presumption that all persons arriving from these nations could be potentially classified as "detrimental to the interests of the United States."[1] While the ninth circuit court ruled in favor of the plaintiffs, the Supreme Court narrowly ruled five to four to overturn the lower court ruling, with the majority pronouncing that the "entry suspension is an act that is well within executive authority" and that "the Government has set forth a sufficient national security justification" for the heightened surveillance.

Writing the majority opinion on the case *Trump v. Hawaii*, Chief Justice John Roberts made a point of distinguishing *Trump* from *Korematsu*, condemning *Korematsu* as "objectively unlawful" and "gravely wrong the day it was decided," yet simultaneously upholding the right of the executive to suspend the entrance of noncitizens into the country when such entry might be deemed to be detrimental to the interests of the United States. By contrast, in her dissent, Justice Sonia Sotomayor argued that the force of addressing *Korematsu* was not to dispute a point about the rights and privileges of citizens versus noncitizens but rather to highlight how the majority rulings in both cases relied upon a "barren invocation of national security" that "redeploys the same underlying logic of *Korematsu* and merely replaces one 'gravely wrong' decision with another." Whether applied to citizens with extranational connections (in the case of *Korematsu*) or noncitizens seeking to join citizen relatives in the United States (in the case of *Trump*), both cases show how the modern US state, from the 1940s through the present, has continued to demand heightened surveillance and increasing expectations of transparency from individuals in the name of military necessity while shielding its own workings and decision-making apparatus from view.

Many scholars have warned how these ever-increasing demands for individual transparency—accompanied by diminished expectations for governmental or structural accountability—have long-reaching consequences for the very ideas of US citizenship and democracy, yet few have taken account of the way that the hypervisibility of racialized or otherwise minoritized individuals has historically marked these same individuals as *transparent citizens.* Legal scholar Joel Reidenberg

(2015: 449) defines a *transparent citizen* as one who "loses informational self-determination in [their] relationship with the state and thus loses an important bedrock of democratic civil society." While Reidenberg argues that this "overexposure . . . reduces the checks and balances on the exercise of government powers," which in turn diminishes *all* citizens' "trust and commitment to the law," in this essay I argue that this now prevalent phenomenon of transparent citizenship has roots in racialized forms of surveillance undertaken in the name of national security against the perceived threat of an enemy within. Drawing from two works by midcentury Japanese American authors— Hisaye Yamamoto's short story "Wilshire Bus" (1951) and John Okada's novel *No-No Boy* (1955)—I show how conflicting commitments to transparency, privacy, and the demands of national security are narrated and held in tension around Asian Americans' ambivalent relationship to citizenship.

If the proper functioning of a democracy relies upon government transparency and individual citizens' privacy, Yamamoto's and Okada's reversals of these terms illustrate how the lingering authoritarian logics of national security, held into perpetuity, can erode both a sense of personal agency and participation in civic life. Both authors render their Japanese American protagonists' inner thoughts transparent through the deployment of psychologically realistic stream of consciousness narrative; by contrast, the state and the systems that support it remain pointedly inscrutable. Yet this does not mean that minoritized communities are doomed to living out a bare life at the margins. Instead, I read these works as offering alternative sites of community repair through narratives and structures that protect and make space for both transparency *and* what Martinican theorist Édouard Glissant (1990: 189) has called the "right to opacity" (*le droit à l'opacité*) as a means of articulating mutual vulnerability, responsibility, and community building, in opposition to systems of enforced exposure that operate as tools of surveillance and control. "Wilshire Bus" and *No-No Boy* not only question the obscuring logics of national security; they critique the fetishization of individual rights upon which popular ideas of citizenship are based. If, as Carrie Hyde (2018: 4) notes, the belated codification of citizenship under the Fourteenth Amendment and its subsequent interpretations increasingly bound individual rights to the figure of the citizen, an "official legal status that describes a person's inclusion in a community . . . defined in national terms," the abrogation of those rights in the case of the large-scale incarceration of Japanese Americans highlights the conflicts that emerge when rights-bearing individuals whose communities exceed or extend *beyond* national borders and boundaries run up against such nation-based, exclusionary definitions of citizenship. In so doing, they test the extent to which the rights conferred by US citizenship can meaningfully protect and preserve not only the personal right to privacy but also the right to opacity.

Before continuing, I want to say a few words about this project's engagement with Glissant's conceptualization of opacity, which responds to conditions of racial, colonial, and national subjectification that are very different from those experienced by Yamamoto and Okada. Glissant's commitments to a decolonial Caribbean and his political and aesthetic engagements with the art and culture of an expansive Black diaspora are quite different from the situations of Yamamoto and Okada, whose experiences of incarceration left them ambivalently attached to the US state and its increasingly global ambitions. Yet following Katherine McKittrick's (2022: 7) reading of Glissantian opacity as a generative *methodology* for the "terrible working through of objecthood and the legible and quiet forms of racist violence," I find opacity to be a useful frame to consider Asian American racialization in relation to other modes of settler colonial and racial violence that have worked to police the boundary between a legitimate right to privacy and a suspicious or threatening inscrutability. When read alongside articulations of illegibility, refusal, and quiet in Black, Indigenous, and queer studies, the ascription of inscrutability or "unfeeling" to the figure of the Asian American individual similarly tests the limits of the politics of recognition upon which liberal subjecthood—and by extension, modern citizenship—is based. Some of the most interesting new scholarship in the field of Asian American studies has emphasized the critical dimensions of Asian inscrutability in terms of its potential to, as Xine Yao (2021: 6) has argued, confound the "demands of sympathetic recognition" that work as gatekeeping mechanisms for the "liberal project of inclusion." This critical turn—which includes recent work by Iyko Day (2016), Stephen Sohn (2018), Kandice Chuh (2019), Juliana Hu Pegues (2021), and Vivian Huang (2022) among others—engages queer, Black, and Indigenous theories of refusal to reframe the trajectory of Asian American studies away from questions of representation and recognition and toward what Lisa Lowe (2015) has identified as the disavowed yet insurgent intimacies among communities differently subjugated by the projects of colonialism, nationalism, and racial capitalism that have shaped global modernity. I engage opacity as one more way to consider how demands for transparency from Asian American citizens perceived as inscrutable might connect to other important conversations around the racialized and gendered dynamics of privacy, personhood, and humanity.

The expectation of transparency as an unofficial requirement of good citizenship certainly did not begin with nor has it been limited to Asian American communities. Jessica Vasquez-Tokos and Priscilla Yamin (2021: 718) posit that the right to privacy exists largely as a "privilege of Whiteness," arguing that this "racialization of privacy" becomes particularly evident today at hypersurveilled sites like the US/Mexico border, where intensified levels of surveillance have eroded individuals' rights to privacy and expanded the reach of the carceral system into the personal and private lives of people in Black, brown, and immigrant communities. This racialization of privacy can be characterized by a divide between individuals whose interior and domestic lives are protected as *private* and individuals whose interior and domestic lives have been perceived as lacking, inscrutable, or opaque: the former individuals are understood as contributing to the basic dignity and individuality necessary for a citizen participating in a democracy, while the latter individuals are seen as a threat to the smooth functioning of the same. In this sense, interrogating the racialization of privacy also requires a reckoning with the racialization of citizenship, as both draw attention to the ways that certain communities' mobility and access have historically been made contingent upon precisely the kind of informational self-disclosure and transparency that encroaches upon the right of the individual to retain sovereignty over their personal lives.

Like other practices of discrimination, the racialization of privacy does not operate in a uniform way: the flexibility of its application speaks to how the right to opacity remains contested across multiple constituencies. Kevin Quashie (2012: 8) notes how historical, legal, and cultural understandings of Black citizens as fundamentally "public subjects with identities formed and articulated and resisted in public" has served to mobilize Black identities in service of social justice while downplaying or eliding the personal sovereignty afforded by privacy and interiority. Yet if Black modes of subject-formation have been historically overdetermined by presumptions of publicity and transparency, Asian American expressions of subjectivity have been rendered suspect by their presumed impenetrability. In contrast to discourses around Blackness that collapse private life into public expression, racial rhetorics around Asian American inscrutability presume, as Sunny Xiang (2020: 38) argues, a "faithless relationship between surface phenomena and inner truths." Indeed, so long as minoritized communities' assertions of rights and personhood are tied to an implicit expectation to publicly perform or narrate emotional or affective transparency, Asian American attempts to perform transparency are always already regarded as suspicious, "faithless," or inauthentic: as Huang (2022: 19) points out, a "racial politics of inscrutability" serves to "stoke anxieties of Asian American apoliticality" in ways that set Asian American communities in tension not only with unmarked ideals of "white comportment" but also with expectations of "POC political affect." In this sense, Asian inscrutability not only limns the legal and structural limits of national inclusion, but it also remains alien and offputting to understandings of social justice that rely upon performances of authenticity.

These racialized ascriptions of impenetrability, inauthenticity, and inscrutability have shaped and been shaped by Asian Americans' ambivalent relationship to both legal and affective forms of US citizenship. As Lowe (1996: 5–6) has observed, the very concept of citizenship has been "defined over against the Asian *immigrant,* legally, economically, and culturally" since the 1850s, when Asians began to emigrate to the Americas in large numbers; even more than a century later, "Asian Americans have remained persistently racialized as "immigrant[s], as the 'foreigner-within,' even when born in the United States and the descendant of generations born here before." Suspicions about the alien inscrutability of Asian Americans certainly contributed to the logic that led to the targeting and incarceration of Japanese Americans during World War II, and later expanded into a more robust surveillance state during the anti-Communist Red Scare of the Cold War years. Although fears of espionage and Communist infiltration were by no means focused solely on Asian American individuals during the postwar era, susceptibility to Communism itself was often racialized as an Asiatic or "Oriental" trait (Kennan 1947: 574). Xiang (2020: 7) points out that the "emergence of two Chinas, Koreas, and Vietnams—combined with the U.S. government's confusion of anticolonial nationalism with global communism" during the dawn of the Cold War era worked to "establis[h] the Oriental as a perfect cross of the racial and ideological unknowns." In other words, rendering the "Oriental" as a racially *and* ideologically inscrutable figure extended and expanded the surveillance logics that had demanded transparency from the Japanese American citizenry during World War II. If the racialized targeting and removal of Japanese Americans during the war was understood as an exceptional wartime measure, the racialized surveillance of the "Oriental" became a part of the way that war itself became incorporated into the fabric of everyday life. Such surveillance practices were key, as Christine Hong (2020: 1) argues, to the transformation of *war* power into *policing* power, as both were predicated upon a framework through which racialized populations were viewed as inscrutable and therefore understood as "suspect terrain" more than rights-bearing "individuals."

Written and set during the rise of these Cold War discourses around race, privacy, and democracy, Hisaye Yamamoto's and John Okada's fictions mark this shift from the specific targeting of Japanese Americans as individuals whose citizenship was contingent upon enforced transparency to the broader suspicion of the more generalized Asian American "Oriental" as a figure whose opacity becomes an excuse for racialized surveillance and policing. Having already been taken from their homes, interrogated about their beliefs and loyalties, and incarcerated, the protagonists of both Yamamoto's and Okada's works begin their stories already understanding the contingency of their right to privacy and the expectations of transparency that attend their reentry into the mainstream of US society. In the sections that follow I explore how Yamamoto's and Okada's depictions of transparent citizenship not only critique its limitations and the burdens of proof that it places on racialized or other minoritized individuals, but also articulate ways to think differently about citizenship itself. What if US citizenship were understood as a formation that did not fetishize the role of individual agency in the process of self-determination? What if the goal of transparency was not to expose or condemn the individual but to better illuminate the parts that individuals play in the construction of our society, and the complexity of their connections to others? How might transparent citizenship be reconceptualized to empower, rather than infantilize, citizens vis-à-vis the state, by giving us information we might need to imagine and remake the power dynamics of this relationship?[2]

The Right to Opacity and the Limits of Transparency in "Wilshire Bus"

Hisaye Yamamoto's short story "Wilshire Bus," originally published in 1950, is a useful parable about how the pressures Asian Americans place on ourselves and others to be transparent refracts across literary, political, and interpersonal contexts. First published within a decade of the author's own release from an internment camp in Poston, Arizona, "Wilshire Bus" focuses on a bus trip taken by the protagonist

Esther Kuroiwa, a young Japanese American woman who is going to visit her husband at the VA hospital in Los Angeles not long after the end of the war. On the bus, Esther witnesses a drunken white man harassing a Chinese couple; although she says and does nothing, she feels anger at the man's belligerent racism mixed with a sense of relief that it is the "Chinese," and not the "Japanese," who are this time being singled out by the man's "exclusion order" (Yamamoto 2001: 6). After the drunken man leaves the bus, a different white man stands up and makes a public apology to the couple, and possibly to Esther as well. This second man's seeming satisfaction with this apology is contrasted with Esther's growing feelings of unease. When she finally arrives at the hospital and sees her husband, he interprets her despair as being about her feelings for him, a mistake that she allows him to believe.

While many readings of "Wilshire Bus" have foregrounded the complexity of Esther's silence in this text, I want to draw attention to how the story's limited omniscient third-person narrator gives voice to Esther's thoughts—if not to her fellow passengers on the bus, then certainly to the reader. Esther's thoughts and emotions, rendered transparent by Yamamoto's vivid stream of consciousness narrative, are in direct contrast to the unknowable thoughts and motives of the Chinese couple on the bus, whose opacity Esther herself finds alienating and off-putting. Yamamoto (2001: 37) shows us that Esther makes repeated attempts to communicate solidarity with the Chinese woman, but all these attempts fall short: Esther's initial attempt to "smile a greeting" is missed because the Chinese woman is looking elsewhere, and when she does finally catch her eye as the drunken man is ranting at them, the woman "presented a face so impassive yet cold, and eyes so expressionless yet hostile, that Esther's overture fell quite flat." Esther reacts defensively to what she interprets as the woman's "hostile" look, withdrawing her own feelings of sympathy as she thinks to herself: "Okay, okay, if that's the way you feel about it," and thereafter avoids even looking at them when they all get off at the same bus stop (37).

All the interactions between Esther and the Chinese couple take place in complete silence, yet the contrast between the accessibility of Esther's interior monologue and the inscrutability of the Chinese couple's response marks them as jarringly other within the context of the narrative. I argue that this contrast works to draw attention to the limits of Esther's perceptions and sympathies. Pushing back against the idea that racial discrimination is experienced in a universal way, the unspoken misunderstanding between Esther and the Chinese couple speaks to the different ways that discrimination operates even among people who are, within the mainstream of US society, racialized as part of a homogenous group. It also demonstrates the difficulty of being able to move beyond one's own biases, defenses, and sense of self-preservation in the work of allying with racialized others—particularly when those others' experiences of and reactions to being racialized within US society do not present as transparent to, or comprehensible from, one's own perspective.

As presented in the story, Esther's narrated consciousness is clearly limited by her own experiences of racial disenfranchisement within the United States. In a brief flashback, Esther recalls encountering a fellow "Oriental" on the street, only to feel betrayed when she sees that he was wearing a large button that said "I AM KOREAN" (Yamamoto 2001: 36) on the lapel of his jacket. This moment clearly parallels and foreshadows the tension that emerges between Esther and the Chinese couple on the bus; however, it also speaks to the complexities of interethnic dynamics that extend far beyond the conceptually closed spaces of the bus, the city, and even the nation-state. David Roh (2021: 22–23) points out the transpacific implications of this scene, noting that during World War II "Koreans, as colonial subjects [of Japan], were technically Japanese citizens," and thus the Korean man's lapel pin operates as "both a declaration against racial persecution at the expense of Japanese Americans . . . and a political act resisting the Japanese Empire's subsuming of his ethnicity." Esther initially interprets the man's gesture as the former, but she is not aware of or does not consider the latter. Trying to come up with a more sympathetic context for his actions, she speculates that "perhaps the man didn't even read English, perhaps he had been actually threatened, perhaps it was not his doing—his solicitous children perhaps had urged him to wear the badge" (Yamamoto 2001: 36–37). Esther's interpretation of the man's decision deprives him of ownership over his own actions ("it was not his doing"); indeed, her attempts to make his motives more understandable to herself further reduce him to object-status within her narrative, unable to speak or act on his own behalf. Ironically, Esther's projection of transparency onto the Korean man evacuates his interiority, as she assumes that his experiences of racialized exclusion must be equivalent to her own.

In just a few short paragraphs, Esther's train of thought demonstrates how transparency is simultaneously demanded of and denied to people who have been racialized as other. If, as Denise Ferreira da

Silva (2007: xxxv) argues, transparency operates as a "ruling ontological premise" that interprets "all that is particular to post-Enlightenment Europe as a signifier of the subject, the transparent 'I,'" those who emerge outside of this particular historiocultural tradition are by contrast *made* to signify through a "descriptive sense that does not and cannot communicate interiority . . . because it remains fully within a scientific (anthropological) terrain of signification." While the interior selfhood of the transparent and presumably universal subject is taken for granted, the interiority of the cultural/racial other is always under question because they are so strongly overdetermined by their exterior appearances, which are subject to description and interpretation by those occupying a subject-position. To put it another way, the ideal of transparency that inheres in the subject—what da Silva calls the "transparent I"—takes for granted the universal applicability of the judgments and interpretations made from their particular subject-position or point of view. Like Ralph Waldo Emerson's (2015: 37) metaphor of the "transparent eyeball" through which the "currents of universal Being circulate," the transparent "I" presumes transcendental detachment from immediate historical, material, or embodied circumstances, allowing for access to "higher" or more abstract truths. By contrast, the transparency projected onto the racialized individual seeks to definitively define or determine their interior state through subjective interpretations of their exterior appearance and actions. It is the latter figuration—the individual whose appearance, actions, and affiliations are not detached from but instead taken to be entirely representative of their interior state—that would come to take the form of the transparent citizen of the late twentieth and twenty-first century, in contrast to the narrating subject, whose private interior life is taken for granted as adhering to a universalized norm or standard.

In terms of narratology, Dorrit Cohn (1978: 29) notes that this implicit division between narrat*ing* and the narrat*ed* subject indexes varying degrees of "cognitive privilege" that "enables [the narrator] to manifest dimensions of a fictional character that the latter is unwilling or unable to betray." Cohn posits that the more strongly the narrative voice asserts itself, the less able it is to grant other characters the right to complexity, precisely because the narrator's "equipoise would be endangered by approaching another mind too closely and staying with it for too long; for this other mind, contrary to [the narrator's] own disincarnated mental existence, belongs to an incarnated and therefore distinctly limited being" (25). In other words, the embodiment and opacity of these fictional characters pose both a challenge and a threat to the universalist presumptions of the authorial voice and its corollary power to "manifest" or reveal obscured elements of their subjects' character or actions without their knowledge or against their will. This narrative power dynamic maps back onto the racial dynamics around transparency and opacity at play in both "Wilshire Bus" as well as in the field of Asian American literary studies more broadly: Sue Kim (2017: 25) points out that Asian Americanist critique has likewise focused on the questions of "*which* minds have been seen to be legible or inscrutable" as well as "how 'minds' (i.e. subjectivity, agency, identity) have been defined" that Cohn articulates as central to narratological inquiry. Authorial privilege, in this reading, might be usefully read as paralleling the rights of the "proper" citizen-subject, a category to which Asian Americans—and in the post–World War II context of this story, Japanese Americans in particular—have had a vexed and ambivalent relationship at best.

Thus, while Esther is presented in much of the story as operating from a position of what Cohn would term "cognitive privilege"—particularly as she imposes her own interpretive views upon the actions of the Chinese couple and Korean man—it is inevitable that she too is ultimately excluded from operating *as* a subject, or a "transparent 'I.'" While she initially feels "quite detached" from the anti-Chinese slurs that the drunken man hurls at the Chinese couple, by the time she gets off the bus she has completely lost this "saving detachment" and she finds herself "filled once again in her life with the infuriatingly sickening sensation of there being in the world nothing solid she could put her finger on, nothing solid she could come to grips with, nothing solid she could sink her teeth into, nothing solid" (Yamamoto 2001: 37). The reference to this feeling as something she is experiencing "once again" operates as a reminder both to Esther and the reader that Esther's status as both a narrating subject and a US citizen is, *and always has been,* conditional at best; despite the relative transparency of her thoughts and her apparent control over the narrative, her status as a racialized figure means that she does not have access to the same level of subjective "detachment" allowed to both the drunken white man and the kind white man who are the only two people to speak up on the bus. The drunken white man is allowed to speak without consequence; because he is drunk, the other riders say nothing, perhaps giving him the benefit of the doubt that his external presentation (a crude racist) is not representative of his real self. The kind white man who speaks up only after the drunken man leaves the bus reinscribes this sentiment on behalf of white American society at large: namely, that one man's racist rant should not be taken as representative of the "real" America. However, Esther cannot help but recall a saying that reminds her that drunkenness is, itself, a kind of transparency: "People say, do not regard what he says, now he is in liquor. Perhaps it is the only time he ought be regarded" (37). Realizing that the drunken man's hostility speaks to the truth of her racial positioning in US society, Esther understands that she can no longer sustain the fiction of detachment or dissociation that allows her to imagine herself as a narrating subject. Esther's realization is both reflected in and emphasized by a subtle shift in narrative style as well. Following Esther's revelation, Yamamoto no longer allows the omniscient narrator to access Esther's interior thoughts; indeed, when Esther reaches the hospital she allows her husband to misinterpret her tears as womanish sentimentality, letting him impose a narrative of faithful wifehood onto her complex feelings of disenfranchisement and subjectlessness.

Esther's shift from a narrat*ing* to a narrat*ed* subject has been interpreted by critics as a signal of her entrapment within the very racialized and gendered norms that have rendered her voiceless throughout.[3] Yet the lingering tension between her only spoken words ("yes, weren't women silly?") and the reader's understanding of Esther's state of mind points equally to the failure of those norms to completely interpret and define her actual thoughts. At the very moment Esther loses her "saving detachment," she also rejects narrative transparency: her emotions are no longer transparent to her husband, to the reader, or even to herself. If the "detachment" that allowed her to imagine herself a transparent *subject* is problematically aligned with what Victor Bascara (2019: 29) calls a "technology of forgetting" that operates "in service of legitimizing racism, wartime hysteria, quotidian militarization, and patriarchy," its collapse allows space for an alternative form of relationality that does not require a subjectivity based on such technologies to assert a form of solidarity. Indeed, by the story's end, Esther's deliberate obfuscation of her emotional state allows her to more closely resemble the other Asian individuals in the story than she did when she imagined herself a speaking subject. Once Esther's thoughts are no longer transparent to the reader, her opacity—like that of the Chinese couple, or the Korean man's before them—implicates the limitations of the social narratives that she and her husband have used to cope with their situations as transparent citizens.

Instead of merely illustrating submission to her husband's narrative, I posit that at the story's conclusion Esther actively refuses transparency, taking shelter instead in Glissant's "right to opacity." This "right" operates as a rejection of the demand to be made transparent or relatable to a single dominant and presumably universal understanding and instead embraces the unintelligibility and confusion that often attends interpersonal communication. While Glissant speaks of the individual choice to respect opacity by resisting the desire to impose one's own viewpoints and interpretations on another's words or actions, in the context of "Wilshire Bus" we might think of how this right applies equally to state policies as well, and the legislative need to impose a requirement for transparency, or singular and presumably universal perspective, upon its citizens' actions. In this context, Esther's turn to opacity articulates the limitations of subjectivity by showing how many of the assumptions around who can and cannot be considered a "transparent I," or an authorial narrating subject, are largely preempted by the racialized and gendered norms that render Esther always already suspect.

If privacy is a property of citizenship that can and has been revoked or suspended when an individual or group is perceived as posing a threat to national security, what might it mean to rethink the right to *privacy*—which, as Vasquez-Tokos and Yamin have argued, has frequently been adjudicated as a privilege of heteronormative whiteness—as the right to *opacity*? While "Wilshire Bus" concludes with Esther's retreat into opacity as a deconstruction (and ultimate refusal) of transparent subjectivity, in the next section I turn to John Okada's novel *No-No Boy* to address the question of what new forms of citizenship might be reconstructed out of this refusal. What might it look like to engage opacity not just as a right but as a central practice of the difficult yet necessary negotiations with difference that sit at the very heart of a democratic society? What kinds of relationships can emerge between citizens who remain opaque and unreadable, not only to one another but also to themselves? How might these new relationships both assimilate to and give new direction to changing interpretations of US citizenship, both during this period and in the present day?

Coming to Terms with the Unknown Within: *No-No Boy*'s Opaque Citizenry

In his reflection on "The Thinking of the Opacity of the World," Glissant (2012: 77) argues that a core element of the right to opacity is the "right to be obscure, first to yourself." Yet from the moment Ichiro Yamada steps off of the bus on the first page of John Okada's 1957 novel *No-No Boy*, he is anything but assured of this right. Tormented by his inability to come to terms with or even fully understand his own motivations for becoming a "no-no boy"—an American-born citizen of Japanese descent who refused to pledge loyalty to the United States and serve in its military—Ichiro arrives back in Seattle feeling like an "intruder in a world to which he had no claim" (1). While Ichiro believes that he made the choice purely of his own "free will," he simultaneously feels alienated from the America that had divided and forced him to choose between his nationality and his ethnicity, and he holds a deep resentment toward his mother, who had demanded that he remain loyal to Japan. This ambivalence dominates Ichiro's interior narrative: at one moment, he is ready to accept everyone's blame and hatred because he made his decision as a "man of twenty-three," but in the next he reflects that he was "just a goddamn kid" who "didn't know enough to wipe my own nose" (1). Ichiro's unwillingness to accept the obscurity, ambivalence, and contingency that inflect his own emotions and decisions lies at the very heart of the rage that drives his internal monologues and interactions with his friends, family, and neighbors.

If the (fictional) Ichiro found the ambivalence and obscurity of his own feelings to be unpalatable to himself, they proved to be equally indigestible to the reading public of the time. *No-No Boy* was rejected many times and was poorly received when it was published at last; its initial run of fifteen hundred copies had not even sold out by the time that Okada died in 1971. Rediscovered after Okada's death by Jeffery Chan, Frank Chin, Lawson Inada, and Shawn Wong, *No-No Boy* became a core literary text for the emergent Asian American movement in the 1970s and 1980s. Since then, Ichiro's dialectical predicament of being entangled within a binary framework that sets his American and Japanese identities in tension with one another has been frequently interpreted as a metaphor or parallel for an Asian American identity that is similarly caught between assimilation and resistance. While Viet Nguyen (2002), Suzanne Arakawa (2005), and Daniel Kim (2005) posit that the resistant potential of Ichiro's initial "no" is ultimately absorbed into psychological or novelistic conventions that valorize a postracial American identity, Jinqi Ling (1995) and Lisa Lowe (1996) have argued that the aesthetic and psychological fragmentation that characterizes Okada's novel refuses or ironizes those very conventional requirements of "development, synthesis, and reconciliation" (Lowe 1996: 51). Building on these arguments about the potential of the novel's narrative aesthetics to push discourses around Asian American identity in a new direction, I argue that *No-No Boy* narrates a shift from an expectation of transparency at the beginning of the novel to an acceptance of opacity at its conclusion. It is only by allowing himself and others the right to opacity in the face of both external and internalized demands for transparency that Ichiro is able to articulate a renewed sense of community-centered identity predicated upon respecting and collaborating across difference.

Unlike Hisaye Yamamoto—who allows her protagonist Esther the right to opacity at the end of "Wilshire Bus" by cutting off narrative access to her thoughts—Okada delves directly into Ichiro's messy, disordered stream of consciousness to emphasize how Ichiro's motives remain opaque to himself and others. Unlike Esther, Ichiro does not cling to preset narrative assumptions to help him navigate the postwar landscape: he has already lost the person he thought he was, and he doesn't yet know the person he is or hopes to be. Ichiro's disjointed and contradictory thought processes express a kind of radical transparency that does not seek to explain or make Ichiro's motivation *clear* so much as to show how difficult it is to disentangle the different motivations, emotions, and contexts that all led up to his individual choice to say "no" to America. While the so-called loyalty questionnaire given to all Japanese Americans living in the United States during the second world war presumed to determine a citizen's loyalty from their answers to a series of yes/no questions with little room for context or nuance— this was the infamous document that gave rise to the pejorative term "no-nos" to indicate the men who refused to forswear Japan and serve in the US military—the reasons that drove people's responses to these questions could be quite complex. In an attempt to explain his thought process to Mr. Carrick, a sympathetic white man who appears briefly in the novel, Ichiro gestures at this difficulty:

> Sometimes I think my mother is to blame. Sometimes I think it's bigger than her, more than her refusal to understand that I'm not like her. It didn't make sense. Not at all. First they jerked us off the Coast and put us in camps to prove to us that we weren't American enough to be trusted. Then they wanted to draft us into the army. I was bitter—mad and bitter. Still, a lot of them went in, and I didn't. You figure it out. (Okada 1978: 152–53)

While Ichiro identifies several things that influenced his decision— the guilt and pressure that his mother exerted on him, his bitterness at the government's treatment of Japanese Americans, and his cynical attitude toward the US military's need for fresh troops—in the end he doesn't know and can't say exactly *why* all of these things pushed him to say "no" when others who were in the same situation ended up saying "yes." If the circumstances surrounding the administration of the questionnaire fundamentally "didn't make sense," it was equally impossible for Ichiro, or anyone else for that matter, to fully explicate the reasons they did what they did in consequence. By concluding with "you figure it out," Ichiro places the onus of interpretation onto Carrick, and—implicitly—the reader as well. The implication is that the reader's interpretation of his motives would be no more or less correct than Ichiro's own understanding of those motives. While he can tell us the many things that informed his decision, the ultimate reason behind his response remains opaque to him as much as to anyone else.

Still, the impossible demands that Ichiro constantly places upon himself to be transparent—marked by his repeatedly stated desire to excise from himself the "thing in him which made him say no" (11) to the government so that he might be able claim a more unproblematic "American" self—is paralleled by the other characters' violent policing of Japanese American identity. Eto and Bull, two Japanese American veterans who had said "yes" where Ichiro said "no," single out Ichiro and other no-no boys for abuse because their choices represent precisely the kind of opacity or inscrutability that marked out *all* Japanese Americans as objects of suspicion. The brutal harassment and bullying that Ichiro and his friend Freddie receive at the hands of their own community members—bullying that eventually culminates in Freddie's death—externalizes the stakes of Ichiro's internal struggle. All four men want to be seen and treated as transparently American citizens, even if that means destroying or denying a part of themselves or their own community to be treated as such. However as the novel progresses Ichiro comes to realize that this drive to transparency is neither an attainable nor a desirable goal; the rage to uproot and remove all traces of ambiguity around the question of how and why one comes to identify as Japanese or American is ultimately a desire that not only partakes in troubling forms of settler colonial and racial capitalism, but also undermines the political and social potential of new modes of citizenship and community that have the potential to emerge out of the postwar Japanese American experience.

Exploring the novel's conflation of American identity with settler colonial property, Viet Nguyen (2002: 73) points out that *No-No Boy* shows how "the ownership of property and commodities . . . [is] a corollary to the willingness to sacrifice one's life and body for that American culture." Kenji, a Japanese American who befriends Ichiro, embodies this sacrifice. Kenji enjoys a great deal of material prosperity; he has a brand-new car, and his family is well provided for. However, he has won this prosperity at the cost of his life: he is slowly dying from an infected leg that was wounded during the war, and unlike Ichiro, he harbors doubts about whether or not the sacrifice was worth it. Ichiro's initial envy of the "fullness" or seeming transparency of his friend's desires and his actions—that is, Ichiro's belief that Kenji was "man enough to *wish the thing* which destroyed [his] leg"—is aligned with his desire for his friend's apparently superior claim to the land itself, summarized by his belief that the "dirt of America . . . is yours beyond a single doubt" (64). Yet while Nguyen argues that Ichiro's yearning to achieve subjectivity established along these settler colonial terms leads him to sacrifice his body in a more metaphorical way by ultimately giving up his opacity and "consent[ing] to the virtual panopticon of American identity" (75), I interpret Ichiro's trajectory as gradually shifting *away* from these desires, moving instead to articulate a form of citizenship or community that does not conceptualize belonging in terms of transparency and access to property and commodities, but rather in terms of an opacity that both recognizes and honors the complexity of one's entanglements.

By the end of the novel, Ichiro comes to a similar conclusion as Esther in "Wilshire Bus"—namely, that subjectivity for *all* Japanese Americans is contingent at best. No matter how they replied on the loyalty questionnaire, they can be equally excluded from occupying the subject-position of the proper citizen. The rights bestowed by this form of citizenship are not (and never have been) fixed and universal but remain profoundly contingent upon shifting power dynamics. Through his encounters with Kenji, Emi, and other Japanese American men and women set adrift in the postwar years, Ichiro begins to realize that although he believes that he was the one who had "dealt himself out" with his own choices, others who had chosen differently— even those who did not have to choose at all, like Mr. Carrick, or the Black men who heckled him on the street—were equally stuck "on the outside looking in" (159). Maybe, Ichiro reflects,

> there is no in. Maybe the whole damned country is pushing and shoving and screaming to get into someplace that doesn't exist, because they don't know that the outside could be the inside if only they would stop all this pushing and shoving and screaming, and they haven't got enough sense to realize that. (Okada 1978: 160)

If subjectivity is most frequently configured or represented as a quality emerging from privacy or interiority, then Ichiro's growing doubt that this interiority or "inside" even exists pushes him to reflect that there may likewise be no universal standard or standpoint from which to narrate or navigate the postwar landscape. Rather than understanding himself as the sole outsider among insiders, Ichiro begins to understand that his community's rejection and dehumanization of no-no boys defers and disavows their own fears of the opacity or obscurity within.

What might a form of citizenship or community *not* mediated by the requirements of transparent subjectivity look like? In the absence of a universalized ideal of subjectivity, Glissant makes the case for an ethics of relationality built on respect for individuals' right to opacity. Such solidarities can lead to a reformed concept of community where, in Ichiro's words, "the outside could be the inside"—or, in Glissant's (1990: 190) interpretation, where "every Other is a citizen and not a barbarian." The last chapters of Okada's novel experiment with articulating this reimagined form of citizenship, and I argue that the difficulty of narrating these forms of solidarity while preserving incommensurable difference accounts for the uneven nature of the novel's conclusion. The penultimate chapter of *No-No Boy* concludes with Ichiro, who has seemingly come to accept his position in postwar society, coming full circle: he emerges from a bus, just as he did at the beginning of the novel, but instead of being consumed by feelings of alienation and anger he feels "a bit more settled in heart and mind" knowing "there was room for all kinds of people. Possibly, even for one like him" (232). Reflecting on a clichéd phrase, "After the rain, the sunshine," Ichiro again waits to cross at the light, this time noticing that "the cluster of people at the bus stop hardly gave him a glance" (232–33). Many critics have observed that the hopefulness that Ichiro expresses as he nears the end of the novel seems a little too pat; it appears to concede to narrative conventions that push its protagonist to resolve his problems by moving beyond them, in that way gaining the kind of transparent subject-position that has eluded him all along.[4] This is certainly the implication of Ichiro's apparent invisibility at the conclusion of this chapter; the journey he has taken through the novel has seemingly transformed him from a highly visible object to a "transparent I," or an all-seeing subject. His apparent invisibility to the people who surround him suggests that he is no longer bound by the opacity of his raced body, a move that implies that he has finally come to both accept and transcend the Japanese American identity that he has been striving for throughout the novel.[5]

However, Okada does *not* conclude Ichiro's story at this moment but instead adds one more chapter focused on events at the Club

Oriental that, I argue, subverts the penultimate chapter's promise of resolution through transcendence and assimilation. The addition of the final chapter shows that Ichiro's personal epiphany is an insufficient conclusion to the complex questions of identity and citizenship that he has been struggling with throughout. It is not enough for Ichiro alone to accept the opacity within himself and others; this work must be undertaken by the entire community. In this context, his return to the Club Oriental represents Ichiro's effort to bring an acceptance of opacity back to his own social group; it is his attempt to bring the "outside . . . in." The Club Oriental operates as a kind of spatial metaphor for the Japanese American community: unlike the warm, all-American interior of Kenji's family home or the rigid, unforgiving order of Ichiro's Japanese one, the club exists in a liminal, semilegal space. The club is located on an "ugly street with the ugly buildings among the ugly people which was a part of America and, at the same time, would never be wholly America" (Okada 1978: 71) and, as befits a nightclub, is depicted as perpetually dim, dark, and smoky. It is the space where Kenji had felt most comfortable to be himself; however, it is also the space that is most heavily policed by Bull and other veterans who remain hostile to no-no boys like Ichiro. In the novel's final chapter, Ichiro's friend Freddie, another no-no boy who has become increasingly erratic and self-destructive, decides he wants to cross that invisible line by going to have a drink at the club. Although he initially tries to dissuade Freddie, Ichiro admits that "there was a hint of logic in his stubborn defiance," reflecting that "they would have to make peace with their own little world before they could enjoy the freedom of the larger one" (244). Similarly, the shift that Okada makes from larger questions of transcendent identity and "freedom" in the penultimate chapter to negotiations with Japanese Americans' "own little world" in the final one signals the author's understanding—however mediated by narrative conventions and political pressures—that Japanese Americans must look to their own community as the place to rethink, renegotiate, and relitigate what it means to be a citizen, rather than seek to individually transcend their racialized histories.

There is certainly little transcendence to be found, as Freddie's challenge to Club Oriental's unspoken exclusion laws ends in more tragedy. Bull's attempt to throw Freddie out of the club begins a brawl that ends with Freddie dying in a grisly car crash as he tries to flee the scene; the novel concludes with Bull sobbing in the alleyway while Ichiro walks off into the darkness. It is Bull—along with the other bystanders who watched the tragedy happen—who now must grapple with and make their peace with the feelings that have rendered them unrecognizable and opaque even to themselves. While Okada's description of Bull sobbing "like a baby in loud, gasping, beseeching howls" (250) might be interpreted as a sign of rebirth, it is a rebirth not into clarity but into obscurity, an emergence not into the light but into the dark. In contrast to how the previous chapter's optimistic invocation of sunshine breaking through the rain appears to parallel Ichiro's brief moment of revelation, the final chapter juxtaposes images of darkness and light to demonstrate how the obscurity and opacity afforded by "darkness" provides a needed space for healing, while the "brightness" of the streets is instead linked to the merciless "morbidity of the crowd" (250). Yet the thread of hope that Ichiro clings to at the novel's conclusion is, importantly, born out of and preserved in this darkness and obscurity; it is what allows him to sympathize with Bull, even if Bull's emotions resist clear articulation. By ending in this way, Okada leaves us with the idea that one way Ichiro and the broader Japanese American community might emerge from the sense of personal and political paralysis incurred by the incarceration is not to run away from but to embrace the opacities that had been violated by the enforced transparency of the loyalty questionnaire and everything that followed. To do so, one must be able to comprehend the impossibility of, as Glissant (1990: 194) would later write, reducing "anyone, no matter who, to a truth he would not have generated on his own."

While Bull, Ma, and the state all refused to grant Ichiro this right to opacity, by the end of the novel Ichiro does his best to extend it to others. He does not condemn Bull as he sobs like an "infant crying in darkness," nor does he attempt to ventriloquize or summarize Ma, as he ultimately acknowledges that "as much as he wished to know where and how the whole business had gone wrong, he could not, for he had never been close enough to his own mother" (Okada 1978: 205). Even the sense of hope that Ichiro feels at the novel's conclusion resists classification as such; rather, it is a sentiment in emergence, something that Ichiro "couldn't see [. . .] to put it into words, but the feeling was pretty strong" (250–51). While Kim (2005) and others have persuasively argued that Ichiro's (and Okada's) emphasis on feeling and sentiment affectively sutures the Japanese American experience to the project of American exceptionalism and expansionism, I posit that this emphasis on the opacity of "feeling" over the ability to "see it to put it into words" (Okada 1978: 250) can also work to push beyond the expectations of informational transparency that such assimilationist projects require, focusing instead on the affective ties that escape or cannot be effectively articulated within official nationalist discourses.[6] Certainly, the grief and guilt that Bull feels over Freddie's death indicates the extent to which—despite Bull's denials and Freddie's nihilism—they had remained profoundly interconnected by their community and experiences, even when their choices positioned them on opposite sides of a nationalist divide. Likewise, the sympathy that Ichiro feels for Bull emerges out of a similar impulse to acknowledge their interconnection, even though they have also remained opposed to one another throughout the events of the book. It is out of these often unspoken and untapped feelings that the possibility for a different understanding of citizenship emerges, one that remains responsive to the ties that bind—both within and across nation, race, and gender—rather than seeking out information that would give further reasons to disavow, deny, and exclude. The model of citizenship that Ichiro haltingly pursues is one that is slowly attempting to move away from the proscriptive and exclusionary forms shaped by more than a half-century of exclusion acts, and more toward something resembling the more inclusive and capacious models theorized in the writings of racialized writers and thinkers of an earlier generation, which Derrick Spires (2019: 5) describes as being characterized by "mutual responsibility, responsiveness, and active engagement, a relation in which membership and individual rights come with moral obligations to a collective," rather than a state that is always "reducible to individual interest." This more expansive model for citizenship emphasizes the relations and obligations that connect different members of the community rather than focusing on the preservation of the rights for certain individuals at the cost or exclusion of others. It is in this simultaneous acknowledgement of interconnectivity and respect for incommensurability or opacity that Ichiro's, and Okada's, aspirations for a new way of defining American citizenship take shape.

(In)conclusion

No-No Boy's partial and tentative invocation of a community that might be forged across—rather than in spite of—opacities and differences remains an aspirational, if often elusive, model for both Asian American and multiethnic solidarity movements whose constituents continue to occupy an ambivalent or ambiguous relationship to the figure of the rights-bearing citizen. Even as Okada's novel has since found itself at the center of emerging debates and discourses around what it might mean to represent Asian America to itself and to others, it refuses definitive answers to these questions, shrouding Ichiro's conclusions in an obscuring darkness. Instead of seeking to search out, expose, or eliminate those qualities of opacity within oneself and one's community, *No-No Boy*—like "Wilshire Bus" before it—encourages us to lean into that inscrutability as a site of refuge and repair. Both Okada's and Yamamoto's texts illustrate how the texture of inscrutability or opacity is not the same thing as an absence, lack, or retreat from feeling: rather, such opacities represent an excess or *plenitude* of emotions, motivations, and information, the full range of which threatens to overwhelm or render incoherent traditional narrative structures focused on the development of character, conflict, and resolution. In both "Wilshire Bus," where Esther retreats to a place where the narrative voice can no longer ventriloquize her, and in *No-No Boy*, where the narrator's access to Ichiro's thoughts reveals not clarity or resolution but only more swirling indecision, Yamamoto and Okada push at the edges of the realist narratives that they work within as they attempt to critique and dismantle the "cognitive privilege" of the authorial voice that aspires to universality and omniscience. Since a single authorial voice or narrator is unequal to the task of explaining the plenitude and complexity of their protagonists' situation, both texts force us to instead confront the opacity that shrouds, and preserves, their characters' multiplicity.

It is perhaps for this reason Ling (1995: 376) observes that, despite *No-No Boy*'s ostensible realism, it was ahead of its time in anticipating the "spreading flame of literary pluralism" that would come to mark the later, more explicitly postmodern and experimental work that would characterize Asian American cultural productions in the decades to come, from Maxine Hong Kingston's *Woman Warrior* (1976) to the recent release of The Daniels's multiverse-spanning film *Everything Everywhere All At Once* (2022). If, as Anne Cheng (2022) writes in a review of the latter, the Asian American experience is comparable to existing in a "fractured multiverse . . . riven with geographic, temporal, and psychical dissonances," such experience can be only partially or incompletely expressed within a narrative form that presumes a singular transparency or narrative trajectory. What these midcentury Japanese American works show us is how even within the structure of an ostensibly realist text, we can see these dissonant energies pushing outward and against narrative frameworks that demand transparency from its subjects while keeping its own structuring logics implicit or out of sight. Reading these narrative tensions against the specific political demands for transparency that had been made of Japanese Americans—demands that were, by the time of these texts' publication, expanding to encompass *all* Asian Americans, and other minoritized and racialized groups—we might certainly extrapolate how both engaging and respecting opacity might operate not only as a narrative strategy but as a practice of citizenship within an increasingly diversifying democracy. If "Wilshire Bus" critiques systems of surveillance and enforced transparency that disempower and encourage citizens to view one another with suspicion while allowing the broader structural logics of the security state to grow more distant and unresponsive to the citizenry it ostensibly serves, *No-No Boy* reimagines citizenship as something practiced from within through the slow and difficult process of developing trust and interpersonal accountability. Taken together, these works show how it might be possible to acknowledge the incommensurability of experiences within a shared citizenry while also continuing to seek out resonances between, rather than explanations for, these differences. These strategies for thinking with, and respecting, opacity and difference remain important for navigating questions of citizenship in the twenty-first century, as technology increasingly renders us all into transparent citizens

Erin Suzuki is an associate professor of literature at University of California, San Diego. She is the author of *Ocean Passages: Navigating Pacific Islander and Asian American Literatures* (2021).

Notes

1   *Trump, President of the United States, et al. v Hawaii et al.*, 585 U.S. 2 (2018)
2   Here I draw from Lauren Berlant's (1997: 27–30) characterization of "infantile" citizenship, a phenomenon where citizens' attitude to government becomes mired in passivity, dependence, cynicism and paranoia (or some combination of these attitudes).
3   See, for example, Mullins 1998; Elliott 2009
4   For example, Ling (1995: 374) posits that the ending of *No-No Boy* reflects "the conflicting concerns of the author, the reader, and the cultural establishment, concerns that imply the author's conscious use of literary strategies in order to be heard—and perhaps also his unconscious conformity to the cultural conventions of his time."
5   Nguyen (2002: 77) interprets this shift from highly visible to invisibilized subject as Ichiro's "disavowal of his body and its significance . . . for Ichiro the narrative of liberation from his imprisonment is the narrative of forgetting his own body," which he can only do through "repenting" his so-called sin against the state. (77)
6   Kim (2005: 80) argues that the turn to sentimentality and "feeling" at the novel's conclusion serves to support and promote the "American way of

life" promoted by the soft-power propaganda that accompanied US expansion during the Cold War, noting that "it is only through the wielding of this sentimental power that a new kind of war can be fought: a war that is as much about the restraint of military violence as it is about its unleashing; a war that is as much about the winning over of hearts and minds as it is about the conquest of territory."

References

Arakawa, Suzanne. 2005. "Suffering Male Bodies: Representations of Dissent and Displacement in the Internment-Themed Narratives of John Okada and Toshio Mori." In *Recovered Legacies: Authority and Identity in Early Asian American Literature*, edited by Keith Lawrence and Floyd Cheung, 183–206. Philadelphia, PA: Temple Univ. Press.

Bascara, Victor. 2019. "Permission to Forget: A Metacommentary." *Verge: Studies in Global Asias* 5, no. 2: 28–33.

Berlant, Lauren. 1997. *The Queen of America Goes to Washington City*. Durham, NC: Duke Univ. Press.

Cheng, Anne. 2022. " 'Everything Everywhere All At Once' Is A Deeply Asian American Film." *Washington Post*, May 4. www.washingtonpost.com /outlook/2022/05/04/everything-everywhere-asian-american-pessimism/

Chuh, Kandice. 2019. *The Difference Aesthetics Makes: On the Humanities 'After Man.'* Durham, NC: Duke Univ. Press.

Cohn, Dorrit. 1978. *Transparent Minds: Narrative Modes for Presenting Consciousness in Fiction*. Princeton, NJ: Princeton Univ. Press.

Day, Iyko. 2016. *Alien Capital: Asian Racialization and the Logic of Settler Colonialism*. Durham, NC: Duke Univ. Press

Elliott, Matthew. 2009. "Sins of Omission: Hisaye Yamamoto's Vision of History," *MELUS: Multi-Ethnic Literatures of the United States* 34 no. 1: 47–68.

Emerson, Ralph Waldo. 2015. "Nature," in *Ralph Waldo Emerson: The Major Prose*, edited by Ronald Bosco and Joel Myerson, Cambridge, MA: Harvard Univ. Press.

Ferreira da Silva, Denise. 2007. *Toward a Global Idea of Race*. Minneapolis: Univ. of Minnesota Press.

Glissant, Édouard. 1990. *Poetics of Relation*. Translated by Betsy Wing. Ann Arbor: Univ. of Michigan Press.

Glissant, Édouard. 2012. "The Thinking of the Opacity of the World." Translated by Franck Loric. *Philosophie de la relation. Poésie en etendue*, 7.

Hong, Christine. 2020. *A Violent Peace: Race, U.S. Militarism, and Cultures of Democratization in Cold War Asia and the Pacific*. Palo Alto, CA: Stanford Univ. Press.

Hu Pegues, Juliana. 2021. *Space-Time Colonialism: Alaska's Indigenous and Asian Entanglements*. Durham, NC: Duke Univ. Press.

Huang, Vivian. 2022. *Surface Relations: Queer Forms of Asian American Inscrutability*. Durham, NC: Duke Univ. Press.

Hyde, Carrie. 2018. *Civic Longing: The Speculative Origins of U.S. Citizenship.* Cambridge, MA: Harvard Univ. Press.

Kennan, George (as X). 1947. "The Sources of Soviet Conduct." *Foreign Affairs* 25 no. 4: 244-61.

Kim, Daniel. 2005. "Once More With Feeling: Cold War Masculinity and the Senteiment of Patriotism in John Okada's *No-No Boy.*" *Criticism* 47 no. 1: 65–83.

Kim, Sue. 2017. "What Asian American Studies and Narrative Theory Can Do For Each Other," in *Narrative, Race and Ethnicity in the United States*, ed. James J. Donaghue, Jennifer Ann Ho, and Shaun Morgan, 13–26. Columbus: Ohio State Univ. Press.

Ling, Jinqi. 1995. "Race, Power, and Cultural Politics in John Okada's *No-No Boy.*" *American Literature* 67 no. 2: 359–81.

Lowe, Lisa. 1996. *Immigrant Acts: On Asian American Cultural Politics.* Durham, NC: Duke Univ. Press.

Lowe, Lisa. 2015. *The Intimacies of the Four Continents.* Durham, NC: Duke Univ. Press.

McKittrick, Katherine. 2022. "Dear April: The Aesthetics of Black Miscellania." *Antipode* 54 no. 1: 3–18.

Mullins, Maire. 1998. "Esther's Smile: Silence and Action in Hisaye Yamamoto's 'Wilshire Bus,'" *Studies in Short Fiction* 35 no. 1: 77–84.

Nguyen, Viet. 2002. *Race and Resistance: Literature and Politics in Asian America.* New York, NY: Oxford Univ. Press.

Okada, John. 1978. *No-No Boy.* Seattle: Univ. of Washington Press.

Quashie, Kevin. 2012. *The Sovereignty of Quiet: Beyond Resistance in Black Culture.* New Brunswick, NJ: Rutgers Univ. Press.

Reidenberg, Joel. 2015. "The Transparent Citizen." *Loyola University Chicago Law Journal* 47: 437–63.

Roh, David. 2021. *Minor Transpacific: Triangulating American, Japanese, and Korean Fictions.* Palo Alto, CA: Stanford Univ. Press.

Sohn, Stephen. 2018. *Inscrutable Belongings: Queer Asian North American Fiction.* Palo Alto, CA: Stanford Univ. Press.

Spires, Derrick R. 2019. *The Practice of Citizenship: Black Politics and Print Culture in the Early United States.* Philadelphia: Univ. of Pennsylvania Press.

Vasquez-Tokos, Jessica, and Priscilla Yamin. 2021. "The racialization of privacy: racial formation as a family affair." *Theory and Society* 50: 717–40.

Xiang, Sunny. 2020. *Tonal Intelligence: The Aesthetics of Asian Inscrutability During the Long Cold War.* Palo Alto, CA: Stanford Univ. Press.

Yamamoto, Hisaye. 2001. "Wilshire Bus," *Seventeen Syllables and Other Stories.* New Brunswick, NJ: Rutgers Univ. Press.

Yao, Xine. 2021. *Disaffected: The Cultural Politics of Unfeeling in Nineteenth-Century America.* Durham: Duke Univ. Press.

Kathryn Walkiewicz The Sentimentalist Terrain of Ora V. Eddleman Reed's *Twin Territories* Fiction

Abstract This article grapples with the messy legacy of Ora V. Eddleman Reed, editor of *Twin Territories* magazine in the Muscogee Nation, Indian Territory, at the turn of the twentieth century. *Twin Territories* vocally opposed US statehood in Indian Territory and furthered the literary careers of many Native writers. It was an important and influential venue of Native literary expression in the early twentieth century that deserves greater attention from Indigenous literary and print culture studies. However, the magazine's ambitions and how we make sense of its legacy are complicated by Eddleman Reed's racial politics, her own (non)citizenship, and the contents of her short sentimental fiction, all of which did as much to reinscribe racialized notions of Indigeneity as they did to challenge prevailing settler assumptions about Native people. Reed has been hailed as a recovered Cherokee writer, but her family's rejected Cherokee Nation enrollment applications and recent genealogical research raise critical questions about framing her in this way.
Keywords Indian Territory, sentimentalism, Ora V. Eddleman Reed

Citizens of Indian Territory and Oklahoma Territory experienced extreme political, social, and cultural upheaval from the end of the nineteenth century until the successful bid for Oklahoma statehood in 1907. During this era, territorial residents witnessed the invasion of an unprecedented number of settlers and the allotment of communally held tribal lands. Within a few short decades, Congress and influential US businessmen became intent on fully incorporating Oklahoma and Indian Territories as a US state and dissolving tribal sovereignty (see fig. 1). In this heated political climate, Ora V. Eddleman Reed, her sister Myrta, and her brother-in-law Walter Sams began publishing *Twin Territories: The Indian Magazine* in Muskogee, Indian Territory. The first issue was printed in December 1898 and proudly declared itself the "only magazine published in the

American Literature, Volume 96, Number 4, December 2024
DOI 10.1215/00029831-11557513   © 2024 by Duke University Press

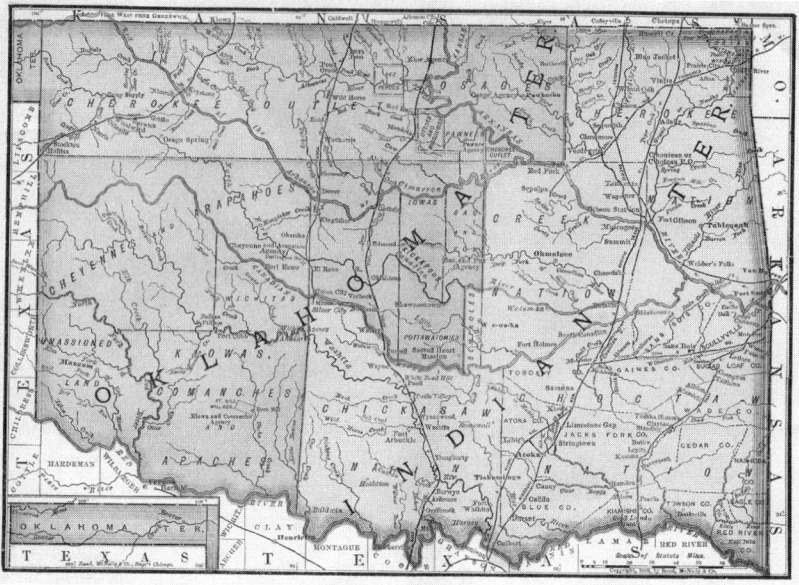

Figure 1 *Oklahoma Territory and Indian Territory.* 1890. Rand McNally. Oklahoma State University Digital Collections, OK—Docs Maps, https://dc.library.okstate.edu/digital /collection/OKMaps/id/3918/rec/1. Accessed September 11, 2022

Indian Territory or Oklahoma" on the cover. The monthly would continue until 1904 and featured everything from "departments devoted respectively to educational interests, religion, the farm and the ranch, fashion, fiction, children, Territorial men and women of note, and a dozen others of equal interest" ("Editorial" 1898: 2). Throughout its publication, *Twin Territories* was a prominent contributor to a thriving Indian Territory print culture with a long Indigenous tradition.

While understudied because few copies of the magazine still exist, *Twin Territories* is a significant archive of Oklahoma and Indian Territory writing, especially of work by Native writers.[1] *Twin Territories* offers valuable insights into how residents of Indian and Oklahoma Territories made sense of their own era and posited itself as a voice for the civic and domestic merits of the territories. As the magazine's editor, Eddleman Reed consistently wrote editorial columns and short fiction that explored territorial identity and political tensions brewing as US involvement in territorial affairs increased.[2] Some of her columns, particularly her opinion pieces, unabashedly responded to anti-Indigenous stereotypes and bigoted assumptions that circulated in mainstream US media, including the narrative that the territories were wild and lawless places with minimal structure, governance, or culture. Eddleman Reed often made *Easterners* the butt of her jokes—accusing them of far greater savageness than any Native person.[3] *Twin Territories* employed sentimentalist tropes to argue that the territories were civilized, domestic havens that epitomized US moral and cultural values and that they would only stay as such so long as Native nations maintained political and economic control. Given the looming threat of statehood and mounting federal policies aimed at dissolving tribal governments and attacking Native families, Eddleman Reed's vocal support of tribal rule ambitiously attempted to sway public opinion and speak back to settler power. To do so, she savvily argued that the exceptional domesticity of Indian Territory was necessary for the continued success of the larger US nation-state, and she did so by playing on prevailing tropes of the territory as feminine, staging the Native feminine frontier as a space of moral excellence.[4]

However, the magazine's ambitions and how we make sense of its legacy are complicated by Eddleman Reed's racial politics, her own (non)citizenship, and the contents of her short sentimental fiction and running editorial columns, all of which did as much to reinscribe racialized notions of Indigeneity as they did to challenge prevailing settler assumptions about Native people. Under her editorship, the magazine operated under a white supremacist logic that reinforced anti-Blackness and eugenic notions of racial difference. It tacitly celebrated a style of Native femininity that was proximate to whiteness and could easily navigate settler society. Eddleman Reed repurposed many sentimental tropes in her writing, especially in her short fiction, to argue for the generative value of territorial domestic spaces and Native femininity. Nonetheless, by reinforcing anti-Blackness, colorism, and blood quantum in the magazine, her work is complicit in what Xine Yao (2021: 14) describes as sympathy's "violent origins in the matrices of domination that produce the system of racial difference."[5] While Eddleman Reed was critical of white feminist weaponizations of sentimentalism used to attack the Native family (and thus Native nations) at the end of the nineteenth century, her work did not disrupt the core ethos of sentimentalist appeals: advocacy through compassion for society's seemingly most vulnerable, most marginalized. She invoked a white settler discourse of civility to argue that because territorial Native women could perform proper middle-class white womanhood through education, manners, dress, etc., the domestic space of Indian Territory must be protected. Nonetheless, this ethic centers the same whiteness and white feelings that drove allotment, statehood, and the dissolution of tribal governments. Therefore, Eddleman Reed's writing employs narrative elements that are incompatible with her political objective: her method—a sentimentalist discourse that affirms white supremacy—undercuts the message of protecting Indigenous sovereignty and thwarting expansion of the settler state.

Yet, Eddleman Reed understood herself not as a white woman savior but as a Native woman writing in support of her community. Unlike settler feminists who advocated *against* tribal self-determination, she vehemently argued on its behalf. During her tenure at the magazine, Eddleman Reed (1902a: 70) identified as a "Cherokee editor."[6] Marketing herself this way gave the publication an air of novelty that drew a readership beyond the territories and helped bolster her reputation, both then and now. When Eddleman Reed and her writings were "rediscovered" later in the twentieth century, scholars reclaimed her as a Native woman writer. She was hailed as one of a handful of activist Native women engaged in turn-of-the-century journalism.[7] However, her mother Mary's application for the Cherokee Nation rolls was denied due to a lack of evidence substantiating her Cherokee heritage (Morrison 1982: 142). What is more, recent research conducted by Kirby Brown (Cherokee Nation) into Eddleman Reed's genealogy finds no definitive evidence of direct lineal Cherokee descent. *Twin Territories* and Eddleman Reed's role at the magazine raise difficult but critical questions about citizenship, especially within Indigenous literary studies.

Twin Territories vocally opposed US statehood in Indian Territory and furthered the literary careers of many Native writers. It was an important and influential venue of Native literary expression in the early twentieth century that deserves greater attention from Indigenous literary and print culture studies. However, uncritically reading Eddleman Reed as a Cherokee editor and author poses a challenge to present-day Cherokee sovereignty and Cherokee Nation's right to determine its citizens. Her noncitizenship matters in how we engage her work because of the long tradition of white sentimental authors "playing Indian" in the name of Indigenous rights and reform.[8] That being said, Eddleman Reed was a good territorial citizen, meaning she advocated for continued Native governance of Indian Territory, as opposed to a good US citizen invested in the dissolution of tribal governance and settler expansion via statehood. These facts inflect how we might read *Twin Territories*, especially within Indigenous literary studies.

Twin Territories' Political and Print Contributions

Although the format and columns of *Twin Territories* changed quite frequently throughout Eddleman Reed's tenure, the overall tone of

Figure 2   Cover, *Twin Territories* (August 1899). Courtesy of the University of Oklahoma Western History Collections

the magazine remained relatively consistent. The magazine posited itself as the first of its kind in either of the two territories and aspired to be a highbrow publication that demonstrated the sophistication, wealth, and education of territorial inhabitants (see figs. 2 and 3). *Twin Territories* marketed itself as the premiere venue for Native writing and published the work of many Native territorial writers of the day. While the publication had ambitions for a wider audience, the magazine framed itself as a publication written by, for, and about territorial people, specifically Native people in the territories. As such, the issues offered a performative function that extended beyond a local audience in the very act of addressing said local audience—to have an entire magazine dedicated to a territorial readership meant that there was a perceived need and interest for such a publication, not only to individuals in the territories but also to a US audience.

The twinning of the territories in the magazine's title not only spoke to Oklahoma and Indian Territory proper but also to the kind of hybrid cultural space developing between disparate populations in both territories as the number of non-Native settlers rapidly increased. Native nations were fighting to protect their people and lands while seeking

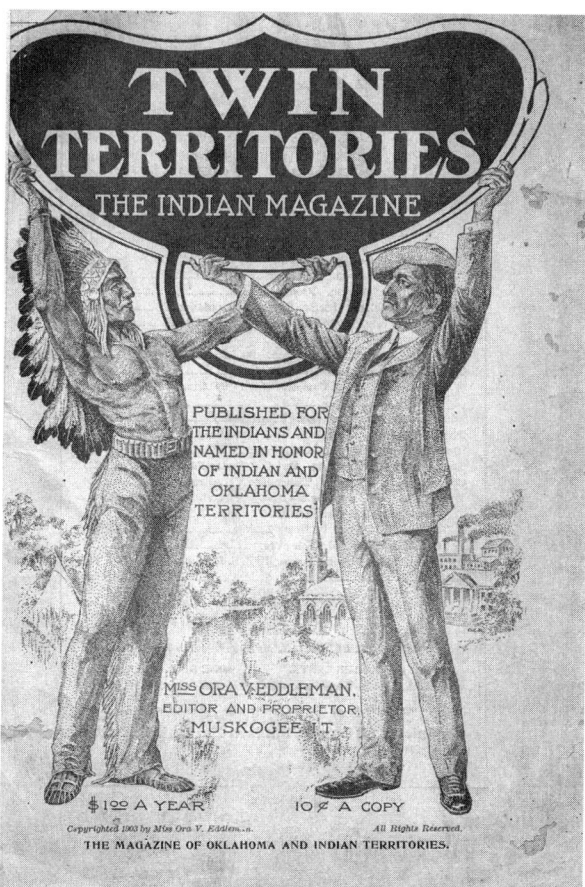

Figure 3 Cover, *Twin Territories* (June 1903). Courtesy of the University of Oklahoma Western History Collections. This cover, or one similar, appeared on most issues published from 1902 until the publication's end.

new tactics to negotiate rapidly shifting demographics on their reservations. Tribal leaders worked tirelessly to fight settler colonial assertions that Indian Territory was an uncivilized place needing guidance. They were vocal that much of the chaos in Indian Territory resulted from settler occupation not Native incivility.[9] *Twin Territories* participated in this discourse by showing the already extant "civility," i.e., colonially legible modernity, of the territories.

While the magazine framed itself as a publication for both territories, it was especially invested in promoting cultural and political life in Indian Territory. Utilizing its pages to show the "progress" at work in Indian Territory through images of new churches, thriving townships, fashion, and so forth, the magazine argued that Indian Territory did not need reform because it was already a domesticated, highly advanced region successfully governed by Native nations.

Although a few years before substantive statehood debates, the February 1899 issue of the magazine, its third issue, uses the "Editorial" column to discuss what it calls *double statehood* ("Editorial" 1899a), later called *single statehood* or *joint statehood*. Here, *double statehood* refers to campaigns for Oklahoma and Indian Territories to enter the United States as one state, instead of *separate statehood*, whereby Oklahoma and Indian Territories would enter as two distinct states. The column inverts the logic of a civilized–savage dialectic by claiming single statehood would not only require Indian Territory to take on the debts of Oklahoma but also argues that settlers in Oklahoma are not as advanced or economically successful as those in Indian Territory: "Oklahoma is a new country; her people, for the most part, came to that region as homeseekers, and in many instances without a dollar; and, instead of 'taking things easy,' and learning to crawl before they walked, they undertook the latter job first" ("Editorial" 1899a: 38). The editorial goes on to say that "*TWIN TERRITORIES* is published for Oklahoma as well as the Indian Territory but it is first, last and all the time, opposed to double statehood, because it is not justice to saddle the debts of one country or one person on the back of another, when only one country or one individual has been the beneficiary. Is it?" (38). The magazine maintained a political bent toward the people of Indian Territory throughout its run, albeit not always in such explicit terms. It is important to note that while Native nations held control over most economic and political affairs in Indian Territory, this was not the case in Oklahoma Territory. As I have argued elsewhere, because Indian Territory was mostly governed by sovereign tribal nations, we must understand it as Native space and the print produced there—even print produced by non-Native people—as part of a Native print public (Walkiewicz 2023).

While a self-conscious advocate for the economic stability and cultural success of Indian Territory, the magazine's framing of "success" is somewhat more inconsistent. Politically charged editorials denouncing white encroachment sit side by side with columns and articles that seemingly poke fun at the stereotyped figure of the so-called Native traditionalist or advocate what might appear to be assimilationist calls to the value of colonial social norms. This contradictory framing positions *Twin Territories* as a rich archive of Indian Territory responses to allotment and statehood. Allotment was an unquestionably traumatic experience that forcibly changed tribal, personal, and intertribal relations through a heightened emphasis on phenotypic features, blood quantum, and other forms of racial categorization.[10] *Twin Territories* projects a sense of domestic stability, both spatially and interpersonally, during this moment of extreme flux to counter the volatility that increased US intervention brought to the territories.

Being a Good Territorial Citizen

Throughout the magazine's run, Eddleman Reed routinely published short fiction, often from the perspective of young Native women, that argued *against* US statehood and *for* tribal sovereignty by contending that under Native control, Indian Territory was already progressively domestic—so much so that it served as a model of proper society that the United States would do well to emulate. I suggest that this fiction allows us to sit with the messy contradictions of *Twin Territories'* legacy, especially the publication's aspirations and limitations. While Eddleman Reed's long-running opinion columns like "What the Curious Want to Know" beautifully excoriated readers' ignorance about Native people, especially Native women, her short fiction acutely delineates the logic of sentimentalist advocacy that informs the magazine as a whole. While her stories adulate Native women as exemplar domestic figures, Eddleman Reed reinscribes what Yao (2021: 11, 10) terms the "emotional respectability required by the politics of recognition" that is critical to the "dominant modes of feeling" that secure settler futurity. In other words, the kind of sympathy that white sentimentalism invites only ever recenters white settler belonging. Eddleman Reed's characters garner sympathy as women and girls through their phenotypical and cultural proximity to whiteness and their marriages to white settler men.

As mentioned earlier, Eddleman Reed's complex relationship to Indigeneity and citizenship is inflected in her literary and editorial work. And, in fact, the biographies of her heroines often bear striking similarities to her own. Ora Veralyn Eddleman Reed, born September 17, 1880, grew up in Denton County, Texas (Morrison 1982: 139). She was the daughter of a prominent cattle ranching father and a mother who claimed Cherokee ancestry. When she was fourteen, the family moved to Muskogee in the Muscogee (Creek) Nation (Morrison 1982: 139). A few years after arriving there, Eddleman Reed's father, David J. Eddleman, bought the nascent *Muskogee Daily Times* and turned the newspaper into a family business venture. Her mother, Mary, "claimed it was the newspaper that stood in the way of the family's enrollment in the Cherokee Nation; the very reason they had come to Muskogee was thwarted. The claim for citizenship was presented to the Dawes

Commission and was rejected" (Morrison 1982: 142). The Eddlemans' version of the story suggests that the judge took umbrage with something written about him in the family's newspaper and decided to decline Mary's citizenship claim as retribution. In this narrative, the Eddlemans' entrance into tribal life via print culture had denied them any claim to allotment or official recognition as Cherokee citizens.

However, Kirby Brown's (Cherokee Nation) genealogical research finds no direct lineal Cherokee descent for the Eddlemans.[11] In addition to never having recognized citizenship in the Cherokee Nation, Eddleman Reed was not writing or publishing in the Cherokee Nation, which was unusual for Cherokee writers at this time (I struggle to think of many others). In fact, the Muscogee Nation, where she lived, is the focus of much of the magazine's content.[12] Likewise, her magazine does not present itself as a Cherokee publication (or a Muscogee one) but as a territorial one, meaning it is representative of a broader discourse in Indian Territory. Finally, her family had recently relocated to Indian Territory from Texas at the end of the nineteenth century to enroll. Therefore, they did not have long-standing, deep cultural connections to Cherokee communities in Indian Territory. Collectively, these facts represent a family who hit very few of the markings of belonging that denoted Cherokeeness in this particular historical moment.

Enrollment was unquestionably a chaotic process for many, and there were huge inconsistencies in the Dawes Commission's methods. However, the Cherokee Nation kept extensive census records from the early nineteenth century, well before the Dawes Rolls, and worked vigilantly to fight false claims to Cherokee enrollment. As Daniel Heath Justice (Cherokee Nation) (2021: 27) explains in describing a non-Native maternal ancestor who falsely claimed Chickasaw citizenship through Cherokee ancestry: "Cherokee kinship ties were extensively documented in over thirty-five separate censuses, rolls, and lists, not counting various treaties, judicial decrees, and other legal documents. If her relations couldn't be found in that archive and she hadn't been granted citizenship to that point, she was, in the light of all available and tribally recognized evidence, not Cherokee."[13] Native nations have the right to determine who their citizens are. While the federal government aimed to gain greater control over how Native nations governed themselves and whose tribal citizenship was recognized at precisely the moment Eddleman Reed was writing, it was also that moment when Cherokee Nation leaders insisted on the Nation's right to determine its own people. As the Digadatseli'i ᎫᏍᎾᏉᏗᎢ Chero- kee scholars' collective (2020) explains, "Cherokee identity is a politi- cal identity that can only be established through documentation by one of the Cherokee governments that an individual is a Cherokee citi- zen. It is not, and never has been, an ethnic or racial identity that is established through self-identification." Rarely did affluent Native peo- ple of white descent get rejected by the Dawes Commission. Far more common was the rejection of Afro-Native people, Freedpeople, and Freedpeoples' descendants.[14] While there are necessary conversa- tions about how citizenship policies excluded Cherokees of African descent at the turn of the twentieth century—as well as at the turn of the twenty-first century—that discussion is not germane to the case of Eddleman Reed.[15]

With all of this in mind, I have spent many years debating the ethics of how to write about Eddleman Reed and her work—and whether or not to do so at all.[16] Instead of avoiding the complexity that she engen- ders, I find it necessary to grapple with the difficult questions about citizenship, belonging, and kinship that she and her work bring for- ward because these are questions that continue to dog Indigenous lit- erary studies in the twenty-first century. Who gets to speak for Native communities? Do a person's political and cultural contributions out- weigh the personal when someone who has claimed Indigeneity has no Indigenous community that claims them? These questions are especially vexing for Cherokees, given rampant unsubstantiated claims to Cherokeeness in academia and, more generally, across the United States. Ultimately, it is up to Cherokees to debate, discuss, and determine our relationship with Eddleman Reed and her relationship to us.

At this time, I cannot call Eddleman Reed a Cherokee author. How- ever, this does not mean she did not make significant contributions to Indian Territory literature, culture, and politics that deserve greater recognition, which is why I describe her as a good territorial citizen. She advocated for the continuation of Indian Territory as a distinct, Native-run geopolity and actively denounced statehood. In other words, she prioritized a political orientation toward Native nations over that of a fealty to the US settler nation-state. However, her narra- tion of Indian Territory as a space of regenerative domesticity—a sentimentalist terrain, if you will—reinscribes many of the stereotypes of Native people used by the US media and Congress to justify the arsenal of attacks on tribal sovereignty that Eddleman Reed and others witnessed at the end of the nineteenth century. In analyzing her contributions to *Twin Territories*, which I turn to for the rest of this essay, I am most interested in how she used sentimentalist tropes to assert the necessity of tribal autonomy under the looming shadows of statehood. She admirably attempted to undermine the settler investments of sentimentalism, even though her efforts reveal the limits of such a project. If Indian Territory's rich literary and media landscapes made essential contributions to Indigenous print because they were produced within sovereign Native nations, then Eddleman Reed was invariably a vital contributor to that ecosystem.

What the Curious *Should* Know

As mentioned earlier, despite the magazine's contemporary influence, there are only a handful of scholars who have delved into the cultural importance of *Twin Territories*.[17] The scholarship that does exist focuses primarily on two running features, "What the Curious Want to Know" and "Types of Indian Girls." The former, began in 1901, and was one of the magazine's most popular running pieces. In it, Eddleman Reed responds to practical questions and concerns sent in by readers—from both the territories and the "East."[18] It becomes a vital space to address Eastern readers' bigotry and prejudice, where Eddleman Reed (1901: 58) will "cheerfully answer questions concerning Indian Territory and Oklahoma" because, according to her, "letters are received every month from people throughout the United States, who wish to know about the conditions prevailing here." Despite the warm invite of her solicitation, some of Eddleman Reed's responses are icy, openly critiquing readers' stereotypical assumptions about Native people, as is the case with her response to "Paddy, Arlington, N.Y.":

> The Indian girls of Indian Territory, or "squaw girl," as you will persist in calling them, do not have to advertise for husbands. Such questions as yours are really getting tiresome. There is no excuse for your not knowing that the Indian girls of the civilized tribes are just as modest, cultured and womanly as their white sisters, and would not think of advertising for husbands. They don't have to do that. Many of them have married white men, and many more will perhaps do so, but as far as chances of marriage are concerned, they aren't compelled to advertise for them. I'm afraid I can't give you much encouragement, for I do not know of any Indian girl who "wants to secure for a husband one who is capable of taking care of

her allotment to her advantage as well as his own, being a good farmer."[19] (Eddleman Reed 1902c: 118)

Responses to questions about the eligibility of young Native women, like the one from Paddy, reveal an explicit, politically charged rebuttal to the perception of women in the territories and the gendering of Indian Territory by those living in the United States proper. "What the Curious Want to Know" suggests that Eddleman Reed was aware of the necessity of framing the territories in a particular way to shape prominent public opinions about the space.[20] In her responses to questions that posit Indian Territory women derogatorily, her typical response is one of educator or teacher lecturing to her uneducated Eastern students. She scolds readers for their ignorant and insensitive questions. At the same time, however, she does not reject interracial marriage, especially between Native women and white men. Instead, what seems most interesting about her response to "Paddy" is that she describes Native women as desirable and attractive but fully capable of determining their own futures. Unlike a magazine, these women do not have to "advertise" themselves and have many suitors to choose from: they are white middle-class women's equals.

Emphasis on Native women's virtue, intelligence, and agency is a thread that runs throughout the magazine's content, including "Types of Indian Girls." "Types" presents photographic portraits and brief biographies of married and unmarried young Native women, sometimes depicted in Indigenous clothing and sometimes in Victorian (see fig. 4).[21] While Alexia Kosmider (1998: 111), one of the first scholars to write about *Twin Territories*, reads the column as "interrogat[ing] existing assumptions about Indian women as 'savage' or 'barbaric' by presenting a new way of seeing Indians"—specifically, Native people who have "turned the camera on themselves to be photographed"—I read it as an argument for Native sovereignty that argues for individual bodily autonomy and self-determination of the body politic, with a recognition that the two were (and are) often conflated. The column's embodied political message is therefore not unlike the performative and photographic work of well-known Indigenous public figures of the era, including Gertrude Simmons Bonin / Zitkala-Ša (Yankton Dakota) and Sarah Winnemucca [Hopkins] / Thocmetony (Northern Paiute). In Kosmider's reading, she also understands the audience for the magazine almost exclusively as a non-Native one, but I want to poke at that assumption. Even if a substantial contingent of readers were Easterners or white settlers in the territories, the publication was invested in

204   TWIN TERRITORIES.

TYPES OF INDIAN GIRLS.

A Beauty of the Cherokee Tribe,
Miss Helen Severs.

Miss Ella Monahwee, in whose veins   Miss Leota Crabtree, a beautiful young
flows only a fraction of white   girl who is proud of her Creek blood.
blood, mingled with that of the
Creek tribe.

Figure 4 "Types of Indian Girls," *Twin Territories* (July 1902), 204. Courtesy of the University of Oklahoma Western History Collections

promoting Native materials self-professedly intended for an audience of Native readers; the title states as much in the early issues. All of the columns in the magazine celebrate modernity in the territories, often attributing advances to the work of influential Native political, economic, and cultural figures. While we may critique the messages about beauty and respectability that "Types" promotes, it was a running feature that was acutely aware of the interplay between settler surveillance of territorial life and intercommunal dialogue. Unlike many nineteenth-century periodicals, *Twin Territories* assumes Native readers and is as interested in how Native people see each other as it is in how others see them. The same is true of Eddleman Reed's sentimental fiction. While she employs the conventions of settler sentimentality, she seemingly does so for an imagined audience of Native readers, not just white settlers and Easterners. She does so partly because she understands herself as a Native writer publishing a magazine in a Native nation.

Like "Types of Indian Girls," the short serial fiction Eddleman Reed pens under the name "Mignon Schreiber" metaphorizes Indian Territory as a young modern woman and challenges statehood and further US encroachment on Indian Territory and affairs.[22] Throughout her fiction, Eddleman Reed pens a sentimentalism that utilizes the domestic sphere and courtship to endorse a political policy intended to mend bigger fissures both among the twin territories themselves and between the territories and the United States. Her heroines, as representations of territorial identity, resignify sentimental tropes to authenticate a Native territorial domestic space, not unlike heroines in the work of contemporaneous Native women writers, including E. Pauline Johnson / Tekahionwake (Mohawk) and S. Alice Callahan (Muscogee).

Similar to Callahan, Eddleman Reed utilizes the sentimental genre to critique settler attacks on Native domesticity in Indian Territory. As Niimiipuu literary scholar Beth Piatote (2013: 49) has demonstrated, "'sentiment' drove Indian policy" during the Allotment era, and "the force of sentiment exerted itself through public policy and domestic fiction alike, working together to define the affective and legal boundaries of the family." Understanding sentimental fiction in this way helps us understand why Indian Territory writers like Callahan and Eddleman Reed might want to subvert the genre's racist undertones and promote a different notion of domesticity, one that opens up a space for Native women as active protagonists. But unlike Callahan's *Wynema: A Child of the Forest* (1891), which Piatote reads as affirming Native maternalism and kinship, the plotlines in Eddleman Reed's short fiction are less preoccupied with the Native family (almost all of the Native mothers in her stories are dead) and more invested in promoting heteropatriarchal marriage between Native women and white men. She utilizes the domestic sphere and courtship to endorse a political policy intended to mend fissures between Indian Territory and the United States, gesturing toward a "separate spheres" approach to US-Indian Territory relations.

Mainstream sentimental fiction depicts Indigenous women's "savagery" as the foil to middle-class white women's civility. Whereas, Eddleman Reed's work not only troubles but often reverses the dichotomy, asserting the notion that the United States and its residents benefit from Native life *as is* in Indian Territory. While she does not necessarily center what Piatote (2013: 4) terms the "intimate domestic," the "Indian home and family," which Piatote argues is "the primary site of struggle against the foreign force of U.S. national domestication," she does center Native feminine domesticity. In other words, as representations of territorial identity, her female heroines resignify sentimental tropes to authenticate a territorial domestic space—a *sentimental terrain*. Because the stock plotline stays (at times painfully) consistent in her fiction, Eddleman Reed's emphasis on the success of these cross-cultural, transnational relationships seems to indicate, in much the same way as her more flagrant editorials, the kinds of policy she is advocating for—a marital one that is as political and symbolic as it is trite and sentimental.

For the rest of the essay, I demonstrate how Eddleman Reed negotiated the inherent tension between her political commitment to Native sovereignty and the sentimentalist literary conventions she employed in her writing by reading three pieces of her short fiction published from 1899 to 1900, the first two years of the magazine's run: "Aunt Mary's Christmas Dinner," "Lizonka, a Creek Girl," and "Only an Indian Girl." All three assert a consistent political agenda and follow a similar plot: Either an Eastern tenderfoot visits Indian Territory for the first time or a Native girl leaves the territory for the first time. There is some deception or confusion of identity, usually of the young Native woman, but in the end, the Eastern man woos her, and the two wed. Often, the heroine is intelligent, ambitious, and an aspiring career woman (usually a newspaper or magazine writer like Eddleman Reed). Her young Eastern beau helps her better her professional interests and personal happiness. In all of these cases, Eddleman Reed stages debates about statehood as marriage plots. She reinterprets the prevailing trope of Mr. Oklahoma and Miss Indian Territory used to present statehood as a happy marriage of the two territories to argue instead that a successful union between the United States and Indian Territory necessitates the continued sovereignty of the domestic spaces of Native nations.[23]

Invading the Settler Domestic

"Aunt Mary's Christmas Dinner," published in the magazine in 1899, follows the experiences of a young Native woman as she enters white settler domestic spaces—the settler nation and the settler home. The story subtly suggests that successful acculturation can allow for "passing" in white society, especially for those who can phenotypically do so. In the narrative, Aunt Mary gets a letter from James Jenkins, her "father's cousin" who had moved to Indian Territory and married a Cherokee woman (Schreiber 1899a: 9). She and her nephews receive a letter informing them of Jenkins' death and his wish that they care for his daughter. After reading the letters, Mary and the nephews laugh as they brainstorm ways to civilize this girl from Tahlequah (the Cherokee Nation's capital). The girl, Nannie Jenkins, is to arrive close to Christmas, so Mary and the nephews begin to prepare as the holidays approach. However, when the girl arrives, Aunt Mary mistakes her for the new cook. When Nannie enters the house, she decides to go along with the error and play a joke on Mary by pretending to be the cook. Eventually Nannie reveals herself, and Aunt Mary and the nephews claim they never suspected because she seemed totally unlike the young girl in "a little red shawl and buckskin moccasins" they had anticipated (10). Nannie's features trouble how she is read racially in the story. When she first appears, the narrator describes her as "a stunning looking cook" who looks more like "one of [Aunt Mary's] acquaintances than a house-maid" (10). While Aunt Mary and her nephews are deep in discussion about what a Native person will look like, they are unable to recognize one when she knocks on the door.

Nannie enacts a literal invasion into the domestic by the foreign when she enters Aunt Mary's house, an inversion of what Amy Kaplan (2002: 25) terms "manifest domesticity." White settler women's national responsibilities are twofold: ensuring the family's and private sphere's stability and serving as imperial agents. By bringing their domestic knowledge to foreign lands as stabilizing, colonizing forces, they are critical components to settler colonial expansion and occupation. Native nations in Indian Territory and Oklahoma Territory inhabit a peculiar space within imperialist discourse because, under federal law, they are understood as both domestic and foreign. Nannie becomes a figure that troubles the line between the two and moves freely between them, "passing" back and forth when necessary. Eddleman Reed plays on this anxiety by making Nannie's "foreignness" illegible. As a woman of mixed descent, she is both inside and outside the domestic and the foreign, in between two territories, and can migrate back and forth. What initially makes her passing so believable is her ability to perform the signature features of a proper settler woman. She speaks English fluently, knows her way around a kitchen, and understands how to keep a proper home (so well that Aunt Mary feels her abilities are "out of the ordinary") (Schreiber 1899a: 11). Nannie exudes a sense of class privilege, and she exemplifies true domestic womanhood.

Nannie's invasion into the domestic sphere simultaneously troubles and repairs it. When she hears Frank, one of the nephews, tell his aunt he has reached financial ruin, she reveals her true identity to offer Frank the money he needs because she has "money enough to keep me always" from her "Cherokee claim" (11). It is Nannie's foreign status, marked as "authentic" by her inclusion on the Dawes rolls that enables her to repair the financial struggles of the settler home and offer Aunt Mary's family money from her allotment. Joe, the other nephew, is romantically interested in her. While we never learn what she and Joe discuss in the kitchen as they prepare for Christmas dinner, they emerge "both blushing and laughing" as Joe tells Aunt Mary that "we'll keep her in the family!" (11). While Joe comments on Nannie's beauty earlier in the story, it is not until she provides economic relief to the family that she becomes a potential mate. She ensures the alluring attributes of a proper Victorian woman and the income from her allotment lands, making her a valuable asset. In addition, as Joe's wife, Nannie can enter the domestic realm of the middle class, her civility verified by his white, patriarchal approval of her.

Nannie's ability to enter the settler colonial home without conflict alleviates white women's fears that allowing the "foreign" into the domestic space threatens settler state values. At the same time, Eddleman Reed offers Native women a guide for economic and personal survival in the face of the increasing influx of white settler interests in Indian Territory. But, "Aunt Mary's Christmas Dinner" does not offer readers a clean outline of cross-cultural relations. The plot emphasizes the ability of interracial marriage to inoculate the colonial desires of white men. However, such moves validate many of the values of white domestic rhetoric, elide the inherent power structure in these interactions, and neglect a long history of conquest via wedlock.

The trope of the white man attracted to the young, unmarried Native woman was a pervasive one in Indian Territory at the time and the most popular conceit to describe joint statehood between "Mr. Oklahoma and Miss Indian Territory" (see fig. 5). As women began to accrue land through allotment, many white men were interested in marriage because under US coverture laws, which fell into effect for most tribes after allotment, a husband acquired control of a wife's property and investments. Because of Eddleman Reed's strong understanding of white men's exploitation of Native women through marriage, which she details in numerous "What the Curious Want to Know" editorials, it is difficult to read Nannie's story as a simple celebration of nuptials between financially strapped white men and propertied Native women. However, the story is also not explicitly critical of allotment as a means of dissolving collective tribal landholdings and eroding Native nations' power. While her pieces advocate for Indian Territory as a sustainable,

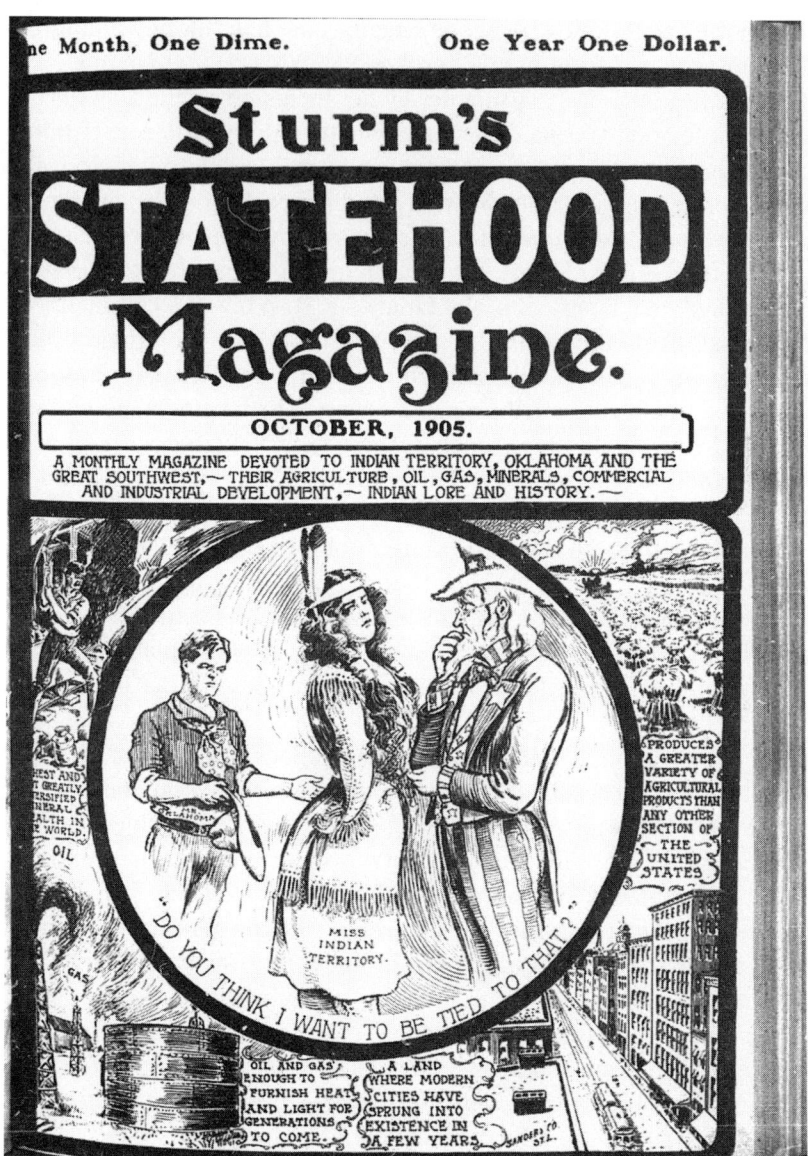

Figure 5   Cover, *Sturm's Statehood Magazine*, October 1905

domestic space under its current rule, Eddleman Reed also invokes the racialist logic that accompanied allotment and its threat to the political status of Indian Territory. It is through allotment, after all, that Nannie accrues the individual wealth that she can then share with the white brothers.

Allotting Marriage

Unlike "Aunt Mary's Christmas Dinner," "Lizonka, a Creek Girl" and "Only an Indian Girl" are set in Indian Territory and situate the territory as the text's domestic locus. While "Aunt Mary's Christmas Dinner" emphasizes Native women's ability to enter the white settler home, "Lizonka" and "Only an Indian Girl" reinforce the self-sufficiency and value of the territorial one. The heroines in these stories advance a territorial domesticity that encourages heightened civility and chivalry in the white men who travel to Indian Territory. As such, Eddleman Reed's territorial domesticity envisions Native women maintaining tribal ties and values while accommodating white settlers into their homes.

In "Lizonka, a Creek Girl" (1899), Lizonka is a free-spirited tomboy raised by the ranchers who lease her father's land. She meets Loren Hurst Jr., the son of a "well-known Texas cattleman," who has come to Indian Territory for the same reason as the others. Almost from the start, a mutual attraction blossoms (Schreiber 1899b: May, 114). After a series of bizarre and unforeseen events, including the death of Lizonka's father, she is sent to Carlisle Indian Industrial School, Richard Henry Pratt's infamous boarding school in Pennsylvania. When Lizonka returns from Carlisle, she is a refined "tall, graceful young girl of twenty" (July, 169).[24] She is happy to see the ranchmen and return home "for a love of her own race and a deep and tender loyalty to her people" (July, 169). She and Loren profess their love for one another. She reveals that if it were not for her devotion to him, she would not have been as dedicated to her education at school. Shortly after her return, Loren's father tells Lizonka and his son that they share the same mother, eliminating any possibility for the two to marry. Lizonka and Loren learn that this is, in fact, a lie. Disgraced following his misdeeds, Loren Sr. dies by suicide, and Loren Jr. and Lizonka can finally wed.

Aside from the serial's twisting plotline and Dickensian web of characters, the story places the young lovers on the frontlines of economic and civic policy during allotment. After white ranchers and farmers settled in Oklahoma Territory, interest in Indian Territory colonization grew, and settlers aimed to seize political and economic control of the territory away from Native nations. The allotment of land aided their efforts, forcing Native nations to dissolve collective landholdings into individual plots. Under the Curtis Act of 1898, the Five Tribes (the Cherokee, Muscogee [Creek], Seminole, Choctaw, and Chickasaw Nations) were required to relinquish their civic authority and comply with allotment policies. As allotments were handed out, "excess" land was opened to settlers, leading to a massive influx of non-Native people.

Twin Territories often portrays "cattlemen" as good territorial citizens, downplaying their impact on the increased settlement of Native land. They are depicted in contrast to bad settlers, who have no respect for tribal governance or Native ways of life. It is important to remember that Eddleman Reed's father had been a prosperous rancher in Texas before her family moved to the Muscogee Nation, so Eddleman Reed had personal experiences with the industry.[25] In multiple editorials, the magazine argued that leasing to the cattlemen was a critical economic enterprise for the territory. A March 1899 editorial asserted that "there isn't the least doubt but that the cattlemen have been a very important factor in the opening-up and development of this country, and it seems rather hard to shove them out in the cold so unceremoniously" ("Editorial" 1899b). Allotment and increased settlement hurt the cattle industry as fencing prevented the herding of livestock across the territorial prairies, so many in the industry were critical of increased US interventions into territorial politics. The magazine's general approach to the cattle industry is helpful to remember when reading "Lizonka" and its entangled romance plot.

Even though the story's central villain is a cattleman, he is an outsider from Texas with no interest in participating in territorial life. Loren Sr. symbolizes the "disreputable Texans" and "multitude of criminals" (Thompson 1986: 37) that came to Indian Territory to profit off the chaos ensuing during allotment. At the same time, his son embodies the desirable white settler—one who is willing to still abide by tribal policies and communal land-sharing. Lizonka and Loren Jr.'s relationship provides a model for how Native people could retain economic and political authority in the territory but endorse commerce with white settlers and cattlemen. The text goes out of its way to display the cruel dealings of Loren's father and the bravery of Lizonka to reinforce the purity of Loren and Lizonka's love. While Loren may have access to Lizonka's land and power after they wed, the text clarifies that he is not only uninterested in that kind of power but unsure of how to wield it. He is willing to participate in territorial economic exchanges but is not interested in changing or subverting tribal rules and policies. He moves from the home of one savvy cattleman (Loren Sr.) to another (Lizonka).[26]

Unlike the typical heroines of sentimental fiction who work to create change in a public sphere they have indirect access to, Lizonka must resist change to keep the power she already possesses. To a territorial audience, Lizonka's fight to maintain the home—both personal and tribal—is a political move. While she does marry a white man, she also decides that he must settle in the territory with her, not vice versa: "The party tarried awhile visiting various places of interest and then returned to the Indian Territory, 'which,' Lizonka declared to her husband as they stood together in their old trysting places, 'is, after all, the only place that's really home.'" (Schreiber 1899: October, 228). Their relationship as Native tomboy and Texas tenderfoot complicates the foreign-domestic dichotomy undergirding manifest domesticity. By making Indian Territory the center of her writing, the East becomes the subjugated, the foreign that is ignorant of the richness and civility of the territory (Kosmider 1995: 52). While the ideology of sentimental domesticity may be grounded in settler society, Eddleman Reed argues that *true* domesticity can be found in Indian Territory, untarnished by the urban life and greed of the East. For both audiences, Eastern and territorial, Eddleman Reed provides a marriage between white leasers and Indian landowners that attempts to demonstrate the benefits of the arrangement to both parties. In so doing, she argues for a policy that becomes as much a civic partnership as a romantic union, allowing for open lines of commerce and intercultural communities that can thrive without incorporating Indian Territory into the United States.[27]

"Only an Indian Girl" (1900), published directly after "Lizonka," elaborates on how territorial Native women can respond to their roles as landowners and housekeepers. Much like Lizonka, our heroine Dannie, a Cherokee girl named after her father Dan Gray, falls in love with a tenderfoot sent to Indian Territory to "rough it awhile" (Schreiber 1900: February, 37). The young man, Lewis Morrison, is a wealthy reporter and newspaper owner who is pursuing a rest cure as far away from city life as possible. Almost as soon as he enters the Gray home outside Tahlequah, his preconceived notions about Native people and the territory collapse. The more he and Dannie talk, the more he realizes his ignorance, and the more she teases him: "'Are you armed, Mr. Morrison?' she called out laughingly. 'Because you know, Tahlequah's a terrible place and you must keep a sharp lookout for the Indians who crave the white man's scalp—not to mention the wild beasts that may attack you from the wayside. Verily, this is a wild county!'" (Schreiber 1900: May, 101). During their conversations, Morrison realizes Dannie's love for writing. He encourages her to send off stories for publication but discovers her confidence was previously shaken. The *New York Ledger*, the newspaper he edits and owns, rejected a piece of hers. He persuades her to write back to the paper. After publishing her work, he reveals his connections to the *Ledger* and asks her to be his coeditor and wife. Their union is both marital and professional—and it is mutually beneficial. Living in the territory literally cures the ails of the city, and Morrison's influence and wealth ensure Dannie can circulate her writing about Indian Territory more broadly, existing separately but in union.

Unlike "Lizonka," "Only an Indian Girl" attempts to confront head-on the gross caricaturing of Indian Territory citizens as lawless and savage in the pages of Eastern newspapers. Morrison realizes the value of what Dannie has to say, that hers is a critical, unique perspective that an Eastern audience must hear. In addition, according to the story, he is enriched by a sense of community and goodwill for the first time in his life while he is in Indian Territory. While Dannie eventually does wed Morrison and moves away to New York, she makes numerous return visits to the Cherokee Nation. She also sends "frequent letters" back home (Schreiber 1900: July, 154). She keeps her maiden name, Dannie Gray, when penning her fiction and "smiles happily as she does so," continuing to negotiate a twinned sense of self, as a woman writer and a wife (Schreiber 1900: July, 154). Dannie must leave the territories to articulate a territorial voice to an Eastern audience, but she tries to stay true to her Native identity by penning under her maiden name. By becoming a wife and coauthor, she can *insert* a territorial voice into a larger Eastern discourse and thus *assert* the merits of Indian Territory to an outside audience.

The Domesticating Frontier

"Lizonka" and "Only an Indian Girl" present Indian Territory as a politically and culturally stable region with a better quality of life for its residents than anywhere in the East. Since the territory is already "civilized," the kind of domestic imperial takeover described by Kaplan is unnecessary. Native nations can be trusted to manage their lands and people as successfully as the United States. Consequently, Eddleman Reed argues for Indian Territory as a locus of true domesticity where the values associated with the home—love, family, care, and nourishment—are powerfully present. The territory becomes an almost hyperdomestic space, a frontier that helps white Eastern women return to an ideal understanding of true womanhood and white Eastern men become good husbands and reinvigorated businessmen. Most importantly, however, the territory can only maintain its purity through Native control. While white immigrants can visit, lease, or marry into the territory, they cannot simply consume. In other words, they must behave as good territorial citizens. Otherwise, by tarnishing the purity of the territorial domestic sphere, they risk the fate of Loren Sr.: personal humiliation and death. However, both stories also romanticize the political and economic partnerships that Lizonka and Dannie agree to when they marry white men. While Lizonka may be in charge of the day-to-day workings of her ranch in practice, Loren now owns her family land on paper. While Dannie continues to write under her maiden name, she nevertheless leaves Indian Territory to work for her husband. In both cases, marriage and the legal coverture it catalyzes make these women's financial security (Lizonka) and their relationship to their Nation (Dannie) more tenuous.

Eddleman Reed's heroines serve as moralistic embodiments of how to navigate a rapidly changing territorial world. While her characters argue for the necessity of maintaining Indian Territory as a distinct geopolity, they encourage a "change with the times" attitude that teeters on the edge of complete assimilation and the reinforcement of colonial hierarchies. Moreover, her stories routinely move dangerously close to reinforcing harmful stereotypes of Indigenous peoples used to justify allotment, statehood, and United States meddling in Indian Territory affairs. Despite the optimism of Eddleman Reed's politics, she neglects to leave a space for Native people who had rejected acculturation or any engagement with white society. In the subplot to "Only an Indian Girl," the Cherokee Nation's election of the "traditionalist" candidate describes him and his supporters unflatteringly. The traditionalists resort to violence to elicit their desired electoral results. Whereas, she describes the more "progressive" candidate of mixed ancestry as "strong, brave and true—a leader among his people" (Schreiber 1900: May, 101). The contrast between the two candidates reinforces the racist notion that the more white-presenting a Native person appears, the more acculturated and capable the person.

Eddleman Reed's romantic plotlines suffer from much of the same racialist thinking. Reading generously, the marriages between white men and Native women model consensual relationships at multiple scales that challenge the gendered, sexualized histories of conquest in the Americas (between non-Indigenous settlers and Indigenous peoples, as well as between the United States and Indian Territory). Or, they detail paths to tribal inclusion for non-Native people in Indian Territory—an Indigenizing of sorts—that argues Indigenous governance benefits all people. However, both of these more generous readings are preoccupied with managing whiteness and white expectations of Native people. The reader is told on multiple occasions that "in Lizonka, the Creeks found a love for her own race and a deep and tender loyalty to her people. And they loved and respected her for it," but very early on in the story, Lizonka's father dies. She quickly becomes the story's only Native character (Schreiber 1899b: July, 169). Instead of demonstrating Lizonka's ties to her Muscogee community, the novel is preoccupied with delineating the specifics of her white ancestry that eventually reveal an unknown white uncle (John Leen, her father's assistant). Much of the plot's suspense is driven by revelations about these white relatives and which white men in the story (John Leen, Loren Sr., or Loren Jr.) will become responsible for managing Lizonka's landholdings for her. The only time her ties to the Muscogee community are evoked is through Mvskoke language conversations we either do not hear or that are translated into English for us or through descriptions of her father's funeral as full of "weird chantings" and "wild carryings on" ostensibly from Muskogee mourners (Schreiber 1899b: June, 138). Indigeneity operates almost exclusively as a racial marker in the story; there are no overt efforts to foreground or celebrate specifics of the Muscogee world where the story takes place.

Reading *Twin Territories*

In her fiction, Eddleman Reed presents Native women characters who are autonomous subjects negotiating their own futures with Victorian morals and New Woman ambition. However, she does so by reinscribing notions of middle- and upper-class femininity predicated on white supremacist logics of proper womanhood. Perhaps this is because Eddleman Reed did not grow up in Indian Territory—she only spent a few years living there before starting the magazine—so she employed the tools of activism she was likely most familiar with from an upbringing in middle-class settler spaces: white feminist sentimentalism. Across *Twin Territories*' content but especially in her short fiction, she neither disrupts the inherently racialist norms of Victorian femininity nor does she interrogate how heteronormative, white-supremacist family structures almost always exclude Native, Black, immigrant, working-class, gender-nonconforming, and of-Color women.[28] Instead, she argues for Native women's *inclusion* in a particular kind of femininity dictated by racial capitalism and settler colonialism by placing Native women in close proximity to whiteness. Eddleman Reed's work is deeply entrenched in a logic of race and blood quantum.[29] She routinely invokes stereotyped tropes of Native life and stages dyads between "civilized" and "savage" or "white" and "Indian" that she inverts more than she breaks. The few representations of Blackness or Black people in the magazine are disturbing racist caricatures, and unlike the friendships she narrates between Native and white women, her fiction never imagines "sisterhood" between Native and Black women. While the magazine dynamically challenges many of the conventions of sentimentalism, it maintains a consistent white supremacist logic. Meaning, the methods of cultural dialogue Eddleman Reed asserts, at best, privilege acculturation, heteronormativity, whiteness, and a particular and limited type of embodied Indigeneity; at worst, they posit redface romances that reinscribe the damaging stereotypes about Native people that structured the aggressive dispossession and cultural genocide of the Allotment era.

Eddleman Reed's fiction provides her readers with rich texts that interrogate, but unevenly answer, problems of cultural translation, colonialism, and assimilation. She used *Twin Territories* to assert Indian Territory as a sovereign, sentimental terrain outside the United States proper whose many positive attributes are due to the self-sufficiency of tribal nations. She was part of a community of writers, many of them deeply entrenched in political campaigns within their nations and in transnational alliances, who utilized newspapers and magazines to critique US intrusion into territorial affairs, craft political tracts (sometimes through literary writing), and shape imagined geographies of the region's future.[30] Their writing was actively invested in the politics of the present but also attuned to the geopolitical futurity of Indian Territory.[31]

This era's rich body of print culture serves as an invaluable archive that faithfully documents the federal government's overreach into tribal affairs and the large-scale protests many in Indian Territory launched in response. While Native people in Indian Territory have always known that their reservations were not abolished upon Oklahoma statehood, the US Supreme Court recognized this fact in its recent *McGirt v. Oklahoma* (2020) ruling, a (re-)recognition of the Indian Territory domestic Native spaces *Twin Territories* celebrated. The magazine is an unrivaled archive of fin-de-siècle Indian Territory literature that makes a far-reaching contribution to Indigenous print and literary studies. While not a Cherokee Nation citizen, Eddleman Reed was committed to fighting against further US encroachment on Indigenous self-determination, as evidenced throughout the magazine's content. Eddleman Reed was not a Cherokee citizen, but she was a good territorial citizen.[32] Meaning, she advocated to protect an Indian Territory governed by sovereign Native nations and worked against Oklahoma settler statehood.

In this essay, I have resisted the impulse to offer a cogent argument about how we should read *Twin Territories* and Eddleman Reed's writing, especially her sentimental short fiction, but emphasize the necessity of reading it nonetheless. Aside from their sentimentalist framing, the essays and fiction penned by Native authors and the images of young Native women in "Types of Indian Girls" provide important snapshots into the lives of Native people during a tumultuous historical moment. Greater access to the magazine will allow Native people to find portraits of their relatives and communities, and for this reason alone, *Twin Territories* is a valuable archive. However, if we continue to read Eddleman Reed as a Cherokee writer and editor, we risk dismissing Native nations' right to determine who their people are—a right that Eddleman Reed defended throughout her writing. Quick moves to legibility threaten to oversimplify what we find in the magazine and echo the dispossessive logics of allotment and statehood that Eddleman Reed herself critiqued. For years, working under the belief that she was Cherokee, I struggled to make sense of the sentimental fiction she published in *Twin Territories*, to justify its romantic racialism and cheesy plotlines because I *wanted* her to be a Cherokee author rooted in a commitment to Cherokee self-determination and story. A young Cherokee woman who supported her community by creating a unique magazine celebrating Native literature, art, and politics? That's a good story—and one I wanted to believe. But better than a good story is a real story. Taking the time to sit with the entanglement of her sense of herself, her political commitments to Indian Territory, and the sentimentalism of her magazine invites us to slow down and take care reflecting on issues that continue to inform Indigenous literary studies. I want to make room for deliberation on how to understand the relationships among Indian Territory, Eddleman Reed, and her work. I want to practice working through complicated Indigenous literary archives in conversation with and attendant to the needs and current political struggles of Indigenous Peoples. Again, one does not have be a tribal citizen to be a good territorial one.

Kathryn Walkiewicz is an enrolled citizen of Cherokee Nation and an associate professor in the Department of Literature at University of California San Diego. She is the author of *Reading Territory: Indigenous and Black Freedom, Removal, and the Nineteenth-Century State* (2023).

Notes

1   I use *Native* and *Indigenous* fairly interchangeably throughout this article. However, I typically use *Native* more frequently when describing the specific experiences of Indigenous people in Indian Territory to signal the particularity of their relationship to the United States. At the time of writing this essay, *Native* is an acceptable descriptor of American Indians, although that may certainly change in the future.

2   No records indicate precisely how involved Eddleman Reed was in the magazine's early years. Still, most scholars agree with Daryl Morrison's (1982: 143) assertion that she consistently took an active part in production and was likely the editor from its inception. Beginning in the April 1900 issue, "Ora V. Eddleman" is listed as *Twin Territories*' editor.

3   *Easterner* was a term used throughout the magazine to denote readers living in the United States proper.

4   This depiction of Indian Territory as Native and feminine and Oklahoma Territory as white and masculine was pervasive at the time. Another magazine staged a series of covers invoking the conceit (I include an example later in the essay). The bronze statue *Statehood* (Frederick A. Olds, 1907) at the entrance to the Oklahoma Territorial Museum in Guthrie, Oklahoma, also invokes this imagery.

5   Here I am also thinking of Kyla Schuller's work on sentimentalism and biopolitics, especially *The Biopolitics of Feeling: Race, Sex, and Science in the Nineteenth Century* (2017).

6   She was also the first woman member and one of the youngest members of the Indian Territory Press Association in 1900.

7   Because *Twin Territories* is still relatively inaccessible, the primary venues where one might encounter her work are anthologies and bibliographies of Native writers. A few prominent examples are Littlefield and Parins's biobibliographies of Native writers (see "Ora V. Eddleman Reed" 1995) and Karen Kilcup's edited collection of Native women's writing (see Kilcup 2000). I am deeply indebted to their work, which has been enormously crucial for my research and to Indigenous literary studies in general.

8   For more on "playing Indian," see Deloria 1998.

9   Ironically, while five of the most populous tribes in Indian Territory were colloquially called the Five Civilized Tribes, this did not quell US suspicions about their incivility.

10   One of the most damaging results of the Dawes Commission's rolls was the attempt to make Native identity something marked on the body that an outside observer could visibly identify. While tracing lineage was also critical, many Dawes determinations, especially for Afro-Native people, were based on what agents "felt" the person was. See Miles 2005; Naylor 2008; Roberts 2021.

11   I am indebted to Kirby Brown (2024) for taking the time to do this research. For me, his findings critically clarified how to understand Eddleman Reed and her work. His findings were the result of research

for the afterword for an anthology of Eddleman Reed's (2024) writing edited by Cari Carpenter and Karen Kilcup that I was lucky enough to read in advance.

12 Muskogee is on the border of the Muscogee (Creek) Nation and the Cherokee Nation. Today, parts of the city are within Cherokee Nation's jurisdiction, but, to the best of my knowledge, that is due to urban sprawl after the early twentieth century. Most of the city is within the jurisdiction of the Muscogee Nation.

13 Justice contrasts these specious claims to Indigeneity through his mother's family to his paternal family member's long-standing, documented, unequivocal Cherokee ancestry.

14 *Freedpeople* were individuals formerly enslaved in the Cherokee Nation. The Dawes Commission created separate rolls for Freedpeople, and they were often the individuals whose inclusion on official rolls and during allotment was the most scrutinized.

15 In the late twentieth century, the Cherokee Nation made the shameful decision to revoke the citizenship of Freedpeoples' descendants. Citizenship was only recently reinstated after a lengthy dispute that lasted the better part of the first two decades of the twenty-first century. When the United States District Court of the District of Columbia ruled in favor of the descendants of Cherokee Freedpeople in 2017, Cherokee Nation decided not to appeal the decision and to honor descendants' citizenship applications.

16 In my dissertation (Walkiewicz 2014), I identified Eddleman Reed as Cherokee. I have changed my position after much reflection, self-education, and growth.

17 Eddleman Reed's work has been republished in a few anthologies. Still, Cari Carpenter and Karen Kilcup's recent edited collection of Eddleman Reed's writing will finally allow greater access to her writings (Carpenter and Kilcup 2024). Otherwise, *Twin Territories* is only available via microfilm or at a handful of archives in Oklahoma, and none of these hold a complete physical copy.

18 Almost all of the write-ins Eddleman Reed responds to have addresses outside the territories.

19 "Squaw" is a highly offensive slur. I reprint it here because it inflects the tone of Eddleman Reed's responses, but I do not use it outside direct quotes or this note. Also, Eddleman Reed's use of the term "civilized" here likely refers to the Cherokee, Chickasaw, Choctaw, Muskogee, and Seminole Nations, also called the Five Civilized Tribes or the Five Tribes (Eddleman Reed 1902c: 118).

20 I am not convinced that all of the letters Eddleman Reed responds to were submitted to the magazine (this was a common trick employed by many editors throughout the nineteenth century). However, I believe they expressed sentiments Eddleman Reed felt were common among Eastern readers.

21 The column is also called "Types of Indian Women" in some magazine issues.

22   Eddleman Reed's 1908 article for *Harper's Bazaar*, "Modern Mistress Lo," succinctly summarizes her overarching argument about civility and virtuous femininity in Indian Territory. It also mimics the imagery of "Types of Indian Girls."

23   These marriage plots also mirror her own life experiences. Eddleman Reed married a white newspaperman, like the character of Dannie in "Only an Indian Girl." She sold *Twin Territories*, and her involvement with the magazine ended. In 1903, Eddleman Reed met Charles LeRoy Reed, then AP writer for the *Kansas City Star*, who had come to Muskogee for work, and they wed a year later. Unlike Dannie, Eddleman Reed mostly gave up her career after marrying, and she focused on raising a family. She had some difficulty selling the magazine (Morrison 1982: 158). After *Twin Territories*, Eddleman Reed wrote a short-lived column, "In Society's Realm," for the *Muskogee Phoenix* newspaper. The column included poetry, the social lives of the Muskogee elite, and news of regional musical and artistic events. According to my research, this *Phoenix* column was previously unknown (or at least unacknowledged) by scholars prior to my stumbling across it while reading copies of the paper. As best I can tell, it ran from 1904–5. In September 1905, she became editor of *Sturm*'s "Indian Department" and continued to run that column until November 1906 (Morrison 1982: 158–60).

24   Eddleman Reed paints a relatively rosy portrait of Carlisle Indian Industrial School in the story, but it was a space of trauma and violence for many students.

25   It should also be noted that some of the most prosperous ranchers in Indian Territory were Native.

26   While I do not have the space to go into detail, there are also delightfully queer undertones to the romance plot between Lizonka and Loren Jr.

27   I intentionally use the word *incorporate* here because Indian Territory was an unincorporated territory. The language of incorporation was central to debates about US empire, territory, and statehood at the end of the nineteenth century following the Spanish-American War in 1898.

28   As Brigitte Fielder (2020: 14) reminds us, "racialization has historically been a gendered affair."

29   Native American and Indigenous studies scholarship has demonstrated the necessity of moving away from the genocidal logics of blood quantum, illuminating how such logics reproduce a privileging of US racial constructs over Native understandings of kinship, autonomy, and culture. See Chang 2010; Sturm 2002.

30   Writers in this community included Mabel Washbourne Anderson, De Witt Clinton Duncan (Too-Qua-Stee), Charles Gibson, Alexander Posey (Chinnubbie Harjo), and others.

31   My insistence on the important contributions of print culture, especially newspapers, to Indigenous fights against colonization is deeply influenced by the field-shaping work of Native Hawaiian scholar Noenoe K. Silva (2004).

32 Here, I am thinking of Derrick R. Spires's (2019) understanding of citizenship and Adam Spry's (White Earth Anishinaabe) (2018) work on settler-Indigenous intertextuality.

References

Brown, Kirby. 2024. "Afterword: Ora Eddleman Reed, Allotment Genealogies, and Cherokee Literary Transnationalism." In Eddleman Reed 2024.

Chang, David. 2010. *The Color of the Land: Race, Nation, and Politics of Landownership in Oklahoma, 1832–1929*. Chapel Hill: Univ. of North Carolina Press.

Deloria, Philip J. 1998. *Playing Indian*. New Haven, CT: Yale Univ. Press.

Digadatseli'i ᏙᏓᏣᎵ. 2020. "Cherokee Scholars' Statement on Sovereignty and Identity." *Think Tsalagi*, February 13. https://www.thinktsalagi.org/blog/2020/2/13/-cherokee-scholars-statement-on-sovereignty-and-identitynbsp.

Eddleman Reed, Ora V. 1902a. "An Indian Territory Magazine." *Twin Territories*, March: 70.

Eddleman Reed, Ora V. 1902b. "What the Curious Want to Know." *Twin Territories*, February: 58.

Eddleman Reed, Ora V. 1902c. "What the Curious Want to Know." *Twin Territories*, April: 118.

Eddleman Reed, Ora V. 1908. "Modern Mistress Lo." *Harper's Bazaar*, October: 1002–4.

Eddleman Reed, Ora V. 2024. *The Selected Works of Ora Eddleman Reed: Author, Editor, and Activist for Cherokee Rights*. Edited by Cari M. Carpenter and Karen L. Kilcup. Lincoln: Univ. of Nebraska Press.

"Editorial." 1898. *Twin Territories*, December: 2–3.

"Editorial." 1899a. *Twin Territories*, February: 38–39.

"Editorial." 1899b. *Twin Territories*, March: 66.

Fielder, Brigitte. 2020. *Relative Races: Genealogies of Interracial Kinship in Nineteenth-Century America*. Durham, NC: Duke Univ. Press.

Justice, Daniel Heath. 2021. "Narrated Nationhood and Imagined Belonging." In *Allotment Stories: Indigenous Land Relations under Settler Siege*, edited by Daniel Heath Justice and Jean M. O'Brien, 17–34. Minneapolis: Univ. of Minnesota Press.

Kaplan, Amy. 2002. *The Anarchy of Empire in the Making of U.S. Culture*. Cambridge, MA: Harvard Univ. Press.

Kilcup, Karen. 2000. "Ora V. Eddleman Reed." In *Native American Women's Writing: 1800–1924, An Anthology*, edited by Karen Kilcup, 350–98. Oxford: Blackwell Publishers.

Kosmider, Alexia. 1995. "'What the Curious Want to Know': Cherokee Writer, Ora Eddleman Reed Writes Back to the Empire." *Literature and Psychology* 41, no. 4: 51–72.

Kosmider, Alexia. 1998. "Strike a Euroamerican Pose: Ora Eddleman Reed's 'Types of Indian Girls.'" *American Transcendental Quarterly* 12, no. 2: 109–31.

Miles, Tiya. 2005. *Ties That Bind: The Story of an Afro-Cherokee Family in Slavery and Freedom*. Berkeley: Univ. of California Press.

Morrison, Daryl. 1982. "*Twin Territories*: The Indian Magazine and Its Editor, Ora Eddleman Reed." *Chronicles of Oklahoma* 60: 136–66.

Naylor, Celia E. 2008. *African Cherokees in Indian Territory: From Chattel to Citizens*. Chapel Hill: Univ. of North Carolina Press.

"Ora V. Eddleman Reed." 1995. In *Native American Writing in the Southeast: An Anthology, 1875–1935*, edited by Daniel F. Littlefield Jr. and James W. Parins, 134–52. Jackson: Univ. Press of Mississippi.

Piatote, Beth. 2013. *Domestic Subjects: Gender, Citizenship, and Law in Native American Literature*. New Haven, CT: Yale Univ. Press.

Roberts, Alaina E. 2021. *I've Been Here All the While: Black Freedom on Native Land*. Philadelphia: Univ. of Pennsylvania Press.

Schreiber, Mignon [Ora V. Eddleman Reed]. 1899a. "Aunt Mary's Christmas Dinner." *Twin Territories* December, 9–11.

Schreiber, Mignon [Ora V. Eddleman Reed]. 1899b. "'Lizonka,' a Creek Girl." *Twin Territories* May, 113–14, 122–23; June, 138–41; July, 167–71; August, 184–89; September, 209–11; October, 227–28.

Schreiber, Mignon [Ora V. Eddleman Reed]. 1900. "Only an Indian Girl." *Twin Territories* February, 28, 37–38; March, 51, 54–55; April, 84–85; May, 100–102; June, 125, 128–29; July, 147, 150–51, 154.

Schuller, Kyla. 2017. *The Biopolitics of Feeling: Race, Sex, and Science in the Nineteenth Century*. Durham, NC: Duke Univ. Press.

Silva, Noenoe K. 2004. *Aloha Betrayed: Native Hawaiian Resistance to American Colonialism*. Durham, NC: Duke Univ. Press.

Spires, Derrick R. 2019. *The Practice of Citizenship: Black Politics and Print Culture in the Early United States*. Philadelphia: Univ. of Pennsylvania Press.

Spry, Adam. 2018. *Our War Paint is Writer's Ink: Anishinaabe Literary Transnationalism*. Albany, NY: SUNY Press.

Sturm, Circe. 2002. *Blood Politics: Race, Culture, and Identity in the Cherokee Nation of Oklahoma*. Berkeley: Univ. of California Press.

Thompson, John. 1986. *Closing the Frontier: Radical Response in Oklahoma, 1889–1923*. Norman: Univ. of Oklahoma Press.

United States District Court for the District of Columbia. 2017. *Cherokee Nation v. Raymond Nash, et al.* August 30, 2017. Civil Action No. 13-01313 (TFH). United States District Court for the District of Columbia. https://ecf.dcd.uscourts.gov/cgi-bin/show_public_doc?2013cv1313-248.

Walkiewicz, Kathryn. 2023. *Reading Territory: Indigenous and Black Freedom, Removal, and the Nineteenth-Century State*. Chapel Hill: Univ. of North Carolina Press.

Walkiewicz, Kathryn. 2014. "Wide Open Spaces: Place, Empire, and U.S.-Indigenous Relations, 1816–1907." Ph.D. diss., University of Illinois, Urbana-Champaign. http://hdl.handle.net/2142/50393.

Yao, Xine. 2021. *Disaffected: The Cultural Politics of Unfeeling in Nineteenth-Century America*. Durham, NC: Duke Univ. Press.

Sidonia
Serafini

"Unquestioned Citizenship":
History, Poetry, and Black and Native
Military Service in Hampton Institute's
Southern Workman

Abstract This article explores how Black race histories, Native American traditionary histories, and tribute poems published in Hampton Institute's *Southern Workman* (1872–1939) used military service as an imaginative foundation for thinking about citizenship beyond legal meanings. In race and traditionary histories, writers make visible the sacrifices of Black and Native soldiers that had been overlooked in official accounts of wars throughout US history. Writers also transform these histories' commemorative aim into tribute poems, which accomplish similar work by recognizing publicly, through imaginative verse, Black and Native military service. These writers share a hope that military service might usher in the benefits of formal citizenship. But that hope is accompanied by a sense of skepticism, in that wartime did not always yield a completely united American front. With such contingencies in mind, writers use the act of military service as inspiration for the act of writing into the historical and literary record the legacy of Black and Native commissioned and noncommissioned men and women, bestowing upon each other a sense of "unquestioned citizenship" that the nation would not.
Keywords African American literature, Native American and Indigenous literature, Hampton Institute, military history, citizenship

Amid World War I, editors of Hampton Institute's central mouthpiece, the *Southern Workman* (1872–1939), printed a speech—"The World War and the Negro"—by Black educator and Hampton graduate William Taylor Burwell Williams (1866–1941). Speaking in December 1917 at the Negro Organization Society meeting in Portsmouth, Virginia, Williams (1918: 9) opens his address with a question: "What has the Negro to do with the war?" His answer? Everything. Drawing a parallel between the past and the present, Williams calls on the legacy of the Civil War, reminding his audience that the Black soldier was instrumental in the fight for freedom. Turning to his current moment amid World War I, Williams confronts the irony

American Literature, Volume 96, Number 4, December 2024
DOI 10.1215/00029831-11557521   © 2024 by Duke University Press

that the United States, which had "so strenuously denied the rights and privileges of democracy" to Black Americans, now "call[ed] upon the black man" to defend it (10). "The Negro," he concludes, "hopes to win, in this war, not only freedom for America, but full and unquestioned citizenship for himself" (16). Williams's desire for "full and unquestioned citizenship" embodies the continual battle fought by Black Americans—as soldiers in wartime and civilians in daily life—to secure the privileges of formal citizenship even after Emancipation and the passage of the Fourteenth Amendment. Military service, as Williams expresses hopefully, offered one pathway to safeguard civil rights and to carve out a position of national belonging, first within the military itself and, by extension, the fabric of the nation.

Hampton Institute (now Hampton University, an HBCU) was a Black industrial school, a Native American boarding school, and a military training ground. It is little wonder, then, that writings like Williams's, which meditated on the ways in which military service might provide a roadmap for Black and Native peoples in obtaining equal rights, recognition, and protection guaranteed legally by formal citizenship, appeared frequently in the *Southern Workman*. Indeed, the idea of citizenship was the lifeblood of Hampton's educational mission. Yet citizenship within the context of such institutions was a complex, and constant, negotiation. The model of citizenship for Black and Native students was crafted by white educators, reformers, and administration officials who often reinforced their nominal positions in the nation. In making and remaking Black Americans and Native Americans "into the dominant culture's definitions of American citizenship," as Kim Cary Warren (2010: 2) has characterized such institutions' educational ethos, military training was front and center. Despite the ethos of subordination underlying Hampton's agenda, however, it did offer students an entry point into enlistment, and Hampton's students-turned-soldiers were highly commended by the US military for their training.

Yet, as writings in Hampton's central periodical demonstrate, the full promises of formal citizenship that Williams describes were not guaranteed by wartime sacrifice. While the military did provide opportunities for national inclusion, it also reflected the precarity of Black and Native peoples' positions as citizens. Even as the Fourteenth Amendment to the US Constitution was extended in 1868 to grant formal citizenship status to all born on US soil, including newly freed people and their children, limited economic opportunities, widespread racial violence, and Jim Crow segregation guaranteed second-class citizenship for Black Americans. Black soldiers fought in segregated battalions and, as veterans, they returned home from overseas to a Jim Crow South.[1] Unlike for Black Americans, the Fourteenth Amendment did not grant US citizenship to Native peoples. While Native American soldiers fought in integrated units with white soldiers, recognition as birthright citizens was legally withheld until Congress unilaterally granted that status to all tribal peoples with the passage of the Citizenship Act of 1924, nearly six years after World War I ended. Further, service for Native enlistees was synonymous with assimilation. Securing formal citizenship by pledging allegiance to the US military was an unequal exchange, as it often meant lessening or severing ties with Native culture through integration into American culture.[2] As Mvskoke/Creek scholar K. Tsianina Lomawaima (2013: 343) has explained, both Black Americans and Native Americans understood that a formal definition of, and granting of, US citizenship did not safeguard the privileges of civil rights and did not promise "exemption from wardship." For Native peoples—even those who served— formal citizenship remained marked by the same "inconstancy, indeterminacy, and variability" that "characterize[d] the uneven ground of federal Indian policy" (Wilkins and Lomawaima 2001: 6).

How, and on what terms, then, did voices in the *Southern Workman* conceive of meanings of citizenship with regard to military service? If serving in the US military was not evidence enough to grant unequivocally for Black and Native peoples the privileges and protections of formal citizenship, then what possibilities of unquestioned citizenship were possible? This article explores how writers used military service as an imaginative foundation—a method and a process—for thinking about citizenship beyond legal connotations. Carrie Hyde's (2018: 7) notion of "the speculative making of citizenship" provides an especially helpful framework for contemplating how both Black and Native writers in the *Southern Workman* harness the written word and the public sphere to imagine extralegal meanings of citizenship. In *Civic Longing: The Speculative Origins of U.S. Citizenship*, Hyde looks to literary and cultural productions to demonstrate how writers in the early national period of the United States articulated visions of "civic longing" when a legal definition of citizenship was not yet conceived (9). Although Hyde's examination of "the speculative making of citizenship" applies to writings that circulated before the Fourteenth Amendment introduced the first formal definition of citizenship, even after the passage of the Fourteenth Amendment—which granted citizenship to persons of African descent born in the United States but excluded Native Americans—formal citizenship was still, for Black and Native peoples, largely "speculative." Educational institutions like Hampton and, by extension, print productions like the *Southern Workman*, became places to "[speculate]," to borrow Hyde's term, how one might live as and enjoy the benefits of formal citizenship when they had been deemed second-class citizens or wards of the nation (7). On the one hand, writers acknowledge the hope that the act of serving in the military would usher in, once and for all, the protections inherent in formal citizenship; on the other hand, bearing in mind a skepticism that that wartime service might not cement that hope, writers wield the pen to make visible the sacrifices of Black and Native soldiers by documenting, commemorating, representing, and circulating it in the public sphere. Writers use the action of military service, then, as inspiration for the act of writing into the historical and literary record the legacy of Black and Native soldiers.

In this way, historical and literary productions in the *Southern Workman* that center military service cohere around a sense of action. Martha Jones and Derrick Spires have theorized the ways in which Black Americans cultivated a sense of citizenship and belonging through extralegal actions. Jones (2018: 10), for instance, examines how Black Americans in the antebellum era asserted birthright citizenship "by acting like rights-bearing people" and "by comporting themselves like citizens," even before the Fourteenth Amendment officially granted them that status. Like Jones, Spires (2019: 3) understands citizenship not through a legal paradigm but instead through a "practice-based theory of citizenship." In convention meetings, on committees, in voting booths, in neighborhoods, and in fleeting interactions in public spaces, Spires writes, Black people "practice[d]" "citizenship" (3). It is this everyday praxis, Spires argues, and not "law and custom," that "shape[d]" and made "citizenship or citizens" (3–4). Like Spires, I am less interested in definitions of the term *citizenship* and more interested in the "processes" by which writers "imagined citizenship"—in particular, what print platforms and historical and literary forms they gravitated toward in doing so (3).

Black and Native writers in the *Southern Workman* used the genres of the race history, traditionary history, and occasional or tribute poem to explore military service as an opportunity for obtaining the privileges of formal citizenship. In Black race histories and Native American traditionary histories—commemorative sketches that chronicle forgotten and/or misrepresented accomplishments of Black and Native peoples—writers make visible the wartime sacrifices of soldiers that had been overlooked in official (white) accounts of wars throughout America's history, from the War of 1812 to the First World War. *Southern Workman* contributors also transformed the commemorative aim of these histories into tribute poems, which accomplish similar work by recognizing publicly the military contributions of commissioned and noncommissioned Black and Native men and women through imaginative verse. From the soldier facing the front lines to volunteer women sewing uniforms back home, Black and Native historians and poets—including Charles Steward (1870–ca. 1967), Eva del Vakia Bowles (1875–1943), Sarah Collins Fernandis (1863–1951), Paul Laurence Dunbar (1872–1906), Arthur C. Parker (Seneca, 1881–1955), Henry M. Owl (Eastern Band of Cherokee, 1896–1980), Arthur Chapman (White Earth Chippewa, years unknown), and Hen-toh (Wyandot, 1870–1927)—share a hope that military service might usher in the equal rights, recognition, and protections of formal citizenship.

But that hope is accompanied by a sense of skepticism that informs their understanding that inclusion into the nation on military terms often meant towing a treacherous line between gain and loss and, further, that wartime did not always yield a completely united or harmonious American front. For example, speakers of poems subversively yoke the violence of wars overseas with racial and cultural violence on US soil, revealing the limitations, temporary expediencies, impermanence, and even impossibilities of formal citizenship. To protect against legal and extralegal violence, harmful stereotypes, and historical erasure, writers harness commemorative race histories, traditionary histories, and tribute poems as weapons of defense. To redeem the unfulfilled promises of formal citizenship, historians and poets intercede through the act of writing to bestow upon Black and Native soldiers unquestioned citizenship. *Unquestioned citizenship*, then, refers to a sense of citizenship that writers themselves produced for the people they represented. In locating citizenship outside of formal definitions and national inclusion, writers' representations of unquestioned citizenship often place value on the formation of social, cultural, racial, and familial coalitions within—but separate from—the larger American nation. Such nations within the nation are united by a sense of citizenship that emerges from the pressing needs of wartime and shared values of communal uplift and protection. These coalitions of Black and Native citizens are responsive to national inclusion. Yet, as Black and Native writers often suggest, they are eager to privilege negotiating inclusion on their own terms and are willing to forgo national belonging. From a coalition of Black women sewing uniforms for Black soldiers overseas to a pantribal coalition of Native soldiers, their labors on and off the battlefield are performed not always in service to the United States as a nation but instead in service to one another. To be a Black American or Native American in the United States, writers suggest, is to be a soldier who must fight to survive in a hostile nation. In writing *about* soldiers, writers, too, became soldiers, fighting not with a gun on the battlefield but fighting with the pen in the public sphere to claim Black and Native peoples' place as unquestioned citizens.

Black Heroism and Singing for the "Unsung Heroes"

A popular genre among Black contributors to the *Southern Workman* was what is known as the race history. In race histories, writers chronicle the forgotten and/or misrepresented accomplishments of people of African descent, pushing back against monolithic stories of white American heroism which, in denying Black perspectives, rejected them as equal citizens of the nation. In describing what he terms "liberation historiography," John Ernest (2004: 8) identifies liberation from white supremacist narratives of American history as "a defining condition of African American historical thought." As Stephen Hall (2009: 10, 186) explains, Black historical writings, including race histories, "transcended and reinterpreted mainstream historical narratives," utilizing "history to tell and shape an alternative textual record of racial possibility." Importantly, the image of the Black soldier, who represented a "courageous, patriotic, physically robust, disciplined, and moral" model of American heroism, Laurie Maffly-Kipp (2010: 225) observes, was documented in the pages of race histories time and time again.

In addition to race histories, the occasional or tribute poem was a staple genre in the *Southern Workman*. The form, which I argue *Southern Workman* contributors adapted as a literary version of the race history, accomplishes similar work by recognizing publicly the contributions of Black enlistees through imaginative verse. Reaching back through multiple wars in US history to make visible the memory of Black soldiers, the verse of poets Paul Laurence Dunbar and Sarah Collins Fernandis undertake one goal of the race history by cultivating a "collective existence" (Maffly-Kipp 2010: 3). These poets also used occasional verse to extend the work of the race history by questioning the value of military service and its ability to not only guarantee the promises of formal citizenship but also to produce a fully united coalition of American citizens.

Making visible Black heroism as a means of ushering in unquestioned citizenship, of protecting the representation, memory, and history of Black soldiers, writers deployed the race history in defense against stereotypes of Black inferiority and criminality with an eye toward the heroism of Black soldiers fighting and laboring for the promises of formal citizenship. In the late 1890s, writer Charles Steward—son of scholar, minister, Army chaplain, and Buffalo Soldier, Theophilus Gould Steward (1843–1924)—published histories of Black military service and heroism in the *Southern Workman*. Lamenting that Black soldiers had "no favorable journalist," the foremost priority of his race history, "Colored Americans as Army Officers" (1899), was adequate representation through "public acknowledgement" (Steward 1899: 376). Nearly a century before Steward penned his histories, abolitionist and journalist William Cooper Nell (1816–74) vowed in the introduction of his own race and military history, *Services of Colored Americans* (1851), "to rescue from oblivion the name and fame" of Black soldiers in the Revolutionary War and the War of 1812 (Nell 1851: 3). Steward heeded Nell's project, with a particular focus on the recently ended Spanish American War. Steward used the pen and the periodical press to defend against the demeaning claim made in Theodore Roosevelt's account of the Spanish American War, *The Rough Riders* (1899), that the "soldierly conduct" of Black men who fought in the Battle of San Juan Hill was "not their own" but instead "inspired into them" by white officers (Steward 1899: 376). To counter such misrepresentations, Steward calls on the record of Black regiments in the Civil War. "The history of our Civil War," Steward writes, "bears many now somewhat familiar instances of Negro officers commanding Negro troops in battle" (378). The possessive use of "our" simultaneously claims Black soldiers' equal participation in the country's war and highlights the specific freedom struggle of people of African descent. Steward lists the names and ranks of Black soldiers in the Civil War, accompanied by citations of honorable mentions and medals for "gallant and meritorious leadership" (378). He also recounts the legendary heroism of the formerly enslaved Captain André Cailloux (1825–63) who, despite a mangled arm shattered by cannon fire, continued to lead the 1st Louisiana Native Guard of the Union Army in the Siege of Port Hudson (1863), "urging his men onward by brave words and braver example" (379).[3]

The record of bravery and sacrifice was no different in the Battle of San Juan Hill, as Steward evidences and honors by listing the names and ranks of Black soldiers of the Tenth Cavalry, also known as the Buffalo Soldiers. "All these examples and many more, of Negro leadership in battle," Steward (1899: 379) writes, "Mr. Roosevelt could have studied before advancing his opinion as to the dependence of Negro troops on white officers." In defending the record of Black heroism that Roosevelt "could have studied" but did not, Steward uses Roosevelt's own description of the experience of war against him to call attention to the historical amnesia, and willful forgetting, of Black participation in America's wars. He singles out a particular line in Roosevelt's depiction of battle: "It is astonishing what a limited area of vision . . . one has in the hurly-burly of a battle" (379). Obscured sight caused by the chaotic experience of battle, Steward notes, was Roosevelt's "explanation of his failure to notice" the competency of Black troops (379). Clouded vision in combat emerges as a microcosm for a much larger historical problem. The act of "fail[ing] to notice" speaks to the greater concerted mainstream neglect of Black participation in America's wars that race histories like Steward's actively attempted to undo. The possibility of the race history, Steward implies, is the restoration of sight: it claims unquestioned citizenship by making visible to the American public an undisputable image of Black heroism.

What writers of race histories also made visible was that the story of Black war heroes could not be told without also bringing to light the female figures on the periphery of the war effort: Black women—often mothers of sons serving their country—who fought in wars by washing, darning, and sewing uniforms for the US military. In "Negro Women and the War" (1918), Eva del Vakia Bowles used her brief race history to foreground the agency of Black women. Bowles draws on the work of women of African descent both nationally and internationally, in the United States and in France, affirming a sense of transatlantic citizenship in which their "spirit of sacrifice" was rooted (Bowles 1918: 425). "In justice to all," she proclaims, "may we not call to mind that the Negro women just now are being given a chance to show the world what they are capable of doing, not because of, but in spite of, apparently insurmountable obstacles" (425). Her phrase, "in justice to all," encapsulates the heart of the meaning of unquestioned citizenship. It underscores an inclusive vision, across gender lines, of Black participation in the war effort. Recognizing Black women's war work as a form of providing "justice to all" implies the following: until America "call[s] to mind" the shared history of Black men and women's heroism in defense of the nation, accounts of the war and, as a result, a portrait of the nation, will remain unjust, incomplete. Furthermore, the phrase reflects Bowles's understanding of her position as a writer as one that bestows justice and grants unquestioned citizenship to those who have been overlooked and forgotten.

In recasting the race history, poets such as Paul Laurence Dunbar and Sarah Collins Fernandis transformed the genre into poetic form. Their tribute poems take the facts, historical details, and litany of names and accomplishments characteristic of the race history and elevate them with the literary imagination in order to depict scenes, emotions, hopes, and fears of soldiers of color in battle and the women who supported them from afar. Dunbar's tribute, "The Unsung Heroes" (1900), reimagines the experiences of enslaved Black men who joined, fought, and died for the Union army in the Civil War. Whereas the southern landscape under slavery locked enslaved people in an unnatural relationship with the environment through forced labor and violence, Dunbar illustrates that same landscape as a site upon which Black heroism is made visible. On the "bloody sod" of battlefields, Dunbar reimagines fallen Black soldiers who "fought their way from night to day," from enslavement to Emancipation (Dunbar 1900: lines 43, 44). From the coasts of South Carolina and Louisiana to the banks of the Mississippi River in Tennessee, in the battles of Fort Wagner and Port Hudson and in the Fort Pillow Massacre, the "rivers," "valleys," "hillsides," and "plain[s]" of the South "saw their glory," "heard their war-cry," and "knew their blood" (lines 25, 34, 21, 23, 21). Dunbar uses the genre of the occasional poem to affirm these Black soldiers' place as unquestioned citizens. The poem's title captures the purpose that galvanized writers to compose race histories: to "narrat[e] a past" that "gave African Americans control over their identities" and "allowed them to refute the pervasive dictum of black inferiority" (Maffly-Kipp 2010: 3). When the promises of formal citizenship persist unfulfilled, it is the poet's place, in other words, to sing for the "unsung heroes," to confer upon them unquestioned citizenship.

Moreover, the poem as genre fills a major void in representations of military heroism in photographs of the Civil War. As Mark Meigs (2012) has noted, in photographs by two of the war's most famous photographers, Mathew Brady (ca. 1822–96) and Alexander Gardner (1821–82), Brady and Gardner give us "white heroes, dead and alive" (Meigs 2012: paragraph 24). When Black subjects are pictured, they are often serving or burying the bodies of white soldiers. Deborah Willis's recently published *The Black Civil War Soldier: A Visual History of Conflict and Citizenship* (2021) acknowledges how such a "lack of images of black soldiers" fighting in battles or standing with regiments continues to "influence our modern perceptions of the war," and she reprints letters from Black soldiers as one means of bridging this gap (Willis 2021: viii). Such firsthand accounts testify to the sacrifices and death toll of Black soldiers on the battlefield. The absence of photographs showing bodies of Black soldiers is a striking contrast to photographs of lynchings that depicted the lifeless, mangled bodies of Black men and women and propagated stereotypes of Black criminality. Dunbar's "The Unsung Heroes" counteracts such historical erasure and violence by creating the image of Black heroism that Brady and Gardner refused to capture and which white Americans who consumed lynching visuals were not willing to accept. Dunbar's poem functions as a kind of proxy photograph, providing the American public with an image of Black heroism that was never produced.

Following Dunbar, Sarah Collins Fernandis's war poems commemorate Black military legacies.[4] A Hampton graduate, Fernandis worked for the War Camp Community Service in Chester, Pennsylvania, where she organized a club for Black veterans, a parade for Black soldiers, and concert programs dedicated to enlistees and veterans during World War I ("Chester's" 1919: 379–80). She also planned the New Era Week, a week-long celebration that "demonstrated that white and colored men and women can successfully engage in constructive cooperation for the all-round advancement of a war-production community and the distinct betterment of race relations" (381). Fernandis must have looked around Chester and saw that the war produced much more than military resources. The war production community was not simply a coalition of Black and white citizens uniting to produce the necessities of wartime. The very act of coming together to produce wartime resources was a form of production in and of itself in building a stronger national coalition of diverse citizens, as was the case at Hampton. During World War I, for example, Black and Native students collected books and fashioned bookcases to be sent to the Library War Service; produced checker-board tables for the Army YMCA; participated in food conservation efforts by canning and baking war bread for the Red Cross; and knitted afghans and sweaters for soldiers (*Hampton in War Time* 1918: 7–21).

Like a military uniform that not only protects but also brings pride to its wearer, Fernandis's tributes bestow dignity upon Black soldiers by celebrating their sacrifice and brotherhood while also protecting their memory in the public sphere. Her poem, "Our Allegiance" (1917), celebrates Black soldiers who took up arms to defend the nation in World War I. The speaker alludes not solely to international strife overseas but also to racial discrimination at home in the United States by deploying the language of social justice. "Our flag, our country!" the speaker proclaims, "tho' our plaint, a meed / Inadequate; tho' justice's delay / Has held us hindered by our urgent need / For equity on progress' steep way—" (Fernandis 1917: lines 5–8). Fernandis projects a hope into the future that "light unprejudiced" will illuminate the nation to see Black subjects not as a problem to be solved but "as citizens of this great land" (lines 11, 12). While the poem may initially seem a testament to Black soldiers' allegiance to the nation, the unbalanced scales of justice—embodied in the phrase "justice's delay"—foreground instead an allegiance to Black brotherhood (line 6). The "our" in the poem's title refers not to a united coalition of Americans but instead gestures toward a coalition of Black soldiers who will grant one another a foremost right of formal citizenship that the nation did not: protection.

Fernandis's most poignant interrogation of formal citizenship through military service is visible in her poem, "The Cry Supreme" (1918), in which she subversively confronts another unofficial and ongoing battle in which racism and discrimination ensure second-class citizenship even for Black veterans returning home from war. "The Cry Supreme" is dedicated to Black women's Red Cross work in Baltimore, Maryland.[5] Like Bowles's history, it foregrounds the agency of Black women who served in official and unofficial military capacities in World War I. It is a tribute to those who "fold[ed] and knit[ted] and sew[ed], and pray[ed]" for soldiers overseas battling the "great counter-strife" of the "brutish invading Hun," or the German army (Fernandis 1918: lines 13, 1, 2). Yet Fernandis's message runs deeper. In the context of racial violence and terrorism, the mass incarceration of Black men and women in chain gangs and convict camps, and Jim Crow segregation, it becomes clear that the violator to whom the speaker refers is not Germany but the United States—a nation that "by force and frightfulness o'er-run[s]" its own "[e]stablished law" by exacting "ruthless devastation" onto subjects who, by legal doctrine, are its citizens (lines 3, 4, 7). To be a Black citizen in America, Fernandis suggests, is to be a soldier. The real "counter-strife," or retaliatory strike, then, is the Black poet's public condemnation, and the occasional poem becomes a gun aimed in combat against the first blows dealt by the nation. Its message is a bullet that aims at, shoots, and shatters the heart of America's beliefs in the sanctity of the inalienable rights of "life, liberty, and the pursuit of happiness" and in the amendments of the US Constitution as the law of the land.

With this criticism in mind, the feminine characterization of "her" that the speaker uses to reference America also gestures toward another female presence to whom the poem is dedicated: Black women whose fathers, husbands, brothers, and sons have been doubly stripped from them by fighting *for* the American nation and by merely living *in* the American nation. "She," a composite of all Black women, hears "her brave manhood's last, dying groan" (Fernandis 2018: line 6). The "ruthless devastation" of racial terrorism seeks the "red blood" of Black people as "womanhood's deep wail / Of nameless torture" and "childhood's frightened scream / All intermingle in the cry supreme" (lines 7, 9–10, 10–11). By the poem's close, it is clear that the women form a coalition to "fold and knit and sew, and pray" not for the larger nation but for another coalition—the "nation within a nation," as Du Bois described of the Black community in his speech, "A Negro Nation Within the Nation," in which he encouraged Black Americans to build autonomous economic and educational resources (Du Bois 1995: 388). Their labors of love are performed for the survivance, safety, and strength of Black soldiers—both official combat soldiers overseas and unofficial soldiers who are citizens fighting to survive in a hostile nation. Black soldiers, Black women in the war effort, and Black poets bestow upon Black Americans, through their actions, unquestioned citizenship.

"Let It Not Be Forgotten": Writing Against the "Vanishing Indian"

Native American contributions printed in the *Southern Workman* also took the form of commemorative histories and tribute poems. Akin to the genre of the race history, the Native American traditionary history protects the memory of tribal histories and the cultural and political contributions of Native peoples. Describing the contours of traditionary histories, Maureen Konkle (2004: 160–61) writes, "Native writers did exactly the opposite of what white writers did when they wrote about their traditions, and histories . . . They not only explained traditions but also explained their experience of whites and that of their tribes generally; they wrote about treaties and broken agreements; they wrote about the progress of Indian nations as they understood it." Whereas the Black race history dispelled stereotypes of criminality or obsequiousness, traditionary histories allowed Native writers to push back against the myth of the contrived "vanishing Indian" narrative, which validated settler colonialism by predicting the disappearance of Native peoples through assimilation or extinction. The histories foster a sense of cultural pride, assert political autonomy, and emphasize the strength of tribal families and communities. Further, they foreground a pantribal vision of "cross-tribal bonds" which, as Musco-gee Creek-Cherokee scholar Craig Womack (1999: 226) has noted, worked against assimilation policies of boarding schools like Hampton, which intended to individualize the culture, family, land, and selfhood of Native peoples. In doing so, the histories center what Chippewa scholar Gerald Vizenor (2008: 1) calls "Native survivance"—"an active sense of presence over absence, deracination, and oblivion."

While boarding schools like Hampton used military training as evidence of the successful assimilation of Native peoples, writers of traditionary histories often throw that ideology into question. Writers towed a thin rhetorical line, blending celebratory accounts of Native soldiers' sacrifices with thinly veiled, and at times blatant, critiques of the hypocrisy of US democratic ideals. As Christopher Capozzola (2014: 725) explains, even though Congress passed an act in 1919 that granted citizenship to Native veterans who enlisted in World War I, and the Citizenship Act of 1924 approved this status unilaterally for Native peoples, "no one took seriously the idea that many Native Americans did not want to be citizens of the United States." At the heart of such hesitancy or outright refusal was that formal US citizenship policies "pushed American institutions and cultural practices toward a citizenship premised on a single allegiance to one state bounded by the territorial limits of the United States" (725). What traditionary histories make visible is that military enlistment was not always synonymous with the renunciation of cultural roots. Further, such writings cast doubt on the idea that inclusion into the US military could offer Native enlistees a sense of citizenship and belonging in a nation that did not already value the sovereignty and subjecthood of tribal peoples. As writers convey, some soldiers did not fight to obtain formal US citizenship but instead to protect their homeland as the First Americans.

One contribution in the *Southern Workman* stands as poignant evidence of the kinds of stereotypes that writers of traditionary histories attempted to dispel. In his address, "A Plea for the Red Man" (1905), a white politician and ex-Governor of Oregon named J. F. Fletcher cautions readers about the erasure of Native heroism latent in American historical memory. "[L]et it not be forgotten," Fletcher urges, "that the white man has been the historian. We have read only one side of the story" (Fletcher 1905: 14). Echoing the saying, "the half has never been told," of the experiences of enslaved Africans, Fletcher concludes, "The Indian side will never be told" (14). While the ex-Governor attempts to combat the "vanishing Indian" myth, he simultaneously encourages assimilation through Christianization and land allotments to "[convert] every Indian into a citizen of the United States" (16). He calls such a plan "the only just, true, and radical solution" to "the problem," reducing Native peoples to an "Indian problem" that must be solved (16). Regarding tribal communities as the nation's wards, rather than as sovereign nations or citizens, was paralleled in dominant white culture's rhetoric of Black subjects. As Alain Locke denounced in his essay "The New Negro" (1925), Black people were disparaged, viewed not as agents or citizens but as sick patients of American society (Locke 1925: 11). Though Fletcher attempts to counter the "vanishing" myth, the irony seems to have been lost on him that he himself is implicated in creating such a stereotype by encouraging the further erasure of Native cultures. Nonetheless, Fletcher's claim that "the white man has been the historian" rang true (Fletcher 1905: 14). But Native voices in the *Southern Workman* made certain that Fletcher's prediction, "the Indian side will never be told," would not.

The traditionary histories of Henry M. Owl (Eastern Band of Cherokee) and Arthur C. Parker (Seneca) counter the "vanishing" stereotype by documenting the past and present military service of Native Americans. Unlike Fletcher's title "A Plea for the Red Man," traditionary histories were not pleas for recognition but affirmative statements of subjecthood. Owl's "The Indian in the War" (1918) documents Native soldiers in World War I, reaching back through history to demonstrate their heroism on the front lines "in every war" that America "has waged" since the war for independence (Owl 1918: 353). The article's opening line positions the Native subject as "a patriotic citizen," and "a loyal and patriotic American," claiming unquestioned citizenship even as the Constitution did not yet recognize about 40 percent of Native peoples as formal US citizens when Owl's article appeared in the *Southern Workman* (353). Importantly, however, Owl's history is inflected by a sense of skepticism about the US military's ostensible campaign for peace overseas and its treatment of Native peoples at home. He confronts the ways in which the US government has hindered the autonomy of and undermined the once "[bright] future" for tribal nations not simply in the "treaties" that "have been broken" but, more importantly, in the "detrimental" treaties that "have been kept" (353). He goes on: "The red man, cooperating with his fellow-countrymen, will fight to the bitter end for an ensured and humane peace, for we cannot enjoy such a state of existence until we successfully abolish that detestable autocratic government which is a tyrannical injustice to civilization" (353). Criticizing the inhumane injustices of oppressive governments outside of the United States and against which the United States waged war, Owl indirectly indicts the hypocrisy of the American federal government. While the United States may be fighting in a global war to bring about "ensured and humane peace," Owl suggests, that same harmony is antithetical to its own ideals of democracy—a discrepancy visible in the centuries-long subjugation of Native peoples, especially by US military conquest and its involvement in Native American genocide and removal. Furthermore, as expressed by Black historians and poets, Owl positions the Native subject, both on and off the battlefield, as a soldier who "will fight to the bitter end for an ensured and humane peace" (353). What that peace is, for Owl, is the nation's acknowledgement of Native Americans as unquestioned "citizens worthy of recognition" in "the body politic" (353).

Turning away from American patriotism, Owl (1918) champions a national cultural pride by commemorating the war work of Native peoples in both official and unofficial capacities. He commends the soldiers trained at boarding schools, including Hampton, Carlisle, and Haskell, who "are an honor to our race" (354). What is more, he expresses disapproval of the integration of white and Native soldiers into the same units. "We shall not hear of an Indian battalion making a spectacular attack or a wonderful raid," he regrets, "for the War Department has decided that there shall be no separate Indian units. But, nevertheless, the Indian is in the ranks, on the seas, and in the trenches . . . side by side with the white man fighting for the same goal" (354). His skepticism of racially and culturally integrated units evidences a desire for national recognition of Native peoples as unquestioned citizens on their own terms, as capable patriots and fighters who do not need or desire fraternity among white troops.

His praise also extends beyond soldiers who are on the front lines to recognize the many men and women whose contributions to the war effort helped to clothe and feed those same soldiers. "The Indians are not only fighting with the rifle," Owl (1918: 354) proclaims. Native American women from all ages had taken up "needles as weapons, and are constantly knitting for the soldiers" (355). Native farmers "increase[d] their production of food" and, as he quotes from Medicine Owl, Chief of the Blackfeet Tribe in Montana, pledged to "'raise more goats and sheep'" to clothe soldiers and "'plant more corn'" to feed them (355). Owl's history showcases an unofficial coalition of civilian troops—seamstresses and farmers—who rallied behind the official front of soldiers to not only produce clothing and sustenance but also something much larger: protection and safety for Native soldiers as well as a sense of community and national pride that signified everything *but* the disappearance of Native peoples. The coalition that Owl describes provides for Native Americans a sense of unquestioned citizenship that the United States as a nation did not.

Such histories did not merely present counternarratives to the erasure of Native presences, cultures, and traditions. Arthur C. Parker, who published multiple traditionary histories in the *Southern Workman*, used the genre to remind readers of the shifting contours of formal citizenship rooted in broken treaties and to highlight the familial, cultural bonds that remained strong within tribal nations, despite land allotment mandates by the government and assimilation policies of boarding schools like Hampton. Further, while Native writers in the *Southern Workman* certainly published tribal-specific articles and sketches, traditionary histories and poems about military service often foreground a pantribal vision. Parker's histories are no exception.

Building upon Konkle's discussion of traditionary histories, Scott Richard Lyons (2010: 130) discusses the ways in which "[t]raditionary histories presented portraits of Indian people that clearly resonated as nationalistic in their own day, not only in their content but through their rhetorical tactics," using as evidence George Copway's (Mississauga Ojibwe) 1850 traditionary history, *The Traditional History and Characteristic Sketches of the Ojibway Nation*. Yet the traditionary histories published in the *Southern Workman* foreground a pantribal vision. One *Southern Workman* editorial in 1917 broadcasted an interesting prediction: "That the Indian will give a good account of himself in the war there is no doubt, but it seems probable that the records will be made by them individually rather than collectively" ("The Indians" 1917: 522). Such an assumption on the part of the *Southern Workman*'s editors projects a desire for staunch individualism ingrained into the American Indian boarding school experience and in federal laws like the Dawes Act of 1887, which parceled tribal lands, transforming them from a collective to an individualized model of property ownership. The prediction was wrong. As Craig Womack (1999: 226) has acknowledged, "cross-tribal bonds" were created in boarding schools, often against "the intended effects" of such institutions. Further, such pantribal visions characteristic of the military traditionary histories align with the circumstances of war which, as Thomas Britten (1997: 84) has discussed of the twelve- to fifteen-thousand Native American and First Nations peoples who served in World War I, brought diverse tribes together in close proximity. Instead of histories centered on one individual or one tribal nation, writers in the *Southern Workman* often offered more expansive, inclusive military histories. They conformed less to the prediction that histories would be focused "individually rather than collectively" and instead reflect the closeness of students from diverse nations in boarding schools and Native soldiers across nations and tribes in the military ("The Indians" 1917: 522). Even Arthur C. Parker's "The Seneca Indians in the War of 1812" (1916), the title of which highlights one nation and one war, broadens outward to reflect on the precarities of wartime service for all tribal nations not simply in the War of 1812 but also throughout America's wars.[6] Further, he recognizes transnational military involvement by both Native American and First Nations tribes.

Parker's traditionary history, "The Seneca Indians in the War of 1812," looks to tribal nations' involvement in a past war to reflect on the current service of soldiers in World War I, recounting specifically the story of how the Seneca became US allies in the War of 1812. Parker makes visible that protecting their *own* homeland as the First Americans, rather than securing formal US citizenship, was the Seneca nation's primary objective. Parker's history highlights a pantribal vision—a coalition of sovereign tribal nations—of the precarities of wartime service for all Indigenous peoples across North America, in the United States and in Canada. In it, he recalls the story of the "league of the tribes," or the Iroquois Confederacy, which consisted of the Seneca, Mohawk, Oneida, Onondaga, Cayuga, and Tuscarora nations. Initially, the Six Nations agreed to remain neutral in conflict between America and Britain. Precipitated by British forces' encroachment onto and occupation of tribal land, however, the Seneca, Oneida, and Onondaga decided to support the US military out of necessity (Parker 1916: 116). While Parker paints the motivations of the tribes in the language of American democracy and patriotism, he makes clear that allyship was agreed upon not out of loyalty to "white settlers" or to the United States but instead out of the tribes' "native love of country" (117). Their declaration, which Parker reprints, makes clear that, as the First Americans, "native love of country" signifies loyalty to sovereign tribal nations and not to the larger United States: "'We know of no other way to preserve peace but to rise from our seats and defend our own firesides, our wives, and our children,'" and, to protect "'our lands,'" the very foundation upon which the home and the family can prosper (120). Like Native soldiers during wartime, Parker acts as a proxy soldier: his history defends and preserves Native memory, positioning Native peoples as unquestioned citizens.

Like Steward's race history, Parker's (1916: 120) traditionary history lists the names on a "roster kept by the survivors of the war," which included soldiers across age and gender, male and female, young and old. In the War of 1812, Parker writes, women, most of whom were Oneida women, "donned uniforms, shouldered muskets, and fought like the patriots they were" (121). Parker reprints their names from "the old army register": "Annie Metoxen, Usena Reed, Polly Antonine, Margaret Adams, Susan Hendrick, Dolly and Mary Schenandoah, Salmo Adggnette, Margaret Stevens, Polly Cooper, Mary Williams, Margaret John, Mary Antonine, and Susan Jacobs" (121). Such histories offered a more detailed, expansive gloss on scattershot news items that featured singular portraits of Native women such as Sarah Valandre, for example, whose knitting efforts on a South Dakota reservation were praised in the *Southern Workman* and in boarding school and mainstream newspapers and magazines across the United States. Her ability, described as a "remarkable record," to knit an entire soldier's sweater in a period of four hours gained her national attention during World War I ("Indian Americans" 1919: 208). Perhaps the most important element of both race and traditionary histories, the presentation of names humanizes and legitimizes soldiers' individual experiences, assuring that their memory would be circulated in the public sphere.

Parker's conclusion gestures toward the larger tensions between hope and skepticism regarding Native peoples' participation in the military and highlights the lack of consensus among tribal peoples regarding the value of enlistment. "More than anything else," he writes, "the War of 1812 cemented the Iroquois to the United States and left them loyal people confident in the integrity and justice of the nation. Their hopes were high and they believed that a new era of good fellowship had dawned" (Parker 1918: 122). This hopeful vision, however, is fleeting. "Alas," Parker laments, "how falsely they were deceived. In fifteen years' time this hope snapped like a bubble. Through a fraudulent treaty, signed by the chiefs elected by a land company, they lost the Buffalo Creek Reservation for which they had spilled so much blood" (122). Though "one hundred years ha[d] passed since the close of the second war with Great Britain," little had changed at the time Parker penned his history in 1916 (122). Though "in every national calamity the Senecas ha[d] supplied men to defend and uphold the Union," the hard truth is that the exchange of service for formal US citizenship, recognition, and autonomy of tribal nations was an unequal and unfulfilled one (122). In place of the United States' lack of formal recognition, Parker understands that the historian, and the genre of the traditionary history, provide for Native enlistees the unquestioned citizenship that the action of military service itself could not.

Like Dunbar and Fernandis, who recast the race history into imaginative verse, Native American poets in the *Southern Workman* adapt meanings of the traditionary history into occasional poems that look to the past, present, and future in questioning Native peoples' relationship to the US military. Printed first in the *Tomahawk* and reprinted in the *American Indian Magazine, Olgala Light,* and *Southern Workman,* Arthur Chapman's (White Earth Chippewa) poem, "Indians in Khaki" (1919), invokes the Wounded Knee Massacre in which nearly three hundred Lakota were killed by the US Army.[7] The poem's refrain encapsulates the sacrifice of Native American soldiers as more than ample evidence for their inclusion into the nation as formal US citizens: "We, too, were not afraid to die" (Chapman 1919: lines 8, 16, and 24). The speaker opens by recalling the nine thousand Native enlistees in World War I, stating that "forgotten, then, was Wounded Knee" (line 5). This seemingly definitive statement poses a question: Who forgot the massacre? While initially this line seems to gesture toward Native enlistees' willful forgetting of the massacre in fighting for the United States, the history of Wounded Knee suggests that it is the US government that suffers from historical amnesia. The massacre was precipitated by the Army's attempts to disarm the Lakota of their weapons. The irony, which Chapman's allusion exposes, is that the United States is now, for its own protection, arming those whom it once disarmed. "Forgotten, then, was Wounded Knee" is really a statement that *Native peoples* will never forget. Although armed today, they could be disarmed tomorrow, and the parallel between Wounded Knee and World War I encapsulates the shifting contours of formal citizenship. When mainstream history narratives misremember, or neglect, the sacrifice of Native soldiers, the poet steps in to make visible their service, defend their memory, and claim their position as unquestioned citizens.

Wyandot poet Bertrand Nicholas Oliver (B. N. O.) Walker, also known as Hen-toh, builds upon Chapman's skepticism of military service. Printed in the *Southern Workman*'s inaugural issue of 1919, Hen-toh's two-stanza commemorative poem, "The Calumet or Peace-Pipe," laments the destruction of war while simultaneously imagining that Native enlistment will generate national belonging and harmony that might logically emerge from formal citizenship obtained in exchange for military service:

Sent from the white lands of the North,
Emblem of peace and brotherhood,
Its first fruits ever are offered
To the Great Spirit, then to the Sun;
To our Mother, the Earth; and the Waters;
To the North, the South, the East, the West;
    Then to each other.

A prayer goes to the One Great Spirit, thus:
Oh that the whole wide World could now
Accept the Red Man's ancient symbol,
Off'ring its incense to the Universe;
And blot out fierce, mad War's red stain
Bringing Good Will to Earth again
    With Peace, White Peace. (Hen-toh 1919)[8]

Titled after the ceremonial event of passing around a peace-pipe, the poem opens by affirming this long-standing cultural tradition. Written within the context of World War I, the speaker's description of the ceremony speaks doubly to Native American service in the war. The "fruits" of military service "offered" in defense of the nation, the speaker hints, might also be extended "to each other" to bring about "peace and brotherhood" (lines 3, 7). In the second stanza, Hen-toh superimposes the history of the peace-pipe ceremony onto the moment following the end of World War I: "A prayer goes to the One Great Spirit, thus: / Oh that the whole wide World could now / Accept the Red Man's ancient symbol" (lines 8–10). The word "now" encapsulates the urgency of the speaker's plea. Now, after the war has ended, the United States as a nation might recognize "the fruits" of Native enlistment "offered" in defense of the nation (line 3).

The speaker's desire for "mad War's red stain" to be "blot[ted] out" from the "Earth," then, gestures to the global war in which the United States was recently engaged. But it also signifies the centuries-long war that settler colonialism and its legacy in Hen-toh's contemporary moment waged upon Native culture, families, and land (lines 12, 13). Importantly, Hen-toh opens and closes the poem with the word "white," which appears only in the first and last lines. Beginning by summoning the calumet's origin in the "white lands of the North," the poem concludes by describing the calumet offering as a "White Peace" (lines 1, 14). The spread of the calumet tradition across geographical regions, and the white color of the smoke, are meant literally. But the language of whiteness also implies racial connotations, particularly in the poem's final line. The phrase "White Peace" implies Hen-toh's understanding that any "[a]ccept[ance]" by white America "of the Red Man's ancient symbol" will be on the colonizer's terms (line 10). The poem's framing with the language of whiteness signals Hen-toh's doubt that becoming a formal US citizen by serving in the military would ensure equal footing in the United States while also honoring the sovereignty and culture of Native peoples.

Yet the poem equally contradicts the sentiment of universal, cross-cultural brotherhood among white and Native soldiers that it initially seems to indicate. The speaker's implied reservation regarding the circumscribed conditions on which national accord might be forged throws into question the closing clarion call for fraternal harmony, asking the reader to reconsider to whom "the fruits" of "peace and brotherhood" of the peace pipe and military service apply (lines 3, 2). The ceremonial event of passing around a peace-pipe, which is both a traditional and political act, represents a brotherhood—a coalition, similar to Du Bois's "nation within a nation"—of Native soldiers who cultivate a sense of unquestioned citizenship through cultural and political practices not within the larger American nation but through a pan-tribal community of enlistees and veterans. Rather than reject tribal allegiance in favor of "a uniform system of citizenship with a single allegiance" to America, Hen-toh reaffirms sovereignty and tribal traditions (Capozzola 2014: 722).

Given the end of World War I, Hen-toh's poem might suggest that national acceptance on military terms is the heart of the "prayer" of the calumet (Hen-toh 1919: line 8). However, the vision of a future in which Native people are acknowledged both as members of sovereign nations and as unquestioned citizens is not grounded in the act of military service but is instead in the hands of cultural tradition. Embodied in the peace-pipe ceremony, Native tradition itself, rather than the act of serving the US military, of garnering public national acceptance, or of being granted formal recognition as US citizens, is what will "[Bring] Good Will to Earth again" (line 13). The poem, like the calumet, is an "[o]ff'ring," an homage to Native history and tradition (line 11). The poem itself, connected to the peace-pipe, is not a "prayer" but is instead a statement. It testifies, in the public sphere, that the "fruits" of citizenship originate not from formal US citizenship but instead from "each other" (lines 3, 7). Native culture is not only *not* vanishing. It is the central source of hope. And the poet, in writing that tradition, safeguards it in service to cultural legacy in the past and present.

The weight of such histories and poems in the *Southern Workman* would have had an immense impact on an often-unacknowledged audience of periodicals published by Black industrial schools and Native American boarding schools: student readers. Used primarily as a fundraising tool to advertise Hampton's agenda in industrial and military training to white donors, the periodical was read by Black and Native students who not only materially produced the *Southern Workman* in Hampton's Print Shop but who also encountered the periodical in Hampton's classrooms. Indeed, the *Southern Workman* was frequently integrated into the school's curriculum as reading material. Such race and traditionary histories, and their literary reimagining in the form of tribute poems, were crafted not merely to provide evidence of Black and Native peoples' worthiness to white audiences contemplating a donation to Hampton. They were meant to inspire and instill race and cultural pride in the next generation of aspiring young Black and Native men and women—in particular, male students who had been trained in the military since Hampton's founding.

And, like the complexities of citizenship that defined the educational model of institutions like Hampton, historical and literary contributions in the *Southern Workman* were not without their own tensions. By and large, race histories, traditionary histories, and tribute poems maintained a racial and cultural dividing line that reflected the separation of Black and Native troops into separate battalions and units at Hampton as well as in the larger US military. Histories and poems were a lens through which Black and Native peoples instilled pride and campaigned for unquestioned citizenship and belonging on their own terms. This meant that writers documented such legacies separately. The desire for standalone recognition in histories and poems was reflected, too, in Hampton's school battalions. Once integrated, Native students campaigned to form their own battalions, for instance (Lindsey 1995: 127). At times, however, military histories referenced one another in ways that replicated the methods by which the United States—in particular, the US military—ensured the oppression of those who had been deemed second-class citizens or had been excluded from the nation's formal definition of citizenship. In citing medals of honor bestowed upon Black soldiers in the Indian Wars, for example, readers of Charles Steward's race history, "Colored American Soldiers" (1899), were reminded of the fraught history of the Indian Wars. Steward cites medals of honor, which recognized and awarded Black soldiers for "bravery in action against hostile [Apache, Ute, and Sioux] Indians" (Steward 1899: 290–91). Such details were reminders of the ways in which the US military historically had weaponized Black and Native peoples against one another.

Despite the lack of overlap between Black and Native histories and poems, it is clear that writers shared a common objective. Military action and the historical and literary commemoration of that action became linked for writers who bestowed unquestioned citizenship upon those whom they represented. As scholars continue to retheorize meanings of citizenship outside of the legal realm, Black industrial school and Native American boarding school periodicals provide an often-overlooked lens through which to examine how writers used print culture, history, and literature to affirm Black and Native peoples as unquestioned citizens. As Stephen Hall (2009: 9) notes in his discussion of Black historical writing, for example, Black educational institutions "suggest new avenues for investigation into the development and dissemination of African American history." Robert Dale Parker (2011) and Jacqueline Emery (2017) have similarly argued the importance of recovering, and reconsidering, literary and cultural productions that circulated in boarding school newspapers. As central sites of military training, schools such as Hampton, which was uniquely positioned as both a Black industrial school and a Native American boarding school, and the print productions that emerged out of such institutions, allow us to think about how writers confronted the shifting and tumultuous contours of citizenship from multiple perspectives within one print space.

Seeking out and examining these perspectives broadens our understanding of how Black and Native writers used military service as an imaginative foundation for thinking about citizenship. Such writings also ask us to consider, or reconsider, how Black and Native writers defined military service. Historical and literary productions, inspired *by* military service, in turn became a kind of service to soldiers whose legacies were at risk of being forgotten and neglected, as well as a service to the larger Black and Native nations within the United States. In essence, writers served service members. Writers themselves provided Black and Native communities unquestioned citizenship that the larger nation did not and would not. Such acts of service allow us to contemplate how writers understood themselves as engaged in a conflict during wartime and in times of ostensible peace. The act of writing race histories, traditionary histories, and tribute poems about military service became, in and of itself, a kind of military service by proxy in defense of unquestioned citizenship. Because military writings in the *Southern Workman* often center the formation and strengthening of social, cultural, racial, and familial coalitions within, but often sepa-rate from, the larger United States, in writing unquestioned citizenship, such historical and literary productions prompt a larger question: *For whom* did soldiers fighting on the front lines and women laboring in the war effort back home serve and sacrifice? We can glean one answer to this question by joining together Eva del Vakia Bowles's race history and Hen-toh's tribute poem. "In justice to all," they served "each other" (Bowles 1918: 425; Hen-toh 1919: line 7).

Sidonia Serafini is assistant professor of English at Georgia College and State Uni-versity. With Barbara McCaskill, she coedited *The Magnificent Reverend Peter Tho-mas Stanford: Transatlantic Reformer and Race Man* (2020). Her work has appeared in the *Southern Quarterly, Women's Studies, Journal of Transatlantic Studies*, and *American Periodicals*. She serves as codirector of *Black Activism: A Transatlantic Legacy*, a website that examines the imprint of Black activism in the United States and the United Kingdom, past and present.

Notes

I am grateful to my mentors, Barbara McCaskill, Cody Marrs, and John Whar-ton Lowe, for providing feedback of early versions of this essay as part of my dissertation.

1   For further reading on Black military service during this era, see Wil-liams 2010; Donaldson 2020.
2   For further reading on Native American military service during this era, see Britten 1997; Krouse 2007.
3   The impetus of Steward's race history resonates, too, with recent literary works and scholarship, including Natasha Trethewey's "Native Guard," the title poem of her collection *Native Guard* (2006), and Cody Marrs's *Not Even Past: The Stories We Keep Telling about the Civil War* (2020).
4   The poems I analyze, "Our Allegiance" and "The Cry Supreme," are only two examples of Fernandis's war poetry published in the *Southern Work-man*. She also wrote "The Troopers at Carrizal" (1916), "Our Colored Sol-diery" (1918), and "A New Vision" (1919), none of which have been reprinted since their original publication.
5   For further reading on Black and Native women's roles in the war effort, see Britten 1997; Dunbar-Nelson 1919; Brown 2006.
6   This history was one of several of Parker's histories published in the *Southern Workman*, including "Progress for the Indian" (1912) and "The American Indian in the World War" (1918).
7   Robert Dale Parker (2011) has questioned the verity of Arthur Chap-man's status as a White Earth Chippewa, citing a lack of tribal records.
8   Hen-toh's poem was later included in his poetry collection, *Yon-Doo-Shah-We-Ah (Nubbins)* (1924).

References

Bowles, Eva del Vakia. 1918. "Negro Women and the War." *Southern Workman* 47, no. 9: 425–26.

Britten, Thomas A. 1997. *American Indians in World War I: At Home and at War.* Albuquerque: Univ. of New Mexico Press.

Brown, Nikki. 2006. *Private Politics and Public Voices: Black Women's Activism from World War I to the New Deal.* Bloomington: Indiana Univ. Press.

Capozzola, Christopher. 2014. "Legacies for Citizenship: Pinpointing Americans during and after World War I." *Diplomatic History* 38, no. 4: 713–26.

Chapman, Arthur. 1919. "Indians in Khaki." *Southern Workman* 48, no. 11: 607.

"Chester's New Era Week." 1919. *Southern Workman* 48, no. 8: 379–81.

Copway, George. 1850. *The Traditional History and Characteristics Sketches of the Ojibway Nation.* Boston, MA: Sanborn, Carter, Bazin and Co.

Donaldson, Le'Trice D. 2020. *Duty Beyond the Battlefield: African American Soldiers Fight for Racial Uplift, Citizenship, and Manhood, 1870–1920.* Carbondale: Southern Illinois Univ. Press.

Du Bois, W. E. B. (1935) 1995. "A Negro Nation Within the Nation." In *Voices from the Harlem Renaissance*, edited by Nathan Irvin Huggins, 384–90. New York: Oxford Univ. Press.

Dunbar, Paul Laurence. 1900. "The Unsung Heroes." *Southern Workman* 29, no. 7: 421–22.

Dunbar-Nelson, Alice. 1919. "Negro Women in War Work." In *Scott's Official History of the American Negro in the World War*, edited by Emmett J. Scott, 374–97.

Emery, Jacqueline, ed. 2017. *Recovering Native American Writings in the Boarding School Press.* Lincoln: Univ. of Nebraska Press.

Ernest, John. 2004. *Liberation Historiography: African American Writers and the Challenge of History, 1794–1861.* Chapel Hill: Univ. of North Carolina Press.

Fernandis, Sarah Collins. 1917. "Our Allegiance." *Southern Workman* 46, no. 6: 348.

Fernandis, Sarah Collins. 1918. "The Cry Supreme." *Southern Workman* 47, no. 9: 426.

Fletcher, J. F. 1905. "A Plea for the Red Man." *Southern Workman* 34, no. 1: 13–16.

Hall, Stephen G. 2009. *A Faithful Account of the Race: African American Historical Writing in Nineteenth-Century America.* Chapel Hill: Univ. of North Carolina Press.

Hampton in War Time. 1918. Hampton, VA: Press of the Hampton Normal and Agricultural Institute.

Hen-toh (B. N. O. Walker). 1919. "The Calumet or Peace-Pipe." *Southern Workman* 48, no. 1: 30.

Hyde, Carrie. 2018. *Civic Longing: The Speculative Origins of U.S. Citizenship.* Cambridge, MA: Harvard Univ. Press.

"Indian Americans." 1919. *Southern Workman* 48 no. 4: 208.

"The Indians and the War." 1917. *Southern Workman* 46, no. 10: 520–22.

Jones, Martha S. 2018. *Birthright Citizens: A History of Race and Rights in Antebellum America*. Cambridge: Cambridge Univ. Press.

Konkle, Maureen. 2004. *Writing Indian Nations: Native Intellectuals and the Politics of Historiography, 1827–1863*. Chapel Hill: Univ. of North Carolina Press.

Krouse, Susan Applegate. 2007. *North American Indians in the Great War*. Lincoln: Univ. of Nebraska Press.

Lindsey, Donal F. 1995. *Indians at Hampton Institute, 1877–1923*. Urbana: Univ. of Illinois Press.

Locke, Alain. 1925. "The New Negro." In *The New Negro: An Interpretation*, edited by Alain Locke, 3–16. New York: Albert and Charles Boni, Inc.

Lomawaima, K. Tsianina. 2013. "The Mutuality of *Citizenship* and *Sovereignty*: The Society of American Indians and the Battle to Inherit America." *American Indian Quarterly* 37, no. 3: 331–51.

Lyons, Scott Richard. 2010. *X-Marks: Native Signatures of Assent*. Minneapolis: Univ. of Minnesota Press.

Maffly-Kipp, Laurie F. 2010. *Setting Down the Sacred Past: African-American Race Histories*. Cambridge, MA: The Belknap Press of Harvard Univ. Press.

Meigs, Mark. 2012. "Photographic Histories of the Civil War and the First World War and Rebirth." *European Journal of American Studies* 7, no. 2. https://doi.org/10.4000/ejas.9515.

Nell, William C. 1851. *Services of Colored Americans, In the Wars of 1776 and 1812*. Boston: Prentiss and Sawyer.

Owl, Henry M. 1918. "The Indian in the War." *Southern Workman* 47, no. 11: 353–55.

Parker, Arthur C. 1916. "Seneca Indians in the War of 1812." *Southern Workman* 45, no. 2: 116–22.

Parker, Robert Dale, ed. 2011. *Changing Is Not Vanishing: A Collection of American Indian Poetry to 1930*. Philadelphia: Univ. of Pennsylvania Press.

Roosevelt, Theodore. 1899. *The Rough Riders*. New York: P. F. Collier and Son Publishers.

Spires, Derrick R. 2019. *The Practice of Citizenship: Black Politics and Print Culture in the Early United States*. Philadelphia: Univ. of Pennsylvania Press.

Steward, Charles. 1899. "Colored Americans as Army Officers." *Southern Workman* 28, no. 10: 376–79.

Steward, Charles. 1899. "Colored American Soldiers." *Southern Workman* 28, no. 8: 289–94.

Trethewey, Natasha. 2006. *Native Guard: Poems*. Boston: Houghton Mifflin Company.

Vizenor, Gerald. 2008. "Aesthetics of Survivance: Literary Theory and Practice." In *Survivance: Narratives of Native Presence*, edited by Gerald Vizenor, 1–23. Lincoln: Univ. of Nebraska Press.

Warren, Kim Cary. 2010. *The Quest for Citizenship: African American and Native American Education in Kansas, 1880–1935*. Chapel Hill: Univ. of North Carolina Press.

Wilkins, David E., and K. Tsianina Lomawaima. 2001. *Uneven Ground: American Indian Sovereignty and Federal Law*. Norman: Univ. of Oklahoma Press.

Williams, W. T. B. 1918. "The World War and the Negro." *Southern Workman* 47, no. 1: 9–16.

Williams, Chad L. 2010. *Torchbearers of Democracy: African American Soldiers in the World War I Era*. Chapel Hill: Univ. of North Carolina Press.

Willis, Deborah. 2021. *The Black Civil War Soldier: A Visual History of Conflict and Citizenship*. New York: New York Univ. Press.

Womack, Craig S. 1999. *Red on Red: Native American Literary Separatism*. Minneapolis: Univ. of Minnesota Press.

Xiomara Santamarina

Market Nation:
Forging Economic Citizenship
in Nineteenth-Century African America

Abstract This essay engages with the civic possibilities African Americans perceived in the social, economic, and political transformations associated with the antebellum market revolution. Against the emerging nineteenth-century hegemony of political and economic liberalism, African Americans formulated an ideal of economic citizenship that translated Black material successes and social mobility into an extra-legal symbolic citizenship; in particular, class stratification among African Americans was mobilized to counter the presumption of immutable, ontological Black abjection that justified ascriptive Jacksonian civic exclusions. The essay engages with two proto-sociological texts designed to challenge these exclusions by depicting stratified African American communities that testified to African Americans' market participation in and contributions to the nation. As insiders of their respective groups, authors Joseph Willson—*Sketches of the Higher Classes of Colored Society in Philadelphia* (1841)—and Cyprian Clamorgan—*The Colored Aristocracy of St. Louis* (1858)—innovate a vernacular sociology that cobbles together political economy, proto-social science, reform and literary discourses to fashion empirical, reparative accounts of their better-off African American communities. Engaging with these texts allows us to understand the role that regional specificity played in formulating race, class, and status across an expanding nation, but more importantly, it makes us aware of the perils and ambiguities involved in making African Americans' participation in the liberal marketplace, or economic citizenship, the basis of African American civic legitimacy.

Keywords African American, economic citizenship, vernacular sociology

In 1852, when Martin Delany inveighed against the African Colonization Society's proposal to repatriate free African Americans to Africa, he took aim at the society's claim that African American communities were of little value to the polity. Justifying the continued residence of freedpeople in the antebellum United States, Delany (1852: 50) specifically grounded the case for African American civic equality in relation to the liberal marketplace: "The legitimate requirement, politically considered, necessary to the justifiable claims

American Literature, Volume 96, Number 4, December 2024
DOI 10.1215/00029831-11557545 © 2024 by Duke University Press

for protection and full enjoyment of all the rights and privileges of an unqualified freeman, in all democratic countries is, that each person so endowed, shall have made contributions and investments in the country." With this civic-economic definition, Delany was "refut[ing] the objections urged against us, that we are not useful members of society. That we are consumers and non-producers—that we contribute nothing to the general progress of man. No people who have enjoyed no greater opportunity for improvement, could possibly have made greater progress in the same length of time than have done the colored people of the present day" (96). For Delany—in line with the classical political economy of the day—the "greater progress [of] the colored people" was analogous to the "the general progress of man" founded on the "contributions and investments in the country" on which an emerging market society was founded.[1]

Notwithstanding Delany's affirmation of African Americans' entitlement to what we understand as "birthright citizenship," his insight into African Americans' market contributions amid the social, political and economic upheavals of the era exemplifies how market participation was perceived as a basis for civic legitimacy; as "useful members of society," free people of color might challenge the ascriptive discourses that linked race to poverty and promoted their social abjection.[2]

When Delany and others shaped socio-economic modes of political affiliation into a form of economic citizenship, they attempted to map compensatory modes of racial legitimacy onto the nation's civic imaginary; for example, they translated African Americans' participation in a national, purportedly impersonal, market in goods and labor into a form of political allegiance to the emerging liberal hegemony of market exchange and property rights. In this way, African Americans tapped into the emancipatory possibilities that were associated with the nation's transition from republican civic membership to liberal economic individualism. As Derrick Spires (2019: 122) observes:

By the 1830 [. . .] citizens had come to understand their economic selves and ideas as coextensive with, and in some cases, the same as their civic selves. [. . .] In the absence of political representation and amid a growing sense that market capital was replacing political capital, African American activists searched for economic representatives, men and women who could earn 'credit' for their communities in the civic economy, advocating for them in a market that was increasingly figured as the space for, rather than a threat to, citizenship practice.

African Americans attempted to mediate their imminent exclusion from the body politic by putting the symbolic credit they earned to work against the premises of immutable ontological racial difference.

But of course, this story is much more complicated. When African Americans took rhetorical recourse to a socio-economic civic register, they were operating in a symbolic field riddled with contradictions beyond those posed by national and state suffrage ambiguities. Because there was no settled a priori in terms of the meanings of African Americans' economic participation, the nation's dependence on African American workers (enslaved and free), their market participation did not automatically confer social and civic legitimacy. For this reason, identifying and claiming economic value was an acutely ideological—rather than a transparent—rhetorical strategy rife with ambiguity. This discursive instability was a feature in all discussions of African American workers, even among African American leaders, including Martin Delany (*Report* 1848 [2002]). One better-known exchange that appeared in *Frederick Douglass's Paper* between William Wilson, writing as "Ethiop," and James McCune Smith, writing as "Communipaw," debated the symbolic and socio-economic value attributed to African Americans, dramatizing the lack of consensus over the value of African Americans' market participation, and offering a sense of the high stakes involved.

The lack of unanimity around economic citizenship as a cultural ideal often raised more questions than answers. Were all African American workers, including the so-called servile rank-and-file manual workers, among the ranks of economic citizens? And were better-off African Americans, often caricatured in national media, really the true representatives of their race? Though firmly embedded in the expanding nation's liberal market consensus, invocations of this extra-legal mode of belonging were radically contingent; while liberal market freedom might in some ways offset the nation's emerging inequalities—racial, sexual, and socio-economic—as compensatory civic practice, economic citizenship was a precarious foundation on which to shape African Americans' cultural and political legitimacy as a social group.

Two proto-sociological antebellum texts written by freeborn African Americans sought to mitigate the perils and ambiguities associated with African Americans' contributions to the nation's liberal marketplace. They showed that it was possible to translate or narrativize African Americans' economic successes and social mobility—as nominal forms of status and material privileges—into an extra-legal symbolic citizenship intended to offset ascriptive Jacksonian civic exclusions. Their authors, Joseph Willson of Philadelphia and Cyprian Clamorgan from St. Louis cobbled together political economy, proto-social science, reform and literary discourses to promote recognition of social and class difference within African American populations as proof of their social mobility and civic competence. They challenged stigmatizing assumptions, like those expressed by a southern congressman in 1830 that "there does not exist on the face of the earth, a population so poor, so wretched, so vile, so loathsome, so utterly destitute of all the comforts, conveniences, and decencies of life, as the unfortunate African Americans of Philadelphia, New York and Boston. . . . Liberty has been to them the greatest of calamities, the heaviest of curses" (Nash 1988: 247). Instead, in their respective texts, *Sketches of the Higher Classes of Colored Society of Philadelphia* (1841) and *The Colored Aristocracy of St. Louis* (1858), Willson and Clamorgan promote recognition of those fortunate African Americans whose enjoyment of liberty included "all the comforts, conveniences, and decencies of life." [3]

Whether describing Philadelphia's "higher classes of colored society" or St. Louis's "colored aristocracy," as insiders of their respective groups, Willson and Clamorgan innovate a vernacular sociology designed to positively frame their stratified communities as proof of African Americans' important market contributions to the nation. Working at the generic intersection of vignette-form "sketches," "condition" reports, and ranked tax lists, these authors tap into the presumed empirical objectivity of an emerging sociology that was tasked with mediating the effects generated by nineteenth-century political, social, and economic transformations.[4] As such lay practitioners of a vernacular sociology, Willson and Clamorgan took on a challenging task: to promote the empirical reality of African American social stratification and class mobility, they had to strategically contend with the difficulties of representing classes that were not known to exist, whose determining criteria were far from agreed on, and which by their very nature comprised by minorities within a minority, could only tenuously be described as even representing or being representative in any way. Against a background of vast social, economic, and political upheavals, these authors offer a lay, or vernacular, voice based in the everyday experiences available to themselves and their class, that captures "life as it is experienced by individuals and groups" (Morgan 1997: 132).[5]

A comparison of these texts, however, also reveals that what counted as class and status—economic and social attributes—were specific to their place of origin; the understanding of who could be identified as an economic citizen reflected the different discursive currencies at play in different regions of the country. Willson and Clamorgan had to contend with problematic lexicons that cycled through "elite," "aspiring," "higher," and "aristocracy" along with the geopolitics of their particular region: why would a writer in a city with both free and enslaved populations figure cultural capital and material prosperity through the figure of a "colored aristocracy?" And why would a Philadelphian opt for a relational term like "higher" for the same purpose? Even as they try to stabilize the meanings of African Americans' economic citizenship, these authors' appeals to literary and empirical authority dramatize the ambiguity of historiographic conceptual schemas like that of respectability: definitions of a better-off class moved along a semantic chain of equivalences that identified elevated social and class difference in overlapping and conflicting ways.

As vernacular sociologists, these authors participated in the emerging social science discourses that were tasked with alleviating the social and economic crises generated by the market revolution; in so doing, they offered literary and social analyses that stake out the methodological and quantitative turf that W. E. B. Du Bois and others would marshal at the end of the nineteenth century. Willson and Clamorgan prefigure the economically successful and "Talented Tenth" demographic that Du Bois and Booker T. Washington would propose as solutions to the so-called postbellum "Negro Problem."[6] These authors' proto-scientific texts, geared toward the emergent social sciences, do not function in the same way as the "fugitive science" developed by African American ethnologists, as formulated by Britt Rusert; yet they do offer a genealogy for the migration of early African American activist discourse from ethnological race science to the civically oriented norms of knowledge organized around purportedly objective "sciences of society" (Gibran 2010; Rusert 2017: 15–22, 29).[7]

Rights and Representations—North

> People of color are too often pre-judged by those unhappy specimens of humanity which are sometimes seen, and from which no people, whatever their color, are exempt. [. . .] their progress in refinement, social improvement [. . .] the moral worth and influence of many in the circle in which they move, pass unobserved—and their true merits become but little known. Their worth, therefore, moral and social, should be

> drawn from its obscurity [. . .]; and if in every community
> some individual would interest himself to gather up the facts of
> this kind which his neighborhood furnishes, and send them
> forth to the world, there would soon be [. . .] an array of proofs,
> under whose influence prejudice would gradually subside.
> —William Yates, *The Rights of Colored Men to Suffrage,*
> *Citizenship and Trial by Jury: Being a Book of Facts,*
> *Arguments and Authorities, Historical Notices and Sketches*
> *of Debates—With Notes* (Philadelphia: 1838): iv

In 1841, wealthy Philadelphian Joseph Willson answered William Yates's call to "send forth to the world" an "array of proofs" that would establish the existence of those he labelled the "Higher Classes of Colored Society." Fulfilling Yates's imperative to "gather up the facts," Willson's own set of "sketches," a literary genre associated with erudition, challenged the stigma that obscured African Americans' "progress in refinement, social improvement, domestic comforts, the moral worth and influence of many in the circle in which they move." He was highly qualified for the task; the son of a rich Scotch-Irish merchant and a formerly enslaved woman, Elizabeth, in 1833 Willson and his family had migrated from Savannah, Georgia, to Philadelphia, where he became acquainted with elite Philadelphians like James Forten and Robert Purvis. (Later, his daughter, Josephine, would marry Blanche K. Bruce, the first African American to be elected to the US Senate in 1878.) In an 1838 census, Willson's mother was listed as one of the city's top three wealthiest African Americans, suggesting that Willson himself would most likely have been an eligible voter prior to Pennsylvania's 1838 constitutional disenfranchisement.

While *Sketches* appeared close on the heels of this disenfranchisement, as author, Willson followed Yates's expository mode in seeking to abolish prejudice with recourse to the power of empirical observations,[8] turning away entirely from an openly political and partisan polemic. He built on the truth-effect of condition books associated with reform movements that featured facts about income, occupation, and property ownership as proof of the environmentalist premises of uplift. Drawing from eighteenth-century compilations by abolitionist Quakers, no less than three extensive statistical inventories describing northern free African Americans had appeared in the five years prior to Willson's writing. Another example of abolitionist documentary realism, Theodore Weld's *Slavery As It Is: Testimony of a Thousand Witness,* appeared in 1839, one of several examples of emergent Anti-Slavery genres, including compendia and almanacs, that were openly committed to an antislavery discourse founded on legalistic corroboration. Willson mimics the empirical aspirations of these proto-sociological subgenres by ethnographically documenting the various polite social practices that characterized a symbolically powerful, though all but invisible and numerically small, class of well-to-do African Americans.[9]

Antebellum Philadelphia had a long history of fugitive slaves and free African Americans in migration, resulting in a large free African American population, second only to that of New York's. In 1840 this population numbered 18,000, just over 8 percent of the city's population (Nash 1988: 247). According to historian Gary Nash, African Americans' household wealth reflected "the crystallizing of an African American upper class and the increasing stratification within the African American community" (248).[10] In this respect, Philadelphia mirrored the social/class stratification of other Northern cities (Ball 2012: 7–9; Harris 2003: 218–19; Peterson 2011: 138–39). Willson's decision to shape the generic language of a "sketch" into a vehicle for vernacular empiricism perhaps reflects his reluctance to add argumentative fire to the often contentious debates taking place among African American reformers over competing forms of the African American convention movement, recent disenfranchisement, and African American communities' vulnerability to racial mob violence.

Willson puts his empirical posture to reparative use by fulfilling Yates's request to counter the "unjust" correlation of a single poor person of color—"one of those unhappy specimens of humanity [. . .] *from which no people, whatever their color, are exempt*"—with all African Americans (emphasis added). Willson (2000: 82) builds on Yates's understanding of demographic similarity among different "people," by analyzing the visual dynamic that underwrites African Americans' singling out and cultural hypervisibility: "The sight of one colored man," he complains, "whatever may be his apparent condition, (provided it is anything but genteel!) is the sight of a community; and the errors and crimes of one, is [*sic*] adjudged as the criterion of character of the whole body." (Subsequent parenthetical citations will refer to this text.) Willson clearly understands the role this perverse representational asymmetry plays in racializing poverty and engendering African Americans' nationwide abject social status.[11] To counteract the stigma derived from this unfairly imposed demographic singularity, he insists that "compared in condition, means and abilities, there are as broad social distinctions to be found here [among African Americans], *as among any other class of societies*" (emphasis added,

83). By establishing the comparative demographic social stratification exhibited by "any other class of societies," Willson tries to undercut the conflation of African Americans' racial difference with economic destitution.

The racialization of poverty is only one dimension of the pertinent representational dialectic at work, however: this dynamic is complimented by the mocking of any evidence of "genteel" prosperity. Willson's angle of attack is directed at racial stigma but also its corollary: the widespread disparagement of better-off African Americans whose class style contradicted the dominant view of African Americans' degradation. A popular theme in the visual culture of the day, caricatures of this class, most notably in lithographs by Edward Clay, depicted well-off African Americans as comic, incongruous, and inauthentic. For this reason, Willson warns his readers that he will disappoint those who "like to see their neighbors' merits caricatured, and their faults distorted and exaggerated" as well as those who desire "burlesque representations, and other laughter exciting sketches" (79). Reiterating the comparative reality of social hierarchy he insists, "The same in these respects [in relation to wealth, deportment and morality- *that may be said of any other class of people*, may, with the utmost regard to truth, be said of them" (emphasis added, 83). Willson's assessment enables us to understand how the visual ridiculing of middle-class African Americans and the visual troping of the poor African American individual as degenerate represent two sides of the same coin: that of the everyday, pervasive, and coercive racial policing of African Americans that was directed at expelling them, if not from the nation, then from the body politic. This same coin, of course, refers to the way that raced class difference—figured through either impoverishment or successful aspiration—was used to justify the inegalitarian exclusion of African American men from the franchise (Lang 2003: 42–46).

Openly aware of how this representative double jeopardy will generate skepticism among his readers, Willson understands his description of an African American "higher" class might provoke "the mirth of a prejudiced community on its annunciation." Yet, he insists, "[this designation] is perfectly correct and proper" (Willson 2000: 79). Establishing the empirical accuracy and propriety of this relational concept, Willson marshals a vernacular social taxonomy that naturalizes hierarchical social stratification and posits the empirical reality of intraracial difference as a social norm, rather than as the incongruous exception to which the Clay caricatures refer.

This association of social hierarchy with empiricism reflected the influence of late eighteenth-century economists—most notably that of Adam Smith whose *Wealth of Nations* had appeared in 1776—who influenced the transformation from earlier "socioconstitutional" divisions of society based on an individual's political status to a "socioeconomic" taxonomy which generalized a tripartite social division reflecting the wealth-creating roles of land, labor, and capital respectively (Burke 1994, 3–7). This general schema was further differentiated by divisions of labor, leading to the eventual dominance of an occupational social matrix in establishing an individual's status and class; but as Stuart Blumin, Martin Burke, and other historians have observed, the multiple terms in this ever-shifting taxonomy— "middling sorts," "better sorts," "upper," "middle" "lower"—reflected the lack of consensus regarding how best to describe the social organization of a liberal market society. Willson partakes of this semantic uncertainty, aware, like many others, of the political stakes associated with social classification and of the ambiguity involved in delineating the different strata.

Into the breach of this terminological political fray and problematic new reality, Alexis de Tocqueville suggested, "A new science of politics is needed for a new world" (Sklansky 2002: 74). This "new science" would be pioneered initially by de Tocqueville's countryman, Auguste Comte. As Jeffrey Sklansky explains: "The intellectual origins of Comtean social science lay in the Enlightenment conception, central to early American social thought, of politics and history as rooted in particular forms of society or social relations, whose laws of motion might be discovered in the manner of the natural sciences" (74). The call for a "science" of society, then, was issued in response to the sense of crisis sparked by the unprecedented and rapid changes to the nation's politics and economy.[12]

This posture of empirical objectivity, established by a "science" of society, would be apposite to Willson's desire to appear politically disinterested, a very important concern considering the ongoing controversies over African American suffrage. And in this effort for transparency, Willson the social scientist lays his cards on the table, explicitly conceding the opaque criteria underwriting his class schema: "It must be confessed," he confides, "that the difficulty of establishing, successfully, a distinguishing line of separation is very great" (86). His painstaking outlining of "the line[s] of separation" reflects the fact that the material circumstances underwriting the separation between groups were extremely nebulous. As he observes,

> The chief grounds of distinction among men are founded upon wealth, education, station and occupation. In other countries, birth, or family connexion [sic] will go a great way towards promotion; but [that] will not stand alone. [. . .] I have not the foundation of wealth; because the number who may be permitted to come under that denomination are too limited to be justly made the standard of the men and manners of the whole body. [. . .] objections will be discernible when it is known that I cannot make moral worth, strictly speaking the standard; for in that case it might be necessary to exclude a number of those who are denominated wealthy! Neither may I erect [sic] upon education nor occupation; as among the higher classes—unless an unjust and illiberal contrast is sought—there is no very remarkable difference any where to be found. (86)

Willson faces a conundrum relating to identifying a "higher" class: he seeks to invalidate the unjust characterizations of well-to-do African Americans, but he lacks an unequivocal empirical basis to do so. Here we can see Willson contending with the analytical murkiness around class that political theorists and would-be sociologists of the period were themselves wrestling. In this case, however, such taxonomic uncertainty is rendered even more ideologically fraught. Singling out one factor, either wealth, birth, occupation, education, or morality, would fail to establish "a distinguishing line of separation," given that the number of individuals ranked under any single one of those headings would be too "limited to be justly made the standard." Hence, we can see Willson negotiating with the complex overdetermination of economic and cultural factors Max Weber (1991: 181–86) would later disambiguate by distinguishing class—derived from economic resources such as property and disposable income—from status, an index of social prestige, honor, and community influence. (The ambiguous criteria of any "higher" class of African Americans continues to be debated among sociologists and historians.[13])

In regard to the parameters of this group, the main attributes of Willson's subjects are culturally derived: the description of this group as "sober, honest, industrious and respectable—claiming neither [the proverbial] 'poverty nor riches' yet maintaining by their pursuits, their families in comparative ease and comfort" (83), identifies a specific style of life that is not necessarily objectively quantifiable. What these attributes do suggest is the ideological foundation of a future, universalized, "middle class" culture (Goloboy 2019: 258). But at this point of uncertainty, Willson again evokes his commitment to empirical disinterestedness, pointing to the care he takes to avoid subjective partiality and to follow a scientific method: "Opinions are founded upon investigation, and a knowledge of facts," he insists. Anticipating the controversial nature of his "facts," Willson tries to preempt readers' interpretation of his taxonomy as positing a "negative opinion against [an excluded individual's'] gentility." Addressing those who might be offended by his classification, he clarifies: "[. . .] this is not necessarily the case [. . .]." If upon examination, it is found that a certain portion of any given class of person have attained to particular positions in society [. . .] in giving a statement of the fact merely, it is not to be inferred, that any opinion is passed upon the merits of those who may not have yet arrived at the supposed point" (Willson 2000: 85–86).

The idea of "not hav[ing] yet arrived" demonstrates how Willson's appeal to contemporary socioeconomic hierarchy reflected the period's contradictory liberal presumption of individual advancement and social mobility. While the period's myriad social, economic, and political transformations generated a desire for greater social stability, paradoxically, the ideology of individualist social mobility and liberal market dynamics protected against (in theory, of course) exploitation and stagnant status. This element of possibility and futurity ensured that all could imagine their current state—presumably not as good as one would like—as just one temporary step on an occupational/wealth ladder. As Martin Burke (1995: 124) explains: "Social mobility moved the worker's horizon conditions of expectations from the present to the future; and it assessed the conditions of the lower classes in terms of circumstances that had not yet occurred. The experience of the working class in the United States was one of anticipation, not exploitation."[14] In this way, Willson's capacious description of the "higher classes" could simultaneously include those delineated therein, and those aspiring from without.

Willson (2000: 87), casting his net wide "to glean the materials from persons of all grades," ultimately upholds his definition of "higher" classes through the auspices of space—in particular, domestic space. He describes his subjects as "that portion of colored society whose incomes, from their pursuits or otherwise, (immoralities and criminalities of course excepted,) enables them to maintain the position of house-holders, and their families in comparative ease and comfort" (87). With the ambiguous criterion of "householder" (which could include both male and female property-owners and tenants), Willson succeeds in legitimizing this class of African Americans as his object

of empirical study: he rewrites the criteria for status through the ful-
crum of a household rich, if not in square feet, then in respectable
domesticity. By invoking leadership in a domestic habitus, Willson off-
sets African American men's lack of political power, allowing for these
men to ideologically recoup the potential loss of manly civic virtue
entailed in their blanket disenfranchisement. As he explains elsewhere, being "deprived of political rights and power," the men must
resort to humiliating behavior: "it is necessary for the people of color
to keep up an incessant *begging* of their *rulers* to legislate in their
behalf" (emphasis in original, 102–3). Given the symbolic capital accru-
ing to domestic space in nineteenth-century America, such a space
could compensate for African American men's symbolic national home-
lessness, as Amy Lang (2003: 42) has observed.

This enshrining of domestic space serves as a springboard for making the case for this class's self-reliance and racial independence;
once this domestic space is secured, another space opens that allows
Willson to describe the "ability of the higher classes of colored society to maintain social intercourse on terms of respectability and dignity" (98). As proof of this decorous "social intercourse," he brings the
robust social infrastructure of support networks maintained by this
class of African Americans onto center stage. This infrastructure
includes numerous churches, benevolent (mutual aid) societies,
schools, and literary societies, along with several cohorts of (male)
professional community leaders comprised by "tradesmen and deal-
ers of various descriptions, artists, clergymen, and other profession-
als; and, last of all, though not the least, men of fortune and gentlemen of leisure" (83). Though Willson opts not to name the latter,
nineteenth-century historians have no trouble identifying these
"men of fortune and gentlemen of leisure" as successful businessmen
like himself, wealthy sailmaker James Forten, Hagar Ballard, and
wealthy community activist Robert Purvis (Winch 2000: 134; Nash
1988: 248).

By deriving respectability from the ability to maintain a family in
the "comparative ease and comfort" that allowed for "social intercourse on terms of respectability and dignity," Willson enables the
members of his "higher classes" to access market-structured liberal
subjectivities located within the prevailing ideal of "social classes without social conflict" (Burke 124).[15] Inasmuch as "respectability" was
purportedly a universally accessible form of social mobility, it derived
legitimacy from its seemingly impartial nature. Just as theorizations of
socioeconomic mobility, like those of Francis Bowen's, prevented the

"crystallization of a fixed class system" and forestalled class conflict, respectability, or what Richard Bushman (1992) has called "vernacular gentility" (Burke 1995: 124; Bushman 182) existed within a supra-political, universalizing, and putatively disinterested discourse that could transcend political conflicts concerned with suffrage, African Americans' disenfranchisement, and growing class disparities.

This analysis shows the critical relevance of African Americans' co-fabrication of and participation in this national ideology of putatively universal liberal respectability; given their sociopolitically disadvantaged position, African Americans' active shaping of and participation in norms for respectability made sense. The potential cultural legitimacy proffered by African Americans respectability was especially apposite to African Americans' national social and political exclusion, and was viewed as a racially autonomous, democratic way of elevating all, including those who occupied the lowest rung of the social hierarchy. Despite the association of respectability with a dominant white middle class, then, it's important to recognize that African Americans as a population, in particular, had the most at stake and the most to gain in aspiring to this social ideal of class status: apolitical respectability served as a key venue through which African Americans reformers could shape and represent their sincere connections to, and investments in, the nation's liberal consensus and class hierarchy.[16]

Willson's impartial sociological posture leverages modern scientific authority to confirm that aspiring African Americans exist as respectable members of the polity, even if they have been booted out of the Pennsylvania constitution. However, his attempt at sociological neutrality has ironic repercussions that also threaten the universalizing and apolitical imperatives of the "higher classes." Willson's introductory promise—"I shall not be forward to magnify the good or to extenuate evil"—demands an impartiality that precludes expressing negative personal judgements, but it also compels Willison to make a clean breast of the political conflicts—the competition and rivalries—that take place among African American leaders. For this reason, Willson's extensive descriptions of African American men's contentious, communal performance of participatory politics threatens his claim of class respectability. In this regard, I build on Samuel Otter's description of Willson's dilemma: "In contriving their status, the higher classes [. . .] succeeded in replicating the strife that comes with social distinction. [but while] Willson values such cleaving as a sign of social development, he also attempts to rectify its excesses, which he views as undermining the exemplary force and political efficacy of the higher classes" (129).

Willson chose not to spell out the basis of this intraracial conflict in the competing convention movements, so it is difficult to know where he stood in relation to these debates. But his method raises a question: If the path to racial enfranchisement through respectability was so clear a universal imperative, how could one explain the jockeying and competition for leadership that existed in 1830s and 1840s Philadelphia? The sociological depiction of political conflict among elite African Americans disrupts the suprapolitical gentility and liberal consensus associated with this class and, consequently, bases appeals for suffrage in racial self-interest.[17] Outed as self-interested political actors in this way, these men were liable to be seen as capable of destabilizing the partisan status quo—at this moment composed of Whigs and Democrats—rather than speaking to their civic fitness (Malone 2005: 189–90). In this regard, the communities of African Americans' close ties to the Whigs signal a threat to Democratic white supremacy in the state: as one Democratic reporter tellingly fantasized after a contentious election, "Fifteen Thousand Negro Balance-of-Power Men Wanted, by the Whigs and Abolitionists!"[18]

Willson (2000: 107) contains this threatening potential by displacing the politics of these conflicts and framing them as personal, stemming from individual "self-exaltation." "There are too many men," he complains, "who might otherwise be useful, who desire to be considered the leaders and the chiefs in every matter of interest that is agitated." Of a piece with his critique, Willson trivializes African American leaders' call to organize by archly commenting, "They never let a subject of peculiar importance to them, that may be agitated in the community, pass without a public expression of their views and opinions in regard to it. Their inability to act with efficiency in the premises makes but little difference with most of the leading men. A meeting they must have" (106). Indecorous open hostility becomes the order of the day: "Blustering, loud speaking and unlimited denunciation, are substituted for reason and common sense" (107). Willson disparages and compares those "educated in a pigstye" from "reasonable" and "honorable" men by attributing it to the "silly" nature of "pretences to superiority" rather than to substantial political disagreement: "Differences are expected and will always arise," he explains. "But it is expected that those differences will be marked by an open, manly and honorable course of procedure" (110). "The spirit of rivalry," he complains, "renders it almost impossible for the people to proceed together in unanimity on any given subject." (110) In a corrective and factual vein, Willson urges adherence to the principal civic currency of respectability, formulated this time as an intersubjective practice: "Until [these rivals] learn to respect themselves, and the rights, feelings and interests of their brethren, they can never hope to gain the respect of others, or attain to any remarkable point of political consideration, or private worth" (111).[19] Willson blames these men's exclusion from the body politic on their failure to privilege respect over self-interest. He does not appear to understand the day's realpolitik: no amount of respectable behavior would effectively supersede the political threat "Negro Balance-of-Power Men" posed to the electoral status quo.[20] Unfortunately, Willson, the sociologist, has inadvertently placed the politics he has tried to evade on center stage.

Rights and Representation—Upper South

In St. Louis, a city with a much smaller free African American population than Philadelphia's, Cyprian Clamorgan offered his readers a somewhat singular perspective on the intersections of race and class in the Upper South. Like Willson, Cyprian Clamorgan descended from enslavers who had passed on property, and through this property, perhaps most importantly, class status. In contrast to Willson's Protestant heritage however, Clamorgan was the grandson of French pioneer Jacques Clamorgan (1734–1814) and as such he invoked a very different cultural and socio-economic heritage. Since the patriarch never married, all of Jacques Clamorgan's children, born of Native and enslaved women, were "natural," i.e. recognized as extramarital offspring, manumitted, and given property. Though perhaps unusual, the grandson's aristocratic identification and genealogical connection to the French settler patriarch most certainly spoke to the publicly recognized, even if extra-legal, social legitimacy of the mixed-race Clamorgans. Furthermore, Clamorgan's French Catholic origins and Missouri's history of French and Spanish colonization explain why he invokes historical racial categories organized on a three-tiered system of Black, mulatto, and white that still privileged whiteness, but which differed significantly from the North's binaristic white/Black schema. While Clamorgan's cultural background shared greater commonalities with Louisiana creoles than with northern free African Americans, St. Louis's participation in immigrant expansion and settlement produced substantial intergroup acculturation among French and Anglo-descended minority groups.

Clamorgan compiles a list of African American "aristocrats" in the South right after the 1857 US Supreme Court *Scott v. Sandford* decision began to reverberate through national public spheres. Whereas *Sketches* projects sincere impartiality, the openly ironic and biased *Colored Aristocracy of St. Louis* offers a fascinating counterpoint that leverages a different set of market/class languages to repair the stigmatization associated with Dred Scott. In its ruling against Dred Scott, the enslaved man who sued for his freedom, the nation's highest court upheld the legitimacy of slavery while effectively also trying to settle, presumably once and for all, the question of African Americans' citizenship. Chief Justice Judge Taney's infamous words, that "blacks had no rights that a white man was bound to respect" represented the effective culmination of decades of racial discrimination and African American voter suppression, seemingly closing the door for good on any possibility of African American citizenship. Clamorgan pointedly challenges this wholesale dismissal of African American political influence, highlighting for us today the obscured importance of regionalist specificity to the ways that antebellum racial identity formation, as well as African Americans' political agency, intersected with, and shaped, national languages for status and class.

In stark contrast to Willson's decorous depiction of an apolitical and genteel "higher class," Clamorgan mobilizes an openly inegalitarian classification to establish African Americans' participation in electoral politics in ways that appear to confound democratic principles. This inference, however, would be missing the point: social and economic stratification among his colored aristocracy is not simply about engendering caste-affirming feelings of social superiority (though it does not exclude those, of course)—this almost satirical account of African Americans' social hierarchy promotes their overlooked civic participation in a nation obsessed with material gains. To this end, Clamorgan structures his text around a vertically organized ranking of individuals according to wealth, mimicking the data format of a Fortune 500 list, *avant la lettre*, which somewhat remarkably, features an entrepreneurial, formerly enslaved woman at its head. (He neglects to tell his readers that the woman, whom he clearly dislikes, is his aunt by marriage!)[21]

While his title, like Willson's, highlights stratification among St. Louis's African Americans, the ideological terms of Clamorgan's classification schema skew openly elitist; paradoxically, he appeals to norms of aristocratic exclusivity even as he upholds the competitive ethos of liberalism.[22] Clamorgan's emphatic sincerity regarding his subjects' "power" builds on an apparently intentional irony: while, he admits, living in antebellum Missouri's slave society "our colored friends have no voice in the elections," he argues that he can prove "in what manner the political influence of the colored man is felt in St. Louis" (47). Another, perhaps unintended irony exists, as well; according to him, Clamorgan's aristocrats are participating—even if indirectly—in a representative democracy.

Understandably, Cyprian Clamorgan approached the issue of African Americans' rights by willfully evading the implications of Taney's decision; instead, he pivots opportunistically to attacking northern reform discourses, singling out abolitionist authors. His description of antebellum St. Louis's largely Creole "aristocracy" explicitly challenges anti-slavery assertions of African American social abjection; astonishingly, it displaces Taney's view of rightless African Americans by challenging the racist and patronizing images of purportedly degraded African Americans circulating in the national media, as if the court decision had not reflected African Americans' public stigmatization. In this way, this hybrid text innovates a vernacular, sociological genre of African Americans' political agency based on a critique of national abolitionist rhetoric and organization.

Even more puzzling, Clamorgan's challenge to abolitionist descriptions of African Americans' abjection specifically targets influential white and African American authors. He vigorously disparages these authors' abolitionist discourse in his opening gambit, attacking what he decries as the sentimental dimensions of anti-slavery publicity: "Thousands have wept over the fictitious sorrows of 'Uncle Tom,'" as delineated by the facile pen of Mrs. Stowe;" he deadpans, "while the imaginary 'Dred,' a monstrous creation of the same morbid and diseased brain, has awakened the sympathies of all classes of readers" (Clamorgan 1999: 45). Clamorgan's contempt also extends to formerly enslaved African Americans: he describes the "romantic autobiographies" of fugitive slaves—among whom Clamorgan identifies Solomon Northrup and Henry Box Brown—and the "oratorical displays" of Douglass and other "compatriots" as "flights of fancy."

Challenging what he denotes as the romantic strain of abolitionist discourse, Clamorgan offers a hardheaded analysis of the "aristocrats'" empirical reality: "In such a state of public affairs," he argues, "the author deems it not inappropriate to take a cursory glance at society as it exists among the colored people of St. Louis; to show the origins and position of a portion of those whom circumstances have placed in the path of comparative respectability, and to whom fortune has been kind in the bestowal of the good gifts of life" (45). With this polemical claim, Clamorgan opens a vital, if tenuous, space for making African Americans' political agency visible: "I will endeavor to show in a few words," he claims, "in what manner the political influence of the colored man is felt in St. Louis" (47). Whereas Willson's critique of US racism focuses on African Americans' disadvantaged status in national public spheres, Clamorgan directly invokes electoral politics to establish the existence of an otherwise invisible African American political agency. [In this regard, we might classify *The Colored Aristocracy* as a Midwest/southern corollary to Robert Purvis's 1838 "Appeal of Forty Thousand," both texts sharing an insistence on historical and existing modes of African Americans' civic participation.]

How can we make sense of Clamorgan's rhetorical maneuver? Despite the controversial national significance of the Dred Scott decision, the reality was that on the verge of the Civil War, slavery in Missouri was on the wane: in fact, 1850s Missouri had seen a distinct decline in the number of enslaved and free African American populations. During that decade, the African American population of St. Louis dropped from 5.21 percent to 2 percent; in 1850 the ratio of free African Americans to slaves was about 1:2; in 1860 it was 1:1.2) (Winch 150). Living in a border city made up of overlapping western, northern, and southern regional identities, free African Americans and especially so-called aristocrats would hardly have been visible to the population at large. In comparison to Philadelphia and reflecting the reality of free African Americans' precarious survival in a slave society, St. Louis had a less robust social infrastructure of African American churches, benevolent societies, or literary societies. This steep vertical social organization and lack of middle ground in African American communities may have justified Clamorgan's claim of class exclusivity as the principal criterion of an established "aristocracy."[23]

When Clamorgan leverages the existence of a "colored aristocracy" to prove that disenfranchised African Americans wield political clout, he figures the bedrock of US civic participation, not in terms of the postulated republican ideal of abstract, disembodied citizenship but in terms of the liberal right to the "pursuit of property," i.e. wealth. Not displaying any cynicism, Clamorgan unequivocally declares his motto: "Wealth is power" (47). Remarkably, just as Willson had, Clamorgan cites the same epistle of Alexander Pope's *Essay on Man* to justify the providential nature of a hierarchical social order; in this case, he tweaks a popular aphorism about wealth. In tune with his elitism, Clamorgan comments: "Wealth makes the man, the want of it the fellow" (29).[24] Nonetheless, he situates the power of African Americans' wealth in the context of a political racial collective, declaring: "There is not a colored man in our midst who would not cheerfully part with his last dollar to effect the elevation of his race. They know who are their friends, and when the opportunity arrives they exhibit their gratitude in a manner most acceptable to the recipient" (47). In the service of this startling claim to African Americans' political influence, Clamorgan names names, listing various wealthy St. Louis African American elites as well as the white politicians—those "friends"—who, he claims, have been rewarded for their efforts in representing this disenfranchised population.

Ironically, if St. Louis's African American social infrastructure was not as robust as that of Philadelphia's, this population benefitted precariously from living in a very unstable political ecosystem. The politicians Clamorgan names represent wide-ranging party affiliations that highlight the persistent contentiousness of slavery in an economically liberalizing nation. With its large number of immigrants, St. Louis had a sizeable portion of elected officials who sought to end slavery in favor of the perceived benefits of expansion: from this perspective one can see Judge Taney's nullification of the Missouri Compromise as a desperate last stab at upholding slavery, rather than its irrevocable affirmation. (Of course, this is not to minimize the critical role that public reaction to the decision played in precipitating the Civil War.) Some of the politicians he mentions, e.g. John How (d. 1888), Benjamin Brown (1826–85), and Francis Blair, Jr. (1821–75), were Democrats who opposed slavery and would go on to support the Union during the war, while others became zealous Confederates (Winch 2001: 69–70). Despite Missouri's status as a state supporting slavery then, St. Louis's politics offered some political opportunities to African Americans who could generously bankroll political campaigns even if they could not vote. When Clamorgan credits "the unwearied and combined action of the wealthy free colored men of St. Louis" as a factor in the rise of the "Emancipation party" (future Republicans) in the city, we should believe it (47).[25] This political ecosphere also accounts for Missouri remaining in the union when other slave states voted to secede.

Affirming the common-sense, if openly crass, belief "wealth is power" allows Clamorgan to pre-empt the potential disbelief and skepticism that would greet his depiction of a southern African American aristocracy. In this respect, Clamorgan has an advantage that Willson, who faced similar disbelief, did not: wealth affords the southern chronicler firm empirical criteria—hence the ranked list—that frees him from having to replicate Willson's painstaking assessment of education, occupation, income, and householder status in designating his class subjects. Basing his designation of "aristoc-racy" without any prevarication in the wealth of his peers, Clamorgan does not offer even the slightest hint that this claim might be a prob-lematic or potentially undemocratic one in a democratic culture that—if only disingenuously—equated wealth with corruption. At no point does Clamorgan's sociological chronicling demonstrate Willson's scruples pertaining to the discriminatory potential of sin-gling out an "aristocracy;" this class, he describes, "form[s] a pecu-liar class—the elite of the colored race" (46). The definition of this subgroup then fits the bill more neatly than Willson's insofar as it fulfills the criteria that "elite" and "aristocracy" imply a small num-ber, without much concern for those thereby excluded. By defini-tion, "aristocracy" is not comparative, i.e. neither "higher," "middle," or "lower," and Clamorgan's use of the term suggests a local reader-ship that holds different assumptions about democracy, racial group, class, and individual identity.

Clamorgan's romanticized depiction of these aristocrats' interracial sexual origins, however, exposes his claim to empirical authority as the patently rhetorical strategy that it is. Despite claiming to be a "faith-ful historian" bearing the "the unpleasant duty to speak of the vile and unworthy, as well as the good and virtuous" (54) he rhapsodically iden-tifies the historical characters and events that spawned his elite:

> When Upper Louisiana was settled by the French and Spaniards, the emigrants were necessarily nearly all of the sterner sex. Stem [ming] the current of the Father of the Waters [the Mississippi] in their light canoes and pirogues and taking up their abode in the wild wilderness, where beasts of prey and prowling savages beset them on all sides, they could not bring with them the soft partners of their bosoms, [. . .] while they undertook the task of exploring a continent. But man without woman, even in the wildest state of soci-ety, becomes a savage, morose and discontented being. He longs for the endearments of a wife and sighs for the prattle of children in the solitude of his forest home. (46)

Displaying his own facile sentiment, Clamorgan glosses the violent social relations that characterized the early settlement of the frontier— relations that coercively assimilated Indigenous and enslaved popula-tions into the national fabric through land dispossession and labor exploitation. In particular, the women, some of whom he describes as "sylvan maids of the forest" (Native American women) and others introduced when "the blood of Africa had crossed the Atlantic" (African women), were critical to the reproduction of life on this settler frontier (46). With this rhetorical flourish, Clamorgan sets up his venerable grandfather, European Jacques Clamorgan (1734–1814), as representative of the entrepreneurial spirit of the "first families" (46) in the state. This claim establishes Clamorgan's credentials within a descent-based citizenship model as a participant (no matter what Judge Taney said to the contrary) in the settling and the building of the region's social order. In this respect, despite claiming to be a "faithful historian," Clamorgan signals his unabashed partisanship to his readers. As a member of the family that claimed the rights to his founding grandfather's extensive land holdings, Cyprian assumes he would be recognized as a privileged insider.[26]

Against this background, wealth empowers disenfranchised African Americans elites, but, perhaps more importantly, this power trumps the cultural capital afforded by respectability. The piquant vignettes in his pamphlet suggest that wealth gives Clamorgan and his fellow aristocrats the privilege of playing more loosely—relatively speaking—with gender norms and discourses of respectability. In *Colored Aristocracy* there is little hint of Willson's concern about the propriety and decorum of this class, nor is respectability enshrined through descriptions of polite socializing and enlightened debate as in *Sketches*. Since elite status is based primarily on wealth, respectability and its liberal corollary—meritocracy—do not feature as Clamorgan's central currency in leveraging the status of his group: in fact, he candidly describes the greed of many subjects, emphasizing the role money serves as key to their distinction. Clamorgan's authority as a southern chronicler thus rests solidly on the tacit understanding that the primacy of wealth in delimiting the "aristocracy" suggests a privilege, which, unlike a right, cannot be compromised by greed, illiteracy, or the absence of respectability.[27]

The prominence of African American women in the list (a total of eleven out of forty-two, not including married couples) displays Clamorgan's indifference to upholding male-centered middle-class respectability. By showcasing many wealthy, self-sufficient women, his list corroborates the day's demographics featuring a significant number of formerly enslaved African American women, whose sources of wealth—frequently originating from sexual associations with white enslavers—remain off stage and who are invisible as "householders" in *Sketches*.[28] These women are correctly represented—if not necessarily in the most flattering light—among the wealthiest of free African Americans, who, incidentally, were highly skilled in growing their inherited money.

In the context of Clamorgan's claims to his class's political clout, the presence of these women suggests a remarkable, even if dubious, equality. Ms. Pelagie Nash, whose estate is worth $5,000, is "very aristocratic in her bearing and takes great pride in her wealth—her motto being, 'Wealth makes the man, the want of it the fellow'" (49). Apparently unaware of the irony of his earlier boast, "wealth is power," he describes Mrs. Pelagie Rutgers, who heads Clamorgan's list as the wealthiest of all, as an "illiterate woman, [who] lives in good style" but who, as a Catholic, hypocritically "worships the almighty dollar more than Almighty God" (49). Likewise, Mrs. Pelagie Foreman—whom Winch has identified as a "courtesan"—makes the list on a pecuniary basis: she "command[s] the cool sum of one hundred thousand dollars," he asserts, though in her case he amplifies his snide critique with a typically rote apology for the fact that he must "with extreme reluctance [. . .] speak in terms of disrespect" (61). Relating at length the "questionable" details of how this "Delilah" acquired her wealth he proclaims, "upon [her name] hangs a load of infamy dark as the shadow of hell" (60).

Clamorgan's description of African American men likewise downplays the propriety and decorum critical to northern African American men's claims to patriarchal authority. One example of this is Marshall Starks, who, Clamorgan states drolly, "is a good businessman, hospitable and kind, but very fond of hoarding money" (61). Samuel Mordecai is "extremely polite" and "quite aristocratic" but also "a most inveterate gambler [with] an incurable passion for games of chance and will bet his pile on anything that has the appearance of uncertainty" (51). One William Johnson, whose knowledge and determination Clamorgan extolls, nonetheless has a notable weakness: "Johnson's greatest fault is his fondness for the gentler sex—the flashing eye and silvery voice of a golden-cheeked beauty, can raise a commotion in his breast almost equal to any eruption of Vesuvius" (56). But he reserves his most pointed language for another wealthy individual whose inclusion might make the reader wonder, until we look at Clamorgan's description of what constitutes his "duty":

> Nothing but [a] sense of duty could induce us to mention in this connection a character so far below the common level of humanity as P. G. Wells. He has been here about twenty years, and in all that time has led the life of a spy and a dog. [. . .] He is a tall, pompous black [sic] man—a great braggart [. . .] He is not only treacherous and deceitful to his own color but has deceived and cheated every white man who has trusted in his promises. (55)

Here, the invocation of "duty" upholds Clamorgan's claim to objectivity, a claim he reiterates notwithstanding his obvious, intermittent salaciousness. In none of his comments does Clamorgan appear bothered by the possibility that these criticisms might countermand his claim to his aristocrats' political influence. From this perspective, these individuals' obvious flaws lend even greater credence to his claim that in St. Louis "wealth is power" since it is entirely on the basis of wealth, and not on virtue or charity, that these individuals qualify for membership in "the colored aristocracy."

Clamorgan's frankness in relation to these accounts of venality and greed brings one contradiction into stark relief in his positive description of Mr. and Mrs. Cox, the single couple "from abroad," i.e. from the North. "Of all the colored men from abroad, Cox is, without doubt, the best," he concedes. But expanding on what appears to have been a singular pet peeve he further asserts:

> As a general remark it may be said that the colored people who have come here, especially from the free States, bring with them more faults and vices than they find among those who have been reared upon the soil. We leave it to abolition philosophers to solve the problem, while we assert it as a fact, that but few of the free colored men among us, who have been raised in those States where the laws make all men literally equal, possess the same amount of honesty, virtue and intelligence belonging to those who have always lived among those whom they have been taught to regard as belonging to a superior race. (57)

At the very least, Clamorgan's speculation about the origins of northern African Americans' purported dishonesty and lack of virtue—"[having] been raised in those States where the laws make all men literally equal"—appears incongruous; after all, his own accounting of colored aristocrats relishes their flaunting of norms for gender and respectability. It also raises a perplexing question relating to his disparagement of northern legal equality (besides that of how he could be so naïve): how can he disingenuously claim that northern African Americans' purported legal parity makes them morally inferior to southern African Americans (presumably including himself) who "have always lived among those whom they have been taught to regard as belonging to a superior race"?

Clamorgan's ironic and dubious observation yields an important paradoxical insight: his text entirely disappears the northern super-respectable "higher classes" that Willson takes such pains to represent.

Furthermore, Clamorgan's damning depiction of northern African Americans reasserts the stigma and degeneracy that Willson, his peer in wealth and education, was working so hard to counter. Given this contrast of southern aristocratic visibility and northern respectable invisibility, it would appear, as Willson's effort showed, that when groups define themselves, they do so necessarily against others, even others like themselves. The paradox here consists of a corruption-tolerating aristocrat openly flouting his difference from, yet outclassing, a middle-class icon of respectability.

The conflicts in logic and rhetoric that appear in these two men's vernacular proto-sociological texts offer insights into the uneven and contradictory nature of the class discourses to which antebellum African Americans appealed when they invoked class stratification as proof of racial heterogeneity. Clearly, inegalitarian ascriptivist claims about ontological and immutable racial difference concerned free African Americans across the nation, whether they were being excluded from voting or were being told "they had no rights which a white man was bound to respect." But these conflicts highlight the importance of regionalism in shaping the spaces through which African Americans across the nation straddled competing residual republican/emergent liberal social orders and the terms of economic citizenship.

Antebellum St. Louis offered a residual social model of ranks that predated but continued to coexist with early republican civic ideals that reflected settler participation in the expanding frontier. In the South, ascriptive descent counted for more than respectability; in the North, the primacy of respectability nullified the ideological purchase of descent. For a St. Louis audience, the racial interdependence of African American aristocrats and white politicians would signal the influence of the African American community—in Philadelphia such a picture would seriously strain readers' credulity. Again, in the latter, the African American community's institutional self-sufficiency would signal the strength of that community, whereas in St. Louis such a picture might seem counterproductively isolationist. While Clamorgan perceives the possibilities in the older (still prevailing) social system of ranks, Willson subscribes to the presumably democratic possibilities in the modern, liberal, one. This makes clear that despite sharing raced identities as men of color, Willson and Clamorgan's classed identities as economic citizens are firmly anchored and produced in relation to different regional social structures.

Yet, for all their differences as African American subjects, Clamorgan and Willson share a political vision of race invested in, or triangulated through, social hierarchies. Hence, their texts offer significantly more nuanced opportunities to broaden our analyses of the various contradictory processes involved in collective Black identity formation; they also encourage us to investigate the origins of Black racial identity in the interstices between civic republicanism, liberal individualism, and counter-hegemonic formulations of subaltern identity. From this perspective, historiographic investments in associating northern Black protest with a unified collective Black identity appear to overlook the uneven claims to citizenship and political fields more broadly, and the internally differentiated situatedness—or locally specific nature—of African American populations.

Epilogue

> As African Americans fought against racial exclusion, they built their own set of barriers to membership, crafting a citizenship that was less than freedom and that reproduced inequalities. Those restrictive arguments continued to shape black protest in the years to come.
> —Christopher Bonner, *Remaking the Republic* (2020)

Framing an extra-legal civic tradition of economic citizenship through the lenses of African American social and class difference, as we have seen, proved to be a contingent and problematic task. Christopher Bonner identifies one often overlooked consequence of the struggle for Black suffrage: activism that pursued market-derived civic virtue in the fight against racial inequality inadvertently truncated—even if it did not entirely eliminate—any democratic urge seeking a universal class equality that would presumably aid all workers, Black and white (Bonner 2020: 37). While Willson's and Clamorgan's texts bring the antebellum period's vexed coarticulations of race, class, and status into sharp focus, they also prefigure today's efforts to align class and race in ways that might effectively attack inequality for the benefit of all (Fields 2014: 256).[29]

An ideal of African American economic citizenship necessarily invokes a reparative mode of racial particularity that appears to harmonize with larger descriptions of African American activists as "posit [ing] all people of African descent as a unified whole" (Rael 2004: 37). But this kind of historiographical unity appears to overlook the sociological realities of nineteenth-century African Americans. As James McCune Smith—an enthusiastic promoter of African Americans' across-the-board market contributions—complained in 1854: "... we are not united as a people; and the main reason why we are not united is that we are not equally oppressed. This is the grand secret of our lack of union" (Stauffer 2006: 98).[30] Smith's analysis of the difficulties African Americans faced in cultivating political unity suggests that a sliding scale of multiple imagined belongings might offer the best political option for a heterogenous African American population seeking to challenge the period's homogenizing racial ascriptivism (Hyde 2018: 32). Lastly, in any historiographic debate about the different meanings and statuses of racial market collectivity vs. intra-racial difference, we should take the opportunity to seek out "thinkable alternatives," i.e. expressions of dissent, existing in Black print culture (Santamarina 2006: 245). In rightly recognizing African Americans' roles as "cofabricators" of the liberal market civic imaginary, we should not overlook those free African Americans who criticized market inequalities and imagined alternatives to market liberalism (Rael 2004: 37).

One individual, the formerly enslaved Sojourner Truth, offered a prescient critique on market liberalism that is an often-sidelined dimension of her abolitionism. In her 1850 narrative (the first of three), she explained her rationale for adopting the itinerant lay preacher persona for which she was later renowned (Isabella Baumfree was her birth name); in so doing, Truth introduced a dissonant note into her slave narrative that bears critical importance to the collective identity the narrative espouses.

In a Poor Richard–like anecdote that relates her waking early to earn the money sidewalk clearing that was earmarked for another, Truth offers a startling insight: as she saw it, there had been no virtue or industry in effectively taking money away from another needy person. According to her amanuensis, Olive Gilbert, this act "troubled her conscience sorely and this insensibility to the claims of human brotherhood, and the wants of the destitute and the wretched poor, she now saw [...] as unfeeling, selfish and wicked" (1993, 79). So jarring is the accusation that Gilbert deflects it with a direct quote from Truth that ironically reaffirms the latter's iconoclastic belief: "'Yes,' she said, 'the rich rob the poor and the poor rob each other'" (78). For this formerly enslaved native northerner, destitute herself, the freedom abolitionists associated with the North obscured the fact that the idealized nation and the capitalist one were not one and the same; instead, Truth refused "the ready conflation of republicanism with capitalism that formed the ideological bedrock of [liberal] union nationalism" (Santamarina 2005: 62). Predictably, Gilbert tries to downplay

Truth's sharp critique—not entirely successfully—by resorting to the ignorant slave trope: "Isabella [. . .] began to look upon money and property with great indifference, if not contempt—being at that time unable, probably, to discern any difference between a miserly grasping and hoarding of money and means, and a true use of the good things of this life" (79). Famous for her labor theory of value claim, "I have plowed and reaped and husked and chopped and mowed and can any man do more than that?" Truth, the abolitionist, sees her labor while enslaved as more "true to God" then her labor for wages once freed: Christian ideals of perfectibility were incompatible with liberal market norms for social mobility or capitalist accumulation (1993, 118). For Truth, "Value inheres in that which circulates, i.e., in that which can be shared with others, rather than that which can be held as private property" (Santamarina 2005: 63).

Given her impolitic critique of the North, it's not surprising that Truth's perspective continues to appear idiosyncratic and non-representative of African American protest. Rather, Truth appears to participate in a transcendent Christian "renunciative impulse" (Hyde 2018: 53). But then dissent of this nature would hardly have made it in the Black press; as diagnosed by "One Who Works" in 1860, however self-sufficient manual labor might prove to be, Black reformers themselves often colluded in the culture's devaluation of the symbolic and material value produced by the rank and file. Still, it is worth pondering where historians might locate alternative visions of political economy and iconoclastic understandings of civic collectivity. Did Christian "human brotherhood" only make sense in an extra-legal renunciative tradition of "expatriation" (Hyde 2018: 53)? Was it even possible for formerly enslaved or free African Americans to challenge the political hegemony of economic liberalism? What would that look like?

Regardless, Truth's dissent does not preclude understanding the lesson derived from Willson's and Clamorgan's chronicling of their social class. For all their similarities and differences, *The Colored Aristocracy* and *Sketches of the Higher Classes of Colored Society* vividly dramatize the potential fault lines in the reconfiguration of Black civic privilege that sought to prevail against the emerging dominance of racially ascriptive citizenship. Ultimately, derived from the hopes and aspirations of a subaltern minority, this discourse in the "political subjunctive" (Hyde 2017:16), of what should or might come to be, was unable to fend off the ascriptive impulse of the Jacksonian political transformation.

Xiomara Santamarina is associate professor of Afroamerican and African Studies and English at the University of Michigan, Ann Arbor. She is the editor of Eliza Potter's *A Hairdresser's Experience in High Life* (1859; 2009), the author of *Belabored Professions* (2005) and essays on nineteenth-century African American print culture and literature.

Notes

1   Adam Smith famously asserts this axiom in chapter 3 of *The Wealth of Nations* (1776): "The extent of the market [in the "produce of all sorts of labor"], therefore, must for a long time be in proportion to the riches and populousness of that country, and consequently their improvement must always be posterior to the improvement of that country."

2   Legal scholar Martha Jones claims that "birthright citizenship was a fully formed idea by the early 1850s" (89), but other scholars speak to the persistent instability of civic discourses more generally: as Robert Levine has argued, a "national position on the question of African Americans citizenship simply did not exist in the early nineteenth century" (75). Carrie Hyde foregrounds the aspirational impulse behind antebellum debates on constitutionally unspecified "citizenship" in *Civic Longing*.

3   Pierre Bourdieu's (1984: 475–76) discussion of social subjects' classificatory tendencies highlights how a community tries to offset "stigma" through "advantageous attributions": "The logic of the stigma reminds us that social identity is the stake in a struggle in which the stigmatized individual or group [. . .] can only retaliate against the partial perception which limits it to one of its characteristics by highlighting, in its self-definition, the best of its characteristics, and, more generally, by struggling to impose the taxonomy most favourable to its characteristics, or at least to give to the dominant taxonomy the content most flattering to what it has and what it is."

4   *Sketches* features in Du Bois's *Philadelphia Negro* and in historian Leon Litwack's *North of Slavery* (1961), both foundational texts in African American studies. In framing *Sketches* as a text aspiring to empirical authority, I diverge from Samuel Otter's astute formulation of the sketch genre as impressionistic, the antithesis of statistics (129).

5   I borrow the formulation, "vernacular sociology," from Saul Cornell (1990: 1159). See Williams and Barlow for further discussions of "vernacular sociology."

6   While W. E. B. Du Bois (1868–1963) receives most of the credit for the emergence of African American sociology and the founding of the American Negro Academy, the ur-text of statistics around Jim Crow's deplorable interracial race relations was authored by journalist Ida B. Wells-Barnett. *Southern Horrors* (1892) and *A Red Record* (1894) marshalled statistics about white supremacy's racial violence to indict white men's barbarity and to counter claims of African Americans racial inferiority and criminality

(Muhammad 2010: 58–60). W. E. B. Du Bois co-founded the American Negro Academy with Alexander Crummell in 1897. His initial, authoritative foray into sociological scholarship culminated in *The Philadelphia Negro: A Social Study* (1899).

7   Jeffrey Sklansky describes the political origins of Auguste Comte's social positivism as directed specifically to containing the disruptive social energies of the market revolution. "The basis of social scientists' new authority lay in their knowledge of the immutable laws that governed the progress of society from the 'theological' stage of monarchy and war, through the 'metaphysical' stage characterized by rude democracy and class struggle, to the 'positive' stage ruled by science and industry. To such a spiritual science of social evolution, as opposed to either revolution or reaction, Comte gave the name, 'sociology'" (Sklansky 2002: 75). Early uses of the phrase "social science," denoting a separate branch of knowledge, appear in the 1820s and 1830s; philosophers and reformers John Stuart Mill, Charles Fourier, and Robert Owen employed the term (Shapiro 1984: 21).

8   Martha Jones (2019: 3) describes the genre of the legal "treatise" as associated with "scientific knowledge" by the late 1830s.

9   In 1838 and 1839 three abolition societies, the Pennsylvania Abolition Society, the American Anti-Slavery Society, and the Ohio Abolition Society, published their own "condition" surveys. See Melish 1999 for how these abolitionist texts were contesting the inventories produced by colonizationists for purposes of delegitimating the presence of free African Americans in the nation.

10   According to Nash (1988: 250), African American householders' property ownership rate in 1840 was 7.7 percent, half of that of white populations, but the degree of social stratification in the 1830s, measured by distribution of wealth "was roughly equal to that among urban whites [. . .] with the wealthiest tenth of the households having amassed two-thirds of the aggregate wealth and richest 5 percent [. . .] controlling more than half the African Americans community's total assets."

11   I borrow the concept of "synecdochal" representation—one for the whole—from Patrick Rael (2002: 179), *Black Identity and Black Protest in the Antebellum North*. Willson's comment appears prescient in terms of the ways the discourse around racialized poverty and African Americans' abjection would morph in the postbellum period into the discourse of racial criminalization or "the stigmatization of crime as 'African Americans'" (Muhammad 2010: 3).

12   Robert Nisbet discusses the paradoxical basis of empiricism in an antimodern conservative "methodological style" that prioritized "the observation of what could in fact be seen and described" over general philosophical formulations about individuals and society. Challenging the Enlightenment's notion of an abstract "natural" man, conservative theorists sought to depict "man in the historically concrete, man as Frenchman or Englishman, as peasant or aristocrat . . . " (Nisbet 1978: 81). This

conservative strain clearly influenced the seminal work of the individual credited with founding modern sociology, Auguste Comte. In his *Positive Philosophy* (1830–42), Positivism would be structured "in clearcut, functionally oriented social classes, with the uppermost being the intellectual-scientific-religious stratum, the business-professional just below it, and the bulk of the population spreading out below these two. There is no pretense of equality in Comte's order, any more than there is of individual liberty" (Nisbet 1978: 107). For the coarticulated development of American sociology and political economy, see Sklansky 2002: ch. 4.

13   The title of Julie Winch's 2000 republication of *Sketches*, "The Elite of Our People," invokes an earlier phrase used by *Freedom's Journal's* editor, John Russwurm; the term does not appear in *Sketches,* perhaps because Willson (2000: 82) was concerned about promoting socially exclusive "invidious distinctions."

14   This liberal ideal of mobility existed in parallel with contemporary moral discourses about Christian perfectibility or "elevation," and the concomitant dynamics of market (Rael 2004: 32). This mode of self-culture would, in the context of African American activist culture, be seminal to discourses of racial uplift.

15   Martin Burke (1995: 124) emphasizes that "Anglo-American liberalism [. . .] did not involve a categorical assertion of classlessness. A 'classless' society [. . .] did not mean one exempt from 'natural' differences, but one without an intergenerational perpetuation of unnatural distinctions."

16   Patrick Rael's formulation captures the material/social convergence assumed to inhere in norms for respectability. "Respectability largely meant that one had, through dint of industry and perseverance, cultivated one's inner character sufficiently to harvest the rewards of material success. Most importantly, this potential was available to all" (Rael 2002: 131). The "politics of respectability" was how Evelyn Brooks Higgenbotham labeled the reforming discourse promoted by end-of-the-century Baptist women in *Righteous Discontent* (1993). However, the phrase now circulates across historical periods and disciplines as a form of shorthand identifying social activities dedicated to individual reform or uplift, as opposed to activities that strive specifically for structural political transformations.

17   Historian Julie Winch has described some of the conflicts that took place over the most effective strategies for promoting racial equality among the African Americans leaders that populate Willson's text. The first African Americans convention movement between 1830 and 1835 sought to establish a national forum for African American activism, principally to regain suffrage. But four years after the initiation of this national movement, Philadelphian minister, William Whipper and other local leaders established a competing convention organization, the American Moral Reform Society (AMRS), devoted to a specifically interracial effort for social reform (Winch 1988: 103). Other conflicts would have concerned which political party would best serve disenfranchised African Americans.

18 Malone (2004: 190) explains the condition of "electoral capture" that placed African American voters in the frustrating position of having nowhere to go politically except to the Whigs. In tried-and-true fashion the Democrats opted for voter suppression, i.e. disenfranchisement, to ensure their dominance over the Whigs. The headline refers to a county election in which African Americans voters were a decisive factor. Reprinted in *National Anti-Slavery Standard*, October 9, 1845. (Cited in Spires 2019: 279 fn. 97.)

19 Willson's vivid description of these interpersonal rivalries raises the question of how else they might be interpreted. Bourdieu's analysis of linguistic "style" suggests that these personalizing characterizations tend to abstract from the social conditions of its production, i.e. power relations. Are these differing interests simply "distinctions between different ways of saying" that bespeak vertical power relations or are they expressions of different content (Bourdieu 1984: 40)? How does one distinguish between the linguistic terms of civic debate aiming for consensus from an empirical reality of agents occupying different positions in the social space? Bourdieu suggests "there are no [. . .] innocent words" (40).

20 Daniel Howe describes the "antiparty strain" of Early Republic and Whig politicians. "In contemporary usage, a 'faction' was a party that pursued its self-interest to the detriment of the common interest. [. . .] Faction represented a group of people not under the sway of conscience and prudence; it was a collective form of 'passion'" (Howe 1979: 52).

21 Clline (1982) documents the general rise of "numeracy" in the nineteenth-century as a political instrument, but she does not shed light on the ranked list Clamorgan uses. To date I have not been able to trace the format's antecedents.

22 Clamorgan's descent from one of the city's founders assimilates him (not unproblematically) to the hereditary legacy associated with titled European aristocrats. Bourdieu (1984) sees aristocracy as "nothing other than seniority which is the birthright of the offspring of ancient families [. . .] this initial status-derived capital [. . .] manifest the rarest conditions of acquisition, that is the social power over time which is tacitly recognized as the supreme excellence: to possess things from the past [in Clamorgan's case a recognized family name], i.e. accumulated, crystallized history" (70–71). Yet, it's clear that the chronicler's use of the term "aristocracy" also refers more generally to the upper layer of a strata in a stratified society.

23 In her scholarly edition of this text, Julie Winch unearths the intriguing fact that Clamorgan seriously inflated the wealth of his subjects (Clamorgan 1999: 18).

24 Clamorgan (1999) silently revises line 203 from epistle 4 in *An Essay on Man,* in keeping with his agenda: the actual line reads "*Worth* (not "wealth") makes the man, the want of it, the fellow."

25 This political interpretation is available on account of Julie Winch's extensive annotations.

26 The entire Clamorgan clan accrued wealth through real estate, barbaring, and catering, but Cyprian and his two brothers' principal occupation was litigating the title (generally unsuccessfully) to the lands which Spain had given his grandfather, the Clamorgan patriarch, for services rendered, but which had not been recognized by the US government. (Winch 2011, *The Clamorgans*, 5–6).

27 Bourdieu (1984: 24) describes a "property of all aristocracies" as "the essence in which they see themselves refuses to be contained in any definition. Escaping petty rules and regulations, it is, by nature, freedom." Another "privilege" Clamorgan exercises as an "aristocrat" is exaggerating the amount of wealth held by these individuals. Julie Winch makes this point in her edition of *The Colored Aristocracy* (Clamorgan 1999: 18).

28 As mentioned above, the group of formerly enslaved wealthy women includes Willson's own mother, Elizabeth.

29 As Barbara and Karen Fields (2014: 266–68) explain in underscoring these complicated realities, the history and social dynamics of race in the United States were constructed on a bedrock of labor inequality that had everything to do with class hierarchies: "Afro-Americans began their history in slavery, a class status so abnormal [. . .] that it required an extraordinary ideological rationale—which then and ever since has gone by the name *race*." "The initial designation of Afro-Americans as a race on the basis of their class position has colored all subsequent discussion of inequality [. . .] In racial disguise, inequality wears a surface camouflage that makes inequality in its most general form—the form that marks and distorts every aspect of our social and political hard to see, harder to discuss, and nearly impossible to tackle." In another context, Stuart Hall (1978: 394) states: "Race is the modality in which class is lived."

30 McCune Smith's analysis of African Americans' lack of unity was itself uneven: compare his "common oppression" perspective from May 12, 1854, in *Frederick Douglass's Paper* with his exasperated assessment elsewhere. A year later, on September 21, 1855, McCune Smith offers a radically different understanding for African Americans' lack of political solidarity: "the reason why we cannot be led by one of ourselves may be found in the fact that whilst we bear a common relation to the whites— attraction—we bear the opposite relation to each other—repulsion. [. . .] This attraction to the whites, and repulsion from each other is but an instance of a general law. [. . .] *it is our natural state*" (Stauffer 2006: 124).

References

Ball, Erica. 2012. *To Live an Antislavery Life: Personal Politics and the Antebellum Black Middle Class.* Athens: Univ. of Georgia Press.

Barlow, Tani. 2021. *In the Event of Women.* Durham, NC: Duke Univ. Press.

Blumin, Stuart. 1989. *The Emergence of the Middle Class: Social Experience in the American City*. New York: Cambridge Univ. Press.

Bonner, Christopher James. 2020. *Remaking the Republic: Black Politics and the Creation of American Citizenship*. Philadelphia: Univ. of Pennsylvania Press.

Bourdieu, Pierre. 1984. *Distinction: A Social Critique of the Judgement of Taste*. Cambridge, MA: Harvard Univ. Press.

Burke, Martin J. 1995. *The Conundrum of Class: Public Discourse on the Social Order in America*. Chicago: Univ. of Chicago Press.

Bushman, Richard. 1992. *The Refinement of America*. New York: Knopf.

Clamorgan, Cyprian. 1999. *The Colored Aristocracy of St. Louis*. Edited by Julie Winch. Columbia: Univ. of Missouri Press.

Cline, Patricia C. 1982. *A Calculating People: The Rise of Numeracy in Early America*. Chicago: Univ. of Chicago Press.

Cornell, Saul. 1990. "Aristocracy Assailed: The Ideology of Backcountry Anti-Federalism." *Journal of American History* 76, no. 4 (March): 1148–72.

Delany, Martin. 1852. *The Condition, Elevation, Emigration and Destiny of the Colored People of the United States. Political Considered*. https://search.alexanderstreet.com/view/work/bibliographic_entity%7Cbibliographic_details%7C4391178.

Du Bois, W. E. B. (1899) 2007. *The Philadelphia Negro*. New York: Oxford Univ. Press.

Fields, Barbara J., and Karen E. 2014. *Racecraft: The Soul of Inequality in America*. New York: Verso.

Goloboy, Jennifer. 2019. *Charleston and the Emergence of Middle Class Culture in the Revolutionary Era*. Athens: Univ. of Georgia Press.

Hall, Stuart et al. 1978. *Policing the Crisis*. Macmillan.

Harris, Leslie. 2003. *In the Shadow of Slavery: African Americans in New York City, 1626–1863*. Chicago: Univ. of Chicago Press.

Hartog, Hendrig. 1987. "The Constitution of Aspiration and 'The Rights That Belong to Us All." *Journal of American History* 74, no. 3: 1013–34.

Howe, Daniel Walker. 1979. *The Political Culture of the American Whigs*. Chicago: University of Chicago Press.

Hyde, Carrie. 2018. *Civic Longing: The Speculative Origins of U.S. Citizenship*. Cambridge, MA: Harvard Univ. Press.

Jones, Martha S. 2018. *Birthright Citizens: A History of Race and Rights in Antebellum America*. Cambridge, UK: Cambridge Univ. Press.

Lang, Amy Schrager. 2003. *The Syntax of Class: Writing Inequality in Nineteenth-Century America*. Princeton, NJ: Princeton Univ. Press.

Larson, John Lauritz. 2010. *The Market Revolution in America: Liberty, Ambition and the Eclipse of the Common Good*. Cambridge: Cambridge Univ. Press.

Levine, Robert. 2008. *Dislocating Race and Nation: Episodes in Nineteenth-Century American Literary Nationalism*. Chapel Hill: Univ. of North Carolina Press.

Litwack, Leon. 1961. *North of Slavery: The Negro in the Free States, 1790–1860*. Chicago: Univ. of Chicago Press.

Malone, Christopher. 2005. "Race Formation, Voting Rights, and Democratization in the Antebellum North." *New Political Science* 27, no. 2: 177–98.

McCune Smith, James. 2006. *The Works of James McCune Smith: Black Intellectual and Abolitionist.* Edited by John Stauffer. New York: Oxford Univ.
Press.

Melish, Joanne Pope. 1999. "The 'Condition' Debate and Racial Discourse in
the Antebellum North," *Journal of the Early Republic* 19, no. 4: 651–72.

Morgan, Gordon. 1997. *Towards an American Sociology: Questioning the European Construct.* New York: Praeger Books.

Muhammad, Khalil Gibran. 2010. *The Condemnation of Blackness.* Cambridge,
MA: Harvard Univ. Press.

Nash, Gary B. 1988. *Forging Freedom: The Formation of Philadelphia's Black
Community, 1720–1840.* Cambridge, MA: Harvard Univ. Press.

Nisbet, Robert. 1978. "Conservatism." In *A History of Sociological Analysis,*
edited by Tom Bottomore and Robert Nisbet. New York: Basic Books.

Peterson, Carla P. 2011. *Black Gotham: A Family History of African Americans
in Nineteenth-Century New York City.* New Haven, CT: Yale Univ. Press.

Purvis, Robert. 1838. *Appeal of Forty Thousand Citizens, Threatened with Dis-
franchisement, to the People of Pennsylvania.* Philadelphia.

Rael, Patrick. 2002. *Black Identity and Black Protest in the Antebellum North.*
Chapel Hill: Univ. of North Carolina Press.

Rael, Patrick . 2004. "Market Values in Antebellum Black Protest Thought." In
Cultural Change and the Market Revolution in America, 1789–1860, edited
by Scott C. Martin, 13–45. New York: Rowman and Littlefield.

*Report of the Proceedings of the Colored National Convention, Held at Cleveland,
Ohio on Wednesday, September 6, 1848.* 2001. In *Pamphlets of Protest,*
edited by Richard Newman, Patrick Rael, and Phillip Lapsansky. New
York: Routledge.

Rusert, Britt. 2017. *Fugitive Science: Empiricism and Freedom in Early African
American Culture.* New York: New York Univ. Press.

Santamarina, Xiomara. 2005. *Belabored Professions: Narratives of African American Working Womanhood.* Chapel Hill: Univ. of North Carolina Press.

Santamarina, Xiomara. 2006. "Thinkable Alternatives in African American
Studies." In *American Quarterly* 58, no. 1: 245–53.

Shapiro, Fred. 1984. "A note on the Origin of the term 'Social Science.' *Journal
of the History of the Behavioral Sciences* 20: 20–22.

Sklansky, Jeffrey. 2002. *Soul's Economy: Market Society and Selfhood in American Thought, 1820–1920.* Chapel Hill: Univ. of North Carolina Press.

Spires, Derrick. 2019. *The Practice of Citizenship: Black Politics and Print Culture in the Early United States.* Philadelphia: Univ. of Pennsylvania Press.

Smith, Rogers M. 1997. *Civic Ideals: Conflicting Visions of Citizenship in U.S.
History.* New Haven: Yale Univ. Press.

Stanley, Amy Dru. *From Bondage to Contract: Wage Labor, Marriage and the
Market in the age of Slave Emancipation.* New York: Oxford Univ. Press.

Stewart, James Brewer. 1998. "The Emergence of Racial Modernity and the
Rise of the White North, 1790–1840." *Journal of the Early Republic* 18, no.
2: 181–217.

Weber, Max. (1922) 2001. "Class, Status, Party." In *Max Weber: Essays in Sociology*, edited by H. H. Gerth and C. Wright Mills, 180–96. London: Routledge.

Williams, Robin. 2000. "Sociology and the Vernacular Voice: Text, Context and the Sociological Imagination." *History of the Human Sciences* 13, no. 4: 73–95.

Willson, Joseph. 2000. *Sketches of the Higher Classes of Colored Society in Philadelphia. By a Southerner.* Reprinted as *The Elite of Our People: Joseph Willson's Sketches of Black Upper-Class Life in Antebellum Philadelphia.* Edited by Julie Winch. University Park: Pennsylvania State Univ. Press.

Winch, Julie. 2011. *The Clamorgans.* New York: Hill and Wang.

Winch, Julie. 1988. *Philadelphia's Black Elite: Activism, Accommodation and the Struggle for Autonomy.* Philadelphia: Temple Univ. Pres.

Ajay Kumar Batra   Becoming "Fellow-Servants":
Slavery, Theft, and Improper Fellowship
in the Nineteenth-Century South

Abstract This article examines the role of theft as a catalyst of communal cohesion and a practice of citizenship in the everyday lives of enslaved African Americans. Historical scholars of
Atlantic slavery largely have portrayed theft as a strategic adaptation that enslaved subjects
made in order to survive the material deprivation and other brutal constraints of enslavement. In
dialogue with this scholarship, this article proposes a different view of theft as a method not
simply of surviving on unfavorable terms but of redefining the art of living. In particular, it suggests that collective practices of theft opened space for the enslaved to forge reciprocal social
and economic relationships that diverged radically from normative customs related to subsistence, creating a state of affairs in which their survival would depend upon their ability not to
endure racialized exploitation as human property, but, rather, to tend to each other's basic
needs as associates, neighbors, and friends. Through analysis of an empirical case grounded in
nineteenth-century Louisiana, this article ultimately develops the concept of *improper fellowship*
to describe the bonds of communal reciprocity that theft could encompass, bonds that prefigured alternatives to dominant, liberal ideals of freedom and models of citizenship founded in
the sanctity of property.
Keywords slavery, freedom, property, theft, citizenship

Is it morally just for a tired, hungry bondsman to
steal a bite of food from his enslaver? Frederick Douglass answered
this question in the affirmative. In his second autobiography, *My
Bondage and My Freedom* (1855), he asserts, "Within the bounds of
his just earnings, . . . the slave is fully justified in helping himself" to
the property of his own, or indeed of any, enslaver; he adds that "*such
taking is not stealing in any just sense of that word*" (Douglass 2003: 104).
Recognizing the potential for this statement of support for ostensibly
criminal activity to scandalize his otherwise sympathetic, law-abiding
audience, Douglass concedes that his view, while sincere, is unorthodox, framing it as a "profession of faith which may shock some, offend

American Literature, Volume 96, Number 4, December 2024
DOI 10.1215/00029831-11557505   © 2024 by Duke University Press

others, and be dissented from by all" (104). Yet despite making this concession, he simultaneously illustrates that his potentially aberrant view about the ethical merits of theft stands in close alignment with traditional ideas about the practice that circulated widely among the enslaved. Across an extended passage, he presents a series of persuasive arguments in defense of enslaved people's acts of theft that resonate deeply and, in some cases, conform perfectly with customary justifications that appear elsewhere in the historical record. In particular, Douglass contends that theft was fundamentally a response to chronic, often extreme material deprivation, undertaken as a "wretched necessity" due to the consistent inadequacy of provisions (103).[1] He argues, moreover, that the enslaved retained an abstract entitlement to steal "the necessaries of life" on the grounds that it was their labor which created them, reasoning that to take such necessities was, simply, to exercise "the right to supply [oneself] with what was [one's] own already" (103).[2] And he suggests that enslaved people, as articles of property themselves, logically could not be accused of stealing, as such, but only of "removing" or "taking" the property of their enslavers—for as he recalls about an instance of food theft from his own past, "the ownership of the meat was not affected by the transaction. At first, he owned it in the *tub*, and last, he owned it in *me*" (104).[3] In reciting this series of customary justifications, Douglass does not only lend credence to an unorthodox belief in the legitimacy of theft as a measured response to unjust, intolerable austerity. Crucially, he shows this belief to be grounded in a robust, alternative intellectual *doxa*, signaling its origins in the moral calculations, critical reflections, and common wisdom of fellow enslaved subjects everywhere. Indeed, he portrays theft not as a bad habit to be excused but, rather, as a mundane form of concerted action that provided occasions for the enslaved to examine, express, and redefine the basic ethical principles and obligations governing their behavior.

Building on Douglass's notion of theft as a medium for the articulation of ethical precepts, this article examines the role of theft as a catalyst for the emergence of new forms of communal cohesion in the ordinary lives of enslaved subjects. In particular, this article discusses the possibility that enslaved people's routine acts of theft generated bonds of trust, interdependence, and reciprocity that accustomed them to addressing their vital needs collectively, through coordinated, solidaristic action divorced from familiar forms of subjugation and toil. Throughout this discussion, I draw on recent historical scholarship that has urged attention to the social bonds enslaved people created in the course of practicing resistance. As Walter Johnson (2003) has suggested, the efforts of African diasporic people held in bondage to contest, subvert, or evade the mandates issued and oppressive structures built by enslavers depended on their ability to forge social and political solidarities in the flux of quotidian life. Each act of collective resistance that primary sources allow us to observe, Johnson contends, was made possible by a broad, ongoing "process of everyday organization," in which groups of enslaved people built the functional alliances and the shared senses of identity and purpose necessary to support the fulfillment of dissident goals (118). In short, for Johnson, as well as for several other scholars writing in his wake, histories of collective resistance to enslavement unfolded in parallel with the continuous and fundamentally creative remapping of day-to-day life.[4] In what follows, I suggest that this organizational work mattered not simply because it prepared the enslaved to resist the system of slavery, but also because, at times, it could express and clarify the rudiments of an existence beyond that system. I contend that enslaved people's widespread practices of theft engendered social and economic relationships that diverged in principle from dominant customs related to subsistence, materializing alternative possibilities for living. Echoing Vincent Brown's (2020: 246) assertion that enslaved subjects often desired "space to develop their own notions of belonging, status, and fairness beyond the masters' reach," I argue, specifically, that theft opened space for them to envision and to begin realizing a state of affairs in which their survival would depend upon their ability not to endure exploitation as articles of property, but rather to uphold duties of communal reciprocity as associates, neighbors, and friends.

As I illustrate below through extended, speculative analysis of an empirical case from nineteenth-century Louisiana, the informal practices of affiliation and belonging that enslaved subjects devised under the sign of theft constituted a communal form of life that stood in contradiction to dominant, liberal ideals of freedom and models of citizenship founded in the sanctity of property. As Saidiya V. Hartman (1997: 115–24) has argued, the formal abolition of slavery and the advent of emancipation did not introduce formerly enslaved people to a condition of substantial freedom but, rather, instigated a "refiguration of subjection" that perpetuated Black subjugation in practice. Throughout this prolonged, deeply quotidian process, the enduring material destitution of racialized ex-slaves rendered their reemergence on the labor market as nominally free, self-possessing individuals an initiation into novel relations of exploitation, as the exigent need to earn a living forced them to accept continued toil and rigid self-discipline as the basic costs of survival. In this article, I contend that theft, a common method of subsistence, made tangible on a daily basis an alternative to this condition of "burdened individuality" (Hartman 1997: 117) defined by constraint, compulsion, and insistent hardship. Through collaborative acts of theft, the collective I discuss below improvised communitarian social and economic relationships that effectively insulated its individual constituents from customary obligations to obtain the means of subsistence through performances of subservience and violent drudgery for the benefit of white enslavers. More specifically, as I demonstrate in sequence, these subjects devised practices of physical and social coordination, informal economic exchange, and mutual protection that made it possible for them to refuse exploitation at the hands of the white ownership class and to ensure their shared capacity to subsist by other means. In doing so, this collective transformed survival from an individual burden into a rigorously communal responsibility, prefiguring a liberated future that would diverge fundamentally from the conventional path leading from enslavement to the constraining self-possession of liberal freedom. In making this argument, I build upon recent literary and cultural studies scholarship that has examined the efforts of politically marginalized African Americans in the early United States to foster senses of belonging and collective identity "from scratch" (Mitchell 2020: 121–24), through the creation of mutually affirmative, life-sustaining bonds in the sphere of everyday interaction. In particular, extending the work of Derrick R. Spires, Koritha Mitchell, and others, I position theft as a hitherto neglected practice of citizenship that radically rejected—and summoned an alternative to— the proprietorial conception of selfhood restricting the terms of Black freedom and civic presence in the wake of emancipation.

Ultimately, this article contends that theft constituted a collective, generative refusal of normative notions of freedom and citizenship rooted in property. In the process, it develops the concept of *improper fellowship* to describe the cherished social bonds that both enslaved and fugitive subjects forged under the sign of theft: bonds of communal reciprocity that promised to engender the independence of Black lives from the white ownership class and from the regime of property relations underpinning coercive, exploitative institutions such as slavery and its successors. In the first of the three sections that follow, I offer a short overview of prior scholarly discourse on theft in relation to slavery. I argue that pervasive interpretations of theft as a means of surviving the degrading conditions of capitalistic enslavement have understated its potential to generate novel physical, social, and economic scripts that prefigured ways of living beyond that system.[5] Building upon this notion of theft as a method of redefining the art of living, the second section traces the efforts of one collective in southern Louisiana to develop a viable livelihood strategy centered around the theft and informal exchange of livestock and agricultural produce. I reconstruct an account of these activities through sustained analysis of a paragraph-length deposition given in 1863 by Octave Johnson, a Black man from New Orleans who had joined the collective in question following his escape from slavery less than two years prior. Reading this short, autobiographical fragment as a kind of fugitive slave narrative, I suggest that its transcription of Octave's language richly illustrates the role of theft in fostering among him and his fellows a sense of capacity, allegiance, and collective identity that transcended their shared status as subjects of oppression.[6] In the third and final section, I reflect briefly on the larger significance of subsistence theft and the bonds of fellowship it encompassed in relation to the different practices of affiliation, belonging, and citizenship documented in recent scholarship on early Black literature and print culture. Here, in closing, I suggest the importance of integrating evidence of the embodied practices of enslaved and formerly enslaved subjects into emerging scholarly narratives about how African Americans theorized and practiced citizenship outside of dominant, exclusionary political frameworks during the nineteenth century.

A Matter of Death and Life

Cursory mentions of theft occur frequently in the documentary record of Atlantic slavery, appearing abundantly in the private papers and public missives of enslavers and in the narratives, testimonies, and literary works of the enslaved. From this diffuse and heterogeneous range of examples, however, historians have distilled a stable, compelling conception of theft as a tool of survival, a pivotal bulwark against probable death by starvation. As initial assessments of theft established, its mundane, widespread occurrence in settings of enslavement was largely a ramification of the caloric and nutritional shortfalls that enslaved people dealt with on a regular basis. For instance, foundational historians of slave resistance argued that the theft of food, money, and valuable items from enslavers was a customary way for bondspeople not only to supplement their paltry rations but also to implicitly oppose their subjugation.[7] Certain others, most notably Eugene D. Genovese (1976: 607–9), echoed and revised this assertion, claiming that theft undeniably afforded access to essential material resources but ultimately conserved the hegemonic authority of enslavers over the social system as a whole.[8] In more recent discussions, scholars have retained this basic notion of theft as a necessary response to quotidian material deprivation in the process of developing more nuanced accounts of its effects. For some, the routine theft of agricultural produce for the purposes of consumption or cash sale was an ongoing assertion of economic autonomy that pressured enslavers to renegotiate terms of bondage, to recalibrate their provision of subsistence goods and other customary entitlements in accordance with enslaved people's implicit concepts of fairness.[9] For others, the acquisition of basic sustenance through theft belonged to a much broader pattern of small adaptations enslaved people made in a grueling effort simply to remain alive in a system dependent on their gradual depletion, such as truancy, shirking, and collusion with authorities.[10] Over time, then, historical scholars have tended to conceive of theft less as an open defiance of slavery's internal logic and more as an intuitive way of ameliorating the intolerable conditions slavery engendered. Yet across this evolution, scholars have maintained the basic premise that theft was born from destitution—that it emerged in response to the grave threat of death which the necropolitical institution of slavery made tangible in the everyday lives of its malnourished, overworked subjects.[11]

To its great credit, this regnant, economistic notion of stealing as a crime of necessity geared toward self-preservation invites recognition of the profound, exigent demands that the prospect of a miserable death placed on the enslaved, demands that ruled their behavior and demonstrably shaped their consciousness. At the same time, however, theft was never simply an effort to outrun mortal danger but also a unique exercise in creativity and vitality. Quite apart from the important material advantages theft could afford, its quotidian enactments provided temporary arenas in which bondspeople could not only break their regular patterns of violent drudgery but also generate new, vital practices of physical dexterity and social coordination. On this key point, Genovese's (1976: 605–6) analysis is singularly illuminating: Although he ultimately concludes that theft was primarily a survival tactic, he recognizes and richly illustrates that it also involved a significant "sporting element," insofar as it often gave its perpetrators scope for exhibiting their ingenuity, skill, and cooperation in dynamic scenarios. For example, tales of theft recorded in slave narratives often describe the improvised steps taken to conceal stolen goods from intrusive surveillance, as in one case Genovese (1976: 606) cites where a woman boiling a stolen hog hid the contraband from an approaching overseer by covering the kettle, placing her young child atop its lid, and claiming that the arrangement was simply "a steam bath for [the child's] terrible cold" (Clarke 1845: 26). In other sources, the routine theft of hogs, chickens, cattle, and other livestock is shown to have required expert levels of timing, agility, proprioception, and situational awareness, as stray animal sounds or forensic evidence such as blood or feathers could prove incriminating (Genovese 1976: 606). Moreover, as demonstrated across numerous testimonial sources (including one that this essay will examine at length), fugitives from slavery who had abandoned farms and plantations for nearby swamps and wooded areas often continued to subsist partly on goods stolen from their old estates and, in doing so, depended on the supportive vigilance and collaboration of friends who had stayed behind (Lichtenstein 1988: 419; Diouf 2014: 136–42). Of course, theft was by no means the only practice which incited such displays of vitality and creativity on the part of enslaved people, from whom the elemental tasks of agricultural and other forms of labor routinely required not only technical skill but also savvy and cooperation.[12] In their acts of theft, however, bondspeople could decouple their vital capacities from the demands of their enslavers, creating habits and forming social bonds that reflected more fully the breadth of their potential as living beings.

Called into existence by the persistent terror of death, the scenes of theft that litter the archives of slavery convey a paradoxical sense of aliveness, illustrating the concrescence of vital patterns of thought, embodiment, and social relation among mortally endangered subjects.[13] In making this point, my aim isn't to revalue certain desperate measures taken by the enslaved as acts of virtue, glory, or heroism; rather, my aim is to elucidate and ultimately name the alternative possibilities for living that such measures, at times, made visible. In a recent article assessing the impact of Orlando Patterson's concept of social death on contemporary studies of Atlantic slavery, historian Vincent Brown (2009) calls for researchers to examine more closely how slavery's constitutive exercises of force served not merely to negate the lives of the enslaved but also, crucially, to form them as living subjects.[14] Echoing the writings of David Scott and other recent theorists of power, subjection, and agency, Brown (2009: 1244) contends that the brutal domination of enslaved people did not simply relegate them to a state of terminal incapacity, but it rather directed them toward vital courses of action that constituted a "politics of survival": a daily,

multifaceted struggle to regenerate life in the face of impending catas-
trophe.[15] On the one hand, theft—as a practice that directly answered
the threat of death with dynamic, life-affirming activity—neatly epito-
mizes this modality of struggle, encapsulating the dual determination
of enslaved people to both defend life and express vitality amid utterly
abject conditions. Yet on the other hand, to incorporate theft into the
politics of survival that Brown conceptualizes is to risk constraining
the significance of the many different expressions of vitality it encompassed. More specifically, locating the practice of theft in the horizon
of survival runs the risk of foreclosing the possibility that its complex,
lively enactments were steps toward other, perhaps liberated horizons
beyond the pale of enslavement. If scenes of theft represent the efforts
of enslaved people to survive the condition of enslavement, do such
scenes ever represent their efforts, or their desires, to create novel,
habitable worlds exterior to that condition? What alternative arrangements of Black diasporic life are prefigured in the dynamic actions,
routines, and social bonds that theft engendered? Under the sign of
theft, how did the enslaved not merely subsist but take small steps
toward redefining the art of living?

As Karl Marx (2021: 70) wrote in reference to the endemic stealing
of wood by destitute residents of the nineteenth-century German
Rhineland, "an instinctive sense of justice lives in [the] customs of the
poor." Building on this assertion, which credits subjects of dispossession and exploitation as prudent judges of right and fairness, I argue
in what follows that enslaved people's customary practices of theft
expressed not merely an instinctive sense of justice but a holistic, if
incipient vision of a just society. I develop this argument through sustained analysis of a specific case drawn from the rural outskirts of
New Orleans, Louisiana, in the early years of the Civil War. Recorded
across two short testimonial sources, the case involves a small group
of fugitives from slavery and bonded accomplices who devised a semi-
permanent livelihood strategy centered around the theft and exchange
of livestock, agricultural produce, and other necessities.[16] In the course
of building and implementing this strategy, this collective contributed
to the rival geography of the plantation system, instituting protean
arrangements of life, labor, and resources that supported its constituents' efforts to get by and intersected with other forms of underground
economic activity.[17] Beyond merely easing the daily burden of survival,
however, this strategy moreover transformed survival into a communal
responsibility: Through routine acts of theft, these subjects developed
lively patterns of collaborative action that affirmed the value of their

basic material needs and, concurrently, engendered bonds of trust, interdependence, and reciprocal obligation among them. In this way, theft served as a medium for these oppressed, pauperized subjects to chart the coordinates of an alternative, communitarian social order, affording them the space to prefigure a postemancipation future in which cherished bonds of communal reciprocity would negate the persistent vulnerability of Black lives to exploitation as burdened, self-possessing individuals. Indeed, as I argue in closing, the collective's transient success in forming this improper fellowship on the edges of the plantation system constituted a practice of belonging that displaced—and expressed an alternative to—the proprietorial notion of selfhood tacitly structuring conventional models of Black citizenship that emerged during the nineteenth century.

"I Called the Party to My Assistance": Octave's "Fellow-Servants"

In 1863, an agent of the US War Department transcribed the deposition of Octave Johnson, a Black man from Louisiana who had fled enslavement and enlisted in the fight against the Confederacy. Octave was born in New Orleans in 1840, began his life as the property of a man named Arthur Thiboux, and, from an early age, came to know slavery as a condition of intimate exposure to the arbitrary whims of whites. During his childhood and adolescence, as he acquired skills in the cooperage trade, he largely remained in Thiboux's good graces, claiming to have been "treated pretty well at home" (Blassingame 1977: 394–95).[18] At the age of only fifteen, however, he lost contact with his mother after her sale to a distant location, enduring a common form of family separation that would have instilled painful awareness of their shared status as commodities. As Octave entered adulthood, he underwent a change of setting that likely expanded this awareness. In 1861, Thiboux sold Octave to one S. Contrell in the nearby rural parish of St. James, where he began fabricating casks for use in storing sugar (*D* 395).[19] Here, under the notorious scrutiny and discipline commonly associated with the intensive process of sugar cultivation and refinement, Octave would have experienced abuse that not only reinforced his position as disposable property but also made visible his concurrent status as an exploited laborer. Indeed, as his deposition indicates, the continued escalation of his twinned obligations as both an object of domination and a source of profit ultimately motivated him to decamp from the plantation and to make a go of subsisting in the nearby swamps. In abandoning this scene of subjection, however, Octave did not simply pursue relief from the gratuitous violence and extreme exploitation of enslavement or from the conditions of isolation and material deprivation that accompanied them. Over and above such relief, he furthermore contributed to the construction of an alternative infrastructure for sustaining Black life on the margins of the plantation system, one rooted in duties not of individual toil but of communal reciprocity.

In the world of enslavement that Octave inhabited, survival was never guaranteed but rather pieced together amid conditions of artificial scarcity. During his time in St. James, his daily activities derived their structure from the basic imperative to earn a living, to procure the means of subsistence through compulsory participation in coerced labor and irregular, market-based exchange. Octave's access to basic necessities depended primarily on his capacity to meet the productivity demands associated with a narrowly defined role in the long, involved process of sugarcane cultivation. In contrast to the overwhelming majority of his fellow workers—who planted, cut, and processed cane in closely monitored gangs—Octave "worked by task," producing fixed quantities of wooden barrels sufficient to house the plantation's anticipated yield (D 394–95). To a degree, this occupation would have insulated him from the brutal excesses of corporal punishment and physical exhaustion that defined gang labor on Louisiana sugar estates, where the imminent dangers of frost damage and other forms of biodegradation during harvest season demanded a work rate that was impossible to sustain (Follett 2016: 74).[20] Yet his relative distance from such brutalities did not shield him from a fundamental obligation—which he held in common with gang laborers—to submit to unreasonable exploitation in the interest of self-preservation. Outside of these performances of labor, Octave and other inhabitants of Louisiana's sugarcane region also attempted to acquire the means of subsistence through the independent production and exchange of agricultural staples. In this context, as in the sugar-producing colonies of the Caribbean, it was customary for the enslaved to maintain small kitchen gardens and provision grounds that yielded vegetables, livestock, and cash crops, all of which proved valuable as sources of nutrition and, more frequently, income gained through sale. Such commerce created markets in which malnourished, cash-poor bondspeople could obtain some of the resources necessary to supplement the inadequate provisions to which their coerced labor nominally entitled them.[21] By addressing such gaps in this manner, however, they in effect absorbed the costs of their own self-maintenance, absolving enslavers of the duty to provide genuine guarantees of subsistence and pinning their hopes of survival on a disorganized array of precarious, self-interested enterprises.[22] Forced to make do under these conditions, Octave would have become accustomed to conceiving of survival as merely a contingent outcome of degrading toil and uncoordinated transaction.[23]

At a certain point, however, Octave abandoned this strenuous pursuit of subsistence. Over time, the pressures that the plantation system placed on his body and his faculties exceeded the limits of his tolerance, motivating him to explore the option of subsisting outside its confines. Octave worked on the Contrell estate for, at most, several months: he arrived at some point in 1861, left on an unknown date, and later surfaced during the Civil War at a Union-controlled fort in 1862 or 1863. Throughout this period, as a new arrival from the city, he would have needed to act quickly to conform his habits to the established patterns of exertion and rest that prevailed in the rural plantation setting. His testimony sheds very little light on his experience of this process of subjectivation—that is, on the granular measures of discipline and coercion that pressured him to internalize the unfamiliar as routine. Yet on one occasion, quotidian forms of physical intimidation and labor management became unbearable for Octave, impelling him toward not compliant action but a bid for escape. "One morning," he recounts, "the bell was rung for me to go to work so early that I could not see, and I lay still, because I was working by task" (*D* 395). Here, in response to an untimely intrusion of sound into his field of perception, Octave passively refused the directive implicit in the peal of the bell, abiding, instead, by the prompt toward continued rest implicit in nature's visual cue of darkness. As he remained motionless, claiming a few extra moments of sleep in his bed or at his workbench, he chose temporary insentience over the alternative of conscious submission to an unjust ("so early") revision of his ordinary routine.[24] In enacting this inert refusal of his duties, however, Octave summoned a threat of violent correction that he could not bear to face: Upon finding that "the overseer was going to have [him] whipped" for his insubordination, he "ran away to the woods" to evade this punishment, and he thus brought an effective end to his term of bondage (*D* 395). In this pivotal scenario, Octave's effort to interrupt his formation as an enslaved subject for only a short interval before dawn incited a drastic escalation in his vulnerability to the prevailing forces of domination. Faced with such escalation, he moved to divest his capacities entirely from the arduous, exploitative struggle for survival mandated by the plantation system, seeking out refuge not in momentary unconsciousness but in permanent decampment.

Octave's instantaneous shift in status from conscript to refugee of bondage released him from the familiar imperative to earn his living through degrading toil but, at first, forced him to tolerate a similarly arduous strategy for obtaining the means of subsistence. As he began to get by not as an exploited worker but as a petty thief, he found that staying alive remained a formidable challenge—a struggle grounded in destitution and saturated with palpable coercion and risk. After his escape, Octave lived in the "woods" or swamps of St. James "for a year and a half" and became associated with a larger group of fugitives from the region (*D* 395). For this reason, his story belongs to the relatively small corpus of narratives from the South that document the efforts of self-emancipated people to build settlements outside the boundaries of local plantation regimes. Indeed, the small number of scholars who have made reference to Octave's deposition have used it to illuminate certain characteristic features of these maroon settlements in Louisiana and across the South as a whole.[25] Contrary to these assessments, however, Octave's deposition is not simply a representative illustration of petit marronage but also, crucially, a rare depiction of how material deprivation persistently encumbered self-emancipated individuals in the initial aftermath of decampment, powerfully determining how they lived their lives. In the time before Octave made contact with other fugitives, a period of "some days," his lack of sustenance compelled him to maneuver in perilous solitude near his old estate to obtain stolen goods for exchange or personal consumption (McKaye 1864: 11). His language in the deposition registers his awareness of the coercive nature of this predicament, suggesting that he "*had* to steal [his] food"—that his acts of theft perhaps did not express defiance but certainly answered a tangible compulsion (*D* 395, emphasis added). As he "took turkeys, chickens and pigs" from livestock pens across the countryside, including, to be sure, some animals kept by enslaved people, he placed himself in jeopardy of detection and punishment, in effect risking life and limb simply to mitigate the threat of slow death by starvation (*D* 395). After his escape, then, as familiar methods of subsistence disintegrated, theft enabled Octave to remain alive amid precarious material conditions. Yet despite the efficacy of this adaptation, it consigned him to continue experiencing survival as, above all, an unwieldy burden, a source of hardship in the form of danger and duress.

This solitary ordeal of self-preservation did not last, however. It formed the context in which Octave encountered and eventually joined the aforesaid group of fugitives, beholding in their habits an alternative vision of survival as a more organized, collective effort, enacted on a broad basis of stability and collaboration. Like Octave, this group of fugitives lived in the uncultivated swamplands that usually bordered Louisiana sugar plantations, maintaining a campsite roughly "four miles in the rear of the [Contrell] plantation house" (*D* 395). Owing to their expanse and impermeability, these swamps were often free of supervision, and thus they provided convenient living space for not solely fugitives from slavery but also poor, landless Acadians, who negated their eligibility for wage exploitation through subsistence-level wood-cutting and moss-gathering (Scott 1999: 114). Octave's comment that he and the other fugitives "slept on logs and burned cypress leaves to make a smoke and keep away mosquitoes" suggests that their own activity may have overlapped with this informal economic sector (*D* 395).[26] Moreover, this image of heavy wooden beds and elaborate routines for repelling pests suggests that their campsite was at least a semi-permanent addition to the extant landscape. Despite setting down roots in the peripheries, however, Octave and his companions in the swamp still resided near enough to prior sites of captivity to maintain connections with the people whom they had left behind. As the collective's "number . . . increased to thirty, of whom ten were women," it inevitably would have included fugitives with lasting ties to multiple different sugar estates and other worksites throughout the region (*D* 395).[27] Covert efforts on the part of the fugitives to perpetuate these ties—bonds of friendship, kinship, intimacy, and religious belief, as well as gendered duties of care and remittance—would have done more than create deep social continuities across nominally bifurcated zones of enslavement and desertion. Furthermore, such efforts would have built practical foundations for the fugitives to access plantation storehouses and livestock pens, incursions which were vitally necessary for their survival but routinely viable only with the support of trusted friends on the inside. For Octave, then, as a solitary fugitive with a tenuous grip on subsistence, the experience of integration into this collective would have recalibrated his habituated conception of what it takes to stay alive. Under these conditions, survival occurred not merely as a sequela of individual struggle but rather as a result of intentional place-making and collaboration, both separate from and in conjunction with plantation geographies.[28]

Octave and his associates in the swamp thus built an infrastructure for ameliorating their individual struggles for survival, remapping the landscape to enable the sharing of resources and of the contacts necessary for procuring them. On a more fundamental level, however, the routine practice of theft that they developed in this setting—the focal point of their shared livelihood strategy—engendered among them relations of interdependence that radically transformed survival from an individual burden into a rigorously communal responsibility. In particular, as demonstrated in their routine efforts to steal heavy livestock from nearby enclosures, theft provided a platform for them to forge bonds of trust and to assume duties of mutual protection that negated their status as individuals solely responsible for their own self-maintenance, placing them into relation, instead, as committed stewards of one another's vital needs and well-being. As Octave recounts in his deposition, "sometimes we would rope beef cattle and drag them out to our hiding place" (*D* 395). Here, the characteristic concision of Octave's language in transcription belies the sensational dynamism inherent in the scenario he is recalling, one which would have encompassed multiple feats of planning, skill, and social coordination. In order to ensure that their raid was feasible, Octave and his accomplices first would have had to gather information about surveillance patterns on the targeted estate, either through illicit conversations with enslaved residents or direct missions of reconnaissance. Then, having identified a viable window of time for action in between patrols, the small, mobile band would have stationed itself to strike quickly during that window, perhaps hiding in some dense growth on the fringes of the targeted estate in anticipation of the proper moment. Once that moment arrived, the appropriation of the cattle needed to unfold across a swift, taut, and brutal series of coordinated movements: In concert and in close sequence, the band would have lassoed the animal, silenced it with a fatal blow, hogtied it, and hoisted it out of its manmade or natural enclosure.[29] As they began subsequently to "drag" the animal back to their campsite or another secret location—carrying one half ton of dead weight across a considerable distance—they might have discussed, in hushed tones, their exact plans for butchering the cattle and storing it underground for later consumption or exchange, a time-sensitive procedure carefully orchestrated to avert prying eyes and canine noses. Across the many phases of cattle theft, then, Octave and his associates faced the dangerous ordeal of subsistence as a cohesive unit, placing immense trust in each other to execute the furtive, highly intricate choreography necessary to secure their livelihood while avoiding detection and certain punishment. Through this conscious embrace of interdependence in pursuit of sustenance, this band of fugitives became practiced in carrying the burden of survival not in miserable solitude but as a capable multitude, unanimous in its determination to provide for and to protect Black life through repeated seizures of private property.

The vital forms of physical and social coordination that the practice of theft encompassed thus recast Octave and his accomplices not only as partners in crime, but as partners in the formation of a nascent communal entity on the margins of the plantation system, a small syndicate of destitute subjects sustained by their practical commitment to preserve and to protect each other. Over time, the fugitives' continued expression of this commitment in their relationships with one another and with their enslaved associates moreover generated a powerful sense of allegiance and collective identity encompassing both groups, a sense memorialized in an ephemeral linguistic excess present at a crucial moment in Octave's deposition. As I have noted, the fugitives' efforts to subsist via theft depended upon access, information, and countersurveillance furnished by allies living inside plantation boundaries. At certain times, however, the support these enslaved allies provided extended beyond mere complicity with incursions and, instead, addressed subsistence needs directly. For example, Octave recalls, "we obtained matches from our friends on the plantation" (*D* 395). Although it is unclear what, if anything, the fugitives provided in exchange for their access to a necessity as elemental as fire—a source of light, warmth, and cooking fuel, and a layer of protection against mosquito-borne illness—this omission does not rule out the possibility that the matches were one end of a reciprocal bargain. Indeed, the fugitives commonly engaged their enslaved "friends" in informal exchanges of stolen goods that displayed characteristics of mutual aid, creating enduring duties of reciprocity between both groups and fundamentally intertwining their disparate struggles for survival.[30] As Octave recounts, "we furnished meat to our fellow-servants in the field, who would return corn meal" (395). In this laconic, yet memorable line, Octave does more than document for posterity the manner in which the fugitives routinely cooperated with enslaved fieldhands to correct imbalances in the distribution of needed nutritional resources, bartering rare, calorie-dense meat products for run-of-the-mill agricultural staples. Crucially, he suggests that this effort on the part of the two groups to shoulder the daily burden of survival in concert undermined the divides of space and status separating their constituents, granting them unity as "fellow-servants." At first glance, this curious term registers as a moment of misidentification, an imprecise, erroneous elision of the significant distinction between Octave, a fugitive from slavery, and his bonded counterparts held in continuous captivity. In the context of the testimony, however, the term reads as an instance of catachresis, in which Octave's misuse of the language of servitude conveys an important suggestion: that the fugitives and their enslaved friends, as *fellow-servants*, modeled a form of fellowship rooted in diligent service—not to the ownership class but, rather, to each other and for the common good.

Following this interpretive cue provided in Octave's own colorful language, I contend that he and his "fellow-servants" of all formal statuses constituted an improper fellowship: Through acts of theft, they wove a fabric of social and economic relationships that negated familiar compulsions to subsist by means of degrading toil or solitary struggle, forging durable bonds of communal reciprocity that could, in theory, perpetuate the independence of Black life from the regime of property relations underpinning exploitative, coercive institutions such as slavery and its successors. In doing so, they showed it was possible to define Black liberation not as a condition of "burdened individuality" rooted in self-possession, but, rather, as a movement toward thriving rooted in belonging to a communal entity. In the process of outlining this new form of life, however, Octave and his accomplices had to contend with breaches of trust and attempts at recapture that imperiled their sense of communal cohesion, placing them at risk of renewed subjugation. Though the fugitives had succeeded in building a trusted network of enslaved accomplices and trading partners, there were occasions when "those at work would betray those in the swamp, for fear of being implicated in their escape" (395). In such cases, the threat of punishment compelled enslaved people residing in climates of terror to give authorities information that would have left the fugitives increasingly vulnerable to apprehension, forcing them to adapt their habits, to alter their usual routes and strategies for trafficking and storing contraband. Octave's deposition offers no precise chronicle of how specific acts of betrayal transformed the livelihood strategy of the fugitives; however, it does discuss one technique of repression used against them that would have gained efficacy from the aid of informants: namely, attack dogs. As he recalls, "Eugene Jardean, master of hounds, hunted for us for three months" (395).[31] Such protracted exposure to Jardean's hounds would have taken a profound physical and psychological toll on the fugitives, likely forcing them to lose sleep, spend time in hiding, veer dangerously away from familiar thoroughfares, suffer injuries, and, at times, run for their lives. Yet, in addition to posing these immediate threats to the welfare of the fugitives, Jardean's hounds also entailed the hazard of reenslavement.[32] The experience of being pursued and terrorized by this pack of hounds would have made tangible the danger not only of dismemberment, but also of sudden disappearance from the microcosmic world of the swamp and from the alternative configurations of life and vital resources that this world encompassed. Thus, as Octave and his associates persisted in their efforts to form a communal entity on the margins of the plantation system, forces of coercion and repression originating in the center of that system exerted a continual, disruptive influence upon their routines, threatening to return them to familiar conditions of domination.

It was under intense pressure from these disruptive forces, however, that the fugitives expressed their status as an emergent class of "fellow-servants" most fully, generating a spectacle of mutual protection in the face of present danger. As Octave endured a dramatic encounter with Jardean's hounds near the end of his eighteen months in the swamp, his fellows embraced his survival as a communal responsibility and, in doing so, assured his continued liberty from racialized subjugation. Before ending his deposition with a few short remarks on his enlistment in the Corps d'Afrique, a segregated Union regiment of Black soldiers from Louisiana, Octave describes the episode in question in unusual detail.[33] He recalls:

> one day twenty hounds came after me; I called the party to my assistance and we killed eight of the bloodhounds, then we all jumped into the Bayou Fanfron; the dogs followed us and the alligators caught six of them, "the alligators preferred dogs flesh to personal flesh," we escaped and came to Camp Parapet [in Jefferson Parish]. (D 395)[34]

As this rendering suggests, Octave's narrow escape from Jardean's dogs was a deeply chaotic fracas of interspecies violence and collaboration. His initial effort to outrun the hounds on his own spawned a larger confrontation in which a group of fellow fugitives and a congregation of predatory alligators combined to dispatch greater than half of the canine assailants. His accounting of the casualties notes that his brethren killed more hounds than the alligators did, in the process "becoming thoroughly exhausted, with their arms and legs torn by the fangs" (McKaye 1864: 11).[35] Yet he also portrays the intervention of the alligators as more decisive in ending the battle, noting, in his own words, that the animals' unaccountable "preference" for dogs rather than humans—a serendipitous quirk of nature—spared the spent fugitives further hardship and allowed time for them to reach safety. In constructing this narrative, however, Octave does not only commemorate the unwitting complicity of nature in delivering him and the other fugitives to salvation from the hounds' menacing pursuit. More than this, he offers one final, enduring image of the fugitives standing together in defense of Black life, moving with a shared proprioception and indivisible unity to rebuff the encroaching forces of recapture. He documents a moment in history when the coalescence of a communal entity—an insistence not to be single—effectively halted the reintegration of poor, formerly enslaved subjects into an oppressive economic system, rendering Blackness not an inflicted condition of exposure to exploitation but, rather, a state of openness to the promise of belonging.[36] Indeed, he enables us to glimpse the precise instant when an assortment of refugees from capitalistic enslavement appears, if only for a moment, to take the form of a political entity—"the party," an improper fellowship of virtuous rogues stealing life to redeem the art of living.

Theft as Citizenship

In the foregoing, I have examined the efforts of a group of enslaved and once-enslaved people to organize a communal form of life on the margins of the plantation system. Our prism for beholding their efforts has been the chronicle of a short period in the life of Octave Johnson, a man who became involved in their experiment through a series of shifts in his experience of subjection. During his years of slavery in New Orleans and St. James, Octave endured conditions of coercion and artificial scarcity that forced him to subsist through performances of toil in deference to white enslavers. His defection from these conditions released him from the intolerable, continually escalating obligations of capitalistic enslavement, holding in merciful abeyance the familiar pressure to earn a living through performances of violent drudgery. At the same time, however, his defection also renewed his vulnerability to starvation, forcing him to subsist through dangerous, solitary acts of theft. His self-emancipation from slavery thus consigned him, at least initially, to continue suffering indignities in his pursuit of survival, as he struggled to obtain sustenance in miserable, precarious solitude. Yet over time—as Octave dove deeper into the groove of the swamp—the relationships he built with the other fugitives he met there acquainted him with an entirely different style of living in which survival, erstwhile an individual burden, would emerge anew as a rigorously communal responsibility. Through repeated acts of theft and economic exchange involving their enslaved "friends," these associates forged bonds of trust, interdependence, and reciprocity that enabled them to live without acquiescing to the customary hardships of enslavement and fugitivity. In the process of constructing this alternative infrastructure for sustaining Black life, they became known to each other as "fellow-servants": subjects bound in faithful, scrupulous service not to owners of property but, rather, to the common needs and desires of their collective. And ultimately, as constituents of this improper fellowship, Octave and his comrades in the swamp made tangible for themselves the possibility of an existence apart from the regime of property relations underpinning coercive, exploitative institutions such as slavery and its successors—modeling, if only for a moment, a liberated future in which the "burdened individuality" of liberal freedom would remain graciously unclaimed.

The movement of Union troops through southern Louisiana in 1862 forced Octave and his unnamed accomplices to vacate their residence in the swamp. Their provisional form of life remained merely transient, and what became of them remains largely uncertain.[37] Yet in spite of this ephemerality, Octave's record of their actions has enduring relevance as a generative, critical engagement with roughly contemporaneous theorizations of Black citizenship recently illuminated by scholars. As Derrick R. Spires illustrates in *The Practice of Citizenship* (2019), the paradigmatic exclusion of African Americans from the prerogatives of formal United States citizenship prompted Black writers of the late eighteenth and early nineteenth centuries to define the concept not merely as a fixed status or set of entitlements conferred by the white supremacist state but, rather, as a dynamic set of practices cultivated primarily in spaces beyond state sanction. More specifically, through their advocacy of local political organizing, economic cooperation, public dialogue, and other collective practices as ideal forms of Black civic presence, these writers envisioned citizenship as a matter not of who one *is* in the eyes of the state but of what one *does* alongside and for the benefit of others.[38] The embodied activities discussed in the preceding case study align closely with these written prescriptions, expressing the willingness of Octave and his "fellow-servants" to respond to their organized abandonment at the hands of the state by building an alternative social order rooted in values of "mutual responsibility, responsiveness, and active engagement, . . . in which membership and individual rights come with moral obligations to a collective" (Spires 2019: 5). Indeed, in Octave's rendering, theft becomes visible as one of many practices of Black citizenship theorized and enacted across the early United States that encapsulated the commitment of African Americans residing on the margins of the nation-state to fostering affiliation, interdependence, and a substantive sense of belonging through the adoption of a communitarian ethos in their daily interactions.[39] At the same time, however, theft did not merely encapsulate this commitment but also, uniquely, demonstrated the potential for this commitment to be radicalized. Under the aegis of theft, as Octave's deposition illustrates, enslaved and formerly enslaved subjects reconfigured the quotidian in a way that unsettled the very roots of Black subordination under racial capitalism, severing the small matter of subsistence from its customary moorings in private ownership, material destitution, and ensuing forms of racialized exploitation. Moreover, through concerted, collective action, they established solidarities and assumed identities that strayed beyond the proprietorial notion of selfhood defining normative, restrictive models of Black freedom and citizenship in the wake of emancipation. In short, becoming "fellow-servants," they arrayed themselves in opposition to the primacy of property in organizing human affairs and, in turn, defined Black citizenship as the practice of building another world in which the predations of slavery and capitalism would be fundamentally unthinkable. Present in every corner of the archives of slavery, stories of theft such as this one stand before us as scattered, luminous illustrations of the determination of the enslaved to pursue justice through radical transformation of the conditions in which life is lived.

Ajay Kumar Batra is an assistant professor of English at Vanderbilt University. His current book project examines the convergences of abolitionism and communism that surface in African diasporic literature and politics in the eighteenth- and nineteenth-century Atlantic World.

Notes

I acknowledge debts of gratitude to the following readers for commentary and conversations that shaped this article profoundly: Isaac Blacksin, Ingrid Diran, and Ana Schwartz, as well as audiences at the USC Society of Fellows in the Humanities, the McNeil Center for Early American Studies, and the UCLA Americanist Research Colloquium.

1   For an illuminating discussion of how formulations of this theoretical bond between theft and material deprivation have evolved across African American literary history, see King 2007.

2   For similar formulations, see Bibb 1849: 194–96; Ball 1859: 218–19; Jackson 1847: 27–28. American landscape architect and journalist Frederick Law Olmsted (1856: 117) famously observed that this justification was widespread on plantations, its popularity stemming from enslaved people's broad subscription to "the agrarian notion . . . that the result of labor belongs of right to the laborer."

3   For other exemplary elaborations of this logic, see Olmsted 1856: 117; Stewart 1823: 249.

4   See, for example, Finch 2015; Roane 2018; Brown 2020.

5   I take the concept of capitalistic enslavement from Sayers 2012: 135.

6   My approach to analyzing Octave's deposition is informed by the recent work of Zachary McLeod Hutchins and Cassander L. Smith (2021: 2–5), who have proposed a critical method for interpreting early, narrative-based African American cultural artifacts that emphasizes how the Black individuals and collectives involved in the creation of such sources "shaped their textual presence" through their speech and actions in the material world. In line with this proposal, I emphasize how Octave's recorded speech in the deposition not only narrates his actions but also, in the process, generates the concepts necessary for understanding them.

7   See, for example, Aptheker 1993: 141–42; Stampp 1989: 126–27.

8   For a similar observation concerning the Jamaican context in particular, see Patterson 1969: 222.

9   See, most notably, Lichtenstein 1988. See also Kay and Cary 1985. Lichtenstein's argument amounts to a compelling case against Genovese's (1976: 608) contention, contra Stampp (1989: 25), that, through stealing, "the slaves could challenge the moral code, but could not readily counterpose a coherent alternative." He formulates this argument using the concept of *moral economy*—a term coined by the British Marxist historian E. P. Thompson (1991a) and further developed by the American anthropologist James C. Scott (1976) to denote the customary ideas of economic justice legible in the grievances and practices of landless workers confronting capitalist and imperialist expansion. For a retrospective overview of the genesis of this concept, see Thompson 1991b.

10   See, for example, Camp 2004: 45–47, 68–71; Browne 2017: 160–83. Randy M. Browne (2017: 158) discusses theft in the context of a broader analysis of what he calls, following Thompson (via Lichtenstein), a moral economy of survival: "a bundle of constantly renegotiated, unwritten rules about economic fairness and material welfare."

11   On *necropolitics* (the subjugation of living beings to the power of death) and chattel slavery, see Mbembe 2003: 21–22. For an empirical study of how death shaped the everyday lives of the enslaved in general, see Brown 2008.

12   On the affective, social, and material bonds that could take shape in scenes of labor, see Johnson 2013: 210–12.

13   My claim here is informed by critical theorist Kevin Quashie's (2021: 8–9) assertion that aliveness comes into view in the flux of Black social life, "the register of black experience that is not reducible to the terror that

calls it into existence, but is the rich remainder." Quashie poses this assertion in dialogue with the work of Terrion L. Williamson (2016: 9).

14 On *social death*, the original condition of deracination from natal ties and supportive sociocultural edifices that partly determined the position and experiences of the enslaved, see Patterson 1982: 13.

15 For an exemplary elaboration of the theory of power and political subjectivity with which Brown is engaging, see Scott 2005: 98–131.

16 I learned the sociological term *livelihood strategy* from Davis 2017.

17 Stephanie M. H. Camp (2004: 7) defines the *rival geography of the plantation system* as the pervasively expressed "alternative ways of knowing and using plantation and southern space that conflicted with planters' ideals and demands." She adapts the general term *rival geography* from recent engagements with Said 1993.

18 Further references to Octave's deposition are to this edition and will be cited parenthetically in the text as *D*. The original source is located in the American Freedmen's Inquiry Commission Papers, RG 94, Letters Received, ser. 12, O–328, National Archives. In addition to this deposition, Octave's biography is discussed in McKaye 1864: 8–12. James McKaye had been one of three individuals appointed by Edwin M. Stanton, the US Secretary of War, to supervise the work of the American Freedmen's Inquiry Commission, an initiative that conducted interviews with formerly enslaved Southerners in an effort to assess their condition and their potential for future economic productivity after Emancipation. His book is a supplement to the commission's official report to Stanton. The summary nature of McKaye's account of Octave's biography suggests that it is based primarily on the content of Octave's deposition; however, McKaye's account does contain certain details and quotations which do not feature in the deposition itself. My own analysis references these additional pieces of information only sparingly, as their exact provenance remains unclear.

19 McKaye (1864: 12) identifies Octave's purchaser using the surname "Coutrell."

20 For a general overview of the organization of enslaved labor on sugar estates in Louisiana, see McDonald 1993a: 276–79. On the task and gang systems in general, see Morgan 1998. Douglass (2003: 174) describes the existence of enslaved workers on Louisiana sugar plantations as a "life of living death." For a vivid first-hand account of this existence and the closely monitored labor of cane-cutters, see Northup 1853: 208–13.

21 For an overview of these activities, see McDonald 1993b: 50–91. See also McDonald 1993a: 279–89. For an exemplary analysis of the comparable empirical setting of the sugar-producing Caribbean, see Mintz 1974. See also Bates 2016.

22 On the preference among proprietors of plantations to internalize the production of subsistence goods as a method of reducing input costs, see Ford 1985; Gallman 1970.

23 My analysis here is shaped by Michael Denning's (2010: 80–81) general observation that the imperative to "earn a living," instantiated through

dispossession and persistent poverty, is what sustains exploitative relations of production.

24 On the accumulated small harms resulting from the suppression of natural rest patterns in favor of artificial ones more suited to modern labor regimens, see Ekirch 2001. I thank Ana Schwartz for recommending this article, which helped clarify the sense of loss Octave might have felt in this moment and others.

25 See, most notably, Dawson 2018: 20–21; Bell 2016: 1; Nevius 2016: 12n19; Diouf 2014: 85, 94–95, 151; Williams 2014: 67–68; Millett 2013: 5–6; Scott 2009: 12–14, 1999: 114; Jung 2006: 50; Cowan 2001: 70–71, 79–80; Booker 2000: 76–77.

26 For a memorable discussion of the participation of enslaved Black Louisianans in the subsistence-level moss trade, see Lynette Ater Tanner's (2014: 218) transcription of the testimony of Hunton Love.

27 Some scholars have asserted in passing that the fugitives all hailed from the Contrell plantation exclusively, but I have found no evidence to suggest this. Regardless, the findings of recent scholarship on the sprawling connections that enslaved people formed across plantation boundaries leads me to the conclusion that an intentional grouping of thirty people would have had personal ties in all corners of the surrounding region. On this point, see Camp 2004; Kaye 2007.

28 Black feminist geographer Katharine McKittrick (2013: 3–5) has theorized plantation geographies—originally, the spatial arrangements of life, labor, and resources that constituted slave economies—as historically perseverant structures of dispossession and exploitation that have set, and continue to set, the terms according to which alternative ways of living may be imagined and enacted. Her work on this topic builds on the prior empirical and theoretical work of the Jamaican economist George L. Beckford (1999).

29 Genovese's (1976: 606) discussion of theft emphasizes the importance that livestock thieves place on silencing their prey with "a single blow."

30 I understand *mutual aid* as organized, reciprocal cooperation aimed at the fulfillment of common needs and desires. For a more expansive definition of this term, elaborated in relation to contemporary social movements, see Spade 2020.

31 McKaye (1864: 11) identifies the fugitives' pursuer as "a famous professional slave-hunter, Eugène Jardeau by name."

32 For an overview of the use of hounds to menace and discipline enslaved laborers (which includes a mention of Octave's deposition), see Parry and Yingling 2020. See also Johnson 2013: 234–40. On the use of hounds against maroons, specifically, see Diouf 2014: 288–92. For representative, narrative-based portrayals of how pursuit by attack dogs disrupted the lives of enslaved people and fugitives from slavery, see Northup 1853: 136–41; Green 1864: 22–25.

33 After receiving asylum at a Union camp, Octave attests, "I was first employed in the Commissary office, then as a servant to Col. Hanks; then I joined this regiment" (*D* 395). For an overview of the history of

the Corps d'Afrique, known originally as the First Louisiana Native Guard, see Hargrove 2003: 97–107; Hollandsworth 1995: 70–93.

34 The site of the fugitives' retreat may have been known as "Bayou Faupron," as a different transcription of Octave's deposition indicates. See Berlin et al. 1985: 217.

35 McKaye's (1864:11) account also adds that the fugitives "carefully rubbed the soles of their feet with the feet of rabbits, with which they had previously supplied themselves for this purpose, and dragging these after them to deceive the scent of the hounds."

36 On insistence not to be single as a defining trait of Black resistance to property and propriety in general, see Moten 2018: 264–67.

37 In the case of Octave himself, John W. Blassingame (1977: 394–95n9) has established (using military service and pension records) that he was discharged from the US Colored Troops in Tallahassee, Florida on April 23, 1866, married twice, had seven children, and died on February 3, 1924, at around eighty-four years of age. None of Octave's conspirators is identified by name, but it registers as plausible that at least some joined him in military service.

38 In addition to Spires, other recent scholars who attend in similar ways to the efforts of Black Americans in the eighteenth and nineteenth centuries to claim and redefine citizenship include Mitchell 2020; Orihuela 2018; Knadler 2010.

39 For an anthropological approach to contemporary Black citizenship that similarly works "to make visible the creative and dynamic ways that people make new worlds out of their own 'bare life,'" see Thomas 2011: 6–7.

References

Aptheker, Herbert. (1943) 1993. *American Negro Slave Revolts*. New York: International Publishers.

Ball, Charles. 1859. *Fifty Years in Chains; or, The Life of an American Slave*. New York: H. Dayton.

Bates, Lynsey A. 2016. "Provisioning and Marketing: Surplus and Access on Jamaican Sugar Estates." In *Archaeologies of Slavery and Freedom in the Caribbean: Exploring the Space in Between*, edited by Lynsey A. Bates, John M. Chenoweth, and James A. Delle, 79–110. Gainesville: Univ. of Florida Press.

Beckford, George L. (1972) 1999. *Persistent Poverty: Underdevelopment in Plantation Economies of the Third World*. Mona: Univ. of the West Indies Press.

Bell, Karen Cook. 2016. "Self-Emancipating Women, Civil War, and the Union Army in Southern Louisiana and Lowcountry Georgia, 1861–1865." *JAAH* 101, nos. 1–2: 1–22.

Berlin, Ira, Barbara J. Fields, Thavolia Glymph, Joseph P. Reidy, and Leslie S. Rowland, eds. 1985. *The Destruction of Slavery*, ser. 1, vol. 1 of *Freedom: A Documentary History*, 3 vols. New York: Cambridge Univ. Press.

Bibb, Henry. 1849. *Narrative of the Life and Adventures of Henry Bibb, An American Slave, Written by Himself.* New York: MacDonald and Lee.

Blassingame, John W., ed. 1977. *Slave Testimony: Two Centuries of Letters, Speeches, Interviews, and Autobiographies.* Baton Rouge: Louisiana State Univ. Press.

Booker, Christopher Brian. 2000. *"I Will Wear No Chain!" A Social History of African American Males.* Westport, CT: Praeger.

Brown, Vincent. 2008. *The Reaper's Garden: Death and Power in the World of Atlantic Slavery.* Cambridge, MA: Harvard Univ. Press.

Brown, Vincent. 2009. "Social Death and Political Life in the Study of Slavery." *American Historical Review* 114, no. 5: 1231–49.

Brown, Vincent. 2020. *Tacky's Revolt: The Story of an Atlantic Slave War.* Cambridge, MA: Harvard Univ. Press.

Browne, Randy M. 2017. *Surviving Slavery in the British Caribbean.* Philadelphia: Univ. of Pennsylvania Press.

Camp, Stephanie M. H. 2004. *Closer to Freedom: Enslaved Women and Everyday Resistance in the Plantation South.* Chapel Hill: Univ. of North Carolina Press.

Clarke, Lewis Garrard. 1845. *Narrative of the Sufferings of Lewis Clarke, during a Captivity of More than Twenty-Five Years, among the Algerines of Kentucky, One of the So Called Christian States of America, Dictated by Himself.* Boston: David H. Ela.

Cowan, William Tynes. 2001. "The Slave in the Swamp: Disrupting the Plantation Narrative." PhD diss., College of William and Mary.

Davis, Mike. 2017. *Planet of Slums.* London: Verso.

Dawson, Kevin. 2018. *Undercurrents of Power: Aquatic Culture in the African Diaspora.* Philadelphia: Univ. of Pennsylvania Press

Denning, Michael. 2010. "Wageless Life." *NLR* 66: 79–97.

Diouf, Sylviane A. 2014. *Slavery's Exiles: The Story of the American Maroons.* New York: New York Univ. Press.

Douglass, Frederick. (1855) 2003. *My Bondage and My Freedom.* Edited by John Stauffer. New York: Modern Library.

Ekirch, A. Roger. 2001. "Sleep We Have Lost: Pre-Industrial Slumber in the British Isles." *American Historical Review* 106, no. 2: 343–86.

Finch, Aisha K. 2015. *Rethinking Slave Rebellion in Cuba: La Escalera and the Insurgencies of 1841–44.* Chapel Hill: Univ. of North Carolina Press.

Follett, Richard. 2016. "The Rise and Fall of American Sugar." In *Plantation Kingdom: The American South and Its Global Commodities*, edited by Richard Follett, Sven Beckert, Peter Coclanis, and Barbara Hahn, 61–90. Baltimore: Johns Hopkins Univ. Press.

Ford, Lacy K. 1985. "Self-Sufficiency, Cotton, and Economic Development in the South Carolina Upcountry, 1800–1860." *Journal of Economic History* 45, no. 2: 261–67.

Gallman, Robert E. 1970. "Self-Sufficiency in the Cotton Economy of the Plantation South." *Agricultural History* 44, no. 1: 5–23.

Genovese, Eugene D. 1976. *Roll, Jordan, Roll: The World the Slaves Made.* New York: Vintage.

Green, J. D. 1864. *Narrative of the Life of J. D. Green, a Runaway Slave, from Kentucky, Containing an Account of His Three Escapes, in 1839, 1846, and 1848.* Huddersfield: Henry Fielding, Pack Horse Yard.

Hargrove, Hondon B. (1988) 2003. *Black Union Soldiers in the Civil War.* Jefferson, NC: McFarland.

Hartman, Saidiya V. 1997. *Scenes of Subjection: Terror, Slavery, and Self-Making in Nineteenth-Century America.* Cambridge, MA: Harvard Univ. Press.

Hollandsworth, James G., Jr.1995. *Louisiana Native Guards: The Black Military Experience during the Civil War.* Baton Rouge: Louisiana State Univ. Press.

Hutchins, Zachary McLeod, and Cassander L. Smith. 2021. "Introduction: Toward a Theory of Black African Mediation, Authorship, and the Early American Literary Archives." In *The Earliest African American Literatures: A Critical Reader*, edited by Zachary McLeod Hutchins and Cassander L. Smith, 1–18. Chapel Hill: Univ. of North Carolina Press.

Jackson, Andrew. 1847. *Narrative and Writings of Andrew Jackson, of Kentucky; Containing an Account of His Birth, and Twenty-Six Years of His Life while a Slave; His Escape; Five Years of Freedom, Together with Anecdotes Relating to Slavery; Journal of One Year's Travels; Sketches, etc. Narrated by Himself; Written by a Friend.* Syracuse, NY.

Johnson, Walter. 2003. "On Agency." *Journal of Social History* 37, no. 1: 113–24.

Johnson, Walter. 2013. *River of Dark Dreams: Slavery and Empire in the Cotton Kingdom.* Cambridge, MA: Harvard Univ. Press.

Jung, Moon-Ho. 2006. *Coolies and Cane: Race and Labor in the Age of Emancipation.* Baltimore: Johns Hopkins Univ. Press.

Kay, Marvin L. Michael, and Lorin Lee Cary. 1985. "'They are Indeed the Constant Plague of Their Tyrants': Slave Defence of a Moral Economy in Colonial North Carolina, 1748–1772." *Slavery and Abolition* 6, no. 3: 37–56.

Kaye, Anthony E. 2007. *Joining Places: Slave Neighborhoods in the Old South.* Chapel Hill: Univ. of North Carolina Press.

King, Lovalerie. 2007. *Race, Theft, and Ethics: Property Matters in African American Literature.* Baton Rouge: Louisiana State Univ. Press.

Knadler, Stephen. 2010. *Remapping Citizenship and the Nation in African-American Literature.* New York: Routledge.

Lichtenstein, Alex. 1988. "'That Disposition to Theft, with Which They Have Been Branded': Moral Economy, Slave Management, and the Law." *Journal of Social History* 21, no. 3: 413–40.

Marx, Karl. (1842) 2021. "Proceedings of the Sixth Rhine Province Assembly, Third Article: Debates on the Law Concerning the Theft of Wood." Translated by Robert Nichols. In Daniel Bensaïd, *The Dispossessed: Karl Marx's Debates on Wood Theft and the Right of the Poor*, edited by Robert Nichols, 59–105. Minneapolis: Univ. of Minnesota Press.

Mbembe, Achille. 2003. "Necropolitics." Translated by Libby Meintjes. *Public Culture* 15, no. 1: 11–40.

McDonald, Roderick A. 1993a. "Independent Economic Production by Slaves on Antebellum Louisiana Sugar Plantations." In *Cultivation and Culture:*

Labor and the Shaping of Slave Life in the Americas, edited by Ira Berlin and Philip D. Morgan, 275–302. Charlottesville: Univ. Press of Virginia.

McDonald, Roderick A. 1993b. *The Economy and Material Culture of Slaves*. Baton Rouge: Louisiana State Univ. Press.

McKaye, James. 1864. *The Mastership and Its Fruits: The Emancipated Slave Face to Face with His Old Master. A Supplemental Report to Hon. Edwin M. Stanton, Secretary of War*. New York: Wm. C. Bryant and Co.

McKittrick, Katharine. 2013. "Plantation Futures." *Small Axe* 42: 1–15.

Millett, Nathaniel. 2013. *The Maroons of Prospect Bluff and Their Quest for Freedom in the Atlantic World*. Gainesville: Univ. Press of Florida.

Mintz, Sidney W. 1974. "The Origins of the Jamaican Market System." In *Caribbean Transformations*, 180–213. Chicago: Aldine.

Mitchell, Koritha. 2020. *From Slave Cabins to the White House: Homemade Citizenship in African American Culture*. Urbana: Univ. of Illinois Press.

Morgan, Philip D. 1998. "Task and Gang Systems: The Organization of Labor on New World Plantations." In *Work and Labor in Early America*, edited by Stephen Innes, 189–220. Charlottesville: Univ. Press of Virginia.

Moten, Fred. 2018. *Stolen Life*. Durham, NC: Duke Univ. Press.

Nevius, Marcus P. 2016. "lurking about the neighborhood": Slave Economy and Petit Marronage in Virginia and North Carolina, 1730–1860." PhD diss., Ohio State University.

Northup, Solomon. 1853. *Twelve Years a Slave: Narrative of Solomon Northup, a Citizen of New-York, Kidnapped in Washington City in 1841, and Rescued in 1853*. Auburn, NY: Derby and Miller; Buffalo, NY: Derby, Orton, and Mulligan.

Olmsted, Frederick Law. 1856. *A Journey in the Seaboard Slave States, with Remarks on Their Economy*. New York: Dix and Edwards.

Orihuela, Sharada Balachandran. 2018. *Fugitives, Smugglers, and Thieves: Piracy and Personhood in American Literature*. Chapel Hill: Univ. of North Carolina Press.

Parry, Tyler D., and Charlton W. Yingling. 2020. "Slave Hounds and Abolition in the Americas." *Past and Present* 246: 69–108.

Patterson, Orlando. 1969. *The Sociology of Slavery: An Analysis of the Origins, Development, and Structure of Negro Slave Society in Jamaica*. Rutherford, NJ: Fairleigh Dickinson Univ. Press.

Patterson, Orlando. 1982. *Slavery and Social Death: A Comparative Study*. Cambridge, MA: Harvard Univ. Press.

Quashie, Kevin. 2021. *Black Aliveness, or a Poetics of Being*. Durham, NC: Duke Univ. Press.

Roane, J. T. 2018. "Plotting the Black Commons." *Souls* 20, no. 3: 239–66.

Said, Edward. 1993. *Culture and Imperialism*. New York: Knopf.

Sayers, Daniel O. 2012. "*Marronage* Perspective for Historical Archaeology in the United States." *Historical Archaeology* 46, no. 4: 135–61.

Scott, David. 2005. *Conscripts of Modernity: The Tragedy of Colonial Enlightenment*. Durham, NC: Duke Univ. Press.

Scott, James C. 1976. *The Moral Economy of the Peasant: Rebellion and Subsistence in Southeast Asia*. New Haven, CT: Yale Univ. Press.

Scott, Rebecca J. 1999. "'Stubborn and Disposed to Stand Their Ground': Black Militia, Sugar Workers, and the Dynamics of Collective Action in the Louisiana Sugar Bowl, 1863–87." *Slavery and Abolition* 20, no. 1: 103–26.

Scott, Rebecca J. 2009. *Degrees of Freedom: Louisiana and Cuba after Slavery*. Cambridge, MA: Harvard Univ. Press.

Spade, Dean. 2020. "Solidarity Not Charity: Mutual Aid for Mobilization and Survival." *Social Text* 142: 131–51.

Spires, Derrick R. 2019. *The Practice of Citizenship: Black Politics and Print Culture in the Early United States*. Philadelphia: Univ. of Pennsylvania Press.

Stampp, Kenneth M. (1956) 1989. *The Peculiar Institution: Slavery in the Ante-Bellum South*. New York: Vintage.

Stewart, John. 1823. *A View of the Past and Present State of the Island of Jamaica; with Remarks on the Moral and Physical Condition of the Slaves, and on the Abolition of Slavery in the Colonies*. Edinburgh.

Tanner, Lynette Ater, ed. 2014. *Chained to the Land: Voices from Cotton and Cane Plantations*. Durham, NC: Blair.

Thomas, Deborah A. 2011. *Exceptional Violence: Embodied Citizenship in Transnational Jamaica*. Durham, NC: Duke Univ. Press.

Thompson, E. P. (1971) 1991a. "The Moral Economy of the English Crowd." In *Customs in Common*, 185–258. New York: The New Press.

Thompson, E. P. 1991b. "The Moral Economy Reviewed." In *Customs in Common*, 259–351. New York: The New Press.

Williams, David. 2014. *I Freed Myself: African American Self-Emancipation in the Civil War Era*. New York: Cambridge Univ. Press.

Williamson, Terrion L. 2016. *Scandalize My Name*. New York: Fordham Univ. Press.

Eve
Eure

Intergenerational Testimonials and the
Politics of Black Cherokee Belonging

Abstract This article extends Tiya Miles's study on the Black Cherokee Shoe Boots family by reading the legal documents they submitted to the Cherokee Nation—citizenship applications and land deeds as intergenerational testimonials. These documents, the article argues, constitute intergenerational testimonials because they record how the Shoe Boots family produced their own archive, their own print record across time and for future generations, as one strategy to build a livable world within and on Cherokee lands. As intergenerational testimonials, they transmit histories of unfinished familial claims and materially contain the fragmentary echoes of a collective set of desires. These testimonials refuse a racial and colonial conception of belonging. The article argues that the collaborative political labor of submitting claims captures the plurality of expression in the documents. What appears as an individual claim, the article contends, is instead linked to a network of familial ties. Put another way, the article reads the use of "I" in a family member's citizenship application, for example, as constituting a collective utterance that embeds the desires of family members, whether living, lost, or dead.
Keywords Black Native studies, Afro-Indigenous studies, African American studies

In 1887, William Shoe Boots appeared before the Cherokee Citizenship Commission (CCC) and narrated a genealogy of Black Cherokee belonging that exceeded legal and national definitions. The CCC assessed citizenship claims through the terms of the Treaty of 1866, which guaranteed that "freedmen," "all free colored persons," and their descendants would have "all the rights of native Cherokees."[1] However, William withheld his former status as an enslaved person in his citizenship application and instead framed his claim to Cherokee citizenship in relation to the family's presence in the Cherokee Nation as long-standing members who were known to the community. William died before his claim was resolved. However, his children, Rufus and Lizzie, working with their father's application,

American Literature, Volume 96, Number 4, December 2024
DOI 10.1215/00029831-11557553 © 2024 by Duke University Press

petitioned the CCC in 1896 to assert their right to belong as Black Cherokees. Their applications, along with the land deeds of William's mother, Doll, demonstrate a Black Cherokee politics of collective place-making that shows how intergenerational community and family knowledge and relationships structured their conceptions of belonging. This article argues that William and his family created what I identify as *intergenerational testimonials,* an emergent literary practice that created a Black Cherokee politics of collective belonging defined by intergenerational community and family knowledge and relationships. Intergenerational testimonials transmit histories of unfinished familial claims and materially contain the fragmentary echoes of a collective set of desires. These testimonials refuse a racial and colonial conception of belonging, and they show how Black Cherokees developed strategies to build a livable world within and on Cherokee lands.

William's citizenship application and the appeals of his descendants replicate the "polyvocal," "fragmentary[,] and embedded" features of eighteenth-century Caribbean slave narratives, while simultaneously developing a distinct form of testimony that is created out of the particular experiences of Black Cherokee communities living in the Cherokee Nation (Aljoe 2012: 18). Their documents share common features with these narratives in the way they use the pronoun "we" to represent a single claim and in how they narrate their story of belonging to the Cherokee Nation through what might be called a fragmentary community testimony that is embedded within multiple archives. My argument follows literary historian Nicole N. Aljoe's (2012: 18) scholarship on West Indian slave narratives, which she argues "manifest the elusive structural form of the fragment" and are texts often "embedded" in other works. William's citizenship application and his children's appeals share some of the characteristics of these texts but also have a particular orientation to family, community, and "authorship" that sets this writing apart. These texts displace the individual petitioner as "author" and instead, present the application as representing a "collective utterance" that, I argue, embeds the political and social desires of family members and friends, whether living, lost, or dead (Hartman 2019: 286).

The Shoe Boots family, especially William's mother, Doll, have been written about in several monographs on Black Cherokee communities in the nineteenth century. Historian Tiya Miles's seminal book, *Ties that Bind: The Story of an Afro-Cherokee Family in Slavery and Freedom* (2005), focuses on Doll and her family's lived experiences of slavery in the Cherokee Nation. In the book's epilogue, Miles (2005:

109) turns to William's testimony to reveal continuities between older traditions of inclusion that emphasized "kinship rather than race" and practices of belonging adopted by Black Cherokee peoples in response to the creation of the Cherokee Constitution of 1827, which denied citizenship to African-descended persons. As Miles (2005: 242) notes, William's citizenship petition highlights the centrality of intergenerational family and community relations, which he used as both "strategy as well as conviction" that "race should not be a determining factor in his right to citizenship." Miles's discussion of William's testimony as emphasizing links among more inclusive, kinship practices of belonging provides the groundwork for this article's discussion of intergenerational testimony. I use the term *intergenerational testimonial* to show how William and his descendants used their family documents—citizenship applications and appeals and land deeds—as a collective act of placemaking. These intergenerational testimonials form an emergent literary practice that I argue William and his family created in the process of producing their own print record, their own archive, through their awareness of the power held by these court documents. My contention is that their testimonial transcription comprises collective stories that disclose models of belonging based on family, community responsibility, and their distinct experiences living in the Cherokee Nation that drew on "long-practiced traditions [of] a socially compassionate ethics of inclusivity" and reciprocal kinship relations that were called into question in court (Nelson 2014: 24). In calling attention to William and his family's documents, and calling these applications and appeals collective, intergenerational testimonials, I seek to reveal the radicality of their insistence on a recognition of themselves as Black and Cherokee, which posed very real political and ethical challenges for the Cherokee Nation.

The article focuses on William Shoe Boots's citizenship claim, the appeals submitted by his descendants, Rufus and Lizzie, and the land applications of his mother, Doll. Her significance to William and his family's petitions for citizenship is critically tied to her status as an enslaved person and the transference of that status to her descendants. The Cherokee Nation, one of the five Nations removed to what was called Indian Territory during Andrew Jackson's presidency in the 1830s, reimagined their society in the context of Indian and African colonizationist ideas through adopting chattel slavery and US governmental structures, both of which were reconceptualized to suit the nation's own ideas of ownership, governance, and belonging. When Cherokees rewrote their constitution in 1827 and 1839, they modeled these documents on the US constitution. Enslaved peoples, as these new constitutions proclaimed, could not marry Cherokees and, thus, remained external to Cherokee cultural and political activities. In this context, enslaved and free Black people were excluded from citizenship and political participation and from the terms of kinship and belonging in the Cherokee Nation. As I will discuss, despite these exclusionary laws, William and his descendants created their own meanings of belonging that were grounded in creating good relations with family and a broader Cherokee community, where they rebuilt severed relations with the land and the other-than-human world.[2]

Throughout the article, I use the term *Black Cherokee* without the hyphen to show how William and his family and mother understood their sociopolitical subjectivities as bound up within Cherokee society. I draw on Reid Gómez's (Diné) (2021: 186) critical writing on unfixing the *and* that is always placed between Black and Native, Native and Black to capture the practice of belonging that William and his descendants adopted to signify their own meanings of Cherokee identity. In using the label Black Cherokee, I also want to highlight how the Shoe Boots family navigated and transgressed US and Cherokee citizenship, land, and enrollment policies that did not grant dual citizenship status to African-descendant persons. As Marilyn Vann (Cherokee) (2021: 3), president of the Descendants of Freedmen of the Five Civilized Tribes Association notes, "tribal freedmen were not entitled to US citizenship under the 14th amendment to the United States Constitution as they were not slaves of U.S. citizens . . . [and] did not receive U.S. citizenship until the 1901 Five Tribes Citizenship Act was passed." Thus, the Shoe Boots family's mobilization of their intergenerational testimony was a collective technique for navigating and refusing a bifurcated system of legal affiliation that narrowed citizenship to official census records, in which African-descended persons were recorded as separate from Cherokee peoples. If we were to view William's insistence on being identified as Black Cherokee in this context, a much wider perspective on Black Cherokee political and social forms of placemaking would be revealed.

Mapping the Limit of Citizenship

William Shoe Boots was the son of Doll Shoe Boots, an enslaved Black woman, and her enslaver, Tarsekayahke Shoe Boots, a Cherokee warrior. He was Doll's fourth child and a twin. William's older siblings— Elizabeth (Lizzie), John, and Polly—were also born to Shoe Boots and

Doll and became Cherokee citizens after Shoe Boots submitted an emancipation petition to the National Council in 1824. The National Council ordered Shoe Boots not to have any more children with Doll, but he had two more, William and his twin brother, Lewis. What this meant was that William and Lewis could not become citizens and their status would be tied to Doll's condition as an enslaved person, and, despite the petitions of Shoe Boots's sisters requesting that the council change their previous ruling, William and Lewis were not granted citizenship. After the Civil War, when formerly enslaved persons were able to petition for citizenship, they were made to do so through the Treaty of 1866, which explained their presence in the Cherokee Nation as the consequence of slavery rather than through marriage or adoption. William's testimony omitted his status as a formerly enslaved person; instead he narrated his own story of the experiences that his family lived as Black Cherokees occupying what historian Alaina E. Roberts (Black Chickasaw) (2021: 65) calls "a liminal space of neither citizenship nor total societal disconnection." His omission then was an act of Black Cherokee placemaking and self-sovereignty that demonstrates the way some refused to honor a treaty which deliberately failed to recognize not only their intergenerational presence in the nation but the fact of their Cherokee ancestry and social relations with Cherokees.

The story William told to the court was based in the deliberate narration of his family's presence in the Cherokee Nation. In his statement, William asserted: "I am the party who has this application on file for children in the Cherokee Nation—I have seven children, named: Lizzie Davis Shoeboot about 32 years old, Willie Shoeboots about 28 years old, Rufus Shoeboots age 23 years old, Flora Shoeboots age 19 years, Jno [John] Shoeboots aged 17 years, Jim Shoeboot aged 14 years, and Sophia Shoeboots aged 13 years . . . " William, then, stated that "My mother was "Dolly"—a black woman—she had six (*sic*) children by Tarsekayahke [Shoeboots]—My brothers and sisters named as follows—Lizzie Shoeboots, Jno [John] Shoeboots, Polly Shoeboots, Lewis Shoeboots, William Shoeboots (myself). Lewis and myself were twins."[3]

In his application, William spoke directly about his childhood. He noted that he was young when his father Shoe Boots died but he remembered him, and that after his father's death, he and his mother "remained with John Ridge," a prominent Cherokee politician and enslaver. William mentions that his twin brother, Lewis, was "stolen and carried off" though he does not add into enslavement or that he was never seen again. William also states that he was apprenticed twice, first "to learn the carpentry trade," then "to learn the Black-smith trade."[4] He indicates that his mother died before the war and that in 1852 his sisters, Lizzie and Polly, were given money and had children. William uses the proceedings to renarrate his own familial history by describing his mother as "a black woman" rather than identifying her as a formerly enslaved person and by mentioning his experiences of apprenticeship and their presence in the Ridge household. William's renarration suggests more than an already-known status as a formerly enslaved person; it discloses the intentionality of his description of Doll and the significance of his elision of her enslaved status in favor of situating her in a broader Black Cherokee narrative in which community belonging, not enslavement, is the key social and legal feature. In the context of William and his descendants, these documents are legal records kept personally or within official archives, which simultaneously repress their voices and bring them into view as challenges to Cherokee marriage laws, land rights, and citizenship and tribal national enrollment policies.

In 1887, William learned that while the CCC agreed that William "was the son of Shoe Boots," because his father "died before the roll of 1835" was created, William was not "entitled to Cherokee citizenship as the evidence showed he deserved." Rather than an outright denial of his claim, the CCC placed William's application on a "doubtful claimants" list that ultimately collapsed the distinction between those cases requiring more evidence and those individuals considered "intruders," as indicated by the title given to the list, "Summary of Colored Citizens and Colored Intruders Resident in the Several Districts."[5] The roll of 1835 was a preremoval federal census roll that anticipated the Dawes Commission's creation of a racialized criterion for determining eligibility for land allotments in the same year the CCC ruled on William's case. This roll was important because the methods of classification that established the presence of Black persons as external became the sole legal record for determining citizenship; in other words, persons had to appear on this roll to "prove" their Cherokee ancestry. The roll recorded Cherokee families in present-day Tennessee, Alabama, North Carolina, and Georgia as either "slaves" or "Black persons" but not as part of Cherokee families.[6] William's testimony asserted his right to belong by narrating his family's relation to Cherokees, and while he omits mention of his status as a formerly enslaved person, I argue that he does so in order to tell his own story, rather than because his status would have already been known. Moreover, his petition is deliberate in situating slavery and colonialism "not [as] a moment but rather an ongoing experience" that structures their family's response (Roberts 2021: 65).

William's petition highlights the tensions created by the external mandate from the US government to draft the Treaty of 1866 that combined with already-present constitutional restrictions on the ability of Black Cherokee persons to become citizens of the Cherokee Nation. These realities intensified the narrowing of citizenship qualifications, on the one hand, and increasingly tethered nearly all claims by Black Cherokees to a treaty that was viewed as an infringement on Cherokee sovereign right to create its own citizenry, on the other. In this context, William's citizenship application and his children's appeal disrupted the CCC proceedings by insisting on their own meanings of belonging which drew from Cherokee kinship traditions, and which William and his children used in their cases to demonstrate the contradiction of the court's ruling against them.

The CCC numbered among many commissions created between 1868 and 1886 to primarily adjudicate citizenship claims pertaining to formerly enslaved and Black Cherokees living in the Cherokee Nation before the Treaty of 1866. In 1870, when the first court cases were heard, the CCC only "admitted 5 freedmen and their families to citizenship and rejected 131 cases, 93 of them because they had not returned within the six-month limitation" period (Littlefield 1978: 77). For many formerly enslaved, Black Cherokees, and free Black persons who had lived in relation to Cherokees before the war, returning to the nation within six months was often not possible, and it was also not how many framed their claims on belonging when they appeared in court. Petitioners invoked kinship networks and frequently submitted collective citizenship applications taken up by individuals who did not claim a biological kin relation to their co-petitioners in order to direct their lives in the nation. Like many that did return and had their petitions denied, they responded by cultivating and sustaining their own meanings of belonging that resonate with Roberts's description of her own family's practices in the Chickasaw Nation. Referring to her great-great-grandmother, Josie, among other Black Chickasaw peoples, Roberts (2021: 63–64) notes, "instead of pursuing citizenship, [many] opted for belonging–creating their own communities through possession of land, the establishment of institutions, and the maintenance of kinship ties." William's testimony and witness affidavits reveal a similar response to the social and political exclusion his family endured, though his petition also demonstrates how obtaining legal citizenship was bound together with Black Cherokee knowledge and memory of their connections and relations to place, land, and Cherokees that William insisted on continuing to honor as a legally recognized member of the nation.

In the US context, formal recognition did not necessarily mean that Black persons had the ability to exercise the "rights and entitlements" of citizenship (Hartman 2022: 271). According to Black feminist literary scholar Saidiya Hartman, "not only was political equality greatly contested and social equality opposed, but even the enjoyment of basic civil rights was unrealized" (217). The recognition of legal citizenship expressed what Hartman calls "the double bind of freedom: being freed from slavery and free of resources . . . sovereign and dominated, citizen and subject" (205). Literary scholar Koritha Mitchell (2011: 54) focuses on how lynching playwrights enacted this "double bind of freedom" that "created opportunities for African Americans to engage in embodied practices of belonging" and claim "a citizenship that was at least two fold: *they belonged in black communities as well as the nation.*" Mitchell's argument that the "practice of belonging" became important to Black community making and national connection recalls William Shoe Boots's assertion of belonging in his insistence on being legally and socially recognized as Black Cherokee. Mitchell's ideas about the "practice of belonging" echo literary scholar Derrick R. Spires's (2019: 5) theorizations of citizenship as a practice of making and collective action. The citizen subject, as Spires contends "invokes a civic ethos and protocols of recognition and justice that call on audiences to think about their relation to citizens and others as one of mutual responsibility, responsiveness, and active engagement, a relation in which membership and individual rights come with moral obligations to a collective" (5).

The model of belonging that I propose is created through a web of social relations that are not defined or given meaning by Cherokee citizenship courts. These social relationships depend on an ethics of reciprocal responsibility to a community, a family, the land where being claimed by members is one organizing principle. This mode of reciprocal recognition describes an active mode of relationality that is built through community acknowledgement and a grounded history and deep relationship with and responsibility to the land. For Black Cherokee peoples, like William Shoe Boots, belonging was lived in part as a practice of "hold[ing] ground as relational" to use literary scholar Jodi A. Byrd's (Chickasaw) (2019: 219) term for a kind of Indigenous relational space-making practice. Black Cherokee petitioners offer models of belonging that emphasized social relationships, reciprocity, and responsibility to a community that encompassed land and an other-than-human world that were not merely shaped by Cherokee citizenship courts. The resonances between Spires's theorizations of Black citizenship practices and my articulations of belonging show how African-descended communities across geographies remade the meanings ascribed to political and social relationships by adopting relations grounded in collective and community responsibility to each other. These were ongoing practices generated from within their own community spaces and did not disappear because of exclusionary Tribal National and US citizenship rules.

Intergenerational Testimonials

Collective writing practices were crucial to the citizenship appeal that Rufus and Lizzie submitted in 1896 to the CCC. This form of writing allowed them to infuse the document with the histories and stories of their Black and Black Cherokee ancestors. They described their citizenship application as a "continuation of one claim" that included "fifteen persons in all," demonstrating the "polyvocal," "embedded," and intergenerational character of their document.[7] This act of submitting collective citizenship petitions was not unique to Rufus and Lizzie or only adopted by biologically related family members. For example, Jeffrey Holt and eleven other formerly enslaved persons collectively submitted an application for Cherokee citizenship in 1875 and declared they should be seen as "equal with the Indians" (Smithers 2015: 221). Collective petitioning was one example of an alternative Black Cherokee placemaking practice that was well-established by the time Rufus and Lizzie brought their case to the CCC.

Despite abundant evidence attesting to claimants' relations to their respective Nations, however, tribal-national courts overwhelmingly rejected citizenship applications of persons with African ancestry or claims that rested on connections with such individuals, as was the outcome in both Rufus and Lizzie's and Jeffrey Holt's case. The CCC ruled that since Jeffrey Holt and his copetitioners possessed "African blood," they were not only ineligible for citizenship but could not be understood in "equal" relations to Cherokees (Smithers 2015: 192). Yet, these court rulings failed to dissuade petitioners from filing citizenship applications and claiming a reciprocal social and kinship relation that they honored in their own communities. In the context of the Choctaw and Chickasaw Nations, historian Barbara Krauthamer describes a similar claiming of citizenship despite the Nation's efforts to deny them legal incorporation. Drawing on historian Michael Vorenberg's concept of *affective citizenship*, a concept that describes the self-fashioning political practices of free Black communities in the post-emancipation United States, Krauthamer (2013: 124–25) argues that "the concept of 'affective citizenship' . . . helps us understand that freed-people might reference their cultural, social, and personal affinity with the Choctaws and Chickasaws and cast themselves as citizens of the nations even though Indian lawmakers insisted they had not and could not become legal citizens." But what legal citizenship offered was the ability to share in political decision-making and help to direct the nation's present and future direction, and, thus, it became necessary for Black Cherokee communities to obtain.

Rufus and Lizzie viewed the CCC's indecision on their father's case as unjust and refused to wait while the court settled the case. That same year, in 1896, they petitioned the Dawes Commission for assistance as many Black Cherokees and formerly enslaved had done when their cases were denied in Cherokee courts. Their petition to the CCC asserted " . . . that if he, William Shoeboots, was entitled to the rights of Cherokee citizenship we his children and grandchildren are entitled also" and that because "William Shoeboots, our ancestor, having died while his application for citizenship was pending, we his children, respectfully submit the evidence presented by him."[8] Their statement forced the CCC to reconsider both their intergenerational presence and how the adoption of race to distinguish "Native Cherokee identity" from their "Black" kin distorted Cherokee kinship traditions. By highlighting their family's long history in the Cherokee Nation, they demonstrated not only how their existence predated the Treaty of 1866 but also how they would continue to fight against the narrowing of Cherokee identity and belonging.

Rufus and Lizzie made strategic use of the CCC's rejection of their application by appealing directly to the Dawes Commission. The Dawes Commission was tasked in 1893 with continuing the imposed process of allotting land that had been communally held by the Choctaw, Muscogee (Creek), Cherokee, Seminole, and Chickasaw Nations in the Southeast into individually owned plots and creating a roll of tribal members. In the CCC's response to Rufus and Lizzie, they argued that the siblings' claim "failed to prove a lineal descendant on any of the authenticated rolls of the Cherokee Nation" and that "there was a weakness in their proof not then discovered [when their father's application was reviewed]. For prior to the [Civil War], descendants of Cherokee men, by women of the African race were not considered by the Cherokee as members of the Tribe."[9] The CCC noted that Rufus and Lizzie "may be entitled under the Treaty of 1866, though the difficulty in the way is that they attempted to establish by their proof that their ancestors, though of the negro race, were free at the time of the birth of William Shoeboots from whom they claim descent."[10] Just like their father, William, Rufus and Lizzie sought to claim their citizenship through eliding their grandmother Doll's enslavement.

The Dawes Commission was the only other governing entity for Rufus and Lizzie to make a legal claim to Cherokee citizenship. After the Cherokee Nation's decision in 1896, they petitioned the Dawes Commission, sending agents a letter that explained their ongoing case and asked for them to review their application. They begin the letter by asserting that their application is a collective document that the Cherokee court has neglected to properly rule on. "The application now made by myself and my brothers and sisters and . . . fifteen persons in all are all in one . . . claim or continuation of one claim." The letter continues that their claim is, " . . . based upon the fact that we are all descendants of William Shoeboots who had a claim for Cherokee citizenship pending . . . before the Cherokee authorities for at least ten years before his death which took place on the 9th of December 1894."[11] Rufus and Lizzie then provide an account of the reasons why their application was rejected by pointing out the flawed logic of the Cherokee Nation's ruling. They note that the Cherokee Nation had determined "Capt Shoeboot was a Cherokee Indian and a citizen of the Cherokee Nation, and that one of his children by . . . [Doll] . . . " was William Shoeboot, [their] father."[12] They proceed to list individuals who had supplied testimony of their relations to Cherokees and include the CCC's justification for its decision which included the acknowledgement of "the validity of William [S]hoeboots claim, . . . [but also how the Commission] was confined by law deciding in favor of those whose ancestors are enrolled on certain Rolls."[13] Rufus and Lizzie use the Cherokee Nation's admission of their father's Cherokee ancestry, naming "Henry Barnes, who was one of the . . . Cherokee Commissioners" that acknowledged this fact, to show the illogical and unjust rationale for denying their applications.[14] Their letter also indicates a carelessness on the part of Cherokee record keeping, as Rufus and Lizzie indicate that they had to acquire " . . . copies of the testimony of JJ Adair and of the decision of the Commission, we submitted as the best substitute we could obtain, the affidavit of Henry Barnes."[15] The letter discloses a Black Cherokee archival practice that situates their writing as a political act linked to Freedpeople's organized conventions held throughout the Cherokee Nation to protest against laws excluding them from financial and land settlement funds. These conventions adopted a similar model of collective action, petitioning the Cherokee Council and the Secretary of the Interior Henry Teller to express their rejection of the unjust distribution of funds. The petition submitted by "fifty residents of Four Mile Branch community and Tahlequah . . . asked the secretary to delay action on the per-capita money and called for an investigation," while in other districts, Freedpeople mobilized a myriad of political responses to the withholding of educational instruction, political participation, land settlements, and shares of per capita funds (Littlefield 1978: 129–30).

In October 1896, the Dawes Commissioners—Henry Dawes, Frank Armstrong, A. S. McKennon, T. B. Cabanis, and A. B. Montgomery— issued an official response to Rufus and Lizzie's citizenship application that refused to uphold their collective actions to not only be recognized as Black Cherokee but also to have their traditions of community and kinship honored. The Dawes Commission's response reinforced the CCC's decision that Black persons could never be considered Indigenous. In a standard typed form letter, the commission relies that:

> Wm Shoeboots, through whom the petitioners claim to derive their right to citizenship in the Cherokee Nation, is not now and has not been a citizen of the Cherokee Nation, since the removal of said Nation, west to the Indian territory at present located and defined; that his name does not appear on any of the authenticated rolls of said Nation; that neither he nor any of his ancestors now reside or ever had resided in the Cherokee Nation and Indian Territory, as citizens thereof . . .

Under this typed section, the commission added a handwritten note in their record.

> That wm Shoeboots mother was pure blood African who was never married to his father an Indian. That said applicants are negroes and not entitled to citizenship in this Nation.[16]

The Dawes Commission further argues that the status of William's application as pending had been made in error because the court overlooked their mother's status as a formerly enslaved person and her unlawful marriage, as the 1824 law prohibited the enslaved from marrying Cherokees or white persons. Cherokee marriage laws before the Civil War criminalized marriages between Cherokee men and

African-descendant women and did not recognize the lineal descendants, children, or grandchildren of "Cherokee men by women of the African race."[17] Thus, Doll's name would not have been listed on "any of the authenticated [citizenship] rolls" because African-descended women could not reproduce Cherokee kin that the Cherokee Nation would legally recognize as Cherokee.[18]

Cherokee literary scholar Daniel Heath Justice (2006: 215) writes that kinship is: "our rights, responsibilities, and relationships as a people, about our sacred relationships to one another, to other people, and to all Creation." Since many African-descended Cherokee families in the postemancipation period were not understood as Cherokee but often described as intruders on Cherokee lands, they were typically not included in the forms of relationality that Justice describes. By the time William and his children petitioned the CCC, kinship had been absorbed into a citizenship that excluded African-descended peoples through legal and constitutional acts. Racial considerations were at the center of kinship's transformation, as possessing African ancestry could dissolve clan membership. Cherokee society was matrilineal and organized around a clan system that linked families across nations and geographies prior to the 1827 constitution. But for African enslaved peoples, as historian Sarah Hill (1997: 27) notes, "clans embraced the entire population, weaving patterns of relationships and responsibilities into the fabric of kinship." Despite the fact that Doll had children who were citizens, because she was enslaved, Doll was not adopted into a clan and so existed outside the clan kinship system. Enslaved persons were not typically adopted into clan networks and, thus, lived with multiple and profound fears about the threat of being kidnapped, brutalized, separated from family, or sold. Tiya Miles (2005: 86) importantly observes, while "Africans could become members of Cherokee clans through adoption, and people of African and Cherokee descent could become members of clans if their mothers were Cherokee, but being an African slave and being a Cherokee clan member simultaneously was unheard of." Yet, this clan kinship system began to shift as the notion of Cherokee citizenship developed along racial lines, wherein even Black Cherokee women were prevented from becoming citizens. In this context, the claims to citizenship made by William and his children represent a radical stance against the racialization of kinship that their testimony reveals through demonstrating models of belonging grounded in social relationships and their Black community. The family's citizenship and land petitions disclose not only a desire for inclusion but contain a belief that citizenship and belonging could move in different directions, adopt different principles, and still create and hold space for them.

Literary scholar Brigitte Fielder shows how Seneca forms of kinship in the early nineteenth century were expressed in similar terms to William and his children's articulations of social relationships. While Fielder is focused on the discussion of the Seneca Nation on Mary Jemison, a white woman who was adopted into the nation and had children who were white-Seneca, her analysis of these dynamics is important because it shows how race and kinship are flexible constructs. As Fielder (2020: 162) notes, "any claims to Jemison's whiteness cannot preclude the Seneca kinship relations that refigure her as Indian." Moreover, Fielder argues that "Indigenous identity and belonging are not reducible to race (162). However, Black feminist literary scholar Tiffany Lethabo King (2019: 160) reminds us in her depiction of Black and Indigenous intimacies in Julie Dash's film *Daughters of the Dust* (1991) that because the stakes of Black and Indigenous "interdependence and cooperation" threaten the US nation-state in ways that white-Indigenous intimacies do not, even when whiteness is "surrendered," they require a different framework of study. Literary scholar Kathryn Walkiewicz (Cherokee) (2023: 26) describes this threat to the US nation-state through noting how "Indigenous and Black collectivity challenges the 'naturalness' of the white supremist state." Thus, the Shoe Boots family's efforts challenge logics of white supremacy and antiblackness within both the US nation-state and Cherokee Nation and deform the constructed mythology of the social and political separation of Indigenous and Black collectivity.

Despite the court's failure to legally recognize Rufus and Lizzie as Cherokee, their documents forced the Cherokee Nation and Dawes Commission to address the presence of Black Cherokees not as a recent history but one that dated to their grandmother Doll Shoe Boots's enslavement and William's apprenticeship. While the CCC and Dawes Commission required that William, Rufus, and Lizzie articulate their claim to legal citizenship through the terms of juridical procedure and the language of their respective commissions, this framing also did not prevent them from creating a "loophole of retreat" to use Harriet A. Jacobs / Linda Brent's (2000: 128) language within the official record. Claims to citizenship were primarily anchored in demonstrating biological connections to Cherokees and were tied to the Treaty of 1866, as the decisions in Rufus and Lizze's application demonstrate. Thus, Rufus and Lizzie were compelled to express their relations to each other in ways that might not have reflected their own practices but rather the protocols of the citizenship commissions. William's statement that his mother, Doll, was "a black woman," is one example of this self-understanding of who should also be considered Cherokee, namely, "black women." I interpret this assertion as a deliberate act of renarrating his family's social relationships that his children continued in their citizenship appeals. When Rufus and Lizzie declared that they were legally entitled to Cherokee citizenship, they also did not redescribe their grandmother, Doll, as a formerly enslaved person or define their father's relation to Cherokees in ways that would erase his status as a formerly enslaved person and his indentureship; instead, they used the testimonies contained in their family records to substantiate their own applications and to challenge the Cherokee courts. Rufus and Lizzie did not rest their claim to Cherokee citizenship on the Treaty of 1866; rather, they showed how their Cherokee father, like them, had maintained good relations with Cherokees but also had constructed his own community and kin relations to the nation that exceeded the restrictive definitions that had come to narrow legal belonging to Tribal National and US rolls. Rufus and Lizzie's appeal placed tremendous pressure on the CCC to address the claims of Black Cherokees who had been living in the nation for multiple generations, building their own conceptions of belonging—which Doll and her family had done for over seventy-two years.

Rightful Claims to Land

The land bounty applications Doll submitted in 1852 and 1855 are part of this print record to claim recognition. They are connected to the family's intergenerational archive and writing, and disclose how she challenged the severing of Black Cherokee people's relations to the land and other-than-human world and the prohibitions against unions between Cherokees and African-descended peoples, free and enslaved. When Doll appeared before an Arkansas court in 1852 to receive land for Shoe Boots's participation in the Creek Wars, she strategically mobilized US and Cherokee law to secure a land deed by reframing her relationship to him from enslaver-enslaved to husband-wife. Doll told the Arkansas court reporter that she had been married to Shoe Boots according to the laws and customs of the Cherokee Nation. She stated they had "lived together as man and wife" until his death but could not provide a "record of said marriage."[19] In accordance with Congress's 1850 act that granted bounty land to widows and descendants of military officers, the Arkansas court issued Doll a warrant of forty acres of land. Three years later, Doll petitioned a Missouri court and told a similar story to the account she gave in Arkansas. The court granted Doll not the one hundred sixty acres Congress promised but one hundred twenty. Taken together, Doll's actions demonstrate how her land deeds sought to craft her own language of intimacy and kinship, her own relations with the land that contrasted with Cherokee and US narratives about the presence of African-descended people in Indian Territory, and the social relationships they created and sustained across generations.

From 1775 to 1855, the United States Congress passed several land distribution acts intended to grant land to military veterans and their descendants for participating in a series of wars that included Indian wars and Indian removals. Doll's awareness of the power held by these land deeds was instrumental in convincing both courts that she was in fact not enslaved by Shoe Boots but had been "married [to him] by the laws of the Cherokee Nation."[20] In order for Doll to submit her land applications, she had to deliberately disregard the 1824 law that prohibited marriages between enslaved persons and Cherokee citizens in her performance of conjugal couplehood. Her applications illustrate how alternative routes to claiming relations to the land were possible through Doll's strategic navigation of the court that created a physical space where her Cherokee kin and community could gather and built relations from within and on Cherokee lands.

Because of Doll's status as a formerly enslaved person, it was unusual that the Arkansas court granted her forty acres and the Missouri court granted her one hundred twenty acres. Even more surprising were the statements from Cherokees attesting to their marriage. Stand Waite, colonel in the Confederate States Army and principal chief, wrote in his affidavit that he was "personally acquainted with the claimant Dolly Shoe Boots" and she "was the widow of Capt. Shoe Boots [who is] deceased."[21] Two other witnesses, Pigeon Halfbreed and Wilson Loowaga, submitted statements testifying to the same marital relations that Waite had described in his affidavit. Miles (2005: 185) suggests that "by attesting to Doll's 'marriage' to Shoe Boots, these men were in effect claiming her, linking her to the broader body of the Delaware District Community." Rather than interpret their statements as an instance of them claiming her, I argue, they disclose how she claimed them, using their testimony to secure her own relations and community in which her family lived. This emphasis on Doll claiming them is important because, as their family's documents reveal, their social relationships were rooted in reciprocal relations rather than one-way recognition.

While Congress forcibly appropriated these lands from Indigenous peoples, Doll's land claim should be understood within the twinned logics of Indigenous and Black dispossession. The logics of which, according to Byrd (2019: 209), "hold two truths in cacophonous balance: U.S. modernity was created through the genocide of Indigenous peoples and the seizure of Indigenous lands, and U.S. modernity was created through chattel slavery." As a formerly enslaved Black woman who had children that were Black and Cherokee, and who were recognized as members of the Cherokee Nation, Doll was entangled in both types of dispossession. As such, her land claims illuminate how she used US courts with the assistance of Cherokees to create not only a space for her Black Cherokee family and community to belong, but through the land claim she created her own meanings of kinship, of her relationships with place, that her descendant's would continue to build on in their own collective citizenship applications.

Doll's performance of normative marriage conventions constituted both an act of self-making and a refusal to live by US and Cherokee legal and social formations. Her successful performance, as Doll was granted land, shows how, when strategically unsettled, interracial restrictions can follow other routes and move toward what Fielder (2020: 20–21) theorizes as "race's different directionalities." Whether Doll understood her relationship to Shoe Boots in terms of matrimony or another mode of intimate arrangement concerns me less than how this performance drew on her own knowledge of racial- and gender-specific prohibitions in order to craft her own story of their relationship. By claiming to be the legal wife of Shoe Boots, Doll asserted what Black feminist scholar Tina Campt (2017: 17) describes as "a belief in what should be true . . . [and] the power to imagine beyond current fact and to envision that which is not, but must be." What Doll produces is a material record of resistance, of building her own conception of place and relations to the land and other-than-human world that created a space of possibility for her son William and his descendants to maintain and build deeper relationships. Without a record of marriage, Doll's statements to the Missouri and Arkansas court reporters were acts of renarration that "imagine[d] beyond current fact," unsettling the prohibitions that erased her presence in the nation.

Even though the family's petitions often failed to transform Doll and her descendants' citizenship status, they no less illustrate how Black Cherokee communities built their own meanings of citizenship and belonging that held tremendous significance for them. Far from simply reporting the most basic information about petitioners, their documents represent a challenge to the racialization of citizenship and demonstrate how Black Cherokee communities responded to this transformation. What we see from Doll and her family's unfinished, intergenerational testimonials is a practice of collective Black Cherokee placemaking that helps us to develop new frameworks for reconceptualizing Black Cherokee belonging and kinship relations. From Doll's assertion that she was entitled to land to her son William and his children Rufus and Lizzie's claim to legal belonging, their family points to the ways they used the law to create space for themselves within the Cherokee Nation, a nation that simultaneously sought to exclude and narrow how African-descended Cherokee persons could claim relations to the land and other-than-human world. Their family's archive of legal records, described as a "continuation of one claim" by Rufus and Lizzie, reflects not only their legal challenge to Cherokee and US courts, but also offers a print record of an alternative model for considering Black Cherokee practices of self-identification that sustained and held future generations on the land.

Eve Eure is a transdisciplinary scholar working across the fields of Black studies and Native and Indigenous studies. She is currently working on a book project titled "The Grammar of Kinship: Black and Native Intimacies in the 19th Century," which explores the literary and legal effacement of Black and Native bonds, along with the new forms of kin-making and literary production that accompanied that effacement in the nineteenth century.

Notes

1   See article 9, Ratified Indian Treaty 358, National Archives Identifier 179015384: Cherokee—Washington, DC, July 19, 1986. American Indian Treaties, "Ratified Indian Treaties, 1722–1869," National Archives. It is important to note that although slavery existed in all five nations, each nation incorporated enslaved peoples quite differently. For instance, the Seminoles absorbed enslaved and free Black peoples within their community.

2   Here I draw on Kathryn Walkiewicz's meaning of *other-than-human world* in *Reading Territory: Indigenous and Black Freedom, Removal, and the Nineteenth-Century State* (2023). In the context of defining their meaning of land, they write, " . . . I mean the other-than-human world that includes language, lifeways, culture, and understandings of how to be in good relation to our other-than-human relatives" (Walkiewicz 2023: 163).

3   Citizenship Application of William Shoeboots. Statement of William Shoeboots. Cherokee Nation Papers, microfilm 1650, roll 51, no. 4422. Oklahoma Historical Society, Oklahoma City.

4   Citizenship Application of William Shoeboots. Statement of William Shoeboots.

5   See "Summary of Colored Citizens and Colored Intruders Resident in the Several Districts 1880," Indian Archives Division, Oklahoma Historical Society, Cherokee—Freedmen (Tahlequah).

6   The census also included information about the heads of households, number of family members, degree of blood, ability to speak English, family possessions, and the number of enslaved and Black persons in each family. Superintendent for the Five Civilized Tribes, Muskogee, Oklahoma. Cherokee-Census Roll of 1835. Volume 14. Oklahoma Historical Society.

7   Citizenship Application of William Shoeboots. Statement of William Shoeboots.

8   Citizenship Application of William Shoeboots, Rufus Shoeboots Appeal, Cherokee Citizenship Commission, Letter to the Dawes Commission.

9   Citizenship Application of William Shoeboots, Rufus Shoeboots Appeal, Hutchings, Hastings and Boudinot, Attorneys for the Cherokee Nation.

10   Ibid.

11   Citizenship Application of William Shoeboots, Rufus Shoeboots Appeal, Letter to the Dawes Commission.

12   Ibid.

13   Testimony also includes "Edna Mona, Ross Thomas Ridge, Nathaniel Fisk, Ed Carey, and William Shoeboots himself," and Rufus and Lizzie also make special note that their application contains "the claims [of]–Adair and Allen Ross, two very prominent and respectable Cherokee citizens [who] testified on behalf of [their father]."

14   Ibid.

15   Ibid.

16   Citizenship Application of William Shoeboots, Rufus Shoeboots Appeal, Response from the Cherokee Citizenship Commission.

17   Ibid.

18   Ibid.

19   Bounty Land Files, file 838:39 (Shoeboots). Military Service Records, Veterans Records, National Archives and Records Administration. Washington, DC.

20   Bounty Land Files, file 838:39 (Shoeboots).

21   Ibid.

References

Aljoe, Nicole N. 2012. *Creole Testimonies: Slave Narratives from the British West Indies, 1709–1838*. New York: Palgrave Macmillan.

Byrd, Jodi A. 2019. "Weather with You: Settler Colonialism, Antiblackness, and the Grounded Relationalities of Resistance." *Critical Ethnic Studies* 5, no. 1–2: 207–14.

Campt, Tina. 2017. *Listening to Images*. Durham, NC: Duke Univ. Press.

Fielder, Brigitte. 2020. *Relative Races: Genealogies of Interracial Kinship in Nineteenth Century America*. Durham, NC: Duke Univ. Press.

Gómez, Reid. 2021. "A Shared World: People of These Stories." *Aztlán: A Journal of Chicano Studies* 46, no. 2: 179–94.

Hartman, Saidiya. 2019. *Wayward Lives, Beautiful Experiments: Intimate Histories of Social Upheaval*. New York: Norton.

Hartman, Saidiya. (1997) 2022. *Scenes of Subjection: Terror, Slavery, and Self-Making in Nineteenth-Century America*. New York: Oxford Univ. Press.

Hill, Sarah H. 1997. *Weaving New Worlds: Southeastern Cherokee Women and Their Basketry*. Chapel Hill: Univ. of North Carolina Press.

Jacobs, Harriet A. 2000. *Incidents in the Life of a Slave Girl, Written by Herself*. New York: Penguin Books.

Justice, Daniel Heath. 2006. *Our Fire Survives the Storm: A Cherokee Literary History*. Minneapolis: Univ. of Minnesota Press.

King, Tiffany Lethabo. 2019. *The Black Shoals: Offshore Formations of Black and Native Studies*. Durham, NC: Duke Univ. Press.

Krauthamer, Barbara. 2013. *Black Slaves, Indian Masters: Slavery, Emancipation, and Citizenship in the Native American South*. Chapel Hill: Univ. of North Carolina Press. Google Book.

Littlefield, Daniel F. 1978. *The Cherokee Freedmen: From Emancipation to American Citizenship*. Westport, CT: Greenwood Press.

Miles, Tiya. 2005. *Ties that Bind: The Story of an Afro-Cherokee Family in Slavery and Freedom*. Berkeley, CA: Univ. of California Press.

Mitchell, Koritha. 2011. *Living with Lynching: African American Lynching Plays, Performance, and Citizenship, 1890–1930*. Urbana: Univ. of Illinois Press. Google.

Nelson, Joshua. 2014. *Progress Traditions: Identity in Cherokee Literature and Culture*. Norman: Univ. of Oklahoma Press.

Roberts, Alaina E. 2021. *I've Been Here All the While: Black Freedom on Native Land*. Philadelphia: Univ. of Pennsylvania Press.

Smithers, Gregory D. 2015. *The Cherokee Diaspora: An Indigenous History of Migration, Resettlement, and Identity*. New Haven, CT: Yale Univ. Press. Google.

Spires, Derrick R. 2019. *The Practice of Citizenship: Black Politics and Print Culture in the Early United States*. Philadelphia: Univ. of Pennsylvania Press.

Vann, Marilyn. 2021. "NAHASDA Reauthorization—Historic Divestment and the Ongoing Plight of Descendants of Freedmen in Native American Communities." Descendants of Freedmen of the Five Civilized Tribes Association. Testimony of Marilyn Vann, Presented to the Subcommittee on Housing, Insurance, and Community Development.

Walkiewicz, Kathryn. 2023. *Reading Territory: Indigenous and Black Freedom, Removal, and the Nineteenth Century State*. Chapel Hill: Univ. of North Carolina Press.

Florencia Lauria

More than "A Matter of Deciding To": Citizenship, Border Positionality, and Irresolution in Louise Erdrich's *The Night Watchman*

Abstract This article considers Indigenous refusal to state-imposed US citizenship through a reading of Louise Erdrich's *The Night Watchman* (2020). The novel follows the Turtle Mountain Band of Chippewa's struggle to remain a federally recognized tribe during the US government's move toward tribal termination in the 1950s. While the characters' appeal to the US government could be construed simply as a plea for state recognition, the novel's insistence on Chippewa kinship structures as a simultaneous and legitimate expression of the characters' political identities suggests otherwise. Taking up conversations in Indigenous studies pertaining to the limits of state recognition and the possibilities of generative forms of refusal, the article expands upon Mohawk scholar Audra Simpson's (2014) model of refusal with an emphasis on irresolution. This irresolution is manifested in the novel's narrative form—which refuses closure. The article uses the term *border positionalities* to describe the unresolved and *un*settled tension between the characters' Indigenous and settler political identities. It contends that the incommensurability of these social and political identities makes Erdrich's novel an important text for reading citizenship as an ongoing site of struggle for Indigenous people.

Keywords Indigenous studies, borders, refusal, kinship, Louise Erdrich

Toward the end of Louise Erdrich's *Love Medicine* (2009: 315), an Indigenous character concludes that "belonging [is] a matter of deciding to," an observation that raises important questions about political belonging in the context of coercive US policy. When in 1924 President Calvin Coolidge signed into law the Indian Citizenship Act,[1] Indigenous peoples living within the territory claimed by the United States were conferred US citizenship, whether they wanted it or not. What can "deciding to" mean when the borders of political belonging are imposed by US law? What kinds of choices are possible in these strangulating conditions?[2] Erdrich's 2020 Pulitzer Prize–winning novel, *The Night Watchman*, engages with these questions by invoking

American Literature, Volume 96, Number 4, December 2024
DOI 10.1215/00029831-11557537 © 2024 by Duke University Press

the history of termination: a Congress-led effort to dissolve tribal identity in the 1950s and, some would argue, finish the project that the Indian Citizenship Act started by incorporating Indigenous peoples living in the territory claimed by the US into the national polity as a minoritized population.[3]

Erdrich's Chippewa characters resist the Termination Bill's totalizing aspiration, claiming that "Law can't take my Indian out of me" and "We can't just turn into regular Americans. We can look like it, sometimes. Act like it, sometimes. But inside we are not. We're Indians" (Erdrich 2020: 45; 211–12).[4] Yet, as it is structured in the novel, refusal is not an individual or collective choice to act or not act as "regular Americans" but rather a demonstration of the difficulty of absolute choice given the characters' *border positionalities*, a term I develop throughout this article to refer to the struggle between US and Indigenous political identities resulting from the tense and irresolute relation between US and Chippewa sovereignties. As Erdrich's characters organize into a delegation to travel to Washington, DC, and appeal to congress in the hopes of halting termination, the novel draws out the lived contradictions between US citizenship and citizenship in the Turtle Mountain Band of Chippewa. This conflict is especially sharp in the novel's depiction of Thomas Wazhashk, who, modeled after Erdrich's own grandfather, works as both the chairman of the Turtle Mountain Advisory Committee to the Indian Bureau and a night watchman at the Turtle Mountain Jewel Bearing Plant.[5] Throughout the novel, Thomas continually uses his status as an American citizen to fight US impositions and thereby assert his Chippewa identity and his kinship relations.[6] These entanglements animate the novel's narrative arc, but Erdrich does not allow for a simple denouement or a resolution between settler and Indigenous political belonging. I argue that while the characters' appeal to Congress engages a framework of recognition, the novel's emphasis on Chippewa kinship as a separate and concurrent form of political membership ultimately refuses the presumed exclusivity of US citizenship. In doing so, the novel moves beyond the binary paradigm of inclusion/exclusion to the national polity, grappling instead with the experience of forced inclusion and the possibilities that emerge within and against those constraints.

Erdrich (2020: 79) thus depicts termination through the Turtle Mountain Band of Chippewas' struggle to "remain a problem" that cannot be "solved" while settler domination continues. This insistence on remaining unsolvable has important historical significance considering the ways in which the United States has tried and failed to resolve the contradiction of American Indian sovereignty vis-à-vis its own sovereignty claims. As James Tully (2000: 40) explains, "Since the beginning, the long-term aim of the administrators of the [colonial] system has been to resolve the contradiction by the complete disappearance of the Indigenous problem: that is, the disappearance of Indigenous peoples *as* free peoples with the right to their territories and governments." In other words, the US government is (and always has been) deeply invested in diminishing the rights of Indigenous nations *as nations* in order to secure control over territory. US law has repeatedly tried to curtail collective Indigenous rights and ultimately to position Indigenous peoples as individualized "wards" of the state.[7] However, despite its best efforts, US policy has failed to completely eradicate American Indian sovereignty. Indeed, the 1924 Indian Citizenship Act (ICA) did little to resolve disputes between US and Indigenous political belonging, and in some ways, it strengthened Indigenous grounds for resistance. The ICA (1924) declared "that all non-citizen Indians born within the territorial limits of the United States be, and they are hereby, declared to be citizens of the United States: *Provided*, That the granting of such citizenship shall not in any manner impair or otherwise affect the right of any Indian to tribal or other property." While the ICA imposed US citizenship onto Indigenous people, the provision that this shall not "impair or otherwise affect" Indigenous rights also cemented some degree of Indigenous autonomy. Although this was not its intent, in essence, the language of the ICA served to legalize the border positionality of the American Indian. Or as Kevin Bruyneel (2007: 99) puts it, "By first conferring US citizenship on Indigenous people en masse and then in the next sentence securing Indigenous rights to tribal property, the ICA codified what amounted to a form of dual citizenship for Indigenous people who maintained enrollment, and thus citizenship, in a tribe." In Erdrich's *The Night Watchman*, this "dual citizenship" is depicted as a site of struggle—a kind of *duel* of citizenships—animating the characters' sense of political belonging.

Much like imposed citizenship, termination was a settler strategy designed to resolve the 'Indian problem,' this time through the abolition of tribes and their total absorption into the US polity. In the novel, when Thomas Wazhashk learns about Senator Arthur V. Watkin's bill to "provide for the termination of Federal supervision over the property of the Turtle Mountain band of Chippewa Indians in the states of North Dakota, South Dakota, and Montana," he is immediately suspicious (Erdrich 2020: 90). The bill promises to fold the Turtle Mountain Band of Chippewa into the American project by forcibly removing their "status as Indians." Without this status, what will become of Thomas and his family? Of the rest of the band? Thomas observes that the United States is trying "in every possible way to absorb" them. He notes that "sometimes the country still actively hated Indians, true. But more often now, a powerful glorious sensation poured forth. Wars. Citizenship. Flags. This Termination Bill." Behind these promises of national inclusion lurks a subtextual threat of elimination.[8] Thomas asks, "how could Indians hold themselves apart, when the vanquishers sometimes held their arms out, to crush them to their hearts, with something like love?" (98). This settler "love" manifests as the attempted erasure of Indigenous political identities. By incorporating Indigenous peoples—assimilating them into the United States—the country threatens Indigenous peoples' right to remain sovereign. Roxanne Dunbar-Ortiz (2014: 174) explains that the resolution called for Congress to "free those tribes listed from federal supervision and control and from all disabilities and limitations specially applicable to Indians." This "freedom" from "all disabilities and limitations" seeks to terminate federal protections (protections that had been guaranteed through various treaties with Indigenous nations). Importantly, the bill's language also negates Indigenous peoples' rights to continue to relate to the United States through a nation-to-nation paradigm. As Thomas says in the novel, this bill aims to "unmake" and to "unrecognize" Chippewa political identities (Erdrich 2020: 79).

The question of recognition is important in the context of Indigenous studies. Yellowknives Dene scholar Glen Sean Coulthard (2014: 1) explains that "over the last forty years, the self-determination efforts and objectives of Indigenous peoples in Canada have increasingly been cast in the language of 'recognition.'" The same might be said of the United States, where the language of recognition has dominated Indigenous struggles for sovereignty. Lately, however, various scholars have challenged the use of "recognition" to address the status of Indigenous self-determination. Mohawk scholar Audra Simpson (2014: 11) theorizes refusal as an alternative to state recognition. She writes that refusal is "a political and ethical stance that stands in stark contrast to the desire to have one's distinctiveness as a culture, as a people, recognized." Simpson's notion of refusal is grounded in an ethnographic study of the Mohawks of Kahnawà:ke's specific experiences as they struggle with settler political boundaries; she shows that by denying the "'gifts' of the state" (refusing voting privileges, passports, etc.), the Kahnawà:ke Mohawks strategically challenge the legitimacy of settler nations as granting authorities (12).

Refusal, in Simpson's terms, is a profoundly political act, "a willful distancing from state-driven forms of recognition and sociability in favor of others" (12).

In what follows, I argue that *The Night Watchman*'s brand of refusal expands upon the model outlined in Simpson's *Mohawk Interruptus* (2014) via an emphasis on irresolution. I take Simpson's definition of refusal as a starting point for understanding some of the decisions that Erdrich's characters are (and are not) making. For Simpson, refusal is a "self-generated" choice, one that allows her subjects to actively disengage from the settler state in favor of their own priorities. Erdrich's brand of refusal in *The Night Watchman* is different. By foregrounding the double-bind of choice under settler colonial conditions, the novel emphasizes that for the Chippewa characters all choices are irresolute, inadequate, and contaminated. This irresolution is also apparent through the novel's narrative form which discourages closure by rendering a repetitive and (at times) anticlimactic plot. I use the term *border positionalities* to describe the unresolved and *un*settled tension between the characters' Indigenous and settler political identities.

In the first section of the article, I discuss the role of American citizenship as a defining feature of settler-imposed political belonging. I consider the limits of this type of political membership for Indigenous peoples, looking specifically at the complications that emerge when American citizenship is placed side-by-side with Indigenous sovereignty. In the next section I focus on Erdrich's structuring of Chippewa-led kinship systems through careful attention to the characters' points of views. I argue that the novel portrays the characters' familial forms of self-recognition as a concurrent and legitimate form of political identity, thereby interrupting US absorption and demanding a different and more unsettled kind of relation.

American Citizenship and Indigenous Sovereignty:
The Limits of State-Sponsored Belonging

Political belonging to the United States is structured through the legal discourse of citizenship. US citizens are supposedly granted equal access to the national community and its dream of security. Yet despite the juridical codification of this term in modern times, in practice the concept is often precarious and inequitable. Lauren Berlant (2007: 44) argues that the relationship between individual sovereignty and citizenship is an essential "hinge" for understanding the concept's contradictions within the United States. She explains that there is an inherent discrepancy between the nation-state's "legal control over what happens in its territory and the presumption that citizens should have control over their lives and bodies." As a result, Berlant points out that "the promise of US citizenship to deliver sovereignty to all its citizens has always been practiced unevenly." The dissonance between sovereignty and citizenship is even more profound when it refers to Indigenous nations. Carrie Hyde (2018: 7) traces the historical development of the concept of citizenship in the United States, showing that it lacked definition from its inception in the early United States, and though the concept's boundaries for determining inclusion and exclusion became clearer with the passage of the Fourteenth Amendment in 1868, "it continues to be an elastic site of political fantasy and debate."[9] Hyde makes an important disclaimer about this "political fantasy" in relation to Native American citizenship (35). She cautions against imposing these fantasies onto a reading of the "monolithic desirability" of citizenship, for although the "legal recognition of Native Americans as 'citizens'" can be viewed as a victory by some, "from the perspective of earlier defenses of tribal sovereignty, it also mark[s] the foreclosure of a different form of political sovereignty." Understanding state-sponsored citizenship beyond the dominant fantasy of its unconditional worth accords with Simpson's (2014: 1) argument that when it comes to Indigenous peoples, "the assumptions and the histories that structure what is perceived to be 'good' . . . shift and stand in stark relief." Simpson adds that "from this perspective, we see that a good is not a good for everyone." These scholars not only stress the asymmetries of US citizenship but also the cracks that make its overall structure less stable than it often appears. By attending to these scholars' work and the fissures they identify, I examine the border positionality that emerges when US citizenship is placed in relation to a competing and simultaneous model for structuring political membership through Indigenous sovereignty.

Sovereignty has been much debated in Indigenous studies and lacks easy definition, but scholars tend to agree that in its recent articulations Indigenous sovereignty is an ethical and political commitment to prioritizing Indigenous determinations of collective relations or belonging. Indigenous sovereignty as a practice, then, reflects Indigenous power to attend to all aspects of Indigenous life independently of the settler state.[10] Yet as Osage scholar Jean Dennison (2012: 132) explains, the term *sovereignty* is not without complications. In her study of the Osage Nation and its dispute with the state of Oklahoma, Dennison notes that while the Osage are redefining *sovereignty* in

Osage terms and using these redefinitions "to build a better Osage future," the term is also "caught up with the unique U.S. relationship with American Indian nations, which at once recognizes American Indian national sovereignty while it claims plenary authority over their citizens, territory, and authority." In this sense, sovereignty alone is not able to resolve the problems that emerge in the grasp of colonial coercion; instead, sovereignty becomes another site through which these problems are enacted and resisted. Thus, one of Simpson's (2014: 11) main claims in *Mohawk Interruptus* is illustrated through the concept of "nested sovereignties," her claim that "Indigenous sovereignties and Indigenous political orders prevail within and apart from settler governance." According to this model, the sovereignty of the state and the sovereignty of Indigenous nations do not cancel each other out, but rather they exist concurrently and in great unsettled tension. In other words, while settler colonial structures undoubtedly stifle Indigenous sovereignty, they have not extinguished it. This puts Indigenous subjects in a border position.

Like many other contemporary Indigenous writers, Louise Erdrich grapples with settler colonialism's failure to extinguish Indigenous lifeways. Erdrich's oeuvre has long dealt with the contradictions that emerge at the borders of settler and Indigenous imperatives.[11] David Stirrup (2010: 201) argues that while Erdrich's work has always been political to some degree in its prioritizing of Chippewa modes of being, Erdrich's later work "has a much more pronounced political edge to it."[12] This "political edge" is evident in *The Night Watchman*, where the entanglements between American citizenship and Indigenous sovereignty are central to the novel's narrative arc. The novel begins by detailing the rhythm of work at the Turtle Mountain Jewel Bearing Plant, a stand-in for the settler state's influence near reservation borders. The plot continues with Thomas finding out about the Termination Bill and beginning the slow process of explaining its meaning to the other band members. The chapters alternate not only points of view but also storylines, with one storyline focusing on Thomas's struggle with the bill and another centering on his niece, Patrice, and her family life, particularly her search for her missing sister, Vera, who disappears after being promised a better life through urban relocation. The novel's middle sections do not chart a consistent rising action moving toward a singular climax, but rather they track a series of entanglements between the more explicitly political aspects of the story (Thomas and the bill) and the everyday experience of the characters (Patrice's storyline). Toward the novel's end, Patrice, Thomas, and the other characters make a trip to Washington, DC, to appeal to Congress; interestingly, the novel does not end with this confrontation. Instead, as if to emphasize the ongoing temporality of settler colonialism, the novel ends where it began, with the characters performing mundane tasks at the Jewel Bearing Plant. Having journeyed with these characters, however, the reader can better appreciate the lived contradictions of Indigenous existence and the stakes of their struggles in their border positions.

In short, the slow and repetitive pacing of the novel emulates the characters' day-to-day existence in the shadow of colonial domination. While there are climactic moments—Thomas's appeal in front of Congress or Patrice's escape from the city—much of the novel dwells in the ordinary. As I mentioned, central to the novel is the characters' work at the Jewel Bearing Plant, where Indigenous women paste "micro-thin slices of ruby, sapphire, or the lesser jewel, garnet, onto thin upright spindles in preparation for drilling" (Erdrich 2020: 3). This is the first US manufacturing job near the reservation, and it provides new economic possibilities for the band's women (and men, like Thomas, who are also employed there). For Patrice, a young member of the band, the repetitive task of placing the jewels onto the spindles creates a "hypnotic state of mind" (10). Here the characters' rhythm of work becomes a way of understanding the novel's narrative irresolution, solidifying the connection between the "slow, calm, mesmeric toil" of the job and the similar ongoing toil the novel charts more broadly. For the workers, the end of the day is only a temporary break from the long and repetitive task at hand. Indeed, when the women go home, Thomas comes to the Jewel Bearing Plant to fulfill his job as night watchman. His task, too, is characterized by a repetitious rhythm perhaps best exemplified in his steady penmanship. In order not to fall asleep on the job, Thomas spends "hour after hour making perfect circles, writing left to right" (16). In this way, the characters' jobs at the Jewel Bearing Plant become a model for Erdrich's storytelling, which takes on a repetitive pace that echoes the slow violence of settler structures that the characters must negotiate at the border of their everyday lives and settler impositions.[13]

Through descriptions of everyday life, the novel establishes a relation between the characters' ordinary existence and the structure of settler oppression. Pauline Wakeham (2022: 339) demonstrates that "although genocidal processes in settler colonial contexts include time-intensive violence, slower, attritional modes of destruction have often been key to such assaults on Indigenous group life." Following this logic, the novel positions characters between the unremarkable everydayness of settler occupation and the remarkable immediate violences that many of the characters experience or have experienced at the hand of the settler state. For example, as soon as Thomas learns about the Termination Bill and its implications, he thinks back to the moment when, as a child, he was taken away from his family and enrolled in an Indian Boarding School. This connection highlights both the US government's forceful attempts to supplant tribal belonging with US national belonging and the protracted timeframe of this event's aftermath. Cary Collins (2004: ix) writes that the "overriding objective" of American Indian residential schools was "the reformation of an entire people, a transformation of identity, advancement from 'savage' to 'citizen.'" In Thomas's case, the reader sees the absurdity of this supposed transformation. Thomas remembers how a boarding school teacher "showed him that he must place his hand on his heart and repeat words the other children already knew. All while staring at the flag" (Erdrich 2020: 99). He follows orders, but in the end these words mean little to him since he does "not know what [he is] saying" (100). In identifying both the long-lasting effects of this violence (so present for Thomas as an adult) and the ultimate failure of this event to "just turn [Thomas] into [a] regular American" (211), the novel draws out the irresolution at the center of Indigenous political belonging in the territory claimed by the United States; namely, the settler state is both inescapable and not entirely effectual. In so doing, the novel emphasizes that, for Erdrich's characters, US political belonging and Chippewa political belonging are always in tension with one another, making resolution between these parts impossible under conditions of settler colonialism. This space of irresolution engages with a politics of refusal.

It also indicates why Erdrich's depiction of refusal in *The Night Watchman* is not identical to Simpson's.[14] Simpson's (2014: 106) brand of refusal is much clearer in its disengagement with settler imperatives. For example, Simpson's subjects refuse passports belonging to UN recognized states, even when this would make their traveling easier. Simpson reads this choice "as a refusal to play the game of being American or Canadian" and as an opportunity to honor the "discourse of being and *staying* Mohawk" (25). By traveling to Washington, DC, to appeal for federal recognition, Erdrich's characters are not refusing "to play the game of being American" (25); instead, they are using their status as Americans to fight for their tribe's continued self-determination. In Erdrich's depiction, recognition and refusal are complementary strategies that Indigenous characters draw from as they interrupt the absolute authority of settler structures. These interruptions, while diverging from Simpson's "refusal," nevertheless gesture toward Simpson's (2014: 3) own emphasis on "interruptus," which she defines as native acts that "fundamentally challenge . . . the structure of settlement that strangles their political form and tries to take their land and their selves from them." Erdrich's novel also "interrupts" but by depicting moments that challenge the notion of a *settled* form of citizenship while the settler state continues to exist.[15]

This irresolution is evident in Erdrich's plotting of the Turtle Mountain band of Chippewa's specific responses to the Termination Bill. Thomas's first suggestion in response to the bill is drafting a formal petition to the US congress. Juggie, the tribal council secretary, volunteers to type it, and Louis Pipestone, another member of the band, says that he "will bring these papers around to everyone" and "get them signed" (Erdrich 2020: 121). At first, the group's procedures follow the kind of organizational methods developed and respected by the settler state itself, engaging with a recognition framework. Thomas's "Palmer Method of penmanship," which he learned in boarding school, becomes a tool for fighting against the bill (16). In fact, he uses what he learned in boarding school (an arm of the settler state) to assert his (and the band's) refusal to the state's plan. Likewise, the whole band relies on Millie, a University of Minnesota graduate student whom Thomas calls, "our Chippewa scholar" to give them the facts and figures necessary to convince the government through settler-approved strategies (202). Moreover, when the characters first learn about the bill and its implications, they agree to attend the meeting at Fargo's judicial building. Rather than refuse engagement with the men-in-suits responsible for this bill and its passage, Thomas helps organize the groups' collective attendance. By arranging responses in this order—first through the characters' participation with settler structures—Erdrich seems to suggest that for her Chippewa characters, engagement with the state is unavoidable. Yet, as I have been arguing, it is through this participation that Erdrich makes room for a different kind of refusal, one that attends to the border-positioned subject, thereby highlighting the state's ultimate failure to *solve* its 'Indian Problem' through its techniques of 'inclusion.'

Although the characters rely on settler strategies in their appeal for federal recognition, their actions ultimately help to unsettle the state's presumed monopoly on political belonging. Consider the way in which the band operates at that first meeting in Fargo, North Dakota. Yes, the Chippewa characters' attendance marks their inclusion into the US national project, but Erdrich follows this inclusion with important interruptions. When Mr. Holmes, the Bureau of Indian Affairs lawyer, tells them, "You will now be equal with whites as far as the government is concerned," Joyce Asiginak, a band member, responds, "Well, equal is not the way we see it. Our rights go down. So this bill does not suit me in any way. The government is backing out of its agreement" (Erdrich 2020: 197). The tension between Holmes's and Asiginak's points is evident, and it suggests that despite the characters' participation in the meeting with the men-in-suits, for them, state-sponsored belonging remains both undesirable *and* out of reach. The reader sees this in the fact that many of the band members in attendance do not speak English, and those who do cannot necessarily understand the bill's legal jargon. This language barrier prevents those characters from participating and marks their exclusion from the polity (despite their formal status as citizens of the United States). The characters' border positionalities manifest outside the binary of inclusion/exclusion, highlighting the ways in which their inclusion is always conditional. When the government men decline to translate the bill into the Ojibwe language for the benefit of the people in the room, bilingual tribal members step in to fulfill the roll of translators and allow Chippewa-speaking members of the community to participate in the discussion. Band members work together to fill the gaps and supplement their collective belonging in a way that supersedes legal belonging to the United States. For them, refusal comes not as opposed to engagement but through careful and contentious involvement with the settler state's inadequate political structures.

By arranging her characters' responses in this way, Erdrich points to the state's unrelenting impositions *and* the band's sustained kinship practices, refusing a settled form of political belonging. Instead of engaging with a settler 'either/or' logic (either inside or outside; modern or traditional; independent or dependent), the novel emphasizes the state of irresolution that emerges in the contact zone between Indigenous and settler sovereignty.[16] This has political implications since, as Bill Ashcroft (2001:16) argues, "The most profound principles of Western epistemology" are "its passion for boundaries, its cultural and imaginative habit of enclosure." In Erdrich's *The Night Watchman*, enclosure is not feasible; instead, the characters live on the edge of various political directives, balancing their imposed American citizenship and their Chippewa political identity. In representing this precarious balance, Erdrich suggests that this may be the only viable form of political engagement for many Indigenous peoples living in the territory claimed by the United States.[17]

Chippewa-led Kinship Practices as Self-Recognition

One of the ways in which *The Night Watchman* refuses a settled form of political belonging is by highlighting Chippewa-led kinship practices as markers of a separate and simultaneous form of belonging. As Laura Peers and Jennifer S. H. Brown (1999: 551) explain, "The Ojibwa family has been, in many ways, the prism through which the Ojibwa have experienced history, as well as their vehicle for response and survival." This is dramatized throughout Erdrich's novel as the strong relational patterns between kin (including members of the band, animals, and the land itself). It also becomes the basis for the characters' form of collective self-recognition, which is always wrestling with imposed federal recognition, and has the power to decenter Western ideas of individual citizenship. That is to say, the novel's insistence on kinship as a *political* relation for the Chippewa characters emphasizes that the settler state does not confer the only effective mode of citizenship.

Chippewa kinship practices are made evident in the characters' points of view throughout the text, though some of the best examples come through the novel's subplot. Early in the novel, Patrice Parenteau travels from the reservation to Minneapolis searching for her sister Vera, who disappeared after relocating to the city. Patrice straddles US and Chippewa expectations, exemplifying a border positionality made evident through the irresolution of these parts. She speaks Ojibwemowin at home with her mother, but she also dreams of career success in Western terms at the Jewel Bearing Plant. This dream of success, however, is deeply tied to her familial obligations, which are ordered by a Chippewa kinship political structure. Patrice often feels "like she [is] stretched across a frame, like a skin tent," responsible for keeping her family intact (Erdrich 2020: 20). She knows that without the money she makes at the plant, her family would "collapse" (291). Given her family's economic situation (imposed by settler structures), Patrice's work at the plant is not always a choice; at times it feels like the fulfillment of duty. If politics is, as Christina Boswell (2020) says, a "contestation over ways of framing policy problems," then through Patrice, the reader sees that this struggle between US and Chippewa ways of framing relations is itself part of Patrice's political identity. When Patrice travels to the city, this framing is challenged. Away from her land and her mother, Patrice finds herself confused and vulnerable to exploitation (which she suffers at the hands of a local bar owner and drug addict who convinces her to work as the bar's exoticizing and exploitative entertainment). Looking at herself in her dressing room mirror, Patrice notes, "I am a stranger to myself" (Erdrich 2020: 132). Patrice's point of view reflects the ways in which, for Erdrich's Chippewa characters, individual identity is deeply tied to familial-tribal relations, even though these relations are also continually affected by the economic and political constraints of settler structures. In the city, Patrice finds herself off-balance; she cannot access kin relations, and thus she feels consumed by settler norms. Not surprisingly, when Patrice finally escapes the city, she does so with the help of another member of her band, Wood Mountain. Her return to herself and her community is also a return to a more balanced border positionality, which reflects her ongoing negotiations between settler and Indigenous structures. Though Patrice does not find Vera during this trip, she does find and bring home Vera's baby boy. Not knowing who the father is or Vera's whereabouts, Patrice's family raises the boy as their own.

Kinship as it is demonstrated between Zhanat—Vera and Patrice's mother—and the baby defies settler familial structures by illustrating a mode of relation that is not dependent on the nuclear family unit, so prevalent in Western imaginaries. The reader is told that Zhanat has a "different sort of intelligence" and "in her thinking there [are] no divisions, or maybe divisions [are] not the same, or maybe they [are] invisible" (Erdrich 2020: 189–90). What Patrice is noting when she discusses her mother's "different sort of intelligence" is an encounter between settler order and Indigenous order and the different effects each produce. Zhanat's Chippewa mode of "division" informs her kinship practices toward her grandson and allows her to breastfeed him. When Patrice sees that Zhanat is nursing him "at her breast," she is at first taken aback. But Zhanat explains that "in the old days, when the baby's mother couldn't nurse, the older women were sometimes able to take over" (191). Saying this, Zhanat is directly alluding to a kinship pattern that precedes (and supersedes) settler occupation. Writing about the Cowessess First Nation in Saskatchewan, Cowessess scholar Robert Alexander Innes (2013: 127) shows that "even though kinship patterns have changed due to outside forces and contemporary realities, aspects of the traditional roles and responsibilities based on family ties have persisted" (116). The same might be said of Erdrich's characterization of Zhanat, which highlights how despite settler influence,

Chippewa responsibilities to one another—their own sense of political and social organization—persists, manifesting in ways that seem to defy biology as understood in settler terms. Erdrich's representation also corresponds to what Peers and Brown (1999: 531) call "immediate extended family" in their description of traditional Ojibwe kinship patterns. These scholars show that customary Ojibwe kinship practices extend beyond the limits of the Western nuclear family and observe intense bonds that defy settler lines. As such, the novel enacts the irresolution between the characters' ongoing struggles under colonial domination and their power to create affirmative ways of knowing and being.

In so doing, Erdrich's representation of Chippewa kinship practices offers a counternarrative to the story of US political belonging. It reminds the reader that, as Audra Simpson (2014: 11) puts it, "there is more than one *political* show in town." The characters' understanding of themselves as a polity is reliant on a deep connection to one another and the land. In this sense, by positioning kinship as political, the novel highlights the ways in which Indigenous affiliative belonging fills the gaps left by settler political imaginaries. In *Red Nation Rising*, Nick Estes (Kul Wicasa) et al. (2021: 117–18) ask, "What does kinship look like as a form of politics?" The authors' answer relies on examples that "defy the narrative of alienation and loss that is commonly used to describe . . . Native life. This narrative presumes that Native people are dying, culturally and physically." The writers argue that kinship can be liberatory by emphasizing Native life over Native death. This emphasis on Indigenous-led practices as a mode of liberation is also related to Indigenous resurgence. Michi Saagig Nishnaabeg scholar Leanne Betasamosake Simpson (2017: 226) explains that "the crux of resurgence is that Indigenous people have to recreate and regenerate [their] political systems, education systems and systems of life from within [their] own intelligence." Indigenous liberation comes from a commitment to privilege Indigenous-led processes. Or, in other words, Indigenous liberation comes from the active practice of Indigenous sovereignty. Erdrich's characters' engagement with settler logic is unavoidable, but by insisting on the importance of Chippewa kinship systems, the novel resists the idea that settler logics are absolute. By focusing on these and other forms of irresolution throughout the novel, the reader can begin to trace a refusal of settler binaries.

One of the binaries that the novel challenges is inclusion in or exclusion from the family unit. This is evident in Wood Mountain's relationship to Vera's baby. Wood Mountain's decision to make the baby's cradle board (a job that traditionally falls to the baby's father) is indicative of a kinship relation that not only exceeds the borders of the nuclear family unit, but of blood-relation as the ultimate marker of Indigenous belonging.[18] He has no direct biological relationship to the baby, and yet he feels a sense of familial responsibility for the child. Wood Mountain's attachment supersedes settler biological or legal assumptions as part of an alternative polity, beyond either adoption or the nuclear family. Audra Simpson (2014: 173) writes that "in spite of the rules of the state, in spite of the governance structure that attempts to implement them . . . there are other workings of citizenship," and we see this embodied in Wood Mountain's actions toward the baby. He beckons an alternative sociality that is not limited by state regulations but instead is defined by an "affective way of being . . . in spite of the lack of recognition" (173). Importantly, Wood Mountain's devotion toward the baby is tied to his feelings for those he refers to as the "way-back people" (Erdrich 2020: 323), allowing us to extend the scope of this familial sociality to what Simpson (2014: 173) calls "feeling citizenship," a sense of belonging to the community that displaces the supremacy of settler law. As he works on the cradle board, Wood Mountain explains to Thomas that he is adding little shells to the bottom of the cradle's sinew. The shells are remnants from when there used to be an ocean in the place where the reservation now stands. "From the endless way-back times," Wood Mountain says, "Vera's baby will be playing with these little things from the bottom of the sea that was here. Who could have known?" (Erdrich 2020: 323). He tells Thomas that the thought gives him a sense of peace: "I feel like they're with me, those way-back people. I never talk about it. But they're all around us. I could never leave this place" (323). Wood Mountain's kinship practices are directly informed by the land in an extended sense, far more than mere soil, connecting him to his ancestors (human, plant, and animal). His love for the baby is practiced through active connection to the "way-back people" and the land (as ecology and history) they share and care for together.

Wood Mountain's notion that the "way-back people" are "all around" emphasizes the affirmative power of Chippewa kinship to enact inclusion beyond exclusionary settler boundaries. His connection to the "way-back people" can be read as a form of kinship that defies settler temporality by establishing connections between the present members of the band and their ancestors. This cross-temporal kinship is also evident in the novel's depiction of Roderick, a ghost who follows Thomas throughout the novel. Roderick's existence blurs the boundaries of settler temporalities and emphasizes Ojibwe storytelling techniques, which are not limited by realism. Or, to go back to Audra Simpson's terminology, Roderick *interrupts* settler frameworks simply by existing. When Roderick triumphantly claims that "you can't assimilate Indian ghosts. It's too late!" the reader sees that, as a ghost, Roderick has a certain degree of power—a power that lies precisely on the refusal of settler boundaries as absolute. Roderick tells Thomas that six boys died at their US-run boarding school, "but not me. I wasn't coming home in no coffin." Thomas argues the point, telling Roderick that they *did* send him home in a coffin. But Roderick counters this version of the story, saying: "They put me in that coffin, sure! Put me on the train. But I was in there laughing. Told myself they'd sure be surprised when I jumped out on them" (163). Although the white boarding school teachers believe him to be dead in the coffin, Roderick's spirit continues to haunt. It is forever ready to "jump out."

Roderick embodies a refusal to the settler notion that the past can be cordoned off from the present. As such, Roderick's existence is also a reminder of the "horror and agony" of his settler-imposed death, which like Roderick, has not disappeared (Erdrich 2020: 372). Roderick died in a US-government-run boarding school after he was locked in the school's cellar by a missionary teacher as punishment for stealing food. He developed a fever and never recovered. Thomas first sees Roderick's ghost during a night shift at the Jewel Bearing Plant. Roderick appears as "a frowsy-headed little boy crouched on top of the band saw" (15). Roderick not only reminds Thomas of his own boarding school past, but he makes it so that Thomas feels this past as part of his present. Confused, Thomas tries to blink the image away, but he sees the boy ever more clearly. In this way, Roderick's haunting presence reminds Thomas (and the reader) that past genocidal practices in the United States continue to impact Indigenous presents. Eve Tuck (Unangax̂) and C. Ree (2013: 642) explain that "the United States is permanently haunted by the slavery, genocide and violence entwined in its first, present, and future days. Haunting doesn't hope to change people's perceptions, nor does it hope for reconciliation. Haunting lies precisely in its refusal to stop . . . this refusal to stop is its own form of resolving." In this sense, haunting is not always affirmative. Rather, haunting can be indicative of the continued trauma inflicted by colonial structures, a "refusal" of resolution that insists that this violence is not over, nor will it ever be over, as long as settler colonial rule continues. In depicting the irresolvable presence of settler domination as it is felt across this Chippewa community, the novel makes reconciliation on settler terms unthinkable. This helps clarify the fact that in this settler colonial context, border positionalities are not necessarily advantageous. While they might produce certain strengths or powers, these positions reflect a broader reality: the impossibility of resolution given the ongoing violence of settler structures.

As a character, Roderick is also notable because of his impulse to continue protecting his kin after death. This is evident when he accompanies the Turtle Mountain delegation to the Congressional Hearing for the Termination Bill. While Thomas speaks before the Subcommittees of the Committees on Interior and Insular Affairs and shares his statement of "strong opposition" to the bill, Senator Watkins continually interrupts him (Erdrich 2020: 400). Thomas thinks, "Oh hell, stick with it, stick with it, don't let him give you the teacher-eye." Thomas is clearly faltering when "suddenly Roderick [enters] the room" (400). Thomas perceives Roderick's presence as the reinforcement he needs to win against the senator. Here again, Roderick's contradictions are exposed; the ghost, a symbol of Indigenous ongoing suffering in the face of settler structures, also becomes a symbol of possibility, the avowal of Chippewa lifeways despite settler constraints. Thomas says, "Is that you, Roderick?" To which the ghost replies, "Yes it's me. Hold out. Don't get mad" (402). He tells Thomas, "Remember how you buttered that white teacher up to the teeth? Called him sir, sir this, sir that, thank him constantly, asked his advice. Then stole the keys from his suit pocket? Then you let me out and slipped back the keys" (405). By calling upon this memory of how Thomas and Roderick resisted settler absorption in boarding school, Roderick urges Thomas toward an indirect refusal, one that *appears* to respect the bounds of settler order. After the hearing, inspired by Roderick's strategy, Thomas finds the senator in his private chamber and thanks him for his time. The reader is led to believe that this gesture buys Watkins's good will and ultimately secures his vote against the termination of the Turtle Mountain Band of Chippewa. After leaving Senator Watkins, Thomas reflects: "I am willing to forgo my dignity to try to butter you up to the teeth. I hope it helps our cause" (406). In Thomas's reflection we see that his individual "dignity" is less important to him than the collective—"our cause"—and sacrificing the former is just another tactic of Thomas's border positionality, an active political strategy for fighting settler absorption.

It must be said that in "buttering up" Senator Watkins, Thomas is not resorting to a new strategy. Although Roderick encourages him to perform this gesture, Thomas does not experience a total transformation during the hearing; he is simply rearticulating a strategy that he has long subscribed to in his dealings with settler structures. He is doing that which he has always done.[19] This is evident earlier in the text when Thomas first starts strategizing against Senator Watkins. Though he admits that "Arthur V. Watkins was clearly an enemy," he decides that he will think of Watkins as his "adversary" instead (Erdrich 2020: 276). Thomas explains his reasoning by saying that "an enemy has to be defeated in battle, but an adversary's different. You must outwit an adversary. So you have to know them very well" (276). In establishing this difference between an enemy and an adversary, Thomas is codifying his strategy of resistance to settler oppressions as one that depends on the semipermeable boundary between self and other. By casting Watkins as an adversary, Thomas is refusing a total separation from the other, choosing (again) to remain in a productive state of ambivalence. This reflects what James Tully (2000: 42) has referred to as a key technique in Indigenous resistance to colonization, that is "their freedom of maneuver within the system . . . to comply and participate in the dominant institutions while refusing to surrender." As such, in establishing the difference between enemies and adversaries, Erdrich is pointing to the lived experience of her characters whose choices are informed by a tense and unresolvable negotiation with the settler state.

Perhaps the best way to understand Erdrich's refusal of settler-imposed belonging as all-encompassing in *The Night Watchman* is through an Ojibwe creation story, a story that Thomas's father tells within the space of the novel. Erdrich's retelling of this story becomes important to establishing the characters' Chippewa identity, reminding the reader of the ways in which storytelling practices are deeply political. The story provides Thomas (and the reader) a frame through which to understand some of the struggles that run through the narrative as a whole. Biboon, Thomas's father, tells him that "in the beginning . . . the world was covered with water. The Creator lined up the animals who were the best divers," to swim down to the bottom to retrieve a piece of earth from the bottom, so the Creator could recreate the land (Erdrich 2020: 172). He sends down the Fisher, the Loon, and the Hell-diver, but they all fail to bring back the earth. Lastly, the Creator sends the "humble water rat . . . He took a long time, a very long time, and then finally Wazhashk floated to the top. He was drowned but his paw was clenched." The Creator "saw that the muskrat had carried up just a little off the bottom. From that tiny paw's grip of dirt, the Creator made the whole earth" (172). The fact that Thomas and the muskrat share a name speaks to the significance of this story in relation to the rest of the novel.[20] Much like the muskrat's dive, Thomas's fight with

Senator Watkins is a fight that will "cost him everything," and one that he cannot win on his own (442). The muskrat's strategy for securing the "dirt" is worth noting. He dives deep into the water in order to secure not only his survival, but that of the other animals. This is not unlike Thomas's strategy against Senator Watkins. Thomas remembers that when he first went to boarding school, Biboon said to him, "study hard because we need to know the enemy." In this sense, by diving into settler structures, Thomas and his classmates aimed to return with the knowledge necessary to fight for the collective survival of their band. Thomas sees the "wisdom" of that strategy, especially since he was able to "use their logic to get improvements in the community school" and to "locate the jewel bearing plant near the reservation." Thomas claims that he was able to use "the education they had given him to advance his people." But these statements are followed by a caveat: "Along the way the word enemy became confusing" (275). This suggests that though at first these structures were "other," they do eventually become part of Thomas's own sense of self. In becoming entangled with "their logic," Thomas struggles to fully separate himself from white settler culture—again emphasizing the semipermeable line between "enemy" and "adversary." To return to the image of the muskrat, in diving down to the bottom, Thomas loses a part of himself. While we might be tempted to read this as a sign of Erdrich's resignation to the power of the state, in Thomas's return, his deep breath once he returns from Washington, DC, we can also find something else.

Much like the muskrat in the Ojibwe origin story, Thomas also drowns after his dive to the bottom of the settler political machine. He has a stroke during the return trip home. Although he recovers, Thomas struggles to find the words and order that previously defined his way of thinking. In the last scene of the novel, he dozes in the lamplight, back to work at the Jewel Plant. He sees "muskrats everywhere. Their small supple forms slipped busily along the floor at dusk, continually perfecting their burrows." He confronts the animals and asks them, "What is my name?" worried that there might "be a time" when he will not "know himself" (Erdrich 2020: 442). This fear is followed by a description of the land surrounding his father's cabin—"the bright popple leaves, trembling and flashing as they swirled thickly off the branches . . . " (443). In this dreamlike sequence, Thomas sees the land "littered with bones" and these bones "assembling into forms" and taking on "shaggy" shapes (443). The nightmarish scene, as evidenced by the "shaggy" and unrecognizable form of these animals, speaks to Thomas's uneasiness at the end of the novel. Despite avoiding termination, the trip to DC has made Thomas and the other members of the delegation even more aware of the difficulties they will face to survive as Chippewa, the high cost of ongoing struggle, as well as the necessity of it. Erdrich's description gives Thomas's personal worry a larger scope; he seems to be wondering not only whether he might forget his name but whether he might ultimately fail to recognize the land as well (and in so doing, lose himself completely *as Chippewa*). This mode of thinking shows a distinct Indigenous inflection, one that understands the land as the source of knowing and being. Leanne Betasamosake Simpson (2017: 43) writes that "Indigenous bodies don't relate to the land by possessing or owning it or having control over it. [They] relate to land through connection—generative, affirmative, complex, overlapping, and nonlinear relationship." In Thomas's characterization at the end of the novel, the reader sees this sentiment figured. Thomas fears the land will disappear, and with it, his and his people's collective identity. The land is a relative, and it is through a relationship with this relative that Thomas and the rest of the band are able to see and understand themselves and their place in the larger world. These kinship structures, so essential to the characters' collective identity, are themselves a form of self-recognition. Much like Patrice, Thomas needs to sustain his relationship with kin—including the land—in order to sustain his own sense of self. In this way, despite Thomas's quest for federal recognition, his worldview at the end of the novel continues to be largely informed by a deep kinship with the land and the other humans and animals who share it, a relationality that escapes settler definition.

Through the narrative arc of *The Night Watchman*, the reader is made aware that the Chippewa characters—given their border positionalities—"can't just turn into regular Americans" (Erdrich 2020: 211). While the characters make important gains throughout—they avoid termination—the conditions of settler colonialism make their complete disengagement from settler-imposed belonging impossible. Instead, at the end of the novel (much as in its beginning) the characters' political identities can best be described through a lens of Chippewa/US irresolution. In the conclusion to *Mohawk Interruptus*, Audra Simpson (2014: 193) says she hopes scholars will continue to investigate how "other people undergoing the stresses of settler colonialism in their territories" are "adapting to this structure." We might say that Erdrich is answering this call in *The Night Watchman*. Like Simpson, Erdrich resists the settler notions that "recognition" and "reconciliation" are "the only options on the table." Simpson calls these "false choices," reminding us that "choices are not choices if they are bestowed rather than self-generated." As we have seen, Erdrich's characters refuse US citizenship as a totalizing form of political and social belonging, but they do so from a space of uneasy irresolution.

There is a moment in the novel when Patrice visits the Capitol. As she walks into the gallery overlooking the House of Representatives, she catches sight of an "extraordinary-looking woman in bold lipstick" (Erdrich 2020: 394). She watches as the woman takes out a pistol from her purse, shouts, "viva Puerto Rico libre!" and shoots into the Capitol, all while waving "a flag of her country." Although Patrice does not understand the full implications of the event—she asks herself, "What was Puerto Rico?"—the event is key to Erdrich's elaboration of what I have been calling border positionality (396). By putting Puerto Rico and the Turtle Mountain Band of Chippewa in close proximity, Erdrich suggests an important connection; namely, the woman's story and Patrice's story both speak of the ways in which state-sponsored forms of citizenship are lacking when it comes to describing those who have endured the United States's colonial machinations. An informed reader cannot help but hear echoes in the language the United States has used to describe its relationship to American Indian nations and to Puerto Rico.[21] In both cases, the US government uses the promise and threat of political belonging to enact its colonial agenda. Both Indigenous nations and unincorporated territories, such as Puerto Rico, straddle a complicated political border between foreign and domestic. This line, which determines inclusion and exclusion from the US polity, is continually drawn and redrawn for the benefit of the settler state alone. When Patrice reflects on the event, she decides that "although it was terrible," she "had been thrilled when the woman stood up and yelled" (396). And how could she not be? Enthralled by this sudden act of violence, Patrice sees her own conflicted relationship to the US government. Regardless of her individual citizenship status, her Chippewa identity makes her an outsider to the US government, a person for whom acting from one's identity in the settler's house is a gesture that must appear simultaneously illuminating and inscrutable to others. With this, Erdrich again shows that for Indigenous people, political belonging is a site of continual struggle, one that cannot be resolved simply by "deciding to."

Florencia Lauria is an assistant professor of English at SUNY Oswego. Her work engages contemporary Latinx and Indigenous literatures and films to consider the tension between Latinx migration and Indigenous sovereignty.

Notes

I am grateful to Scott Manning Stevens, Silvio Torres-Saillant, Jason Zencka, Corinne Noble, Alex O'Connell, Lauren Cooper, Jeffrey Adams, and Susan Zencka for their helpful comments and engagement with this piece at various stages of composition. I am especially indebted to Crystal Bartolovich, whose mentorship and feedback were essential to the success of this essay.

1 "Indian Citizenship Act." 1924. *US Statues at Large* 43:253.

2 I am borrowing the term *strangulating* from Mohawk scholar Audra Simpson's (2014: 3) claim that Indigenous nationals belong to "a strangulated political order."

3 For more on the problem of reading Indigenous peoples as minoritized subjects within the US national polity instead of as distinct nationalities, see Jodi Byrd's (Chickasaw Nation of Oklahoma) *Transit of Empire* (2011). Byrd (2011: xxiv) writes that when "indigenous identity becomes a racial identity," American Indian "national assertions of sovereignty, self-determination, and land rights disappear into U.S. territoriality." See also Mark Rifkin's *When Did Indians Become Straight* (2011) where he explains that US law constructed "racial Indianness" as a means of interpolating Indigenous nations through a racial category, thereby displacing clan belonging as the political organizing method of many Indigenous nations.

4 Louise Erdrich is a member of the Turtle Mountain Band of Chippewa. Following Erdrich's own usage, I use the words *Ojibwe* and *Chippewa* interchangeably.

5 Erdrich addresses the connection between Thomas and her grandfather, Patrick Gourneau, in the novel's foreword and afterword. She explains that although she drew heavily from her grandfather's actual letters in constructing the novel, "the book is fiction." Framing the novel this way suggests that fiction is a powerful venue for unraveling the fraught and complicated conditions at the center of the "real" story.

6 The roots of the term *kinship* are tangled with settler anthropology, and, as a result, the term is not always adequate for describing Indigenous relations. Still, because of the way the term has been reclaimed by Indigenous critics (see Innes 2013; Estes et al. 2021), I chose to use it throughout this article.

7 I am thinking here of the US Supreme Court cases *Johnson v. McIntosh* (21 U.S. [8 Wheat.] 543 [1823]), *Cherokee Nation v. Georgia* (30 U.S. [5 Pet.] 1 [1831]), and *Worcester v. Georgia* (31 U.S. [6 Pet.] 515 [1832]), which are foundational to the relationship between the US state and Indigenous nations. In *Cherokee Nation v. Georgia*, for example, Chief Justice Marshall defined the status of American Indian tribes as "domestic dependent nations." Moreover, he declared that the federal/tribal relationship was analogous to "that of a ward to his guardian." For more on Indigenous peoples' relationship to US law, see Pommersheim 2012; Bruyneel 2007.

8   For more on "elimination" in relation to settler colonialism, see Wolfe 2006.

9   With the passage of the Fourteenth Amendment in 1868, the notion of jus soli, which grants citizenship to those born within the geographical territory claimed by the nation, became established within the American legal framework. Although this did not apply to Indigenous peoples (who were named as an exception in the 1868 amendment), it set the stage for their eventual absorption. For more on the historical development of the US concept of citizenship, see Hyde 2018.

10 As Lenape scholar Joanne Barker (2005: 26) writes, "sovereignty is historically 'contingent,'" meaning that although the term originates from a European context and is thereby "incomplete, inaccurate, and troubled" in its relation to Indigeneity, post–World War II, it took distinct meanings for Indigenous peoples rearticulating the concept to secure their rights to self-determination. For more on the problematics of sovereignty, see Alfred 2006. For more on the value of critical sovereignty, see Simpson 2020.

11 Throughout the Love Medicine series Erdrich takes engagement with the reservation to be irreducible for her Ojibwe characters, but she seems to resist the idea that the logics of the reservation are total. In *The Bingo Palace* (Erdrich 1994: 127–28), for example, Lipsha says he is "waiting for proof-positive self-identification, a complicated thing in Indian Country." However, when he sees Fleur coming, he "shoves" the "duplicates of applications and identification papers" toward the "government building" secretary and tells her to "file it under 'L' for Love Child," suggesting a refusal of the absolute power of state-sponsored belonging.

12 It is worth noting that Erdrich's political engagement throughout her career has not necessarily been consistent, nor is it widely agreed upon among critics. Most notably, in 1986, Laguna Pueblo writer Leslie Marmon Silko wrote a review of Erdrich's second novel, *The Beet Queen* (1986), in which she argued that while the novel "has an ethereal clarity and shimmering beauty" this is only "because no history or politics intrudes to muddy the well of pure necessity contained within language itself" (Silko 1986: 178, 179). Elizabeth Cook-Lynn (Crow Creek Sioux) (1996: 85) supported this claim by saying that in her estimation Erdrich's fiction belongs to a category of cosmopolitan Indigenous writers whose work "seem[s] to leave American Indian tribal peoples in this country stateless, politically inept, and utterly without nationalistic alternatives." Still, other critics have disagreed with these assessments. See Pérez-Castillo 1991; Owens 1992.

13 For more on the ways in which Rob Nixon's (2013) idea of "slow violence" applies to settler colonialism, see Wakeham 2022.

14 It is also important to note that Erdrich writes in an Ojibwe context and, as such, her characters encounter a different set of relations than that of Simpson's (2014) Kahnawà:ke subjects. Yet, like the Mohawks of Kahnawà:ke in Audra Simpson's work, the Ojibwe people in Louise Erdrich's novels are positioned by the US and Canadian states in ways that render a "politics of refusal," as Simpson describes it, relevant.

15 Audra Simpson (2014: 11) writes that Indigenous politics "challenge what most perceive as settled." She continues on to say that "by settled [she] mean[s] 'done,' 'finished,' 'complete' . . . the presumption that the colonial project has been realized."

16 Mary Louise Pratt (1991: 34) defines *contact zones* as "social spaces where cultures meet, clash, and grapple with each other, often in contexts of highly asymmetrical relations of power."

17 Kevin Bruyneel (2007: 25) calls for a "politics-on-the-boundaries" or a "third space of sovereignty" as a necessary framework for understanding US and Indigenous relations and as a possibility for "defining and seeing expressions of citizenship, and sovereignty that are not confined by dominant political boundaries, that refuse the imposition of such boundaries."

18 In her novels, Erdrich tends to privilege affiliative modes of belonging over purely biological ones. For more on Erdrich's suspicion of settler biopolitics, see Erdrich 2010 where she declines to have her DNA tested for the PBS show *Faces of America*. For more on the mixed consequences of genetics as means of assessing belonging to Indigenous communities, see Sisseton Wahpeton Oyate scholar Kim TallBear (2013).

19 In *What We Have Always Done*, Michi Saagiig Nishnaabeg scholar Leanne Betasamosake Simpson (2017: 9) argues that an "intense love of land, of family, and of [their] nations . . . has always been the spine of Indigenous resistance."

20 Erdrich (2020: 4) explains this significance in the novel itself, where she writes, "Thomas was named for the muskrat . . . Although the wazhaskag were numerous and ordinary, they were also crucial . . . In that way, as it turned out, Thomas was perfectly named."

21 In 1831 Chief Justice Marshall (*Cherokee Nation v. Georgia*, 30 U.S. [5 Pet.] 1 [1831]) defined Indigenous tribes as "domestic dependent nations," marking Indigenous people as existing both inside and outside of the United States. In 1901 Justice Edward Douglass White (*Downes v. Bidwell*, 182 U.S. 244 [1901]) made a similar claim about unincorporated territories, such as Puerto Rico, by claiming that these were "foreign to the US in a domestic sense." For more on the Insular Cases, see Burnett and Marshall 2001. Also, for more on the connections between Indigenous and Puerto Rican experiences vis-à-vis citizenship see, Román 2010.

References

Alfred, Taiaiake. 2005. "Sovereignty." In *Sovereignty Matters: Locations of Contestation and Possibility in Indigenous Struggles for Self-Determination*, edited by Joanne Barker, 33–50. Lincoln: Univ. of Nebraska Press.

Ashcroft, Bill. 2001. *Post-Colonial Transformation*. New York: Routledge.

Barker, Joanne. 2005. "For Whom Sovereignty Matters." In *Sovereignty Matters: Locations of Contestation and Possibility in Indigenous Struggles for Self-Determination*, edited by Joanne Barker, 1–32. Lincoln: Univ. of Nebraska Press.

Berlant, Lauren. 2007. "Citizenship." *Keywords for American Cultural Studies*, edited by Bruce Burgett and Glen Hendler, 44–48. New York: New York Univ. Press.

Boswell, Christina. 2020. "What Is Politics?" *The British Academy Blog*, January 14. https://www.thebritishacademy.ac.uk/blog/what-is-politics/.

Bruyneel, Kevin. 2007. *The Third Space of Sovereignty: The Postcolonial Politics of US-Indigenous Relations*. Minneapolis: Univ. of Minnesota Press.

Burnett, Christina Duffy, and Burke Marshall. 2001. *Foreign in a Domestic Sense: Puerto Rico, American Expansion, and the Constitution*. Durham, NC: Duke Univ. Press.

Byrd, Jodi. 2011. *The Transit of Empire: Indigenous Critiques of Colonialism*. Minneapolis: Univ. of Minnesota Press.

Collins, Cary C. 2004. "Editor's Introduction." In *Assimilation's Agent: My Life As a Superintendent in the Indian Boarding School System* by Edwin L. Chalcraft, edited by Cary C. Collins, ix–lxii. Lincoln: Univ. of Nebraska Press.

Cook-Lynn, Elizabeth. 1996. *Why I Can't Read Wallace Stegner and Other Essays: A Tribal Voice*. Madison: Univ. of Wisconsin Press.

Coulthard, Glen Sean. 2014. *Red Skin, White Masks: Rejecting the Colonial Politics of Recognition*. Minneapolis: Univ. of Minnesota Press.

Dennison, Jean. 2012. *Colonial Entanglement: Constituting a Twenty-First Century Osage Nation*. Chapel Hill: Univ. of North Carolina Press.

Dunbar-Ortiz, Roxanne. 2014. *An Indigenous Peoples' History of the United States*. Boston: Beacon Press.

Erdrich, Louise. 1994. *The Bingo Palace*. New York: Harper Perennial.

Erdrich, Louise. (1984) 2009. *Love Medicine*. New York: Harper Collins.

Erdrich, Louise. 2010. "Faces of America: Interview with Louise Erdrich." Interview by Henry Louis Gates Jr. *PBS Television*, February 1–March 3. www.pbs.org/wnet/facesofamerica/profiles/Louise-erdrich/10/.

Erdrich, Louise. 2020. *The Night Watchman*. New York: Harper Collins.

Estes, Nick, Melanie K. Yazzie, Jennifer Nez Denetdale, and David Correia. 2021. *Red Nation Rising: From Bordertown Violence to Native Liberation*. Oakland: PM Press.

Hyde, Carrie. 2018. *Civic Longing: The Speculative Origins of U.S. Citizenship*. Cambridge, MA: Harvard Univ. Press.

Innes, Robert Alexander. 2013. *Elder Brother and the Law of the People: Contemporary Kinship and Cowessess First Nation*. Winnipeg: Univ. of Manitoba Press.

Nixon, Rob. 2013. *Slow Violence and the Environmentalism of the Poor*. Cambridge, MA: Harvard Univ. Press

Owens, Louis. 1992. *Other Destinies: Understanding the American Indian Novel*. Norman: Univ. of Oklahoma Press.

Peers, Laura, and Jennifer S. H Brown. 1999. "There Is No End to Relationship among the Indians." *The History of the Family* 4, no. 4: 529–55.

Pérez-Castillo, Susan. 1991. "Postmodernism, Native American Literature and the Real: The Silko-Erdrich Controversy." *Massachusetts Review* 32, no. 2: 285–94.

Pommersheim, Frank. 2012. *Broken Landscape: Indians, Indian Tribes, and the Constitution*. New York: Oxford Univ. Press.

Pratt, Mary Louise. 1991. "Arts of the Contact Zone." *Profession*, 33–40. http://www.jstor.org/stable/25595469.

Rifkin, Mark. 2011. *When Did Indians Become Straight? Kinship, the History of Sexuality, and Native Sovereignty*. New York: Oxford Univ. Press.

Román, Ediberto. 2010. *Citizenship and its Exclusions*. New York: New York Univ. Press.

Silko, Leslie Marmon. 1986. "Review of The Beet Queen." *Studies in American Indian Literatures* 10, no. 4: 177–84.

Simpson, Audra. 2014. *Mohawk Interruptus: Political Life across the Borders of Settler States*. Durham, NC: Duke Univ. Press.

Simpson, Audra. 2020. "The Sovereignty of Critique." *South Atlantic Quarterly* 119, no. 4: 685–99.

Simpson, Leanne Betasamosake. 2017. *As We Have Always Done: Indigenous Freedom through Radical Resistance*. Minneapolis: Univ. of Minnesota Press.

Stirrup, David. 2010. *Louise Erdrich*. Manchester: Manchester Univ. Press.

TallBear, Kim. 2013. "Genomic Articulations of Indigeneity." *Social Studies of Science* 43, no. 4: 509–33.

Tuck, Eve, and C. Ree. 2013. "A Glossary of Haunting." In *Handbook of Autoethnography*, edited by S. H. Jones, T. E. Adams, and C. Ellis, 639–58. Walnut Creek, CA: Left Coast Press.

Tully, James. 2000. "The Struggles of Indigenous Peoples for and of Freedom." In *Political Theory and the Rights of Indigenous Peoples*, edited by Duncan Ivison, Paul Patton, and Will Sanders, 36–59. Cambridge: Cambridge Univ. Press.

Wakeham, Pauline. 2022. "The Slow Violence of Settler Colonialism: Genocide, Attrition, and the Long Emergency of Invasion." *Journal of Genocide Research* 24, no. 3: 337–56.

Wolfe, Patrick. 2006. "Settler Colonialism and the Elimination of the Native." *Journal of Genocide Research* 8, no. 4: 387–409.

Joseph Isaac Miranda   The Suspended States of Latinx Literature

Abstract This article lingers in the suspended time of Justin Torres's *We the Animals* (2011), a story of loss, alienation, and an errant desire to remain underwater. Written in the long durée of US coloniality, Torres's novel resists the narrative conventions of the bildungsroman to contend with the ways Latinx literature is bound to narratives of forestalled self-development and failed incorporation. Such uneven relations are traced back to the ethnographic frameworks emplotted in the Insular Cases—which are a set of Supreme Court decisions that have suspended Puerto Rico into statelessness since 1901. This article argues that Torres's refusal of narrative convention reveals how the dictates of the Insular Cases have seeped into ethnographic understandings of Latinx as suspended from normativity at large. However, Torres's tactical use of suspension refuses to move toward legible subjecthood or linger in despair. Rather, the novel tarries with the irregular conditions of Latinx life to posit shared alienation as the groundwork for a larger, vibrant brown sociality in the ongoing muck of the Insular Cases.
Keywords law, queer, Justin Torres, Latinx literature, Supreme Court

The final line of Justin Torres's bildungsroman, *We the Animals* (2011), is uttered by an institutionalized adolescent narrator. He professes: "'Upright, upright,' I say, I slur, I vow" (Torres 2011: 125). This desire for the kind of individual autonomy typically associated with normative subjecthood arrives at the end of a coming-of-age novel that does not progressively move toward adulthood. Rather, it concludes with the narrator's involuntary admission into a mental health facility and an intoxicated craving for rectitude. Haunted by an impossible desire for liberation, the narrator does not find freedom in the slurred dream of self-possession; instead, the narrator is held in a state of suspended maturation that mirrors the United States' reduction of Puerto Rican independence to a state of infantilized political pupilage and deferred sovereignty. The novel, told in nineteen episodes,

American Literature, Volume 96, Number 4, December 2024
DOI 10.1215/00029831-11557529   © 2024 by Duke University Press

is stitched together by the narrator's growing alienation from his family and his desire to escape their isolated, rural working-class community. Its description of childhood is marked by a loss of familial belonging and a longing for a scene of queer Latinx life. Failing to reach either the apotheosis of liberal subjectivity or a space of minoritized belonging, the novel's final line suspends the reader in two distinct yet imbricated problems: the false promise of incorporation at the center of the Latinx bildungsroman and the muck of coloniality that constricts Puerto Rican freedom.

First, for most of the twentieth and twenty-first centuries, US Latinx literatures have been suspended in a narrative of development. From the dangling of Latinos as the next generation of Americans to the predominance of the bildungsroman in the Latinx canon, latinidad eludes formal coherence and is presented as an ephemeral event (see the ever-shifting terminology that hails *Latino/a/x/e* into contested relation). *We the Animals* torques these frameworks that shape latinidad as an imminent identity in need of political regulation, confinement, and capture; consequently, it arrests our literary attention in states of stasis. By withholding becoming, the novel identifies a dissatisfying relation that the canonical novels of Latinx literature (like Piri Thomas's *Down These Mean Streets* [1967] or Sandra Cisneros's *The House on Mango Street* [1984]) have to the genre; as their conclusions attest, the novels end with a lingering sense of loss and alienation instead of incorporation.

While these canonical narratives fail to produce a feeling of liberation, *We the Animals* resists the call toward legible subjecthood altogether. Instead, the novel is punctuated by images of the unnamed narrator in confined spaces of movement (lingering in perpetual pupilage and suspended underwater). I claim that this resistance to development turns analyses of the bildungsroman away from individual growth to register the contested relation between narrative form and citizenship; therefore, the novel's embrace of suspension exposes how the nation ensnares the Latinx subject within discourses of perpetual lack and dependency.

Second, this repertoire of suspended life haunts the particularities of the Puerto Rican imagination. Specifically, the institutionalized narrator reflects the ongoing US occupation of the archipelago and the dispossession of Puerto Rican self-determination codified in the Insular Cases. The Insular Cases, decided between 1901 and 1925, legitimized a colonial government in Puerto Rico and denied constitutional rights for those on the archipelago. Although citizenship was later granted in 1917, it created an irregular form of incorporation that withheld sovereignty for increased individual mobility; taken together, these policies reveal an obfuscated state of colonial rule that sedimented Puerto Rican dependence on the United States. As such, the Insular Cases generated perpetual deficiency to justify continued control. The legal frameworks for thinking about Puerto Rican sovereignty—delayed incorporation and incomplete citizenship— undergird how the nation saw Puerto Rican people as contingent outsiders and subservient nationals. I do not see the Insular Cases as a primal wound that shapes all Latinx literature. Instead, they show how the state's legal maneuvers are entrenched in Latinx literature's concern as primarily about recognition and development. By extension, thinking with the Insular Cases alongside *We the Animals* reveals how the novel's captive narrator registers how Latinx claims to belonging are stuck to these narrative conventions of perpetual growth and deferred incorporation—attenuated between foreign and domestic, citizenship and statelessness.

And yet, the Insular Cases have faded from cultural memory. By bringing the Insular Cases back to the surface, and taking up suspended sovereignty as a formal problem, *We the Animals* upends our common understandings of Latinx literature. Set in rural upstate New York, the novel also revises—and is geographically and thematically displaced from—common narrative frameworks for understanding latinidad. Through the particularities of Puerto Rico, we approach Latinx literature through the US's racializing tactics, not solely through narratives of migration and nationalism. The novel is landlocked: it is a narrative neither of becoming nor of arrival; it is held in an abeyed state of growth. Rather than move toward maturation, one hundred of the novel's one hundred twenty-five pages are stuck to the narrator's childhood; such a lack of velocity undermines the bildungsroman's teleological imperative, which equates plot progression with experience. Instead, the solitary narrator emerges over the course of the novel against the disillusion of belonging held by the collective voice in the text's title. The narrative follows the narrator's alienation from his family as he becomes aware of his own queer desires. Loss pervades the text; his growing isolation is predicated on the novel's understanding that queerness is a transgression against the delicate contract the Latino family has with the United States.

Therefore, the narrator, who is estranged from his family and a larger sense of latinidad, is held in a state of impossible movement and misrecognition. By refusing mobility and maturation (two values central to the bildungsroman), the novel does not simply linger in the irregular status of Puerto Rican citizenship. The novel repeatedly suspends bodily autonomy (as a compulsory narrative desire) in order to resist the relation between self-dependency and knowledge. This form of resistance registers what Sandra Ruiz (2019: 2) defines as a sense of *ricanness* as an "ongoing endurance" to US coloniality. In finding tight spaces of freedom in "limited self-control," Puerto Rican performance works against an ontology that is incomplete and always deferred (9). Rather than succumb to failure, Torres moves with abjection to "rehearse another relentless death scene [in] a broad pause for the Rican future" (170). In the contested relation between citizenship and queer latinidad, the novel lingers in despair to ask how we might imagine living on when the arrival of a decolonial future seems forever deferred and withheld from reach.

If Ruiz attunes us to the ways coloniality continues to weigh down the Rican body, I extend Ruiz's focus in performance studies to contend with the ways the Insular Cases set the stage for collective relations over time. By grappling with the novel and citizenship, my focus on the suspended conventions of *We the Animals* offers a repertoire of resistance to history and the law as a compulsory and settled linear plot. Therefore, I argue that *We the Animals* refuses a narrative of becoming (which reproduces stereotypical frameworks of incomplete Latinx subjects) to embrace states of submersion that emplot the narrator in the long durée of American coloniality. By engaging with the ways the law structures affective and material relations, I chart the emergent structures of obligation (aside from the nation, the heteronormative family, and the individual) that survive alienation despite despair.

I return to the novel's scenes of suspended life in three ways. First, I reveal how the novel resists the dictates of the Insular Cases, which have made Puerto Rican incorporation into the nation impossible. Second, I trace how this dynamic becomes the architectural framework for the novel's resistance to the bildungsroman in scenes of failed maturation; I argue that Torres's suspension of narrative progression disidentifies from the genealogical and the national as frames of linear inheritance for a queer latinidad seen as abject. Finally, I argue that the novel deploys a tactical use of suspension to refuse normative fixity and maturation and to move with alienation as the groundwork for a larger, vibrant queer brown sociality. Put differently, I argue that *We the Animals* eschews development and embraces states of constriction and entanglement to recontextualize literary forms that appear fragmented within a lineage of policy making that promised rights yet withheld sovereignty. Despite negation, the novel resists despair by positing forms of queer brown refuge as a means for survival in the absence of state recognition and in the ongoing muck of the Insular Cases.

Law of the Father

Nuyorican literature's relationship to the law is not new. As Miguel Algarín (1981: 91) suggests, this literature is about "establishing patterns of survival" in response to the US disarticulation of Puerto Ricans from history, inheritance, and self-dependency. *We the Animals* extends this legacy by offering suspension as a "structure of feeling"; to sit with the narrator's "isolating" sense of confinement is to register a collective Puerto Rican body under duress (Williams 1992: 132). *We the Animals* follows the wounds of childhood that accompany the expectations of normative masculinity and racial alienation amid class precarity. The narrator's working-class parents (themselves teenagers when their children are born) are overwhelmed by the responsibilities of adulthood and parenting without a financial or communal safety net; often, the boys are left by themselves while their parents go to work. When the parents are present, the boys witness scenes of abuse. When they are absent, the boys' needs go unmet; such a precarious relationship to food, shelter, and work destabilizes the family form into a state of crisis. The novel elegizes an absent innocence and registers the shared feeling (among parents and children) of being trapped by circumstance. Over the course of the novel, the narrator loses the state of dependence that binds him with his two brothers in an act of mutual survival. In the novel's final twenty-five pages, the plot shifts to the narrator's adolescence. Here, instead of a narrative of self-making, the narrative orchestrates the narrator's self-destruction (recall the narrator's alienation from his family and bodily autonomy by novel's close). Thus, the novel is less a story of accumulative growth or liberation than it is a recording of collective endurance despite the "shared wounding" of the law (Muñoz, Nyongó, and Chambers-Letson 2020: 6).

By disidentifying from the formal conventions of narrative development, the novel assembles a repertoire of suspended relations that impress the everyday feelings of coloniality on form. For example, early in the novel the unnamed narrator tells us how his father left him to drown.

The incident itself played and played in my mind, and at night, in bed, I could not sleep for remembering. How Paps had slipped away from us, how he looked on as we flailed and struggled, how I needed to escape Ma's clutch and grip, how I let myself slide down and down, and when I opened my eyes what I discovered there: black-green murkiness, an underwater world, terror. I sank down for a long time, disoriented and writhing, and then suddenly I was swimming—kicking my legs and spreading my arms just like Paps had shown me long before, and rising up to the light and exploding into air, and then that first breath, sucking air all the way down into my lungs, and when I looked up the sky had never been so vaulted, so sparkling and magnificent (Torres 2011: 23).

Abandoned by his parents—who knew he could not swim—the narrator sinks without resistance, desiring, at least for a moment, negation. What drove him to find such tight spaces of fugitive cover? Estranged from the world, the boy replays this scene of fraught development born from his father's abandonment and his mother's panic. In this traumatic memory that "played and played" (23) in his mind, the novel lingers with the image of the boy shoved to the bottom of the lake. Set up to fail, the narrator sinks instead of fighting his mother's dependence on him to survive. He would "rather let go and [slip] quietly down to the lake's black bottom" than "admit fear" (21). This lesson in forced maturation reveals the limitations of arriving at adulthood in a normative way. Rather, he sinks to escape from his father's "meticulous" pedagogy that seeks to prepare his children for "the other side of pain"—an adulthood marked by the cruelty of the nation toward Latinx (2). Although the narrator learns to swim despite his parent's obstruction and neglect, his desire to escape this violent education—by sinking to survive—signals a different kind of refusal.

The narrator's initial resistance accompanies the text's embrace of suspension in order to find spaces of queer refuge. The novel's stylistic embrace of the long-line and the extended meditation on the text's vast "underwater world" (23) identify the novel's fraught relationship to normative subjecthood, as well as its aversion to the developmental discourses of the bildungsroman. These moments of suspension were dismissed by critics who praised its "sinewy and lean" (Simon 2011) form, which felt like "punching out your relatives" (Gordy 2011). The reviews reaffirm conventional stereotypes of Puerto Rican masculinity (as hyperviolent and hypersexual) by celebrating the animality found in the novel's opening pages; there, the boys cry out in collective voice for "more density [. . .] more flesh, more blood" (Torres 2011: 1). By attaching spectacular value to these motifs, the reviews miss how the novel ambivalently reproduces a sense of Latinx difference by identifying the boys as a "pack" (125). The boys, hailed as "locusts" (33) by their white neighbors, are interpolated into the national imaginary as parasites. Seen as both nonhuman and outside the nation, the brothers represent stereotypical thinking about Latinx as an unruly multitude dependent on others to survive. Compare these representations to the narrator underwater. The *New York Times* described such moments of suspension as "showy" and "unnecessary when [the] novel relates such an affecting story of love, loss [and] irreversible trauma" (Isherwood 2011). Rather than read moments of stillness as a desire for a ruptured aesthetic form and antinormative temporal progression, I read with these moments of suspension to claim that this scene queerly teaches us (and reproduces) the infantilizing logics of racialization at the center of the Insular Cases.

The novel's embrace of constriction maps onto the ways the Insular Cases are built on discourses of delayed maturation in order to suspend Puerto Rican difference between belonging and abjection, foreign and domestic. The Insular Cases affirmed US desire for empire within a judicial framework that limited the US Constitution to keep the acquired territories (Puerto Rico, Philippines, and Guam) in a state of dependence at the end of the Spanish American War. For those living in these new colonies, the United States denied citizenship, withheld constitutional protections, and subjected them to US sovereign and military rule. The question in the foundational 1901 case of *Downes v. Bidwell* was whether duties were applicable on a shipment of oranges as they arrived in New York from Puerto Rico. However, contrary to common sense, the US Supreme Court decided that the territory was outside the nation. The decision, authored by Justice Brown, reaffirmed a logic of separate and unequal treatment that he established years earlier in *Plessy v. Ferguson*. Brown claimed the territories were not subject to the uniformity clause of the Constitution because Puerto Rico was not imagined as part of the phrase *United States*. Therefore, he produced another segregated geography and irregular subject "subject to the jurisdiction of the United States, [but] not *of* the United States" (*Downes v Bidwell* 1901: 278).

With these constitutional limitations, the unincorporated territories were not imagined as on a path to statehood. Rather, in *DeLima v. Bidwell* (argued the same year) the Supreme Court declared Puerto Rico a collection of "savage tribes" "unfit" for civic participation (*DeLima v.*

Bidwell 1901: 182). Colombian Anthropologist Arturo Escobar (2012: 23–26) describes how the West deployed discourses of development to turn "the poor into objects of knowledge and management" to save them from "darkness" through the technologies of modernity as part of a project to sediment racial difference. The West thereby developed a circular narrative in which it would "reform" the "natives" while also reaffirming their need for intervention (53). Removing agency for subjects "in waiting," the United States affirmed colonial rule through a language of perpetual pedagogy. The notion of suspended development in *We the Animals* is perhaps most explicit when the mother tells the narrator to "stay six forever [. . .] Promise me [. . .] you're not seven; you're six plus one. And next year you'll be six plus two. Like that, forever." (Torres 2011: 16). In much the same way that Torres's narrator remains in a state of unrealized manhood due to his mother's imperative, Puerto Rico is stuck in the time of colonial acquisition "plus one."

As contemporary accounts reveal, Puerto Rico was visualized as a racialized child and an "adopted heir" to US governance (Jiménez García 2021: 27). These representations captured a national sentiment that the territories were incompatible with US culture "absent a long apprenticeship under American rule" (Sparrow 2006: 10). In 1899, Theodore Roosevelt rallied support for American imperialism by recasting citizenship as a project of individual development in service to the nation. With the conjoining of individual cultivation with national growth, Roosevelt (1901: 6) collapsed the obligations of citizenship into a simple analogy: "as it is with the individual, so it is with the nation." With a commitment to national development, Roosevelt believed that a hegemonic US position demanded an expanded project of global influence. Such "responsibilities" (8) justified colonial expansion as a moral good, as "Puerto Rico is not large enough to stand alone. We must govern it wisely and well, primarily in the interest of its own people" (18). Representations of the United States as pedagogue and Puerto Rico as pupil informed the Supreme Court's imagination. And yet, if the normative course of territorial incorporation required a transformation of a state from "infancy advancing to manhood" (*Loughborough v. Blake* 1820: 324), this reframing of Puerto Rico as a perpetual child produced a state of legal limbo to justify America's imperial ambitions. However, the court needed to create a larger framework to disarticulate Puerto Ricans from citizenship in perpetuity. In his concurrence, Justice White argues that Puerto Rico is "foreign to the United States in a domestic sense" (*Downes* 1901: 341). By positioning Puerto Rico as foreign yet domestic, the court created a sphere of domesticity to hide from view its desire to delimit the Constitution yet extend its control. White legitimized this scheme by minting the category of "unincorporated territory," claiming Puerto Rico's status would remain in limbo until Congress expressed direct intent to integrate it into the United States.

By rendering Puerto Rico both foreign and domestic, the "paternalistic tenor" of the court revealed how the archipelago is "denied a place both within the United States and outside of it [. . .] [they] became foreign relative to states [. . .] and domestic *relative to* foreign countries" (Burnett and Marshall 2001: 13). Puerto Ricans became subject to a regime of colonial assimilation (work programs, forced Americanization, and medical experimentation, for example) without incorporation. Catherine S. Ramírez details how accounts of assimilation (normatively understood as the end goal of immigration) are complicated by racialization because of the nation's need to produce regimes of difference to uphold racial and class hierarchies. She reveals how the state, at this imperial moment, tried to emplace a Puerto Rican people between conceptions of Indigeneity and Blackness to uphold (and work in service of) an Anglo-Saxon nation (Ramírez 2020: 43). This counterintuitive regime of assimilation became a violent tool for erasure instead of incorporation.

Tracing this history reveals the ruse of territoriality, which acts as a protracted form to support the US Supreme Court's "ideological commitment to an Anglo-Saxon conception" of citizenship (Perea 2001: 159). Citizenship promises a normative relation between a subject and the nation, yet the Jones-Shafroth Act (1917), which granted Puerto Ricans conditional citizenship (lacking federal representation and control over the islands' finances and future), obscured the state's tactics of dispossession which sought to decimate labor markers and force migration (Barreneche, Lombardi, and Ramos-Flores: 2012: 18). By increasing the ease of individual mobility, the state disguised territoriality as an exceptional mode of cultural hybridity that is the "best of both worlds" (Allen 2017).[1] This notion of cultural hybridity is resonant with Juan Flores's (1993: 104) conception of Puerto Rican culture as defined by movement and a flow "between two intertwining zones." And yet, the Jones-Shafroth Act did not bring normativity; rather, it highlighted an "ideological rift between citizenship and nationality" (Duany 2000: 9) that renders Puerto Rican identity as either an idealized subject of cultural hybridity or a "fragmented" subject of diaspora (22).

The legacy of the Jones-Shafroth Act (made possible by the precedent established in *Downes*) hides from view the ways the United States deploys narratives of deferred liberation to enact new forms of exploitation and domination—keeping Puerto Ricans in states of proximity and relation, suspension and delay. This period of abeyed development would be resolved when, as Justice White said, "an inquiry into the situation of the territory and its relations to the United States" could be established (*Downes* 1901: 372). By withholding self-governance, the Insular Cases established a cultural desire for narratives of the affinities between the United States and its colonies that demand development but rely on a particular kind of stasis. The novel represents this dynamic by situating the father's refusal to teach alongside the mother's abandonment in the name of self-preservation. The narrator is caught between a paternal tenor that, on one hand, demands a narrative of learning and incorporation (in this case into the heteronormative family) while actively fighting against the hand of his mother who nearly drowns him. The parents render the narrator foreign in a domestic sense (within the confines of the house but not part of the household) and his later institutionalization codifies this state. Novels like *We the Animals* disrupt this infantilizing logic by refusing to progress toward a false promise of incorporation. Yet, this scene's critique of developmental discourses is still caught underneath the weight of the law. By resisting generic convention, the novel reaffirms the importance of the bildungsroman to emplotting Latinx literature (and latinidad itself) within racializing narratives of underdevelopment and perpetual becoming.

Submerging Development

As a bildungsroman, *We the Animals* engages one of the foundational narrative forms through which minoritarian citizenship is evaluated and attenuated. By reproducing the infantilizing logics of Latinx racialization, the chapter is haunted by the Insular Cases and their language of impossible development. My attention to this legal history asks: if citizenship and incorporation are foreclosed for Puerto Rican literature, how does *We the Animals* disrupt the demands for maturation and mobility as the central procedures for Latinx recognition? The narrative of acculturation is often told alongside the narrative of development; as such, they are often limited to individual narratives that trade in sentimentality to render their protagonists worthy of incorporation through displays of suffering and resiliency. In the twentieth century, the development of human rights discourses relied on the conventions of this genre to "provid[e] the normative literary technology by which social outsiders narrate affirmative claims for inclusion in the franchise of the nation-state as a person before the law" (Slaughter 2006: 1411). The rise of human rights also coincided with the formalization of Latinx literary study. Long Le-Khac traces how the ethnic bildungsroman transformed to reflect neoconservative beliefs in radical individualism in the post–civil rights era. With the collapse of a public politics and the ascendancy of personal responsibility, a bildungsroman framework reflected a political shift away from systemic changes to the law and an embrace of "individual opportunity [to] suggest [] that individual rights are enough" (Le-Khac 2018: 150).

The embrace of the bildungsroman as the genre of political recognition reaffirmed stereotypical notions of latinidad while celebrating the exceptional few that embodied the values of "mobility and interiority" (Moretti 1987: 5). Torres's *We the Animals* joins a chorus of works by contemporary Latinx writers—like Elizabeth Acevedo's *The Poet X* (2018), Jennine Capó Crucet's *Make Your Home among Strangers* (2015), and Junot Díaz's *The Brief Wondrous Life of Oscar Wao* (2007)—that disidentify with the ways narratives of individual mobility became the expected representational regime for ethnic writers in the second half of the twentieth century (Moretti 1987: 5). This dissent illustrates what Glenda R. Carpio (2023: 14) sees as a contemporary shift in the aesthetic practices of migrant fiction that "reject the empathy model" (which demands narratives of identity formation) to "turn[] our attention to the larger historical, political, and economic conditions that produce migration"(15). Such aesthetic strategies can be traced to Chicanx literature's origins. A founding intervention is "understand[ing] the nation as already internally divided" and therefore Chicanx literature puts "pressure" on these divisions to critique nationalism and borders (Cutler 2015: 17–18). While literature by Puerto Ricans shares many conventions of migrant and Latinx fiction, its colonial relation to the United States complicates the turn to the transnational to disrupt the sovereign pull of the nation. By "staging the encounter" (18) between the novel and the Insular Cases, my attention to suspension builds on Carpio's and John Alba Cutler's attention to systemic critique (over narratives of individuals) to resist a hermeneutics of development.

We the Animals' embrace of suspension illuminates the association between a deferred Puerto Rican freedom and states of perpetual pupilage through the figure of the child. Foundational to the genre is the relationship between plot and maturation—where the narrative stages a child's loss of innocence in exchange for the accumulation of experience. In this pedagogical inheritance, the bildungsroman ends with the newly matured subject as "icon for the nation-state, as emblem of settler sovereignty and liberal governmentality" (Brady 2022: 10). For those denied a period of innocence yet seen as perpetual children, Mary Pat Brady tells us that the bildungsroman works to secure racial capitalism by "anchor[ing] articulations of freedom and citizenship" against an unincorporated other (10). The novel's focus on childhood and refusal of rectitude reveals how the United States sustains liberal democratic governance by attenuating the bodily autonomy and freedom of a racial-gendered other (Naimou 2015: 97).

Therefore, the violent pedagogy in "The Lake" represents the infantilizing relationship of domination between the United States and Puerto Rico. Instead of liberation, the moment of maturation entangles racialization with queerness, thereby producing co-constitutive frameworks for control and a constricting anxiety on the Puerto Rican subject. By resisting the structural imperative to grow up, the narrator's near-drowning evokes the ghosts of the Insular Cases and the ongoing US thirst to sediment Puerto Ricans as perpetual dependents. The scene begins with a stereotypical moment of adolescent pedagogy. However, the parents, both unable to safely guide the narrator into knowledge, leave him to fend for himself; "how do you expect to learn?" his father taunts him (Torres 2011: 21). Richard T. Rodríguez (2019: 276) reads this scene as affirming the father's belief that he has helped his son on his path "toward normative development." However, in the moment where the self-sufficient citizen should emerge and "rebuke the demands of reciprocity [and] reinforce a liberal ensemble of governance," the novel sinks into despair (Brady 2022: 240).

As the conflicting ideologies around incorporation in *Downes v. Bidwell* reveal (1901: 339), the possibility of the foreign territories "form[ing] a part of the American family" clashed with the majority's beliefs in liberal governance as an Anglo-white enterprise. The image of the nation as a family reveals the Supreme Court's fear of an invasive multiracial assemblage changing the character of the domestic. As Justice Harlan states in his dissent, "I am constrained to say that this idea of 'incorporation' has some occult meaning which my mind does not apprehend. It is enveloped in some mystery which I am unable to unravel" (391). The possibility of incorporation required a narrative that charted the journey from dependence to self-governance mirrored by a protagonist's journey from childhood to masculinity. The long-standing stasis of the Insular Cases reveals what Justice Harlan sensed in his dissent—that the un-incorporation doctrine was impossible to unravel. The deferred promise of sovereignty became a suspended time of statelessness.

Moreover, as Chief Justice Fuller predicted, Puerto Rico's new status granted "Congress [the] power to keep it, like a disembodied shade, in an intermediate state of ambiguous existence for an indefinite period" (*Downes* 1901: 372). It is interesting to note that Fuller does not side with the majority like he did in *Plessy*. However, his decision was not provoked by an anti-imperialist politics. Rather, his dissent mirrors contemporary concerns that the nation had extended beyond its ability to settle new states with white citizens. As legal scholars debated, the United States could not annex a territory "irredeemably unfit for statehood [where not enough] Americans will migrate [. . .] to justify its admission as a State" (Randolph 1898: 304). In Carman F. Randolph's assessment, the geographic and collective character of the territories were too distant from the tactics of "settler-imperial politics" (Rana 2020: 320) to successfully integrate these overseas territories; by the end of the nineteenth century, such anti-expansionist sentiment reflected a fear that an "overseas empire" would not be "properly American at all" (321). Such antiexpansionist sentiment exposes the fragility of legal citizenship and the ways a sense of "common feelings" with the other was a precondition for enfranchisement (*Loughborough* 1820: 324).

Moreover, if Puerto Rico is imagined as "a disembodied shade," the islands are stuck in time and foreclosed from the future (*Downes* 1901: 372). To be in the shadow of the United States reaffirms the United States as superior in a racialized chain of matured governance. Less than thirty years after the end of slavery, Puerto Rico was imagined as too distant from the normative subject of liberalism and too proximal to slavery (and the unsettled ethnographic discourses of racial hybridity) to be imagined as an independent nation or integrated state. In his temporary refusal to come up for air, the narrator registers the impossible position of colonial constraint. The novel embraces a suspended narrative time to critique a hermeneutics of development that renders the narrator stuck, "like a disembodied shade," (372) to the racializing tactics of the law.

Such occult transformations of the law have profound implications for the ways we read the Puerto Rican bildungsroman. If a Puerto

Rican nation is abeyed in a state of development or disarticulation, Torres's novel contends with interiority and mobility as similarly foreclosed conventions of the genre. At the level of form, the novel suspends a linear move toward belonging to arrest our literary attention in the uneven relations Puerto Ricans, and Latinx at large, have with the nation. By staging this metaphorical transmission of Puerto Ricanness, the father, in the figure of the "mad scientist," embraces the colonial position—reifying a suspended form of self-possession and forcing a lesson in robbed maturation and abandonment (Torres 2011: 23). This scene is therefore not about maturing into liberal subjectivity but about the trap of its suspension for Latinx subjects, whereby survival is not expected—revealed by the mother's use of her son as a tool for her survival and the manic celebration of the father's repeated "He's Alive! He's Alive! He's Alive" (23). An object of his father's "creation," the narrator is confronted with a denied inheritance, and the conditions of Puerto Rican life are revealed as without innocence and in submission. By attaching maturation to robbed innocence, the novel arrests narrative form in the ongoing present of the Insular Cases.

What then do we make of *We the Animals*' resistant suspension in relation to Arnaldo Cruz-Malavé's (1996: 136) reading of the Nuyorican canon as resisting yet falling into "abjection's tangled web?" Cruz-Malavé unspools how the Nuyorican bildungsroman functions as a narrative attempt to "gain authority" through performances of masculinity. However, he highlights how these novels are caught trying to contain and "transfigure" the abjection of Puerto Rican national identity as racialized and queer (143).[2] These novels attach to masculinity as the route to incorporation only to fail to overcome the abject stereotypes of Puerto Rican hypermasculinity at the heart of racial difference. "The Lake" acts as a metacritique about identity, latinidad, and the queer trace of a Puerto Ricanness as a dependent relation of submission to the United States. However, in Torres's novel, it is queerness as a desired relation that disrupts such conventions, asking us to linger in abjection without desiring assimilation.

Torres suspends narrative time to linger with negation and loss as a structure that does not rupture the subject but structures relation. Rather than move toward liberation, the narrator finds a tight space against the demands of literary form to inherit a sense of shared alienation. This sense of shared negation approximates what José Esteban Muñoz (2006: 677) articulates as a sense of brown, or "how might subalterns feel" and "feel each other" as a "productive [way] in which to consider relationality." By tracking how the novel moves toward shared relation from social estrangement, I examine how the novel resists developmental narratives to advance a form of belonging that exists without state recognition or incorporation.

Freedom with Every Move

If the narrator's near-drowning presents a traumatic pedagogy in becoming brown, the novel insists on this lesson's reemergence. In an earlier chapter entitled "Heritage," the novel lingers in the isolation the brothers share with their father and his father's loss of a home. All struggle with the distance they feel from each other and a larger sense of community. Such feelings of shared alienation bind them together. However, constructing a sense of belonging through such negative affects is not always a welcome relation. One day their father is home dancing while his three sons watch. They attempt to mimic his movements and find their relation to their father (and their heritage) in the rhythm of music:

> "Mutts," he said. "You ain't white and you ain't Puerto Rican. Watch how a purebred dances, watch how we dance in the ghetto." [. . .] He danced, and we tried to see what separated him from us. He pursed his lips and kept one hand on his stomach. His elbow was bent, his back was straight, but somehow there was looseness and freedom and confidence in every move [. . .] "This is your heritage," he said, as if from this dance we could know about his own childhood, about the flavor and grit of tenement buildings in Spanish Harlem and projects in Red Hook, dance halls, and city parks, and about his own Paps, how he beat him, how he taught him to dance, as if we could hear Spanish in his movements, as if Puerto Rico was a man in a bathrobe, grabbing another beer from the fridge and raising it to drink, his head back, still dancing, still stepping and snapping perfectly in time. (Torres 2011: 10–11)

Rather than teach his children to dance, the father has them imitate a sense of authenticity they cannot inhabit; despondent, he calls them "mutts" and unmoors them from the rhythms of masculinity his dance signifies. They linger in shame and the father reproduces the dynamics of failed pedagogy seen in the lake. As the father dances, the boys' sense of temporal and cultural alienation grows. Time elides and the pasts of the father and the spaces of diaspora merge with the present. What does it mean for the boys not to inherit their father's movements, or to know the places of Spanish Harlem, or to recognize the rhythms Tito Puente asks you to hear that make up the "flavor and grit" of latinidad?

Through the long line we get another sense of suspension; it is as if the boys are set adrift, too far away from the projects and dance halls of their father's youth. As the line accrues memory, heritage emerges in the subjunctive mood. The text transmits latinidad in a chain of "as ifs," searching for an impossible origin of cultural identity through a series of metaphorical proximities that can never cohere. The chapter ends on this vision of heritage lost in stereotype, "as if Puerto Rico was a man in a bathrobe [. . .] still dancing, still stepping and snapping perfectly in time" (11). The father's refusal to teach his children to dance is another alienating lesson of heritage. Rendered "foreign" and "domestic," the boys are estranged from a scene of inheritance. As if it were impossible to learn without being thrown into the deep end, the boys—constrained by authenticity—learn what it means to be Puerto Rican through the barrier of suspended knowledge and discourses of impossible development. Moreover, the scene suggests a critique of essential understandings of identity and posits a sense of obtaining a relationship to latinidad through stereotypes—stereotypes that are flat surfaces (or a set of predefined movements) but point to a place of relation in a larger brown commonality imagined somewhere over there.

A sense of shame accompanies this alienated inheritance. However, as Eve Kosofsky Sedgwick (2002: 37) tells us, shame is painfully individuating yet uncontrollably relational. Her insight, that shame attunes us to the relational, shapes identity as performance instead of as an essential possession. As Frances Negrón-Muntaner explains, Puerto Ricans, through a history of colonial resistance (to both Spanish and American empire) have negotiated a history of refusal that does not conform to a liberal politics of respectability. Rather, Puerto Ricans deal with the shame of colonial control by reorienting an ethnonationalism based on the performance of a "cultural subject" to subvert the relations among sovereignty, citizenship, and personhood (Negrón-Muntaner 2004: 5). However, this cultural nationalism as resistance is rooted in an elite Puerto Rican class that sought to "ward off shame of a nationality at once deemed queer, black and impoverished" at the beginning of the twentieth century (15–16). Therefore, the novel's articulation of latinidad occurs in the resistance to incorporation yet reifies a "colonial/gender system"—where the father's performance of freedom reaffirms the normative constraints of gender, sexuality, and race (Lugones 20016: 16). By rejecting his son's ability to dance, he reinscribes the conditional contract latinidad has as a ethno-national project resistant to US control.

The narrator's father grew up in a New York that was shaped by the Puerto Rican boom and the advent of urban sociology. Influential sociologists Nathan Glazer and Daniel P. Moynihan claimed that cultural assimilation never occurred across various ethnic groups in New York. In their chapter on Puerto Ricans, they claim Puerto Ricans were "weak" and "defective," prone to mental illness and a refusal to assimilate (Glazer and Moynihan 1970: 100–101, 132, 142). In their survey of Puerto Rican neighborhoods, they identify the antinormative behaviors of these families as factors that would keep their children from becoming self-sufficient citizens.[3] The representation of an incapable Puerto Rican family in the postwar period developed from earlier discourses of "overpopulation" on the archipelago. By the mid-century, social scientists shifted to a "culture of poverty" to frame Puerto Ricans as "not poor because of racism, jobs, markets, or colonialism, but because they had the wrong sort of family" (Briggs 2002: 165). Such cultural narratives framed Puerto Rican difference as a destabilized family form incapable of reproducing normativity (14). This shift—from governing a Puerto Rican colony to managing the Latinx family—altered the terrain of racialization from "biology to social science" (165). Therefore, Puerto Rican's perceived difference from normativity invited government surveillance to correct a sense of behavioral difference. In the Insular Cases, Puerto Rico was imagined as an infantilized state in need of US control; by the 1960s, this logic seeped into pathological understandings of Puerto Ricans as in need of government intervention at large. Narratives of national development collapsed with narratives of maturation to promote the policing of the heteronormative family.

In *We the Animals*, the narrator's family tries to succeed but ultimately fails to reproduce this structure. As reflected by Glazer and Monihyan's (1970: 90) writing, "adolescence did not exist for most Puerto Ricans, who moved directly from childhood to adult responsibility." In such a conception of growth without experience, Puerto Ricans are imagined as unprepared for the problems of adulthood. The teenage mother marries the narrator's father amid their flight from Brooklyn and despite his abuse. They flounder to meet the demands of familial responsibility. Here, both the individual and the Puerto Rican nation are incapable of becoming a self-governing form and need a parental figure in the nation. With the mid-century ascendancy of urban sociology, the nation, the novel, and the hetero-normative family are robbed of the narrative accumulation necessary for Latinx incorporation.

What then do we make of the bildungsroman that does not reaffirm these systems of control? A sense of freedom within constraint emerges alongside alienation in this scene of failed pedagogy. The boys reach for belonging (without recognition) through the history of salsa. Despite the father denying them a sense of "freedom and confidence in every move," he models a particularly racialized sense of freedom within constraint (through dance as a repeating pattern of move-ment) that emerged in the ensemble of Black and brown communi-ties in early twentieth century New York (Torres 2011: 10). In dance the novel senses freedom, but salsa also invites relation (in the wel-coming of a partner based on shared knowledge). The boys stumble toward but cannot arrive at a racialized understanding of self-possession; however, with the father's refusal of linear relation between parent and child, they shape another sense of mutual alienation together. A collective inheritance endures despite the infantilizing grip that the United States has on an immobilized sense of a Puerto Rican identity under pressure from the law.

The affinity the boys share emerges in a moment of suspended time; this moment of shared alienation reinforces the novel's resis-tance to the call for legible subjecthood. Torres's narrative resonates with Kandice Chuh's (2019: 95) articulation of an illiberal humanism that disidentifies with the "*sensus communis*" as it shifts the terrain of the bildungsroman away from the nation and toward the production of a sense of entanglement borne from a "shared recognition of misrecog-nition." As I argue in the conclusion, this shared recognition through alienation suggests a queer opening that insists on relation and on proximate connections (however disjunct or disjointed) as the frame-work for understanding Latinx literature.

A Child of Mist

Rendered an orphan, the narrator finds a route back toward social rela-tion by negotiating a queer latinidad without a hereditary or national structure of inheritance. The penultimate chapter thrusts the character into adolescence and is marked by the loss of a collective voice for an isolating first-person narrative. This change is precipitated by two experiences where the narrator's agency is robbed from the expected liberation of a developmental framework. First, the character's sexual maturation happens as the passive object of someone else's pleasure. After he has sex with an older man he screams: "He made me! [. . .] I'm made" (Torres 2011: 115). This passive construction marks the arrival of identity as another moment of reception instead of action. But to be made also signifies a moment of capture. The narrator is caught validating a sense of identity under the confines of "what we are made to be" (Viego 2007: 29). Both the novel and Antonio Viego position the Latinx subject as the passive product of a dominant culture—Latinx are "dead subjects." Against the apotheosis of liberal thinking about the upright subject, the narrator becomes knowable in the act of submission to another. This moment of becoming is therefore a moment of suspended annihilation, echoing the father's making of his son in "The Lake" and the submission of Puerto Rico to colonial rule.

Second, this change is precipitated by the forced disclosure of his sexuality; when the narrator returns home, his family is reading his journal. The narrator says: "I felt trapped and hateful and shamed. Secretly, outside of the family, I cultivated a facility with language and a bitter spite. I kept a journal—in it, I sharpened insults against them, my folks [. . .] I turned new eyes to them, a newly caustic gaze" (Torres 2011: 108–9). The narrator's disclosure of a journal is withheld as a site of knowledge and signals a failed belief in the recognition found in self-authorship or coming out. The narrator lashes out, retaliating against his family and his impending confinement. "I said and did animal, unforgivable things [. . .] we were, all of us [. . .] mongrels" (118). In the moment of self-making, the novel sticks to the language of the animal. Determined a danger to himself and others, he is placed in a mental institution. In a final reversal of the bildungsroman, the narrator is suspended from bodily sovereignty and kept as a ward of the state. His understandable, yet violent, reaction to this violation of privacy pathologizes both his sexuality and his resistance. With its protagonist captured and confined, the novel resists any good feeling of liberation and marks adolescence as a barely represented scene of the narrator's development.[4]

Yet unlike earlier chapters, the novel ends in a brief lyrical paragraph entitled "Zookeeping." It is in this dark opacity where the narrator waits until he can be rehabilitated into an "upright" citizen (125). However, the ending's abstraction resists majoritarian frames for engaging Latinx narratives. While literary critics note that the conclusion finds a space of "utopian citizenship [in the] possibilities of lingering in limbo" (Rohrleitner 2017: 3–4) or "queer liberation [in resistance to] recognition and difference in the terms granted by the normative order" (Rivera Montes 2020: 232–33), I suggest a more ambivalent relationship to the use of abstraction at the novel's close. By refusing to narrate the protagonist's institutionalization, the ending moves beneath the surface of literary realism to conceal as much as it reveals about his uncertain future.

What the narrator calls "the zoo" is ambivalently anarchic and animalistic. By retiring among "peacocks and lions," the narrator sticks to the imagery of wild things that haunts the book's opening, yet it returns renewed with a queer difference (Torres 2011: 125). Torqueing the early associations between Latinx racialization and invasive species (locusts), the animals of the conclusion are pack or flock animals noted for their beauty. While a representation of his institutionalization, "the zoo" also reads as a space of nightlife, as the language of "sleep[ing] with other animals in cages and dens" welcomes queer desire (125). He invites the animals to "paw" and "own" him, to "crown [him] prince" (125). Here, the novel suggests a space that moves beneath literary realism (expected of Latinx literature) to oversee a tight space of refuge through another form of submission. In this turn to abstraction, the novel identifies the ephemerality of queer socialities that thrive despite ongoing coloniality; this space of desire allows the narrator to move with abjection but without despair in this suspension from the nation and the bildungsroman.

If growing into maturity means the loss of a collective voice, a resistance here may be his futile gestures toward a belated return to literary testimony; "upright, upright" he "say[s], slur[s], vow[s]" before the novel's final blackout (125). The novel ends with an utterance of infelicitous impossibility of incorporation, denying rehabilitation as a method for liberation; rather, it reproduces the ethnographic logics of Latinx as incapable of self-care. However, in this momentary refusal to be an upright citizen, the narrator embraces a self in relation to those that share social abjection, together, as the condition of belonging. Recalling the subversion of Puerto Rican resistance between sovereignty and personhood, Torres suspends narrative impulses by refuting the connections among testimony, incorporation, and self-dependence. In this turn to communion, the novel ends in a sense of identity without individuation; however, this conclusion's ephemerality still reifies certain stereotypes. Recall how reviews of the novel find the conclusion an example of how Latino families experience queerness as an "irreversible trauma" or transgression (Isherwood 2011). En route to my own conclusion, I read queerness backward to offer a reparative potential for queer latinidad in two scenes underwater.

Before the father sends the narrator to the hospital, he gives him a bath. The father calls the "boy son again, *Mijo*" (Torres 2011: 121). This moment of intimacy marks a delay of the son's pathologized exile from the Latino family as he is hailed back into relation alongside the singularity of Spanish. Gesturing toward a place where queerness and brownness coexist, the text lingers in this bathtub where a metaphorical "waterfall [emerges] from the tub's faucet [. . .] there is the wet and the cloth and the touch, all of it so brand new and so familiar" (121–22). This sense of deferral drags us, like a slow riptide, into the novel's past; through touch, we sense the waves of heritage, the lessons of "The Lake," and a gesture toward the intimacies that exist outside the pain of hypermasculinity. Moreover, this scene pulls us toward a different narrative resolution, as if pulling us backward to the "rising ride" that swallowed the narrator in the previous chapter (121).

"Niagara" is the last chapter before the blackout to adolescence. This chapter holds an anticipatory potential buried underneath the demands for normativity. While the father leaves the narrator to wander the Niagara Museum alone, the narrator watches a film about stunt men jumping into the Falls:

> the waterfall projected across my face [. . .] swallowed me up and I danced. I pretended I was a mer-boy prince and it was my job to try and catch all the men in barrels and save them from their deaths [. . .] When they disappeared over the edge, I danced a special underwater dance [. . .] Soon I stopped trying to save them at all because I was consumed in the death dance; spinning on my toes and looking down at my body, the water slopping and rushing over me, I slithered my arms and wiggled my hips against the current. (100)

This daydream presents the boy as he falls out of community, with the arrival of a nascent queerness, imagining a space that sidesteps maturation and "grows sideways" into the half-human fantastical animal (Stockton 2009: 52).[5] Suggesting a path aside narratives of development, the boy dances as he crowns himself an adolescent ruler of the sea, an alternative to personhood while also below the surface of narrative expectations. "Niagara" offers a form of imaginative salvaging as the narrator creates his own relationship to latinidad through stereotypes, to move on rhythm, and the rhythm of style, where queerness does not come with the loss of community.

Here, we sense echoes of earlier moments of the long line as a mode of resistance to create a space of refuge. Remapping the geographic imaginary of latinidad, this scene complicates the motif of water in contemporary Latinx writing. Normative accounts of the sea "illustrate the fragility and fluidity of identity constructs in transnational relations" (Figueroa-Vásquez 2020: 22). This scene of the boy in a confined body of water underscores the separation the family feels from a larger diasporic community, but the lingering alienation underscores Puerto Rican constraint. Although not the normative border associated with latinidad, this geographic turn torques Gloria Anzaldúa's (2012: 25) theorization of "los atravesados" or the borderland subjects who traverse "una herida abierta" or "the open wound" that is the border. Rather than privileging transgression as method, the narrator sinks into dance (25). Inhabiting an interstitial space of development, he renegotiates and revises the earlier chapters of "Heritage" and "The Lake" (that signaled an impasse or impossibility of queer latinidad). Suspended, the narrator traces latinidad and queerness as enmeshed socialities under threat of normativity.

Later, the father recalls watching his son dance in the museum. "I was thinking how pretty you were," he says. "I was standing there, watching you dance and twirl and move like that, and I was thinking to myself, *Goddamn, I got me a pretty one*" (Torres 2011: 102). What is leftover and unsaid in this disclosure? The statement that comes to us slowly in italics both recognizes his son's queerness and quickly lets it go. In these quiet touches of intimacy, the novel departs from the bildungsroman's demands for visibility to offer a moment of witnessing without disclosure. As the novel careens to a close, the characters find themselves stuck in a series of confined spaces against this shared vision of Puerto Ricans, amid constraint, finding "freedom and confidence in every move" (10).

Plotting Constraint; or, Desire under the Law

Let us return to the bathtub scene. Before he is institutionalized, the narrator mounts a futile protest by engaging discourses of citizenship, human rights, and the law. "'I'm an adult,' the boy says. 'I got rights.'" (120). The narrator's insistence that he is an adult is undercut by the novel's reframing of the narrator as a perpetual child. This failed dissent is reinforced by the father's bathing of his son, returning the narrator to a state of infantilized dependence. The father tells him, "'Everybody's got rights. A man tied to a bed got rights. A man down in a dungeon got rights. A little screaming baby got rights. Yeah, you got rights. What you don't got is power'" (120). Here, in the difference between rights and power, the literary is particularly useful to tarry with forms of irregular life that are left suspended between foreign and domestic.

The father's response registers the contradictions inherent to territorial citizenship. The narrator's attempt to authorize himself is met with the infantilization of withheld sovereignty and perpetual childhood. In his father's final lesson, rights are meaningless. Rather, what matters is the power to suspend Puerto Rico in a matrix of colonial control that sediments statelessness and alienation through discourses of perpetual underdevelopment. Torres's wrestling of literary attention away from the teleology of the bildungsroman reveals how the Latinx novel is bound to identity narratives (that testify to individual harm and resiliency) that end in fragmentation or failed incorporation. Across these moments of suspended time, what emerges from the stuckness of withheld Puerto Rican self-possession is an insurgent reimagination of political and aesthetic forms of mutual obligation that advances collective relation from shared loss.

If the Insular Cases sustain a colonial order, what do we make of communities that withstand regimes that are built to fracture and confine life? The father tries to sooth his distraught son. In the absence of sovereignty, he pulls the son's focus to what he can still control. "'Breathe, boy, just breathe'" (Torres 2011: 122). Like when one hunkers down in a bathtub to shelter from a storm, this scene at the end of the novel lingers in an ethics of care in anticipation of coming annihilation and without hope for a decolonial future. Read in the aftermath of Hurricane Maria, the narrator's institutionalized disempowerment reads as an inevitable conclusion against the narratives of development that keep Puerto Ricans in a state of perpetual pupilage. After witnessing the government's deadly response to the storm, political anthropologist Yarimar Bonilla (2020: 156) identifies how Puerto Ricans are "contend[ing] with the idea of losing something they never really obtained [. . .] They find themselves mourning a fiction." Connecting the period of colonial acquisition to the current debt crisis, Bonilla advances a Puerto Ricanness unmasked from any optimism in the US promise of a sovereign territorial future. In this suspended temporality of US coloniality, she asks how Puerto Ricans can live on without such a future drawing developmental teleology. She suggests that queer communities in the archipelago are moving with a "hopeful pessimism" to construct alternative structures of obligation in the collapse of a public infrastructure in "the here and now" (162). Despite state failure and without recognition, what can a politics of "hopeful pessimism" toward the Puerto Rican bildungsroman, and Latinx literary study at large, hold?

As the Insular Cases have not been overturned, my methodology throughout this essay has queerly turned backward to think with these legal frameworks that sustain a colonial order. By lingering with this penultimate scene—that insists on care without incorporation—the novel provides a framework for Latinx literature that exists proximately to, but not incorporated within, nation or citizen. This acknowledgment of failure admits that the "the future is only the stuff of some kids. Racialized kids, queer kids, are not the sovereign princes of futurity" (Muñoz 2009: 95). Without the future, the text's thinking about constraint, respiration, and bodily comportment haunts the novel's conclusion. What appears tragic, when read alongside the legal suspension of Puerto Rican sovereignty, also appears inevitable. The narrator's failure to achieve self-possession is contrasted with the novel's sense that resistance to the teleological demands of its genre is futile. In his 2016 essay "Don't Get Used to It," Torres articulates his ambivalence about narratives of progress. He says, "the only future worth dreaming is [. . .] a future where injury is expected [. . .] a future scarred by the past, and one that makes space for the scarred, for the backward-looking, the bent. To put it another way: Fuck progress" (Torres 2016). In concert with Torres's critique of developmental hermeneutics, *We the Animals*' resistance to the bildungsroman reclaims suspension from the Insular Cases as a method to sustain relation under duress.

The novel's insistence on just breathing registers a host of anxieties for Latinx narratives about the delimiting terms of belonging and normativity. The US Supreme Court's formulation of foreign in a domestic sense produced an unsettled statelessness of a Puerto Rican people (and an occult sense of Puerto Rican difference). Yet it also produced a shared sense of collective knowledge that endures despite the law's demand for individuation. In the text's turn toward transmitting this alienated inheritance, it shifts the novel away from possession of the self and toward a sense of collective recognition that comes from shared alienation. And yet, the novel cannot overcome the ephemeral and fleeting nature of this reconciliation. The novel lingers with father and son suspended in the impossibility of repair; submerged in the ruins of history, they cling to each other, knowing they must let go.

Joseph Isaac Miranda is an assistant professor of English at Yale University. His research and teaching interests converge at the intersection of Latinx literature, queer of color critique, and legal and political theory. His work also appears in *MELUS* journal and has been supported by the Ford Foundation.

Notes

1 Taken from media coverage that "celebrated" the centennial anniversary of the Jones-Shafroth Act, these sentiments mirror the ways circular migration defined a diaspora culture in the midcentury. This culture of mobility is enshrined in the title of Luis Rafael Sánchez's "La guagua aérea" ("The Flying Bus") (1994) and the film by Frances Negron-Muntaner *Brincando el Charco: Portrait of a Puerto Rican* (*Jumping the Pond*) (1994).

2 *Down These Mean Streets* (1967) by Piri Thomas shares many parallels to *We the Animals*. With the narrator's desire for queer sociality and attachment to his father's Afro-Latinidad, *We the Animals* attempts to repair the alienated relationship the novel has with others (both novels have scenes where the father abandons the child in the bathtub, for example) and its conclusion.

3 Published one year before "The Negro Family: The Case for National Action" (1965) by Moynihan, *Beyond the Melting Pot* by Glazer and Moynihan shares similar ethnographic concerns. Its comparative methodology reveals the ideological entanglements that emplaced Puerto Rican difference in longstanding racial hierarchies in the United States.

4 The figures around the narrator are affirmed in their actions and, in the novel's final pages, restore a picture of a heteronormative family form. In their brothers' acts of care, they end the novel affirming growth and maturation: "look, they're opening doors. They're stepping out. Here they go" (124). In this moment of repair, the family achieves an affirmation of their humanity at the expense of the narrator. Such alienation of the queer child from the Latinx family delimits latinidad as inherently normative.

5 Kathryn Bond Stockton's (2009: 52) theorization of the queer child elaborates how growing sideways occurs when the future cannot be "envisioned." Queerness escapes confinement by seeking "forms of arrest [which are] suspended in the amplitude of 'more'" (52). There is an affinity of method here between Stockton and Torres's theorizations of the queer child reaching for other ways to be under the suffocating pressures of the social and aesthetic order.

References

Algarín, Miguel. 1981. "Nuyorican Literature." *MELUS* 8, no. 2: 89–92.

Allen, Greg. 2017. "Puerto Rico Celebrates 100 Years of U.S. Citizenship." *NPR*, March 2, sec. Latin America.

Anzaldúa, Gloria. (1987) 2012. *Borderlands / La Frontera: The New Mestiza*. Fourth edition. San Francisco: Aunt Lute Books.

Barreneche, Gabriel Ignacio, Jane Lombardi, and Héctor Ramos-Flores. 2012. "A New Destination for 'The Flying Bus'? The Implications of Orlando-Rican Migration for Luis Rafael Sánchez's 'La Guagua Aérea.'" *Hispania* 95, no. 1: 14–23.

Bonilla, Yarimar. 2020. "Postdisaster Futures: Hopeful Pessimism, Imperial Ruination, and La Futura Cuir." *Small Axe* 24, no. 2: 147–62.

Brady, Mary Pat. 2022. *Scales of Captivity: Racial Capitalism and the Latinx Child.* Durham, NC: Duke Univ. Press.

Briggs, Laura. 2002. *Reproducing Empire: Race, Sex, Science, and U.S. Imperialism in Puerto Rico.* American Crossroads 11. Berkeley: Univ. of California Press.

Burnett, Christina Duffy, and Burke Marshall. 2001. "Between the Foreign and the Domestic: The Doctrine of Territorial Incorporation, Invented and Reinvented." In *Between the Foreign and the Domestic: The Doctrine of Territorial Incorporation, Invented and Reinvented,* 1–36. Durham, NC: Duke Univ. Press.

Carpio, Glenda R. 2023. *Migrant Aesthetics: Contemporary Fiction, Global Migration, and the Limits of Empathy.* New York: Columbia Univ. Press.

Chuh, Kandice. 2019. *The Difference Aesthetics Makes: On the Humanities "After Man."* Durham, NC: Duke Univ. Press.

Cruz-Malavé, Arnaldo. 1996. "'What a Tangled Web!': Masculinity, Abjection, and the Foundations of Puerto Rican Literature in the United States." *differences* 8, no. 1: 132–51.

Cutler, John Alba. 2015. *Ends of Assimilation: The Formation of Chicano Literature.* New York: Oxford Univ. Press.

DeLima v. Bidwell, 182 U.S. 1 (1901).

Downes v. Bidwell, 182 US 244 (1901).

Duany, Jorge. 2000. "Nation on the Move: The Construction of Cultural Identities in Puerto Rico and the Diaspora." *American Ethnologist* 27, no. 1: 5–30.

Escobar, Arturo. 2012. *Encountering Development: The Making and Unmaking of the Third World.* Princeton, NJ: Princeton Univ. Press.

Figueroa-Vásquez, Yomaira C. 2020. *Decolonizing Diasporas: Radical Mappings of Afro-Atlantic Literature.* Evanston, IL: Northwestern Univ. Press.

Flores, Juan. 1993. *Divided Borders: Essays on Puerto Rican Identity.* Houston, TX: Arte Público Press.

Glazer, Nathan, and Daniel P. Moynihan. 1970. *Beyond the Melting Pot: The Negroes, Puerto Ricans, Jews, Italians, and Irish of New York City.* Second edition. Publications of the Joint Center for Urban Studies. Cambridge, MA: MIT Press.

Gordy, Graham. 2011. "The Best Short Novel You'll Read This Year." *Arkansas Times; Little Rock,* September 7.

Isherwood, Charles. 2011. "'We the Animals,' by Justin Torres—Review." *New York Times,* September 1, sec. Books.

Jiménez García, Marilisa. 2021. *Side by Side: US Empire, Puerto Rico, and the Roots of American Youth Literature and Culture.* Children's Literature Association Series. Jackson: Univ. Press of Mississippi.

Le-Khac, Long. 2018. "Bildungsroman Hermeneutics in the Post–Civil Rights Era." *American Literature* 90, no. 1: 141–70.

Loughborough v. Blake, 18 U.S. 317 (1820).

Lugones, Maria. 2016. "The Coloniality of Gender." In *The Palgrave Handbook of Gender and Development*, edited by Wendy Harcourt, 13–33. London: Palgrave Macmillan UK.

Moretti, Franco. 1987. *The Way of the World: The Bildungsroman in European Culture*. London: Verso.

Muñoz, José Esteban. 2006. "Feeling Brown, Feeling Down: Latina Affect, the Performativity of Race, and the Depressive Position." *Signs* 31, no. 3: 675–88.

Muñoz, José Esteban. 2009. *Cruising Utopia: The Then and There of Queer Futurity*. New York: New York Univ. Press.

Muñoz, José Esteban, Tavia Amolo Ochieng' Nyongó, and Joshua Takano Chambers-Letson. 2020. *The Sense of Brown*. Durham, NC: Duke Univ. Press.

Naimou, Angela. 2015. *Salvage Work: U.S. and Caribbean Literatures amid the Debris of Legal Personhood*. New York: Fordham Univ. Press. Accessed via Project MUSE.

Negrón-Muntaner, Frances. 2004. *Boricua Pop: Puerto Ricans and the Latinization of American Culture*. New York: New York Univ. Press.

Perea, Juan F. 2001. "Fulfilling Manifest Destiny: Conquest, Race, and the Insular Cases." In *Fulfilling Manifest Destiny: Conquest, Race, and the Insular Cases*, 140–66. Durham, NC: Duke Univ. Press.

Ramírez, Catherine S. 2020. *Assimilation: An Alternative History*. Berkeley: Univ. of California Press.

Rana, Aziz. 2020. "How We Study the Constitution: Rethinking the Insular Cases and Modern American Empire." *Yale Law Journal Forum*, November 2. https://www.yalelawjournal.org/forum/how-we-study-the-constitution.

Randolph, Carman F. 1898. "Constitutional Aspects of Annexation. Part First." *Harvard Law Review* 12, no. 5: 291–315.

Rivera Montes, Zorimar. 2020. "'For Opacity': Queerness and Latinidad in Justin Torres' *We the Animals*." *Latino Studies* 18, no. 2: 218–34.

Rodríguez, Richard T. 2019. "Oedipal Wrecks: Queer Animal Ecologies in Justin Torres's *We the Animals*—Record Details—EBSCO." In *Latinx Environmentalisms: Place, Justice, and the Decolonial*, edited by Sarah D. Wald, David J. Vazquez, Priscilla Solis Ybarra, and Sarah Jaquette Ray, 267–80. Philadelphia: Temple Univ. Press.

Rohrleitner, Marion Christina. 2017. "Refusing the Referendum: Queer Latino Masculinities and Utopian Citizenship in Justin Torres' *We the Animals*." *European Journal of American Studies* 11: 1–13.

Roosevelt, Theodore. 1899. "The Strenuous Life Speech. Before The Hamilton Club, Chicago, April 10, 1899." In *The Strenuous Life*, edited by Theodore Roosevelt, 3–22. New York: Collier.

Ruiz, Sandra. 2019. *Ricanness: Enduring Time in Anticolonial Performance*. New York: New York Univ. Press.

Sedgwick, Eve Kosofsky, and Adam Frank. 2003. *Touching Feeling: Affect, Pedagogy, Performativity*. Durham, NC: Duke Univ. Press.

Simon, Scott. 2011. "'We the Animals' Delivers a Fiery Ode to Boyhood." *Weekend Edition Saturday; Washington, D.C.*, September. ProQuest, https://search.proquest.com/docview/887285236/citation/67B1CCC7B1 A74619PQ/1.

Slaughter, Joseph R. 2006. "Enabling Fictions and Novel Subjects: The 'Bildungsroman' and International Human Rights Law." *PMLA* 121, no. 5: 1405–23.

Sparrow, Bartholomew H. 2006. *The Insular Cases and the Emergence of American Empire*. Lawrence: Univ. Press of Kansas.

Stockton, Kathryn Bond. 2009. *The Queer Child; or, Growing Sideways in the Twentieth Century*. Series Q. Durham, NC: Duke Univ. Press.

Torres, Justin. 2011. *We the Animals*. New York: Mariner Books.

Torres, Justin. 2016. "Don't Get Used to It: Queer Literature in a Time of Triumph." *Salon*, June 22. https://www.salon.com/2016/06/21/dont_get _used_to_it_queer_literature_in_a_time_of_triumph.

Viego, Antonio. 2007. *Dead Subjects: Toward a Politics of Loss in Latino Studies*. Durham, NC: Duke Univ. Press.

Williams, Raymond L. 1992. *Marxism and Literature*. Oxford: Oxford Univ. Press.

Edlie
Wong

Afterword:
A "Citizen of the Ocean"
in an Empire of Small Islands

In 1901, Baptist minister and writer Sutton E. Griggs published *Overshadowed* through his recently established Orion Publishing Company in Nashville, Tennessee. Perhaps the least well-known of his five novels, *Overshadowed* launched Griggs's early efforts to develop a viable Black literary print culture in the post-Reconstruction South; it anticipated the subsequent endeavors of J. Max Barber's Atlanta-based *Voice of the Negro* (1904–7) and W. E. B. Du Bois's short-lived, Memphis-based *Moon Illustrated Weekly* (1905–6). As we reconsider the meaning and methods of work on citizenship, Griggs's novel helps us think beyond birthright, territoriality, and political rights at the very moment when these concepts became widely accepted as fundamental to the definition of US citizenship. Described as the "most claustrophobic" of all his novels, *Overshadowed* features a bewildering array of intersecting subplots that end in the deaths of multiple characters, including the mixed-race heroine, Erma Wysong, and her half brother John (Fabi 2012: 120). The novel's preoccupation with death extends even to the opening dedication, which memorializes Griggs's sixteen-year-old sister, Alberta, who died earlier in the year (Gruesser 2022: 84). Griggs also confines nearly all the events to one setting—Richmond, Virginia—which further enhances the pervasive sense of closeness and closure.[1] As Griggs (1901: 3) explains in the opening proem added to the later version, *Overshadowed* is "a tragedy—a story of sorrow and suffering" that "does not point the way out of the dungeon which it describes, but it clearly indicates the task before the reformer when he comes." The proem provides an interpretive key to the relentless accounting of failure, malignity, and exploitation in the novel, which builds to an unexpected climax. In the penultimate chapter, Erma

American Literature, Volume 96, Number 4, December 2024
DOI 10.1215/00029831-11611088   © 2024 by Duke University Press

marries her beloved Astral Herndon, gives birth to a son who shares "the soul of the mother," and is briefly reunited with John (whom she had thought long dead by execution) before they both succumb to death in the most qualified and short-lived of happy endings (201). Inconsolable, Herndon attributes Erma's premature death to "the havoc which living side by side with" the white race has wrought and refuses to allow her body to further "enrich" the United States by being interred within its domain for "her dust would help to compose . . . this land" (207, 211). Entitled "The Funeral," the final chapter juxtaposes the vastness of the ocean against the containment of Black opportunity and aspiration on US soil. In it, Herndon bids the United States "an eternal farewell," vowing that Erma's "son shall not be confronted with the same unequal conditions that she so often encountered" (212).

Published during what historian Rayford Logan later termed the nadir, as antiblack violence and racial segregation became entrenched in American daily life, the original two-hundred-seventeen-page version of *Overshadowed* culminates with Herndon and son purposively "adrift upon the ocean" (217). After consigning wife and brother-in-law to the sea, Herndon makes an extraordinary final proclamation that ends the novel:

> 'My son,' said he, 'your mother has been buried in these domains, because here there abides no social group in which conditions operate toward the overshadowing of such elements as are not deemed assimilable. And now, I, Astral Herndon, hereby and forever renounce all citizenship in all lands whatsoever, and constitute myself A CITIZEN OF THE OCEAN, and ordain that this title shall be entailed upon my progeny unto all generations, until such time as the shadows which now envelope the darker races in all lands shall have passed away, away and away!' (217)

A complex aesthetic and political gesture, Herndon's pronouncement serves as the long-sought-for release from the disquieting confines of the novel. In resisting narrative closure, this final scene positions the ocean as an alternative to the overdetermined conditions and limitations upon Black life, family, and community-formation in the United States. Griggs reclaims an oceanic space associated with the histories of the Middle Passage, alienation, and death and reimagines it as the site for new forms of homemaking, belonging, and community-formation. However, by constituting himself a "citizen of the ocean" and conferring this membership upon his son and future descendants, Herndon also engages in a radical act of deracination that renders himself and his "progeny unto all generations" stateless. In this self-described tragedy, Griggs seizes upon the idea of statelessness, in Derrick R. Spires's (2019: 17) words, "to generate new ways of understanding citizenship and being citizens outside of rights discourse." *Overshadowed* thus leaves us with an improbable yet extraordinary proposition, one that emerges from the political and societal failings that accumulate throughout the tale: a citizenship freed from the state.

In going even further than Griggs's earlier *Imperium in Imperio* (1899) to remove Black belonging from US territoriality altogether, the radical proposal of *Overshadowed* puzzled, angered, and even horrified some of its readers. The suggestion of an alternative, oceanic citizenship was not yet imaginable for these frustrated readers who saw in Herndon's pronouncement only a repudiation of Black citizenship. According to John Cullen Gruesser (2022: 112), Griggs likely added the epilogue and the proem to the later edition to address readers who found the ending unsatisfying and too challenging.[2] For example, one disgruntled female reader based in Washington, DC, identified as L. G. A. objected to the novel, claiming that it had received an unwarranted recommendation from John E. Bruce (writing as "Bruce Grit"), who reviewed it for the North Carolina-based AME Church's *Star of Zion* newspaper. Among other faults, she found the conclusion to be not "healthful or indicative of good judgement," for "the concluding scene shows the reader that Mr. Sutton Griggs finds there is no place in America for the Negro" (L. G. A. 1901). She drew particular attention to Herndon's final proclamation, declaring, "With these grandiloquent words, 'Overshadowed' ends. The writer could only repeat in dull amazement, 'A citizen of the ocean! What kind of citizen is that?' Does the author mean that *all* Negroes should 'renounce citizenship in *all* lands whatsoever and become citizens of the ocean?'" (L. G. A. 1901). L. G. A. dismisses Griggs's suggestion that we think beyond the givenness of citizenship. Oceanic citizenship is simply unthinkable as a model of belonging, membership, or affiliation. She sees in Herndon's pronouncement a wholesale rejection of national belonging and the hard-won rights of Black legal citizenship in the Fourteenth Amendment, which established birthright citizenship in the principle of jus soli (or right of the soil) as the national standard. In fact, the US Supreme Court had just delivered its landmark clarification of the territorial scope of the birthright citizenship clause of the Fourteenth Amendment in *U.S. v. Wong Kim Ark* (1898), which declared that otherwise racially excluded Chinese Americans like Wong became automatic citizens by virtue of birth on US soil.[3] In his "citizen of the ocean," Griggs insists that citizenship remain, in Carrie Hyde's (2018: 7) words, "an elastic site of political fantasy and debate" at the precise moment when it underwent further legal codification.

By highlighting the fundamentally vexed nature of citizenship and its contested terrain, Griggs's *Overshadowed* participates in the critical work featured in this special issue of *American Literature* on new citizenship studies and its collective effort to open up new approaches to the study of citizenship through literature and culture. Fiction allowed Griggs to explore the unthinkable: what citizenship might become once freed from the state, daring us to consider forms of social belonging that need not entail a juridical or state form of recognition (Simpson 2014: 189). As Robert Levine (2013: 80) has argued, *Overshadowed* also offered critical Black commentary on the most influential and oft-reprinted literary text of citizenship from the era, Edward Everett Hale's hugely popular "The Man Without a Country" (1863). Unlike Hale's traitorous Philip Nolan who is court-marshaled and sentenced to a life at sea until his death, Herndon voluntarily embraces the statelessness of the ocean in his momentous decision to "renounce all citizenship in all lands." Furthermore, this renunciation does not serve to idealize US citizenship and national belonging as in Hale's didactic example of the contrite Nolan.[4] In pointed contrast, Herndon challenges the idea that despite "all its faults, this country is by far the greatest on earth," determined in his purpose to "abandon" the United States and the racist and racializing "conditions" it places upon Black life (Griggs 1901: 214, 215). Statelessness becomes the precondition for a radical new form of affiliation that derives its value from something other than yearning for civic inclusion and white recognition. Earlier in the novel, a self-destructive revenge subplot featuring Erma's unknown maternal aunt Dolly revolves explicitly around the public exposure and recognition of white paternity. In fashioning a protagonist who selects the statelessness of oceanic citizenship as a self-affirming alternative to US citizenship, Griggs moves beyond the inclusion/exclusion binary of citizenship to place critical pressure on the incorporative telos of the "American Dream" (Hyde 2018: 8). Oceanic citizenship thus names a desire for the building of a new society rather than the amelioration or repair of a broken one. It also contributes to a different understanding of Blackness, one that remains in "a state of openness to the promise of belonging," to borrow from Ajay Kumar Batra in this special issue.

Griggs ends *Overshadowed* with a paradox that even readers from his era acknowledged as such. A stateless person is someone who "under national laws, does not enjoy citizenship," according to the US Department of State (Bureau of Population n.d.). As a literary device, paradox engages the reader through temporary confusion to provoke deeper consideration and thought. According to Margaret Cuonzo (2014: 18), paradoxes can even "force us to question whether our intuitive understanding of the world is really accurate." In demanding that we think about Black citizenship outside the limited discourses of political rights and the law, Griggs's literary provocation aligns with the various considerations of the collected essays. Positioned at different flashpoints along the long nineteenth century, Ajay Kumar Batra, Eve Eure, Xiomara Santamarina, and Sidonia Serafini delineate, in differing and at times antagonistic ways, new forms of Black belonging, membership, and affiliation that alternately utilize, participate in, or exceed the nation-state built on racial capitalism. Like Griggs's *Overshadowed*, they reveal Black Americans simultaneous exclusion from and centrality to the idea of citizenship. Eure offers a powerful example of Black Cherokee place-making and kinship in reading the Shoe Boots family's failed tribal citizenship applications. Spanning three generations, their petitions, appeals, and land deeds form a collective writing and archival practice contesting the exclusionary antiblackness that came to delimit membership in the Cherokee Nation. Such exclusions prompted other formerly enslaved, self-emancipated, and free Blacks writers and thinkers to redefine citizenship "not merely as a fixed status or set of entitlements conferred by the white supremacist state but, rather, as a dynamic set of practices cultivated primarily in spaces beyond state sanction," as Batra writes.

While Batra sets out to contest the fundamental idea of possessive individualism that defines the citizen as a rights-bearing subject, Santamarina and Serafini embrace a different approach by outlining the promise and perils of making either economic or military participation in the nation-state the basis of Black civic legitimacy. They examine rhetorical strategies rife with productive contradictions and ambiguities—not unlike Griggs's proposal for a stateless citizenship. In reading two early sociological texts by Joseph Willson (1841) and Cyprian Clamorgan (1858), Santamarina develops a concept of "economic citizenship" that positions the market—rather than civil society—as the privileged site for Black citizenship practices and civic identity formation. Serafini turns our attention to the Hampton Institute's *Southern Workman* and reads it as a repository for Black and Native discourses on military service as a pathway to "full and unquestioned citizenship." These writers negotiated the histories of

US domestic wars of pacification against Indigenous peoples and its imperial wars abroad, which deepened existing exclusions and created new barriers to US membership. Taken together, these essays ask us to focus not only on those who do not belong but also on what it means to belong and how belonging is defined in the first place.

As Griggs was writing *Overshadowed*, the annexation of Hawaii followed by Puerto Rico, Guam, the Philippines, and American Samoa after the Spanish American War (1898) and the Philippine-American War (1899–1902) helped propel the United States into the so-called American Century. In renouncing the United States, Herndon constitutes himself as a citizen of perhaps the last remaining unterritorialized space in this era of New Imperialism: the ocean. Asked whether he intends to return his "fatherland," Herndon pointedly replies, "'It, too, is overshadowed. Aliens possess it'" (Griggs 1901: 216). In referencing western imperialism on the African continent, Griggs explicitly distinguishes Herndon's experiment in oceanic citizenship from popular Black emigration or colonization projects. The literary turn to the ocean is not accidental. Griggs's "citizen of the ocean" also speaks to the study of citizenship since the transnational turn in American literary studies. The fluid, deterritorializing impulses of the seas and oceans have created new methodologies for nonlinear and nonplanar thought and novel ways of thinking about surface and depth and the human and nonhuman. As Hester Blum (2010: 3) writes, such a "reorientation of critical perception" calls boundaries into question and decenters nations, and it has helped further challenge the "landlocked" imaginary of American literary studies. As literary criticism moved beyond the nation-state, it turned toward a host of other geopolitical configurations, from the Black Atlantic to the global South, borderlands, hemispheres, the oceans, and most recently, the archipelago. In particular, the wide adoption of Paul Gilroy's influential *The Black Atlantic* (1993), which centered the transatlantic slave trade and Black diaspora in the making of the modern West, shifted attention from continents as defining geographical entities to oceans as hybrid, complex cultural spaces. Thirty years of transnational American studies has firmly established the nation-state as an insufficient unit of comparative analysis, yet the conceptual problem of state-regulated citizenship persists. Popular discourses and news media continue to conceive of the citizen in terms of status, rights, and identities bound to territoriality and protected by the nation-state (Shachar 2009: 6).

Emphasizing a wide range of literary texts and approaches, the other essays collected in this special issue challenge such popular notions of citizenship, shaped by law, legalism, and politics, which remain stubbornly tethered to the territorialized nation-state. They examine extralegal, symbolic, or resistant formulations of citizenship, often in dynamic tension with the existing legal codification or political status of national citizenship. For example, Erin Suzuki delves into the fictions of formerly interned Japanese American writers to highlight the "conflicts that emerge when rights-bearing individuals whose communities exceed or extend *beyond* national borders and boundaries run up against such nation-based, exclusionary definitions of citizenship." Belatedly codified in the Fourteenth Amendment and its subsequent interpretations, the figure of the state-regulated, legal citizen has long been tied to an idea of territoriality and defined in national terms. Numerous legislative acts and judicial rulings, including the Treaty of Guadalupe Hidalgo (1849), the Supreme Court decision in *United States v. Wong Kim Ark* (1898; 169 US 649), and the Indian Citizenship Act (1924) helped establish the incorporative logics and the land and border-based limits of ascriptive citizenship (or citizenship by birth). As historian Daniel Immerwahr (2019: 10) argues, the unproblematized concept of the rights-bearing legal citizen evokes an immediate association with the contiguous United States as a "politically uniform space: a union voluntarily entered into, of states standing on equal footing with one another," which contributes to the twofold erasure and intensification of US empire. Yoked to forms of race and racialization that largely envisioned the inhabitants of the continental United States as white English-speaking Anglo-Saxon Protestants, this influential "logo map," writes Immerwahr, borrowing from Benedict Anderson, naturalizes the history of federal systematic expropriation, removal, and displacement of Indigenous peoples from North America. It also does not include the overseas territories, including Hawaii, Puerto Rico, Guam, American Samoa, or any of the other smaller Pacific Islands that the United States annexed throughout the long nineteenth century and whose racialized populations were once declared unfit for citizenship (Immerwahr 2019: 8–9).

In this special issue, Florencia Lauria, Kathryn Walkiewicz, and Joseph Isaac Miranda ask us to reconsider the relationships among birthright citizenship, land, and sovereignty as they call into question the territorial projects of US settler colonialism and overseas empire. US citizenship remains a defining feature of settler-imposed political belonging, and the Indian Citizenship Act reveals the problems of ascriptive US citizenship for Native peoples. As Lauria argues, such forms of coerced, settler-imposed inclusion may not be a desired or desirable form of political belonging. Ascriptive citizenship defies the meaning and processes of individual and collective self-determination. In reading Ora V. Eddleman Reed's writings in the *Twin Territories: The Indian Magazine* (1898–1904), Walkiewicz explores the complexities of dual and competing allegiances and affiliations for Native peoples in Indian Territory and Oklahoma Territory prior to Oklahoma statehood in 1907. During the allotment era and beyond, Native nations in these territories inhabited a peculiar space within settler-colonial and imperialist discourses that positioned them as simultaneously domestic and foreign to the US nation-state. Miranda's reading of Justin Torres's *We the Animals* (2011) shifts our attention to the colonial histories of Puerto Rico to further challenge these land-based paradigms of US sovereignty and citizenship. The interrelated and overlapping contexts of US settler colonialism and overseas empire have long troubled the fetishized figure of the rights-bearing citizen and the territorialized logic of birthright citizenship. Placing pressure on the rift between citizenship and nationality or latinidad, Miranda explores the "irregular status of Puerto Rican citizenship" as part of the complex legal afterlife of the (as yet unchallenged) Supreme Court rulings in the 1901 Insular Cases, which infamously judged these annexed archipelagoes and their nonwhite inhabitants as "foreign to the United States in a domestic sense." As Amy Kaplan (2002: 2–4) has argued, such legal contortions strained to redefine these unincorporated territories as lands under US sovereignty but not subject to the same jurisdiction as the territories and states on the continent. These essays chart the complexities of race, territory, and belonging that take place within and extend beyond the conceptually closed spaces of the US logo map.

In Herndon's renunciation of state-imposed US citizenship, we also see an earlier iteration of the refusals found in Suzuki's discussion of John Okada's *No-No Boy* (1955) and Lauria's reading of Louise Erdrich's *The Night Watchman* (2020). The protagonists of these novels reject US citizenship as a totalizing form of political and social belonging. In reading Okada's originally unpopular novel of Japanese internment, Suzuki resists the enforced transparency of racialized and suspect Asian American personhood to limn a form of citizenship that recognizes opacity and the complex entanglements of community-centered identity and identifications. As alternatives to state recognition, these mechanisms of repudiation, rejection, and refusal help construct new understandings of citizenship that challenge the disciplinary and regulatory processes of national assimilation and incorporation.

In fact, many of the essays in this special issue caution against inclusion as the sole or primary mode of response to past and present forms of racialized exclusion from the nation-state. Subject to heightened surveillance and security demands, racialized populations in the United States, as Suzuki reminds us, have been made hypervisible and historically marked as "transparent citizens," whereas the racialized populations of America's hidden internal *and* external empire have long been relegated to erasure and the invisibility of an elsewhere citizenship. Consider the popular hashtag #PuertoRicoIsTheUSA formed in response to President Donald Trump's remarks questioning whether Puerto Ricans are "real Americans" eligible for US aid after Hurricane Maria made devastating landfall in the archipelago, as Miranda also mentions (Oprysko 2019; Kwong 2019).

In highly uneven ways, legislative acts, following the incorporative logic of the Indian Citizenship Act, have extended the birthright citizenship (or jus soli) once limited to the continental United States to these outlying territories. Annexed in 1898, Hawaii was finally admitted as a state in 1959, despite longstanding fears over its large Asian population, yet the Pacific archipelago remains liminal to the national imaginary (Byrd 2011: 151–52). Recall that President Barack Obama's Honolulu birthplace—in addition to his identification as a Black American—spurred public debates over his status as a "natural-born citizen of the United States" (*New York Times* 2011). While American Samoans remain noncitizen nationals (and deeply divided over the issue of US citizenship), individuals born on the four remaining major unincorporated territories of the United States—Puerto Rico, Guam, the US Virgin Islands, and the Northern Mariana Islands—are now considered US citizens by birth, although only certain parts of the US Constitution apply to them (Wiessner 2022). The persistence of such racialized and territorialized asymmetries of US citizenship provoked (and continues to stir) novelists like Griggs, Okada, Torres, Erdrich, and the other writers and figures discussed in this issue to challenge, critique, and imagine otherwise.

Despite the intensification of modern globalization (and the transnational paradigms studying it), state-regulated citizenship and the highly controlled and exclusive membership that it conveys has become even more entrenched in this century (Shachar 2009: 2). The recent COVID-19 pandemic lockdowns made us painfully aware of the territorial borders that delineate nation-states and the boundaries of restricted belonging in the state. New approaches to citizenship studies are even more urgent now as we witness an unprecedented global migrant and refugee crisis that has further attenuated the meaning of belonging and made the distinction between citizen and stranger even more marked. Global conflicts, natural disasters, food insecurity, poverty, persecution, and accelerating climate change will continue to drive the movement of dispossessed peoples across oceans and borders. As stateless populations worldwide continue to surge, we might return to the question that Griggs posed in 1901 under a different set of historical circumstances: What might citizenship become once freed from the state? Is oceanic citizenship now thinkable? In moving beyond the territorialized nation-state, Griggs's oceanic reorientation might even begin to challenge the anthropocentrism of citizenship thinking itself. Indeed, marine conservation discourse and environmental organizations such as the World Ocean Network have recently taken up the concept of "Ocean Citizenship" to promote marine protection, preservation, and sustainability through raising public awareness and education.[5] In a likeminded fashion, the literary and cultural approaches gathered in this special issue of *American Literature* insist that we consider citizenship through different and interrelated historical contexts, discursive registers, and territorial scales to push us to think beyond the givenness of citizenship.

Edlie Wong is professor of English at the University of Maryland, College Park. She is the author of *Racial Reconstruction: Black Inclusion, Chinese Exclusion, and the Fictions of Citizenship* (2015) and *Neither Fugitive nor Free: Atlantic Slavery, Freedom Suits, and the Legal Culture of Travel* (2009).

Notes

1   Andreá N. Williams (2013: 89, 90) sees the "serial endings" (of individual storylines that abruptly end throughout the novel) and lack of narrative closure as constituting a "deliberate and provocative" aesthetic of racial uplift through nonviolent political activism.

2   The new epilogue foresees the return of Erma's son Astral Herndon Jr. as the catalyst for the transformation of the United States. His long-awaited arrival also signals a possible reconciliation with the state by bringing about the racial justice that his mother was unable to experience during her lifetime (Gruesser 2022: 19).

3   The federal government, which prosecuted the unsuccessful test case against Wong, alleged that his birth on US soil did not make him a citizen because his immigrant parents (as Chinese subjects) remained under Chinese jurisdiction even while in the United States. *United States v. Wong Kim Ark*, 169 U.S. 649 (1898).

4   Hyde (2018: 117) identifies Nolan as a highly influential model of "negative" or nonimitative civic instruction. In Hale's tale of a traitor who finds redemption in perpetual exile, the "pathos of political exclusion is used to lend affective meaning to the prospect of political membership, understood as a privilege rather than a circumstantial fact" (Hyde 2018: 158).

5   The World Ocean Network website states the following: "Since 2002, the World Ocean Network has been developing and promoting the concept of Ocean Citizenship. Being a Citizen of the Ocean means being aware of our relationship with the Ocean, of all that it brings us and our impact on its health" (World Ocean Network 2020).

References

Blum, Hester. 2010. "The Prospect of Oceanic Studies." *PMLA* 125, no. 3: 1–14.

Bureau of Population, Refugees, and Migration. "Statelessness." n.d. U.S. Department of State website. https://www.state.gov/other-policy-issues /statelessness/ (accessed March 5, 2024).

Byrd, Jodi A. 2011. *The Transit of Empire: Indigenous Critiques of Colonialism.* Minneapolis: Univ. of Minnesota Press.

Cuonzo, Margaret. 2014. *Paradox.* Cambridge, MA: MIT Press.

Fabi, M. Giulia. 2012. "Desegregating the Future: Sutton E. Griggs' *Pointing the Way* and American Utopian Fiction in the Age of Jim Crow." *American Literary Realism* 44, no. 2: 113–32.

Griggs, Sutton E. 1901. *Overshadowed.* Nashville, TN: Orion Publishing Company.

Gruesser, John Cullen. 2022. *A Literary Life of Sutton E. Griggs: The Man on the Firing Line.* Oxford: Oxford Univ. Press.

Hyde, Carrie. 2018. *Civic Longing: The Speculative Origins of U.S. Citizenship.* Cambridge, MA: Harvard Univ. Press.

Immerwahr, Daniel. 2019. *How to Hide an Empire: A History of the Greater United States.* New York: Picador.

Kaplan, Amy. 2002. *The Anarchy of Empire in the Making of U.S. Culture.* Cambridge, MA: Harvard Univ. Press.

Kwong, Matt. 2019. "For Trump White House, Belittling Puerto Rico Might Be More Than a 'Slip of the Tongue.'" *CBS News*, April 4. https://www .cbc.ca/news/world/trump-puerto-rico-voters-1.5083666.

L. G. A. 1901. "Disappointed in 'Bruce Grit.'" *Star of Zion*, August 1.

Levine, Robert. 2013. "Edward Everett Hale's and Sutton E. Grigg's Men without a Country." In *Jim Crow, Literature and the Legacy of Sutton E. Griggs*, edited by Tess Chakkalakal and Kenneth W. Warren, 69–87. Athens: Univ. of Georgia Press.

New York Times. 2011. "Barack Obama and the Psychology of the 'Birther' Myth." April 21. https://www.nytimes.com/roomfordebate/2011/04/21 /barack-obama-and-the-psychology-of-the-birther-myth.

Oprysko, Caitlin. 2019. "Trump Accuses 'Grossly Incompetent' Puerto Rican Politicians of Misusing Federal Hurricane Aid." *Politico*, April 2. https://www.politico.com/story/2019/04/02/trump-puerto-rico-hurricane-aid-1247759.

Shachar, Ayelet. 2009. *Birthright Lottery: Citizenship and Global Inequity*. Cambridge, MA: Harvard Univ. Press.

Simpson, Audra. 2014. *Mohawk Interruptus: Political Life across the Border of Settler States*. Durham, NC: Duke Univ. Press.

Spires, Derrick R. 2019. *The Practice of Citizenship: Black Politics and Print Culture in the Early United States*. Philadelphia: Univ. Pennsylvania Press.

Wiessner, Daniel. 2022. "U.S. Supreme Court Won't Hear American Samoans' Bid for Full Citizenship." *Reuters*, October 17. https://www.reuters.com/legal/government/us-supreme-court-wont-hear-american-samoans-bid-full-citizenship-2022-10-17/.

Williams, Andreá N. 2013. "Moving Up a Dead-End Ladder: Black Class Mobility, Death, and Narrative Closure in Sutton Griggs's *Overshadowed*." In *Jim Crow, Literature and the Legacy of Sutton E. Griggs*, edited by Tess Chakkalakal and Kenneth W. Warren, 88–110. Athens: Univ. of Georgia Press.

World Ocean Network. 2020. "Our Projects and Programmes." https://www.worldoceannetwork.org/en/about-us/our-programmes/.

Rodrigo Lazo   When Citizenship and National
                     Belonging Diverge

From Slave Cabins to the White House: Homemade Citizenship in African American Culture. By Koritha Mitchell. Urbana: Univ. of Illinois Press. 2020. xi, 274 pp. Cloth, $34.95; paper, $24.95; e-book, $14.95.

The Makings and Unmakings of Americans: Indians and Immigrants in American Literature and Culture, 1879–1924. By Cristina Stanciu. New Haven, CT: Yale Univ. Press. 2023. x, 370 pp. Cloth, $45.00; e-book, $45.00.

Minor Transpacific: Triangulating American, Japanese, and Korean Fictions. By David S. Roh. Stanford, CA: Stanford Univ. Press. 2021. xv, 214 pp. Cloth, $120.00; paper, $30.00; e-book available.

Represented: The Black Imagemakers Who Reimagined African American Citizenship. By Brenna Wynn Greer. Philadelphia: Univ. of Pennsylvania Press. 2019. xiv, 312 pp. Cloth, $104.95; paper, $34.95; e-book, $34.95.

Scales of Captivity: Racial Capitalism and the Latinx Child. By Mary Pat Brady. Durham, NC: Duke Univ. Press. 2022. xi, 297 pp. Cloth, $107.95; paper, $28.95; e-book available.

Most contemporary theoretical considerations of citizenship and political organization touch on citizenship's antecedents in ancient Greece. To participate in the body politic, Athenian citizens had to be property owners, heads of a household, and male. In *Citizenship* (2015), Étienne Balibar turns to the Greek term *politeia* to trace the linguistic resonance in contemporary conceptions of political organization, including postnational and deterritorialized conditions. "The Romans 'translated' this as *res publica*, and the British of the classical period translated it first as *polity*, then as *commonwealth*, adopting alternate ancient etymologies," Balibar writes (*Citizenship*, trans. Thomas

American Literature, Volume 96, Number 4, December 2024
DOI 10.1215/00029831-11611101   © 2024 by Duke University Press

Scott-Railton; 2015; Malden, MA: Polity). Out of this emerges a universal conception of political organization that has expanded to include more than propertied males in the more contemporary arena, leading Balibar to wonder "to what extent this category contains an unchanging kernel of meaning, and whether its application to a context that is now quite removed from its initial articulation might not in truth involve a great deal of illusion and ideological mystification." We might pose that question in the United States, which originally also formed a constitution of citizens whose participation was predicated on a set of economic, gender, and racial attributes. The Naturalization Act of 1790, for example, required that an "alien" admitted to citizenship be a "free white person," which effectively denied naturalization to Asian Americans, Blacks, and Native Americans. Today birthright, jus soli and jus sanguinis, and naturalization (an increasingly bureaucratized process) form the basis of legal US citizenship, even as discursive emphases on the policing of borders create assumptions, many of them territorial, about what groups should be accepted in the nation-state. And yet the kernel of racial, gender, and economic limitations of both Greek and US foundations, the organization of who is in and out of national participation, continues to hang over discussions of the US nation.

Five recent books take up questions on how different groups that were historically excluded from US participatory democracy or limited in their rights or participatory abilities have produced literary and cultural texts that resonate on matters of citizenship and national belonging. Koritha Mitchell's *From Slave Cabins to the White House*, Brenna Wynn Greer's *Represented*, and Cristina Stanciu's *The Makings and Unmakings of Americans* emphasize the role of US citizenship with a focus on historical conditions for Black and Indigenous populations and European immigrants. David S. Roh's *Minor Transpacific* and Mary Pat Brady's *Scales of Captivity* turn to global dimensions and the reach of empires to consider questions of belonging and exclusion in Asian/Asian American and Latinx fiction. Roh emphasizes transnational interactions that situate the United States (and its notions of citizenship) as a third point in fiction that approaches the historical experiences of Japan and Korea. Despite the different contexts discussed in these books, it becomes clear that a variety of different subfields within US literary study continue to analyze the force of marginalization at the heart of the US constitution of citizens, a force that today inspires a proliferation of border policing and right-wing attacks on voting rights as well as a limited view of who can and should be a citizen.

One of the questions that runs through these books is about the relationship of legal citizenship to national belonging. As a whole, the books show that at various points in history and in different contexts there is a divergence between the possessive investment of citizenship and how people experience being part of a body politic and having access to presumed rights. Historically in the United States, participation in democratic processes such as voting was premised on holding certain subject positions (e.g., male gender) and thus a wedge was driven between the legal category of citizen and a large segment of the population that could not belong. As we move into the twentieth century, the sense of belonging is increasingly tied to questions about who can become a citizen, how citizens called Americans are supposed to behave, what citizens can contribute to the nation, or how the media imagines various populations within the nation-state. Putting that another way: What does it mean to be an American in a national US sense? How do writers and other cultural producers from minoritized groups respond to the hostility of a system that did not start from egalitarian frames and instead poses ongoing challenges to full recognition and participation?

For one, cultural forms introduce other types of belonging and present contiguous spaces of association that are not necessarily at odds with the political dimensions of citizenship. In *From Slave Cabins to the White House*, Mitchell starts from a premise that the United States was founded on the denial of Black citizenship, and the result is ongoing hostility to Black success that prevents civic inclusion. In turn, Blacks develop what Mitchells calls *homemade citizenship*, which provides a sense of success and belonging that does not abide by the discursive terms of a political realm. "Black people pursue and achieve success, white aggression counters their progress, and then violence becomes part of any accurate representation of African American communities" (3), she writes. One of the most persuasive examples Mitchell provides is the racist backlash with threats of violence against the Obamas. Homemade citizenship counters with a turn to community traditions, and cultural producers direct their work toward presenting racial self-affirmation. Focusing on Black women writers, the study derives its force from the argument that their texts foment conversation within African American communities rather than respond primarily to white America's discourse about Blacks.

As her title implies, Mitchell considers a broad historical swath, starting with Harriet Jacobs's and Elizabeth Keckley's nineteenth-century writing, continuing with the work of prominent twentieth-century writers such as Octavia E. Butler, and concluding with a chapter on Michelle Obama. Chapter 1's discussion of *Incidents in the Life of a Slave Girl* (1861) by Jacobs exemplifies Mitchell's approach, namely identifying the negation inherent in what she describes as "know your place" responses to Black accomplishment—in this case Linda Brent's attempt to succeed within the system of slavery. Mitchell writes, "Jacobs highlights the fact that enslaved people define achievement, so her text does not simply protest in hopes of recruiting abolitionists; it affirms black people with a spotlight on their various strategies for claiming success because they routinely focus more on that than on white people" (48). Those strategies contribute to homemade citizenship in a realm that is adjacent to but not contained by a type of national citizenship that is often conflated with whiteness.

From Slave Cabins to the White House is propelled by Mitchell's clear voice and sustained emphasis on the historical and present-day exclusionary injustices and insults foisted on Blacks. Homemade citizenship is an act of communal affirmation. Mitchell's readings of various narratives, including Toni Morrison's *Beloved* (1987), are powerful in their affirmation of Black agency. I wondered about the relationship of *homemade citizenship* to other forms of nonlegal belonging such as *cultural citizenship*, the term popularized by Renato Rosaldo in the 1990s. Mitchell does not develop this type of question, but I would draw a significant distinction between homemade and cultural forms of citizenship, the latter offering an alternative for migrant populations that may not be eligible for formal citizenship. Cultural citizenship arguably is not "citizenship" at all in a juridical sense whereas homemade citizenship can be parallel to legal citizenship, keeping in mind that the attainment of legal citizenship for Black men and women changes from the nineteenth to twentieth centuries. That is not to say that legal citizenship is tantamount to inclusion or even a guarantee of full rights, as various forms of discrimination can prevent people from participatory democracy and other types of national interaction. Voting rights are not commensurate with citizenship. For Indigenous populations, we learn in Stanciu's book, the ability to vote at certain points were under the purview of state rather than national laws.

Subtitled *Indians and Immigrants in American Literature and Culture, 1879–1924*, Stanciu's book opens with a historical conjunction: in 1924, the US Congress passed both the first comprehensive immigration legislation and the Indian Citizenship Act, which first granted citizenship to all Native Americans on and off reservations. Prior to that, Indigenous people had been granted citizenship only through treaty rights, Congressional legislation related to specific tribes, or naturalization for individuals. Stanciu considers the three decades leading to the change in 1924 with a premise that the United States is a "settler nation, not an immigrant nation, but one built on the displacement and genocide of Indigenous people and uninhibited westward movement" (17). She writes that the ultimate goal of Progressive-era Americanization campaigns supported by federal, state, and private agencies was to make "good citizens" of immigrants and Indigenous people. Her book is a cultural history of responses to those efforts, including the work of Indigenous and European immigrant writers. The comparative frame shows how the history of settler colonialism was erased in the myths of an Anglophone nation as presented in Americanization campaigns. Attempts to change the cultures and languages had very different meanings and effects for Indigenous people forced to assimilate—sometimes violently—and, on the other hand, immigrants trying to establish themselves in a new country.

Stanciu's book is a compelling look at examples from a vast and dispersed archive of Progressive-era Americanization projects. Less driven by argument than by a plethora of textual examples, the book will be of interest to scholars of migration and immigration. Chapters focus on the history of Americanization with analyses of cartoons and advertisements from periodicals, student responses from the Carlisle School, published writing by Jewish immigrants, the political work of the Society of American Indians, and representations of immigrants and Indigenous people in silent film. The book keeps at the forefront the challenges posed by Americanization ideology and how certain forms resisted its assumptions. In one of the film chapters, for example, Stanciu analyzes productions of the Ford Motor Company, which, as it turns out, was "the first American industrial company with a motion picture department" (225). The goal of many Ford efforts was to turn its largely immigrant workforce into productive laborers, and to that end, the company also ran an English-language school. But its efforts went far beyond its plants and into newsreels: "In 1917, Ford films were shown in three thousand theaters a week to an audience of four to five million people; in 1924, *Ford News* claimed that sixty million people worldwide had seen Ford films" (225).

What makes the book compelling is the depth and range of examples that address the era's assumption that in order to be included in the American nation, one had to speak English and adopt US-based cultural practices. Stanciu sums up her study's scholarly contributions nicely toward the end of an early chapter: "Although we can never know the sum of immigrant and Native voices, however distinctive they may be, the fragments available to us in writing and print, visual art, materials objects, and ephemera help tell a story that challenges the myth of American exceptionalism" (73). *The Makings and Unmakings of Americans* is sensitive to the agency of Indigenous people and immigrants without negating ideological forces. The question of individual agency also informs Greer's historical recuperation of work by African Americans.

Greer's *Represented* is lucid, informative, and interesting. It emphasizes the role of images and image making in the struggle for Black civil rights and the attainment of the full privileges of citizenship. Rather than emphasize well-known civil rights figures such as Rosa Parks, *Represented* turns toward the little-known work of advertising workers, marketers, and mediamakers whose work changed the way Blacks were portrayed in the media. The book opens with the problematic representation of the first time a Black person was featured on the cover of *Life* magazine (in 1936), a photo that trafficked in stereotypes. Greer then traces changes brought about by the influence of public relations officers, artists, and periodical publishers. The chapters span from the Great Depression through World War II and the Cold War to conclude the book with the question, "What is a civil rights image" (248)? *Represented* offers a prolonged and complicated answer by delving into the ways black entrepreneurs portrayed their communities.

Greer is a master storyteller who organizes her narrative along the life trajectories of public relations executive Moss H. Kendrix, photographer Gordon Parks, and *Ebony* publisher John H. Johnson. Contextualizing their individual decisions and projects in light of conditions for US Blacks as well as international events, including the two world wars, Greer weaves in her analysis of how their work on New Deal information programs, journalistic endeavors, and private companies supported the creation of new images. "Their image work circulated through the marketplace, re-presenting African Americans in keeping with prevailing notions of Americannes and challenging denials of their belonging and their equality," she writes (6). The book offers a fresh look at how participants in commercial enterprises contributed to the changing of national perceptions that prevented Blacks who had legal citizenship from the full rights of belonging. Rejecting a binary opposition between activist activities and participation in capitalist enterprises, Greer shows how the image-making work was effective in creating new views of Blacks for white publics but not without its problematic elements, such as the use of sexualized black womanhood to increase readership at *Ebony*.

The chapter on Gordon Parks is exemplary in that it shows his various rhetorical efforts, which at times were critical of racialized capitalism and at others contributed to new visions of Blacks participating in the national war machine. Parks emerges as both an artist and a participant in enterprises that called for portraying African Americans in ways that were palatable to a country wanting its citizens to be patriotic and industrious. "As war propaganda, these images infiltrated popular visual culture as state-sponsored challenges to conceptions of black inferiority and *dis*belonging," Greer writes (108). World War II thus becomes an important moment when a photographer such as Parks contributed to the conjunction between Black aspiration to full citizenship rights and the country's desire for Blacks to support the national project. Like Stanciu's book, *Represented* includes a significant number of illustrations—photos, advertisements, magazine covers—that allow readers to see the images she discusses.

Not all will be sympathetic to Greer's arguments. While offering an alternative vision to the work carried out by grassroots organizers, the participants in these marketing and journalistic efforts were throwing in with the rampant consumerism of the post–World War II era. While featuring Blacks in Coca-Cola ads (the first one in 1953) may change perceptions, the goal was getting Blacks to buy a product. I once heard someone in a revolutionary society outside the United States refer to Coca-Cola as "imperialist water," and therein is the rub. At what point does inclusion in the US national project entail celebration of capitalist excesses, including the pin-up photos in *Ebony*? My question is not rhetorical. The examples in *Represented* differ in important ways, and that question has to be approached in relation to specific illustrations, as Greer does. In addition, we might consider to what extent media images actually affect the attainment of full rights.

Brady's *Scales of Captivity* is also concerned with the ways minoritized people respond to the pressures of racialized national conceptions of belonging. The category of citizenship is a vexed issue in contemporary Latinx studies, and the notion of cultural citizenship has been important for the field. For Latinx people, citizenship is intertwined with questions about legal residency and work permits, and citizenship has different resonance depending on whether a person is a recent immigrant or born in the United States, sometimes a descendant of those who have been in the United States for decades or centuries. Brady is more focused on belonging than citizenship, although the latter does inform her take on the denial of full integration for Latinx people. Brady de-emphasizes the dynamic of inclusion/exclusion in US society and instead turns to a theoretical exploration of how the cultural treatment of Latinx children reflects a broader negation of Latinx full participation in political and legal systems. Childhood denies a person full rights on the premise that children do not have the reasoning and maturity to exercise those rights and thus are under the care of their parents. Starting with the contemporary US-Mexico border and news reports about children being taken away from parents and guardians, Brady turns to different forms of captivity throughout US history to unpack how racialized capitalism and imperial states restrict the movement of certain populations and constrain the life trajectories of non-Anglo peoples.

Brady then takes it up a notch in a theoretical gambit that brings in *scale* at a massive level and positions it as a colonial residue that "populates, renames, reconceives, possesses, brands, markets, and demeans" (18). For Brady, scale allows for a seemingly rationalized abstraction, a monovision of the world that denies multiplicity and makes difference disappear. Scale is at once an imperial logic and what motivates economic and geographic power that locks up people (captivity) and creates the "cast-out child who does not get to assimilate and integrate as a citizen" (243). The critique of scale challenges scholarly tendencies in recent decades to focus on large geographic areas—hemispheric, transnational, and global—as an antidote to the limitations of nation-based approaches. Brady seeks to challenge such geographic expansion as part of logics that reinforce capitalism's hierarchies and size fetishism. Instead, Brady seeks perspectives that engage with a notion of many worlds and many life-affirming affiliations without resorting to family, region, or nation. To develop these arguments, Brady turns to a variety of contemporary fiction, including Helena María Viramontes's *Their Dogs Came With Them* (2007) and Reyna Grande's *Across a Hundred Mountains* (2006) among many other texts, and discusses how they attend to reciprocal, communal, and specific ways of relating that resist scale and offer new ways of being in the world. "These texts' attention to the cast-out child who does not get to assimilate and integrate as a citizen, and their focus on the way practices of rescaling economic and geographical power entail new iterations of captivity, ultimately also suggests that scale itself is a masquerade," she writes (243).

The strength of the book is in the powerful discussion of the fiction. Brady is a magnificent reader, as evident in chapter 1's discussion of María Amparo Ruiz de Burton's *Who Would Have Thought It?* (1872). Since the 1990s, Ruiz de Burton has inspired a variety of critical work, including a collection of essays and dozens of articles and book chapters about her writing. It seemed like nothing new could be said, but Brady offers a historical interpretation of the "captivity" narrative in the book. As Brady points out, Ruiz de Burton may have been engaging with the captivity and parading of circus-style performers and previously enslaved people. Brady reads *Who Would Have Thought It?* in great detail and effectively complicates discussions of a writer who has been criticized widely for what appears to be a celebration of white Mexicans.

I am skeptical of Brady's turn to scale, in part because some of her associations seem to be built on scaling. Is scale really "beloved by scholars" (239) and does it hold a "lien on the Western academic imaginary" (239)? The more historically minded studies in this review offer a counterpoint. What is the distinction between scaling and other comparison methods, for example the shift from one historical context to another, a language that makes Mary Rowlandson's captivity open to a comparison with *captivity* in boarding schools for Native American children in the late nineteenth and twentieth centuries. What Brady calls scalar logic seems to inflect her use of eighteenth-century *casta* paintings to set up racialized exclusion in the twentieth-century United States. While casta art provides an attractive visual for racialized taxonomies, it is not clear how influential those paintings were, and scholars of Latin American studies have questioned whether casta paintings have been granted undue influence in twentieth-century scholarship. Racialization takes many different turns historically throughout Latin America and parts of the United States. Brady is right that casta paintings narrate "sexualization and racialization" as one and the same process, but they do not work "to create a concept of a Latinidad" (21), which has different antecedents in the nineteenth century and functions in different ways in the contemporary United States.

Reading Brady's book alongside Stanciu and Greer, one can see how different approaches—historical or theoretical—contribute to conversations about the influence of national belonging on the legal aspects of residency and citizenship. Mitchell raises the following question: "When a person's experience falls short of what counterparts enjoy, do they accept the nation's message that they are not a citizen—or do they devise a more complex definition of citizenship" (18)? The studies here offer a range of responses—homemade citizenship, representative imaginaries, reciprocal engagement—but for people without immigrant rights, the path to citizenship might be long and arduous or even impossible. With more and more populations migrating and seeking refugee status, does citizenship offer a legal privilege to participate in a capitalist economy rather than a democratic form of organization? How does citizenship relate to those whose experiences include historical and familial affiliations with more than one nation-state?

Roh's *Minor Transpacific* differs from the other studies in important ways. It reminds us that integration into US (or other national) systems is but one dimension for writers concerned with transnational experiences that are inextricable from a second or third country outside of the home nation. The most important common ground for the texts in Roh's book is not the United States but Korea in its diasporic dimensions. This is a comparative study of Korean American fiction and Japanese literary texts that focus on the experiences of Zainichi, people of Korean descent in Japan. The term "Korean Japanese" is not operative here; it is not commensurate with US hyphenated identities because of the status of the Zainichi, who are not granted birthright citizenship even if they are born in Japan. (Learning about the way Japan treats its residents of Korean descent sheds light on the limitations of birthright citizenship in different countries.) Roh's study is less concerned about citizenship as a nationalizing force and more with the role of a shifting third nation in his panorama of historical interpretation. A multiplicity of triangulations in fictions that deal with Japan, the United States, and Korea, Roh writes, is "the result of minor literatures that emerges in the gaps, the inchoate and nebulous spaces between defined forms of national identity and empire—an emergent third space" (12).

Roh's reading of fiction picks up on the projects of King-Kok Cheung, Joseph Jeong, and other scholars of Asian American literature seeking to bridge the distance between US ethnic studies (national paradigm) and Asian studies (area). The chapters include discussions of Younghill Kang's 1937 novel *East Goes West* in relation to Japanese industrialization, Kaneshiro Kazuki's *GO* (2000), which tells of a Zainichi high schooler in relation to US racialization, and US novels about Korean comfort women in Japan, including Chang-rae Lee's *A Gesture Life* (1999). Roh opens his chapters with memorable scenarios that involve transpacific social interactions, and he thus sets up the analyses as approachable for nonspecialists (such as myself) without being reductive. Since his project is to bring together novels that might otherwise be framed as Asian American or Asian, Roh presents his arguments for multiple readerships. The analyses of the novels focus on sociopolitical interactions, and the discussions could use more attention to language and questions of translation. Like much of the best work in transpacific studies, Roh's book keeps the historical contexts of numerous nations in play as the discussions are developed.

Taken together, these books raise the stakes for the future of political membership in light of increasingly mobile populations. On the one hand, the history of citizenship rights in the United States is also a history of racialized discrimination, as is made evident by Mitchell, Greer, and Stanciu. On the other, domestic racial histories affect and get transposed onto new populations that come in and out of the United States with global capitalist flows and imperial conquest, a matter considered by Brady, Roh, and Stanciu. If we return to Stanciu's strong argument that the United States is a settler and not an immigrant nation, then citizenship functions as an imposition and a mechanism of expansionism, as well as a birthright or an opportunity. Along the US-Mexico border today, US citizenship (or belonging through legal residency) is an ideology that justifies a militarized response to migrants looking for a new place to live. Theorists have considered how external borders help foment internal borders whose effects might be discriminatory treatment and even violence. Increasingly laws are being proposed that would allow police to check the residency status of people suspected of being in the United States without authorization. We also see the developing of internal borders through attacks on voting rights in the United States. Given the long and troubled history of citizenship's disconnection from participatory democracy, recent efforts to curtail voting rights offer yet another possibility for people to feel marginalized despite having citizenship as a legal status.

But there is another matter, one brought out by Roh's transpacific approach. People who feel deterritorialized or live in two or more nations during their lives have complicated responses to unitary nationalism. The US naturalization process is based on a teleology that begins with years of residency and culminates in a ceremony that involves renouncing allegiance to all other states. Those with affection for or a birth connection to another country might see that US loyalty oath as predicated on an either/or binary that clashes with their experiences. In that case, citizenship functions as a cudgel cutting off transnational connections. A first step away from this would be for the United States to recognize dual nationality as not necessarily disloyal. Other countries do so. To admit that someone could be a citizen of one nation (the United States or Japan) and another country throughout a life trajectory would recognize the increasing movement of populations and the complexities of belonging in a national setting.

Rodrigo Lazo is professor of literature at the University of California, Santa Cruz. His books include *Letters from Filadelfia: Early Latino Literature and the Trans-American Elite* (2020) and the coedited collection *The Latino Nineteenth Century* (2015). He has published more than thirty articles on nineteenth-century literature of the Americas, Latinx literary history, and archival theory. Lazo is working on a history of Spanish-language newspapers in the United States.

Book Reviews

Black Madness :: Mad Blackness. By Therí Alyce Pickens. Durham, NC: Duke Univ. Press. 2019. xvi, 152 pp. Cloth, $94.95; paper, $24.95; e-book available.

Disabilities of the Color Line: Redressing Antiblackness from Slavery to the Present. By Dennis Tyler. New York: New York Univ. Press. 2022. xvi, 317 pp. Cloth, $89.00; paper, $32.00; e-book, $32.00.

Since Douglas C. Baynton's often-cited 2001 essay on "Disability and the Justification of Inequality in American History," the assumption that corporeal and mental disabilities have been wielded as disqualifiers for citizenship has been foundational to the field of critical disability studies. African American writers, as a result, it is frequently argued, distanced themselves from representations of disabilities that further pathologized Black people and justified the negation of their rights. The emergence of a robust Black disability studies over the last decade, however, complicates and reimagines these conceptual framings of disability and citizenship with their embedded white liberal biases about Black writers' and activists' strategic repudiation of disability. In field-changing books, *Black Madness : : Mad Blackness* and *Disabilities of the Color Line*, Therí Alyce Pickens and Dennis Tyler trace out how Black writers and activists have long been having their own anti-ableist and anti-racist conversations about disability in relation to racial justice and citizenship on their own terms and in ways that did not follow—*could not necessarily follow* given the distinctive entanglement of antiblackness and ableism within the grammar of US whiteness and citizenship—a mainstream identity politics model of visibility, rights, and access to racial capitalism. Both Pickens and Tyler offer innovative methodologies and critical orientations for scholars in African American cultural studies and disability studies investigating questions of racial justice and citizenship. Their books should be essential reading.

In *Black Madness :: Mad Blackness* Pickens starts with the foundational insight that disability was/is not just another additive intersectional positionality like class, gender, or sexuality that alters Black people's fitness for

American Literature, Volume 96, Number 4, December 2024
© 2024 by Duke University Press

citizenship. Blackness and disability, as Pickens astutely notes, are inter-connected master tropes of human disqualification central to formations of a white Western humanism. By borrowing the analogous sign in her title, Pickens signals her dismantling of the assumption that disability is analo-gous to race, or that Black madness is just another identity making margin-alized Black folks doubly oppressed. As Pickens posits, Blackness and mad-ness are "mutually constituted" (24), though she later complicates this logic. Drawing on theories within Black studies that the ontological formation of Western post-Enlightenment ideas of the human arose during the Middle Pas-sage and depended on the abjection of a malleable Black otherness, Pickens contends that this abjected Blackness was simultaneously viewed as inferior, defective, irrational, or "disabled." Thus, Blackness and disability, particularly cognitive disability, are inseparably intertwined as a part of a Black dehuman-ization and disenfranchisement. As Pickens elaborates, Black madness (a term referencing an intersectional identity) is not analogous to a mad Blackness, for to speak of a mad Blackness is "to intensify Blackness," to conjure Black excess, to make Black otherness more unapologetically Black and abject to a white universalized rational human that determines full rights and citizenship (57). In the "fissures, breaks, and gaps" within Black cultural production, how-ever, this mad Blackness haunts and disturbs notions of whiteness, reason, and self-determination underpinning qualifications for citizenship (3).

Pickens's *Black Madness :: Mad Blackness* is organized around four "conver-sations," which are intended to open generative connections between Black studies and disability studies and to trouble assumptions within both fields. In these four conversations, Pickens turns to the speculative fiction of Black writ-ers (Octavia Butler, Nalo Hopkinson, Tananarive Due, and Mat Johnson) as a set of theoretical sources and not just as literary texts to analyze. In the sec-ond conversation Pickens weaves a cautionary tale about the reduction of Black madness to a counter representation within African American cultural histories. These "sociogenic" theories read Black madness as a symbolic and tragic outcome of systemic racial injustices, which once mitigated, would usher in a supposedly more just and "sane" world (53). Such sanest arguments within African American liberationist thought, however, turn mad Blackness into a politically utilitarian identity that diminishes individuals' actual lived experiences of cognitive or psychiatric disabilities and reduces these disabil-ities to abnormalities that ought to be cured for future racial equality.

Throughout *Black Madness :: Mad Blackness* Pickens seeks to disrupt the way Black mad subjects largely exist to shore up the value and agendas of others. Consequently, Pickens argues we need new interpretive strategies for mad Blackness that may overlap with but not always align with the practices of resistance and agency called for within (white) critical disability studies. In her reading of Octavia Butler's *Fledgling* (2005), for example, Pickens exca-vates how Butler depicts Black madness as too-often coopted within white lib-eralism as merely a critical tool to destabilize normative identities of race or ableism. Such employments of the agency of Black madness ignore the mate-rial reality of mad Black folks and their demands for racial, social, and political transformation beyond deconstructions of the normal. As Pickens expands in her reading of Nalo Hopkinson's *Midnight Robber* (2000), mad Blackness comprises a more capacious analytic tool that interrogates how impairments are the result of "politicized, sexualized, and raced violence" (66).

To further this work of political transformation and a redefined citizenship, thus, Pickens argues in her third conversation, critics need to reclaim mad Blackness as an analytical tool of "Black excess" that overturns the entanglement of Blackness, animality, and disability. Through a reading of Tananarive Due's African Immortals series, Pickens unpacks how an innate Black disability has also been connected to animality and to a lack of reason (cognitive disability) that further configures African-descended people's dehumanization. Although critical disability studies has largely sought to depict disability as an "extra-ordinary" human variation—and, thus, has seen Western post-Enlightenment ideas of the human as potentially inclusive of disabled bodies and minds—Black writers and activists have used mad Blackness to rethink a universalized white and ability-driven concept of the human since these figurations have proven so destructive to so many people of color. As a result, in her fourth and final conversation, Pickens poses the question of what the meaning and value of mad Blackness might be if it were completely uprooted from abjection. In the novels of Mat Johnson, Pickens contends Johnson gestures toward what a reimagined mad Blackness might look like if unsettled from Western logics of time, linearity, and ocularity (103).

In contrast to Pickens's rich provocative theorizations about the intersections of Blackness and disability, Dennis Tyler's *Disabilities of the Color Line* provides a meticulous and richly contextualized literary history of key African American writers from the antebellum period to the present (David Walker, Henry Box Brown, William and Ellen Craft, Charles W. Chesnutt, and James Weldon Johnson) who have engaged disability in complex ways to resist and resignify the figuring of Black people as inherently disabled and thus incapable of freedom, self-governance, and citizenship. In recuperating the disabilities of the color line, Tyler begins by arguing for a more expansive definition of *disabilities* that goes beyond the ADA definition rooted in individualist notions of impairment and that more accurately reflects how early African American writers and activists invoked disability. As part of their more expansive understanding of disabilities, Black writers, Tyler argues like Pickens, grappled with the entanglement of "blackness, disability, unfitness, and inferiority" (115). But Black writers and activists, as part of what Tyler terms an "aesthetics of redress," also focused on the politics of "disablement" (126). As Tyler shrewdly argues, Black writers depicted Jim Crow as more than a social or legal system of segregation. Jim Crow imposed disabilities on Black Americans: Black women and men were maimed and injured by racial violence (often state-sanctioned) and rendered vulnerable to injury, madness, or contagion to protect the "privileges and immunities" of whiteness (167).

Although dominant social models of disability often resist medical frameworks that define disabilities as injuries and impairments rather than proud variations, Tyler, like other recent Black disability scholars, demonstrates that such a singular identity politics perspective trivializes the way African American writers testify to the racialized violence of becoming disabled. Thus, in astute close readings of Charles W. Chesnutt's conjure stories and James Weldon Johnson's autobiographical *Along This Way* (1993), in chapters 4 and 5, Tyler recovers how post-Reconstruction Black writers dramatized the relation between the color line and the "restrictive systems" of disablement, all the while avoiding reproducing white supremacist beliefs in Black bodies and minds as inherently defective (3).

Like Pickens, Tyler offers some of his shrewdest interventions by reclaiming Black writers' own theorizing of disability. For early Black writer/activists such as David Walker, for example, the discursive figuring of Black people as cognitively disabled could not be separated from their *disablement* as illiterate. Thus, Walker did more than talk back to Jefferson's Query XIV, which perpetuated the idea that Black people suffered from defective constitutions making them incapable of citizenship. Walker also, Tyler argues, worked to make his appeals accessible to a Black audience disabled by illiteracy through an elaborate system of typographical symbols indicating how his work should be read aloud according to a Black oral tradition. Thus, Black writers, as part of their aesthetics of redress, also implemented practices of care and radical accessibility. Among the innovative methodologies that Tyler offers in *Disabilities of the Color Line* are new approaches for bringing a disability analytic to Black print culture.

In such a short review, I can hardly do justice to all the rich and nuanced examinations of specific early African American literary histories that Tyler offers. In his final chapter, however, it is important to note, Tyler shifts from the disabilities of the pre-Civil-Rights-era color line to the disabilities of color-blindness. Taking his cue from theorists who contend that the twentieth-century problem of the color line shifted to the problem of colorblindness in a twenty-first-century era of neoliberal racism, Tyler ends by opening a new and vital conversation about how color blindness and antiblackness work as "co-conspirators" (207). As Tyler deftly traces out through a rereading of the murders of Emmett Till and Eric Garner, racial violence has often been associated with the performance of a disability (colorblindness) or the feigning of an inability to see race. Thus, Mamie Till-Mobley's insistence on keeping her son's casket open, for example, represents the continuation of a long Black aesthetic tradition of redress to disrupt a politics of disablement that ensures racial inequities through the manufacture of black people's social and literal death.

In their paradigm-shifting books, thus, Pickens and Tyler examine the role a naturalized and allegedly inherent Black disability has played in the political dynamics around race, rights, justice, and citizenship. They recover a lineage of Black writers who created a Black disability studies that had its own approaches, interpretative strategies, and orientations that were not just an extension of, or response to, a politics of citizenship framed within a white liberal tradition of access and rights. In tracing out generative connections between Black studies and disability studies, they raise important questions about the differential debilitations and incapacitations of Black life as a part of US state violence, while at the same time recovering the anti-ableist imaginings within Black liberationist thought, creative production, and worldbuilding for a reimagined citizenship.

Stephen Knadler is a professor of English at Spelman College. He is the author of three books, including most recently *Vitality Politics: Health, Debility, and the Limits of Black Emancipation* (2019), which won the Tobin Siebers Prize for Disability Studies in the Humanities. His current project (tentatively titled "Crip Counterintelligences: Early African American Literature and Dis/abling Black Futures") recovers a genealogy of mad and neurodiverse Black personhood in early African American literature. Three articles related to this manuscript were previously published in *American Literature*, *M.E.L.U.S.*, and *Cusp: Late Nineteenth/Early Twentieth-Century Cultures.*

DOI 10.1215/00029831-11611114

Space-Time Colonialism: Alaska's Indigenous and Asian Entanglements. **By Juliana Hu Pegues. Chapel Hill: Univ. of North Carolina Press. 2021. 232 pp. Cloth, $95.00; paper, $32.95.**

Giving Form to an Asian and Latinx America. **By Long Le-Khac. Stanford, CA: Stanford Univ. Press. 2020. 264 pp. Cloth, $120.00; paper, $30.00.**

What would it look like to decolonize solidarity? Is there a place for comparison in such an endeavor? In an essay on the "Afro-Asian analogy," Colleen Lye suggests that Asian Americanists have used a method of racial comparison and a rhetoric of cross-racial solidarity to overcome rather than theorize indeterminate and illegible modes of racialization. "Asian as a racial concept requires comparative thinking," she writes, but in rushing from comparison to coalition, analogical treatments of Black and Asian experience have minimized the material effects of differential racialization and, in the end, exposed "the Asian American's attenuated relation to racial conceptualization" ("The Afro-Asian Analogy," 2008, *PMLA* 123, no. 5: 1732–36; 1732, 1733). Native studies scholars, meanwhile, have challenged the tendency to conflate the experiences of colonialization and racialization. In this vein, Jodi A. Byrd observes that Asian and Native peoples' differing relations to sovereignty dampen "some of the optimism of comparison" ("Arriving on a Different Shore: US Empire at Its Horizons," 2014, *College Literature* 41, no. 1: 174–81; 177). For her, *cacophony* is more apt than *coalition* for describing the interactions among Natives, settlers, and arrivants in the lands known as the United States.

Despite such cautionary words, Asian American scholarship on comparative racialization is more robust than ever and continues to be galvanized by cross-racial solidarity. Indeed, in the 2022 essay "Where is the Reciprocity?," Naoko Shibusawa wonders why others have not shared in this comparative work: "I have no interest in arguing against the Afro-pessimist insistence that Blackness is sui generis, incomparable at some base level with other oppressions. My main concern is *what incomparability means for solidarity*" (*Journal of Asian American Studies* 25, no. 2: 261–82; 267, emphasis mine).

Juliana Hu Pegues's *Space-Time Colonialism: Alaska's Indigenous and Asian Entanglements* and Long Le-Khac's *Giving Form to an Asian and Latinx America* in some sense continue the work of pursuing solidarity through comparison. Pegues's monograph opens with the parallel internments of Japanese migrants and Alaska Natives, and Le-Khac's study opens with the parallel migrations of Asians and Latinxs. Yet these side-by-side considerations are less comparisons of two peoples than efforts to clarify the operations of the United States as a settler state with imperial ambitions. *Comparison*, in these opening examples, is a preeminent technique of colonial racialization: it is an interpretive habit of white American lawmakers, missionaries, tourists, and pundits that renders commonsensical the separation between the transient alien and the immutable native (in *Space-Time Colonialism*) and the model minority and the illegal migrant (in *Giving Form*). Pegues and Le-Khac trace these comparative maneuvers in their analyses of racial and colonial power, often emphasizing their uneven effects. However, I would say that their own critical practices are more invested in connecting than comparing. Connection is rangier than solidarity. In exploring the heterogeneity of connections that colonial racialization has obscured, Pegues and Le-Khac summon a different political vocabulary: one of entangled and intimate coexistence in *Space-Time Colonialism* and one of transfictional and formal interdependency in *Giving Form*.

Space-Time Colonialism theorizes and reframes the colonial typologies of Asians as "forever foreign" and Natives as "never modern" (13). These typologies describe Asians' and Natives' respective relationships to settler space and time. The spatiotemporal logics of settler colonialism, meanwhile, have obscured the relationships *between* Asian immigrants and Native peoples: "Relationships remain unrecognizable when Asians can never be 'here' and Natives can never be 'now'" (14). Part of Pegues's task is to recover how Asians and Natives in Alaska were racialized relationally. She shows how popular and scientific efforts to deduce the Asian origins of Alaska Natives served to rationalize land dispossession. These fantasies of racial origins operated in tension with the influx of Asian laborers to Alaska: "Ironically Asian origins yielded the possibility of citizenship for Indigenous subjects while Asian origins for immigrant workers during the same period foreclosed such possibilities" (31). Such ironies position Orientalism and Indianness as operating in the same imperial key. Pegues's more crucial interest, though, is examining how Asians and Natives lived and labored together in Alaska. A vital resource for such an examination is Alaska Native and Asian immigrant literary and cultural production. For example, Ernestine Hayes's memoir *Blonde Indian* (2006) portrays Asians as quotidian presences rather than mystical abstractions, and Nora Marks Dauenhauer's and Carlos Bulosan's depictions of Asian and Native cannery workers displace "productive subjectivity" with "unproductive intimacies" (84). In these literary examples, Asians and Natives cultivate different land and kinship relations, yet they "might have recognized each other outside of settler colonial optics" (81).

I am especially compelled by *Space-Time Colonialism*'s provocation that Asians might conceive of their migration story in relation to Indigenous lands rather than American society. Shoki Kayamori, the focus of chapter 4, offers a revealing case of what this might look like. Between the 1910s and 1940s, Kayamori lived in a majority-Native community and was welcomed into Native social and political circles as an unofficial photographer. In exploring Kayamori's photography, Pegues finds that he took pictures with a specifically Native viewership in mind: the photos in his archive once appeared on the walls of Native homes and were often sourced from the personal collections of Native families. This orientation toward a Native viewer means that Kayamori rendered his subjects with humor, familiarity, ambivalence, and life—qualities that are noticeably absent in the exotic-erotic genre of "vanishing Native" photography. Did other Asian migrants also view the world through Native rather than settler optics? How might this alternative mode of seeing inform an Asian Americanist reading practice? Pegues's study of the Gold Rush–era folk figure "China Joe" attempts to answer such questions. Whereas public history guides us to view China Joe primarily through his benevolence to white miners, Pegues situates this figure in relation to the lynching of Tlingit men. Reading historical newspapers against the grain, Pegues identifies Natives as "the most numerous and longest lasting of all [China Joe's] customers." The white settlers, she proposes, were the "exceptions to China Joe's regular associates, the Tlingit community" (81).

Like Pegues, Le-Khac writes against the siloing of marginalized peoples. But while Pegues draws from documentary archives, local papers, oral histories, and cultural production to demonstrate the lived intimacies between Asians and Natives, Le-Khac assembles a specifically literary corpus to argue that the formal relations in narrative fiction might inspire unity among "minority communities that currently see their fates as separate" (3). Literature, in other words, gives expression to "an emergent formation that Americans do not yet perceive" (3). There is some ambiguity about whether Le-Khac believes Asian-Latinx relations are nonexistent or unsatisfying or whether his strong claims for form require strategically sidelining them. I was surprised that Le-Khac purposely excludes literary texts "that center on Asian American and Latinx characters interacting" (19). He thus opts to read Maxine Hong Kingston's experimental memoir *The Woman Warrior* (1976) instead of *China Men* (1980), a text that references numerous encounters between Asian and Latinx laborers across the Americas, and when analyzing Junot Díaz's short story "Drown" (1996), he has little to say about a Dominican character stationed on a Philippine military base. If the rationale for such omissions is to "develop methods of comparative ethnic study beyond overt connections of social content" (19), then Le-Khac's fine-tuned literary analyses certainly demonstrate the payoff of reading for "transfictional form." Transfiction refers to narratives that are "neither interconnected into a single narrative nor unconnected, as in a story collection" (11). Whether novels such as Cristina Henríquez's *The Book of Unknown Americans* (2014) or story cycles such as Rishi Reddi's *Karma* (2007), transfictional narratives attune readers to latent, indirect, remote, and noncausal links between characters and stories. Such narratives imbue distance and open-endedness with political import, guiding readers to see and feel beyond their immediate family, ethnicity, and race. A "transfictional solidarity" is, in this sense, a "community of fate," forged through not blood or contact but "diffuse networks of effects" (77).

The oft-occurring metaphor of a "horizon" captures the politics of possibility that *Giving Form* advocates. In the book's final case study, the formally weak links of transfiction lead Le-Khac to reconceive the historically loose bonds of panethnicity as a potential asset rather than an abiding weakness. What the prefixes *trans-* and *pan-* share is an investment in futurity: "panethnic identity is powerful not as a premise but as a promise"—as something "not yet available" that one must "struggle for" with "unity as a horizon" (181–82). Le-Khac's eloquent readings of literary texts offer concrete examples of what this struggle might look like. The argument implicit throughout the book, though, is that *reading* itself is one key strategy for struggling toward a unified identity. To address the conundrum of "how might minority groups adjust their visions to see relationally across a divided racial order," Le-Khac proposes "looking to imaginative works" (16). In casting Latinx and Asian Americans as—above all—readers, Le-Khac suggests that a formally sophisticated practice of transfictional reading can produce the vision necessary to connect and unite.

Pegues and Le-Khac show how deeply entangled, primarily formal relationships can transform comparison as a practice of racial analysis. More specifically, by reimagining comparison as connection, these critics give new meaning to a politics of recognition, one in which seeing each other is more important than being seen. At stake in this mutual recognition is challenging the givenness of "the United States of America." For Pegues, displacing the colonial formation called the United States with the primacy of Indigenous nations allows for Asians and Natives to be copresent in the here and the now. For Le-Khac, the United States is being eclipsed by an emergent "Asian and Latinx America" in which "interminority coalitions" give possibility to "a more racially egalitarian future" (6). Reading Pegues and Le-Khac together, one must conclude that "a more racially egalitarian future" cannot take citizenship-qua-settlement as the horizon for "combating perceptions of foreignness" (Le-Khac, 7). How might a coalition of immigrants orient their bid for belonging away from pursuing assimilation or naturalization and toward honoring Indigenous concepts and lifeways? Can one conceive of emplacement beyond the ideological norms of settler citizenship and its cultural rubric of inclusion and exclusion? Such questions neither preclude nor lay claim to solidarity. Instead, they move us to devise better ways of seeing each other—of recognizing our connections as well as our incommensurabilities.

Sunny Xiang is an associate professor of English at Yale University. She studies the styles and sensibilities of US military empire in Asia and the Pacific. Her first book, *Tonal Intelligence: The Aesthetics of Asian Inscrutability during the Long Cold War*, was published in 2020.

DOI 10.1215/00029831-11611127

Extent and Nature of Circulation

Average number of copies of each issue published during the preceding twelve months; (A) total number of copies printed, 428; (B.1) paid/requested mail subscriptions, 297.75; (B.4) Paid distribution by other classes, 0 (C) total paid/requested circulation, 297.75; (D.1) samples, complimentary, and other nonrequested copies, 0; (D.4) nonrequested copies distributed through outside the mail, 65; (E) total nonrequested distribution (sum of D.1 & D.4), 65; (F) total distribution (sum of C & E), 362.75; (G) copies not distributed (office use, leftover, unaccounted, spoiled after printing, returns from news agents), 65.25; (H) total (sum of F & G), 428.

Actual number of copies of a single issue published nearest to filing date: (A) total number of copies printed, 408; (B.1) paid/requested mail subscriptions, 284 (B.4) Paid distribution by other classes, 0(C) total paid/requested circulation, 284 (D.1) samples, complimentary, and other nonrequested copies, 0; (D.4) nonrequested copies distributed through outside the mail, 73; (E) total nonrequested distribution (sum of D.1 & D.4) 73; (F) total distribution (sum of C & E), 357; (G) copies not distributed (office use, leftover, unaccounted, spoiled after printing, returns from news agents), 51; (H) total (sum of F & G), 408.

THE ANTHOLOGY OF BLACK MOUNTAIN COLLEGE POETRY

Edited by Blake Hobby, Alessandro Porco, and Joseph Bathanti

"Like the experimental college whose poetic heritage it documents, this collection is a marvel, literally the best presentation of any literary phenomenon we have had in the United States. This book raises the bar for everyone."

—**Ron Silliman**, author of *The Alphabet*
288 pages $34.95

BROWN WOMEN HAVE EVERYTHING

Essays on (Dis)comfort and Delight

Sayantani Dasgupta

"Essay collections by people of color are hard to find; those from a non-Western perspective are even rarer. Dasgupta offers both and reinvents herself with each essay, making this book a gem."

—**Ira Sukrungruang**, author of *This Jade World*
192 pages $22.00 paper

ANOTHER THROAT

Twenty-First-Century Black US Persona Poetry and the Archive

Ryan Sharp

"Sharp's book offers an incisive and valuable portrait of African American poetry's powerful historical imagination."

—**Keith D. Leonard**, American University
288 pages $34.95 paper

ALL Y'ALL

Queering Southernness in US Fiction, 1980–2020

Heidi Siegrist

"An exciting and robust study of queerness in the US South and southern literature from 1980 to the present."

—**Michael P. Bibler**, Louisiana State University
240 pages $27.95 paper

SHY OF THE SQUIRREL'S FOOT

A Peripheral History of the Jargon Society as Told through Its Missing Books

Andy Martrich

"This book makes a bold and counterintuitive argument for understanding how the failure to publish certain works allows us to understand the project of a press. All of this is in addition to offering a phenomenal demonstration of the bibliographic arts."

—**Daniel Scott Snelson**, University of California, Los Angeles
200 pages $24.95 paper

INDISCIPLINE

Reading Collaboratively Written Native American Autobiography

Alicia Carroll

"Carroll addresses the long history of collaborative Native-white life writing texts while deftly moving beyond them to center Hopi voices and knowledge production."

—**Stephanie Fitzgerald**, Arizona State University
224 pages $34.95 paper

INSCRIBING SOVEREIGNTIES

Writing Community in Native North America

Phillip H. Round

"This book puts to rest any lingering narratives of a divide between oral and written culture as it traces a number of ways in which Indigenous peoples brought spoken languages and linguistic practices into writing and back out again, sustaining living, vibrant vernacular languages."

—**Laura Mielke**, University of Kansas
304 pages $34.95 paper